University of Cambridge Department of Applied Economics

OCCASIONAL PAPER 32

Effects of Selective Employment Tax
Final Report

Effects of Selective Employment Tax

Final Report

by W.B. Reddaway
and
D.R. Glynn
J.D. Sugden
P.M. Croxford
C.H. Fletcher
J.S. O'Donnell

CAMBRIDGE

AT THE UNIVERSITY PRESS 1973

Published by the Syndics of the Cambridge University Press
Bentley House, 200 Euston Road, London NW1 2DB
American Branch: 32 East 57th Street, New York, N.Y. 10022

ISBNs
0521 08496 2 hard covers
0521 09718 5 paperback

Set in cold type by E.W.C. Wilkins & Associates Ltd,
and printed in Great Britain by Alden & Mowbray Ltd,
at the Alden Press, Oxford

Contents

Tables

Preface

This is a book which raised acute problems as to what should be put in the preface, and what should be in the introductory chapter. Since the points in question are mostly of considerable importance for a proper understanding of the book, it seemed best to put most of them in the introductory chapter: experience with our First Report, which included some important points in the'preface, suggested that readers either skipped it or forgot about its content.

Two points do however need to be clarified here. First, this Report is a *sequel* to our First Report, and does not in any way supersede it: indeed, the best advice which I can give to anyone who has got this far in the present book but has not read the First Report is that he should start by doing that.

Secondly, the fact that this Report is being published as an Occasional Paper of the Department of Applied Economics in no way implies that there is any change in its status or objectives as compared with the First Report, which was published by HMSO; nor does it imply any change in the independence with which the research was done — which was complete, in both cases — or in the extent to which the Government is committed by the findings — which was *nil* in both cases.

The reason for the change in publisher is the coming into power of a Government which was committed to abolishing SET; this also led to a major change in the length of our research grant — a point discussed fully in the introductory chapter. Under these circumstances it seemed more logical that the Report should be published by the Cambridge University Press, in a series devoted to making available the results of other objective research projects, rather than appearing to be associated in some way with the Government: this was always our first choice, but as the Government had paid for the work and wanted the speed which HMSO publication was thought to bring we naturally agreed in 1970 to publication of the First Report by HMSO. For the Final Report we have the benefit of CUP's greater experience on the publication of books based on academic research and of their more appropriate distribution system.

Despite the change of publisher, however, this Report seeks to maintain its somewhat special character of strict impartiality, in which its model is the report of a Royal Commission: it does not seek to engage in economic controversy or to establish any particular conclusion. With this objective the Report has again been deliberately written (to quote one of our reviewers) 'in the flattest of flat prose'.

Acknowledgements

A book of this kind could not have been produced without the willing cooperation of a long list of people, and it is impossible to name all of them.

I must again record my gratitude to Her Majesty's Government, both for financing the research and for adhering scrupulously to the principle that it should be done on the basis of strict independence: we decided what we should do and how we should try to do it, and the Government's only 'interference' was to ask us to make construction the next on our list after distribution and its allied trades. In the event this proved an unhappy request, for reasons explained in Chapter X, but it did not affect the independence with which we executed our research.

Next, we could not have produced the Report without the information supplied by Government Departments, by Trade Associations and the like (listed in Appendix B), and above all by the firms which filled in our questionnaires and answered our supplementary questions. To all these I offer most grateful thanks for their cooperation.

Finally, on the academic side I have had magnificent support from so many people that it is almost invidious to attempt to make a list. Each of the five men formally classed as associates had responsibility for some part of the work, and it would have been easy to lengthen the list by including others, notably A. Fels, D.E. Moggridge and B.C. Moore. As always, the rest of the Department's staff gave unstinting support of the highest quality, whether as statistical assistants, or on data-processing, or on the typing of this Report and of the high-quality questionnaires which brought in so much of its information. And on many issues I have had invaluable advice from my successor as Director of the Department, Wynne Godley.

Neither Her Majesty's Treasury nor the Controllers of Her Majesty's Stationery Office is in any way responsible for anything expressed in this book.

W.B. Reddaway
November, 1972

I
Origin and Nature of Our Two Reports

The selective employment tax (SET) was announced by the then Chancellor, Mr. Callaghan, in the 1966 Budget, and became effective from September of that year. Its basic object was to impose on employers in certain industries a tax of a certain amount per week for each person they employed (varying accordingly as the employee was adult or juvenile, and male or female); this result was secured, however, by the indirect method of adding these sums to the weekly National Insurance stamp for *all* employees, and then letting the employers in defined industries obtain a refund (sometimes with a premium). There were various other provisions, but the main effect was to leave employers in most service trades and in construction effectively paying the tax on all their employees, except those who worked for less than 8 hours a week or who also worked for another employer who was responsible for their national insurance.[1]

This fiscal innovation aroused a great deal of opposition, and on the other side it was also claimed that it would achieve great things for the economy. The opposition was partly directed against various administrative and logical problems arising out of the selective principle, but was concentrated mainly on the basic principle of selectivity itself and the reasons given 'for taking selective action against the service trades'. The fact that the tax was a relatively small one compared with even the lowest rate of purchase tax (itself pre-eminently a selective tax) seemed to be regarded as of no consequence, perhaps because little effort was made to portray the tax in that sort of way: it is an interesting subject for speculation (which does not however fall within our terms of reference) to assess how great the opposition would have been if the tax had been described simply as an extension of the purchase tax, which was to be assessed for reasons of administrative convenience by reference to the number of employees rather than the value of what was sold,[2] and charged at a specially low 'concessionary' rate. The absence of the emotive word 'selective' (and perhaps of some of the claims about the benificial effects of the tax on the economy) might have avoided much opposition, and might thereby have deprived the Department of Applied Economics of a very interesting piece of research.

---

1 Strictly speaking, it is not therefore correct to refer to employers in these industries as 'paying SET' or 'liable to SET', because *all* employers are liable to SET: the 'selection' comes at the refund stage. Nevertheless these expressions are so convenient that we have used them on occasions in our Reports, where the meaning is clear.

2 See First Report, pages 15/16, for a discussion of 'employment as the basis of the tax' which brings out the difficulty of a tax on certain kinds of service as such (e.g. those rendered by an insurance office). The same point has of course emerged over the value added tax.

Institution of an Independent Enquiry

Be that as it may, the Department was in fact approached informally at the end of 1967, when Mr. Callaghan was still Chancellor, to ask whether they would undertake an independent and strictly impartial enquiry into the effects of the tax. The change of Chancellors led to some delay over the formal arrangements, but Mr. Jenkins announced in his 1968 Budget speech that it was being launched, with the following terms of reference:

> To examine and report on the effects of the Selective Employment Tax on prices, margins and productivity in industries on which the tax falls as a net burden and the consequent effects on the economy generally.

The Department was under no illusions about either the difficulty of the task or its vast size. Both these matters were discussed at some length in Part 1 of the First Report, but it may be useful to summarise very briefly some of the main points.

'The Effects of SET'

First, as to the meaning of the simple-sounding phrase 'the effects of SET' we need to remember the following *negative* points:

(a) These effects cannot be assessed simply by comparing the position in (say) 1969 with that in a pre-SET year. Such comparisons (which we refer to as 'the historical record') reflect all manner and kind of things besides SET — 'normal' growth of productivity, devaluation, squeezes and freezes, inflation and many more things besides.

(b) One cannot normally find out what action was taken by a businessman 'because of SET' simply by asking him, however willing he may be to help and however reliable his memory. Actions taken by businessmen reflect their reaction to *all* the various things which are affecting their business, *taken in combination*: SET may well have been a contributory factor in a decision (e.g. to install a computer), and the businessman may accurately report that fact, but it will usually be quite impossible to arrive at meaningful conclusions about the number of computers installed as a result of SET on the basis of reports of this kind.

(c) The short-run effects of the introduction (or increase) of SET are not neccessarily the same as the longer-run effects — so that in 1970, for example, the 'total' effects of SET were a combination of what we might loosely call the 'fourth-year' effects of the introduction, the 'second-year' effects of the 1968 increase and the 'first-year' effects of the 1969 increase.

On the *positive* side we have two very important points:

(1) The logical meaning of 'the effects of SET' on (say) prices in a given year is the difference between the *actual* price in that year and what it *would have been,* in the absence of SET'.

(2) The phrase 'in the absence of SET' should be more precisely defined as 'if some other tax of a general character had been imposed (or increased) which would have had the same consequences for the over-all balance between

aggregate demand and potential supply for goods and services taken as a whole.[1]

The second of these positive points perhaps deserves a little elaboration. SET was in fact introduced as an addition to taxation, not as a replacement for some other tax: indeed, its actual introduction came just after the Government had introduced a whole package of measures (in July 1966) which were also designed to reduce aggregate demand. We are *not* concerned to assess how effective SET was as a disinflationary weapon: we take the amount of disinflation which the Government was trying to produce as given, and assess the *other* effects of using SET as an instrument for securing it, rather than using some other tax.

For any practical decision, of course, one would need to know what alternative tax was under consideration, so as to allow for *its* special consequences as well as those of SET. This is clearly outside our terms of reference — no alternative tax has been suggested, and if one had been the assessment of its effects would be a formidable addition to our task. Nevertheless, it is necessary to make one point rather strongly, which is particularly relevant to what we say about anomalies arising out of SET: one must not fall into the mistake of assuming that the alternative tax would be perfect in this respect. No tax is free from anomalies, and the reader must set his own standard of what would be expected from an *extension* of some other tax(es) which would produce the same effect on the balance of aggregate demand and supply.

Finally, a few words are perhaps needed about the meaning of the expression 'what one might have *expected* to find in the absence of SET', though we have little to add to what was said in Chapter IV of the First Report. In brief, the 'expectation' is of a statistical or econometric kind. Ideally, one seeks to find, from a study of the pre-SET period, a set of statistical 'rules' which explain the behaviour of (say) productivity in distribution in terms of a number of variables which would be unaffected by the use of SET rather than some equivalent tax. These 'rules' are applied to the values found in each post-SET year, to assess what was to be 'expected'. The logic of the idea is fairly simple, but of course it may be impossible to establish any good 'rules'.

Problems of Measurement

The previous section was concerned with the logical problems of what one should be trying to measure. The difficulty of the Department's task lay much more, however, in the problem of actually measuring anything with sufficient accuracy. This was discussed in Chapter III of the First Report, on Data Problems, but in view of its transcendent importance we follow this introductory chapter with a brief one which again bears the title Data Problems. This does not supersede the chapter in the First Report, but reflects our further experiences in a part of the field where the statistics are even worse than they were for the distributive trades.

Given the poor quality of the basic data it was inevitable that we had to use very rough methods for filling in some of the elements needed to complete a particular

---

1 We will be exploring the implications of this definition later in the Report. The criterion is the *balance* between demand and potential supply: SET appears to have raised the latter, through its effect on productivity.

statistical picture. It is useful to stress again two points about our procedure which were made in the Preface to the First Report:

(a) We have not attempted to record the innumerable tests which we applied to see whether some other methods of arriving at a particular figure would give an answer which was sufficiently different to affect the general conclusion.

(b) We have followed the system of arriving at what seemed likely to give the 'best estimate' for each separate figure, rather than the one which gave the most consistent *set* of figures. Readers can therefore apply whatever tests of plausibility or consistency appeal to them in the knowledge that the various figures were arrived at *independently*.

Organisation of Our Work

Apart from the problems set out above, the Department was confronted with a truly mammoth task. SET falls as a net burden on industries which account for about one-third of the total economy, whether one judges by the number of employees or the share of the gross domestic product. Moreover the number of separate trades with separate problems is, literally, uncountable: one can count the number of headings in the Standard Industrial Classification, but even if this is done in terms of Minimum List Headings (or even sub-headings) these units are liable to be made up of innumerable sub-units which raise different problems in terms of SET.[1]

Given this state of affairs, it was clearly not satisfactory to produce a general form applicable to all trades and send it to a sample of the whole SET field — even if we could have mounted such an operation. The form would inevitably have been unsatisfactory, because it would *either* have asked about a lot of things which were meaningless to many firms, *or* been confined to general questions about 'effects', many of which would be incapable of proper answer. SET does not necessarily have the same effects on hairdressers as on civil engineering contractors making motorways, and the same questions and method of study will not do for both.

In some ways, it would have been desirable to launch enquiries simultaneously into all the industries affected, or at least a large number of them, taken as being capable of reflecting the field between them: this would have enabled us to produce one report on the field as a whole, with separate treatments of the various industries, but it would have required a vast staff at all levels, and its coordination might have presented an unmanageable task; it would also have provided no opportunities for using the experience of the trades done earlier to improve our investigation of the later ones. We therefore decided to break down the research, by concentrating first on the distributive trades, and then to work through the remaining industries. This allowed us to produce our First Report at the beginning of 1970; but it also meant that this report on the distributive trades had to include a preliminary view of a number of 'general' matters — e.g. the method of collecting the tax and the exemption of the self-employed — without which the Report would have been seriously ill-balanced.

---

1   To take a simple-sounding example, MLH 881, sub-head 1, bears the simple-sounding title 'cinemas': but it also covers film studios and film distributors and 'the developing and printing, etc., of cinematographic films'. Parts of this were exempted from SET, part even obtained a premium - but there are no labour statistics even for the whole sub-head (because it is a *sub*-head).

Our strategy of producing a series of reports on industries or groups of industries to be followed by a general Report on the conclusions reached about the overall effects of the tax, was disrupted by the change of Government in 1970. The new Government were committed to abolishing SET, and so were understandably unwilling to support a large programme of research into its effects. Moreover, the declared policy of the new Government also made it unreasonable for us to expect cooperation from industry with our inquiries on the scale which we had enjoyed up to that time.[1]

The outcome was a decision that we should produce one more report, which would do a number of separate things:

(a) Analyse the data which we had already collected on 'near distribution' – a group of industries having some characteristics in common with distribution, which we had thought might be covered in the First Report, until we realised that their inclusion would lead to substantial delay and make the First Report unmanageably big.

(b) Report on the preliminary work which we had been doing on construction, including anything which we could deduce from published statistics or other evidence.

(c) Extend the work which we had already done on distribution to cover later years wherever possible.

(d) Give any other conclusions which could be reached on the basis of available statistics and other evidence, to cover as much of the SET field as possible.

This has inevitably meant that some of the questions which we hoped to investigate could not be covered at all, and in particular that we have not been able to do much in detail on any trades other than distribution and near-distribution: in particular, we have not been able to obtain systematic direct evidence from people in other trades which are subject to the tax. Furthermore, the limited period for which our research grant was continued meant that some things which *could* have been done, or done much better, have had to be left on a tentative basis, or not brought up to as late a date as would have been desirable.

Within these limitations, however, our basic objectives have been the same as were set out on page 6 of the First Report, in a passage which can usefully be quoted in full.

Thus the object of the present enquiry is to examine, in quantitative terms, such questions as:

(i) How the tax is borne, as between higher prices, worse services, lower profits (and possibly wages) in the trades affected, or higher productivity in the use of labour and/or other inputs (as a means of avoiding any of the above burdens).

(ii) What changes (if any) the tax has caused in the types of labour employed, the methods of organising the business, and so on.

(iii) The market mechanisms by which these results have been produced (since this throws some light on what is to be expected in the future).

---

1 There had already been some signs that cooperation would not be so easy to secure after the publication of our First Report had revealed that 'an impartial inquiry' was not synonymous with a demonstration that the effects of the tax were disastrous: however, the argument that traders should welcome an honest attempt to reveal the true facts was still proving fairly powerful as a means of securing cooperation, so long as the future of the tax was uncertain.

In all these matters we are concerned with the *effects* of SET and not simply with a historical comparison between the position in (say) 1965 and 1968. Moreover there is no reason to expect the answers to be the same for each of the various trades, or even for the various types of business within a trade.

Relationship between the Two Reports

Having said this, it seems best to leave this final Report to speak for itself, rather than to outline its contents — the plan of which is readily visible from the Table of Contents. The one point which does seem to need emphasis is that this Report is *a sequel* to the First Report, and in no way supersedes it, except that a few later statistics are given in Chapters VIII and IX. Nothing which was said in the First Report seems to need amendment, and we have not included its findings in the present Report, except where this helps to give a more rounded treatment of the subject. Any reader who has reached this point without having read the First Report is advised to do that before proceeding further with the present one: and those who have read that Report may find it helpful to re-read Chapter II ('The Line of Approach') at this stage.

II
Data Problems

Problems connected with the availability, reliability, and best use of data took a much larger share of the work of our enquiry than they need be given in the Report. They are referred to *passim* in the text, and rather more detail on some major points is given in the appendices. The purpose of this short chapter is to make some general points at the outset, to avoid unnecessary repetition.

The official statistics relating to SET-paying industries are generally sparse. This is probably due in part to a traditionally greater interest in the economic performance of manufacturing than service industries, partly to the problems for official statisticians in recording developments in industries characterised by large numbers of small firms, and partly to problems raised by some of the concepts involved. (For example, the 'output and input' of many service industries are not unambiguous even in terms of value (e.g. for bookmaking or insurance), and the division between a quantity element and a price element presents great difficulties). Whatever the reason, the result is that most service industries outside the distributive trades have never been covered by statistical exercises corresponding to the Censuses of Production even in benchmark years, and that many published statistical series show service industries only in a few aggregated figures of very doubtful reliability, constructed from scraps of information with the object of covering the whole economy somehow, rather than for use in their own right. Construction industry statistics present peculiar problems which are discussed in Chapter X.

In these circumstances, very little can be deduced from existing statistics about 'the effects of SET on prices margins and productivity' in the industries outside distribution. Nor was it possible to do much to fill the gap by our own data-collecting efforts: even in the few trades in which we were able to carry out our surveys, we could not ask respondents to go back beyond 1965–6, so that there is only the sketchy evidence of the official statistics to serve as the 'pre-SET' record. Clearly, without reasonably detailed and reliable data for several years before the tax was introduced, it is not possible to discover the econometric rules which would allow confident forecasts to be made of what would have happened in the absence of SET. And without such forecasts, there is no basis for precise conclusions about the effects of the tax, even in the industries in which we could collect our own data for the post-SET period.

The official statistics provide almost no information about costs and profits in the industries which we had to investigate. Employment statistics (which are subject to serious limitations discussed below) are available, from the Census of Population and the Department of Employment; and the Central Statistical Office (C.S.O.) made available to us the estimates of 'real net output' which they use for the compilation of the aggregate production estimates of national income, so that we could attempt an examination of changing productivity trends. However, some of these output estimates are based on changes in the numbers of employees classified to the industry, and so are useless for the purpose of measuring productivity, while others are clearly subject to a wide margin of error for other reasons (See Appendix E). Thus the estimates of changes in productivity which we made are necessarily very imperfect.

These difficulties with the output estimates are compounded by problems with the employment statistics. Outside the field of the Censuses of Distribution, these are not based on the same returns as the output data, but on the Department of Employment's analysis of the counts of National Insurance cards exchanged and on Censuses of Population. As a result, one can never rule out the possibility that the coverage of employment and output figures which purport to relate to the same industry may not in fact be the same. The sources impose further limitations on the employment data. Firstly, an employee with two jobs is classified to the industry of his main employer, so that the labour force of industries which employ 'double-jobbers' in their secondary activity is understated – and this is important in industries such as catering. Secondly, National Insurance cards do not provide details such as the hours worked by each employee and they are unreliable as measures of the number of self-employed people, many of whom do not pay National Insurance contributions. The Censuses of Population give more detailed estimates, and better figures for the self-employed, but these Censuses are at best carried out only at 5-year intervals, and the results are not available until some time after the Census date. Thus the latest Census information available when this Report was being compiled related to April 1966, which is before the introduction of SET.

Official statistics on price changes for a few items produced by the SET-paying industries are collected as part of the index of retail prices and are available monthly. However, for many items the concept of price is hard to define – which is doubtless one reason why so few prices are collected and the Government make little or no attempt to allow for changes in quality.

Finally, it is as well to be clear about the limitations of our own survey data. It was beyond our resources to conduct censuses or scientific samples of the industries we were investigating so that we had to rely on evidence from an 'indicative sample' of businesses in each.[1] The results of these surveys give reasonable indications of changes over time in business ratios – such as profits per unit of turnover; but they cannot be used to measure changes in aggregates such as the output of the industry. For this purpose we would have needed a larger coverage, a more strictly representative sample and a system for taking account of firms which closed and new entrants to the industry. The level as distinct from the changes in ratios may also be different in our sample and in the rest of the industry.

Examples of these general data problems (and others) will be noted in the text when this is necessary. In a very real sense they set the framework for the enquiry, and they account for the fact that we have been unable to assess the effects of SET separately for individual trades outside distribution, and have been forced to confine our conclusions to rather broad and tentative statements about the rest of the service sector as a whole.

1 Appendix B describes how we obtained our samples.

III
SET in Perspective

This part of our Report deals with the effects of SET in catering (including public houses, hotels etc), shoe repairing, hairdressing and the motor trades. We can discuss these trades more fully than others, because we were able to carry out our own surveys in them before the 1970 General Election. These surveys are described in detail in Appendix B; and Appendix D gives some background notes about the trades.

These trades together account for nearly 15 per cent of the employees liable to SET. In June 1968 catering had 571 400 employees in employment, the motor trades 423 200, hairdressing 98 100 and shoe repairing 9900, a total of 1 102 600. It should perhaps be noted at this stage that we did not attempt to cover the whole of 'catering' (as defined in MLH 884 of the 1958 SIC) with our own enquiries: fields which were not covered at all were fish and chip shops, holiday camps, clubs and the letting of furnished apartments; fields which were only partially covered, or were not rigorously analysed, were tenanted and free public houses and industrial catering.

Our purpose in this introductory chapter is to give a broad quantitative idea of the importance of SET in near-distribution as preparation for discussion of changes over the SET period in the firms' costs, prices and behaviour. This can be done first by showing SET payments in relation to the cost of hiring a full-time employee, since it was as an addition to labour costs that SET affected firms.

SET in Relation to Wages

The rates of SET were increased quite sharply between its introduction in 1966 and 1969, and wages were also increasing, so that the relative size of SET changed over time. Broadly, it added rather less than 7 per cent to labour costs in 1966 and 1967, and about 10 per cent in later years, for both male and female employees. This is shown in Table III.1, where SET payments in October of each year are expressed as a proportion of the average earnings plus employer's share of the National Insurance stamp for adult men and women in 'miscellaneous services'. The over-all picture would be much the same if allowance were made for the different earnings, National Insurance stamps and SET liability for younger employees.

Table III.2 concentrates on the comparison between SET and other increases in labour costs. It shows the percentage addition to labour costs of SET in October each year, compared with the percentage addition caused by the increase in earnings and National Insurance contribution which took place over the following twelve months. It can be seen that SET in 1966 added rather more to costs than did the increase in earnings over the subsequent 12 months. The highest rate of SET, in October 1969, was equal to about two-thirds of the increase in earnings which had taken place over the three years October 1966 – October 1969, and rather less than the

9

Table III.1   *SET and Labour Costs in 'Miscellaneous Services'*(a)

Date	'Labour cost excluding SET'; i.e. full-time manual employees' average earnings plus employer's N.I. contribution.		SET		% Addition	
	Men (21+) £	Women (18+) £	Men (21+) £	Women (18+) £	Men	Women
Oct 66	18.07	9.33	1.25	0.63	6.9	6.8
Oct 67	18.95	9.73	1.25	0.63	6.6	6.5
Oct 68	20.24	10.31	1.87	0.94	9.2	9.1
Oct 69	21.88	11.07	2.40	1.20	11.0	10.8
Oct 70	24.84	12.39	2.40	1.20	9.7	9.7

(a) I.e, laundries and dry-cleaning, motor repairers and garages and repair of boots and shoes. Earnings tend to be higher in the motor trades than in the other trades covered.

Source: D.E.P. Gazettes (for earnings).

Table III.2   *Percentage Addition to Labour Costs in 'Miscellaneous Services'*

Date	Males (21+): Addition due to		Females (18+): Addition due to	
	Increase in earnings + N.I. over subsequent year	SET	Increase in earnings + N.I. over subsequent year	SET
October 1966	4.9	6.9	4.3	6.8
October 1967	6.8	6.6	6.0	6.5
October 1968	8.1	9.2	7.4	9.1
October 1969	13.5	11.0	11.9	10.8

increase in earnings over the year starting October 1969.

The figures given above relate to full-time workers, and their average earnings. Through our own survey we were able to ascertain more closely the addition which SET had made to total labour costs; we asked for the amount of SET payments made (whether in respect of full- or part-time workers) and for other expenditure on 'payroll', including N.I. and pension contributions as well as wages. These results are combined with figures for turnover, profits and other expenses in the next section.

A Wider View of SET

The importance of SET cannot be judged simply from the amount it added to labour costs, since a given increase in these costs has quite different implications for selling prices or profits in different types of business. A business selling goods will almost certainly have a lower proportion of total expenses taken by payroll than one selling mainly services; thus the quantitative importance of an increase in labour costs would be likely to be less for (say) a car saleroom than for (say) a hairdressing business.

We show in Table III.3 the SET payments made in 1967–8 in relation to the main accounting analysis of the businesses covered by our surveys. Figures are expressed as a percentage of turnover, defined as the total value of sales in the period in question. The SET figures can of course be compared with the other expense items or profit, as well as automatically showing what percentage SET was of turnover. We have *not* included interest or rent paid or taxes other than SET as expenses, so that the residual 'net profit' is the amount available for the proprietor's income (apart from any

Table III.3 *Some Key Relationships, 1967–8*
(All figures are percentages of turnover)

Trade	Turnover	SET	Payroll	Cost of goods sold and materials used	Rates	Other	Total	Net Profit[a]
Hotels	100	1.9	25.4	35.8	2.1	21.8	87.0	13.0
Restaurants	100	1.6	24.6	45.4	1.8	14.8	88.2	11.9
Managed Public Houses	100	0.7	11.9	72.7	1.8	6.4	93.5	6.5
Motor Traders	100	0.5	8.1	84.2	n.a.[b]	3.9	96.7	3.3
Hairdressers	100	3.4	47.0	n.a.[b]	2.5	26.3	79.1	20.9
Shoe repairers[c]	100	2.6	40.6	28.3	2.1	14.2	87.6	12.3
Unweighted mean of above	100	1.8	26.3	44.4	1.7	14.6	88.8	11.3

(a) Before charging rent, interest or direct taxes.
(b) Included in 'other expenses'.
(c) With turnover over £5000 p.a.

salary he may draw), for paying income or corporation tax and for remunerating the capital invested in the business, whether that capital is supplied by the firm itself, or obtained as a loan, or by renting the premises from a landlord.

The categories of expenses shown are fairly self-explanatory. 'Payroll' includes wages, salaries, N.I. and pension contributions, but not SET. 'Other expenses' consist of fuel and lighting, stationery, accountants' fees, etc.

Table III.3 shows the position in our respondents' accounting years ending between October 1967 and September 1968[1] in which year SET was at the original rate of 25/- for a man and 12/6 for a woman. In later years SET was generally rather larger in relation to the other magnitudes shown, as is brought out elsewhere; our present purpose is to show the broad relationship between turnover, profit and the various types of business expense in one year

The line at the bottom of the table must be used with caution; it is simply the arithmetic average of the figures in each column, (taking figures not available as zero) without any attempt at weighting. Its only merit is that it is easier to appreciate than ratios for all six of the trades shown: it would have been possible to calculate a weighted mean, but we have not attempted to cover all the trades in the field of near-distribution, so that the figures would then seem to be claiming a precision which is not justified. Both here and elsewhere in the Report we have stuck to an unweighted mean as a crude 'summary' which clearly makes no such claim: the *total* for near-distribution is not in fact a very useful concept.

The table brings out the point already made in Chapter I, that SET did not in general represent a very large proportion of turnover. In the case of motor traders and public houses, much of whose business is the sale of goods produced elsewhere, the tax amounted to less than 1 per cent of sales. Even for hairdressers, where labour costs are most important, SET payments amounted to only 3.4 per cent of turnover.

1 Appendix B explains in detail the relationship between the firms' accounting years and the years '1967–8' etc. for which our results are given.

It was thus lower than the lowest rate of purchase tax, and it is interesting to speculate on the reactions of the traders if they had been made subject to purchase tax at these 'selective' rates instead of to SET.

The size of these payments increased in later years, and of course they were always larger in relation to profit or payroll expenses than to turnover. These relationships are quantified in later chapters. The main point to be made at this stage is that SET typically amounted to some 2 per cent of 1967–8 turnover in the near-distribution trades, which was about the same as Local Authorities' rates.

IV
Near-Distribution— The Historical Record: Costs and Profits

This chapter deals with the changes which took place between 1965—6 and 1968—9 in the main business ratios in near-distribution, which were summarised for 1967—8 in Table III.3. We start by comparing the size of SET payments in relation to turnover, payroll and net profits in 1967—8 and 1968—9. This brings out the general increase in the importance of SET payments between these two years. We then show the main trends between the pre-SET year 1965—6 and 1968—9, the last year covered by our surveys.[1]

Table IV.1 shows SET payments as a percentage of turnover. These figures indicate the approximate amount[2] by which average selling prices would have been increased if SET had been exactly passed on to customers, without of course any implication that this is what happened. They conform to the obvious expectation, that if SET were passed on, it would cause the largest percentage price increase in trades where what is sold is substantially the product of the trade's own workers (e.g. hairdressers) and much smaller increases where most of the cost of what is sold is made up in other ways (e.g. pubs).

It can be seen from this table that, measured as a proportion of turnover, the importance of SET generally increased by about one-fifth between 1967—8 and 1968—9. This was of course primarily the result of the increase in SET rates in September 1968 of 50 per cent for all employees except those over 65 years old (whose SET rate was reduced) and part-time adults (whose rate was unchanged): as against this, prices were rising and so raising the value of turnover per worker, and the higher rates of SET did not apply to the whole of 1968—9 as reported by our sample. It should also be noted that the 1968—9 figure for hotels is slightly lower than might be expected because some hotels in our sample were situated in Rural Development Areas and received full refunds of SET from September 1968.[3]

---

1 The result of our surveys shown under the headings '1967—8' etc. are based on accounts for firms' financial years ending between October 1967 and September 1968. Thus '1965—6' was the last year wholly free of SET, and 1967—8 was the first year wholly subject to SET, which was, for all firms, payable throughout the year at 25 shillings for a man. The results for '1968—9' cover some months at the higher rates of SET introduced in September 1968. Appendix B gives details of the average terminal date of the pre-SET year in each of the near-distribution trades.

2 The indication is slightly too low, since the value of turnover was itself raised by SET.

3 See Chapter XVI.

Table IV.1   *SET as a Percentage of Turnover*

Trade	1967–8	1968–9	Average number of months in 1968–9 to which increased SET rates applied
Hotels	1.9	2.2	7½
Restaurants	1.6	1.8	7
Managed Public Houses	0.7	0.9	9½
Motor Traders[a]	0.5	n.a.	n.a.
Hairdressers	3.4	4.1	7
Shoe Repairers[b]	2.6	3.1	6½
Unweighted mean of above	1.8	2.1[c]	7½

(a) As explained in Appendix B, the motor trades survey did not cover 1968–9; if it had, the average number of months in the third column would have been 8.
(b) With turnover over £5000 p.a. Unless we specify otherwise, all figures for shoe repairers refer to this group. Smaller repairers are excluded since many are not liable to SET; the results obtained from analysing their returns are used later in the Report for purposes of comparison, where this is appropriate.
(c) Assuming 0.6 per cent for motor traders.

When SET payments in these years are expressed as a percentage of payroll, excluding SET, the figures are of course larger. They again show the increased weight of the tax in the second year, but this was partly offset by the rise in wages and kept down by the timing factor noted above.

Table IV.2   *SET as a Percentage of Payroll (Excluding SET)*

Trade	1967–8	1968–9
Hotels	7.5	8.8
Restaurants	6.4	7.5
Managed Public Houses	5.9	7.6
Motor Traders	6.7	n.a
Hairdressers	7.2	8.9
Shoe Repairers	6.5	7.8
Unweighted mean of above	6.7	8.0[a]

(a) Assuming 7.5 per cent for motor traders.

Table IV.3 compares SET payments with net profit + SET in 1967–8 and 1968–9. SET is added to net profits for this comparison so that one can see how much the tax reduced profits from what they would have been, other things being unchanged, in its absence. Other things would not, in fact, have been the same if the tax had not been levied, so that these figures do not show how much profits were reduced by SET in any causal sense. However, the ratios shown seem the most appropriate to give an indication of the size of SET in relation to profits – which may be important, in so far as it is this which leads businesses to act, whether by increasing prices, raising productivity, or in any of the other ways which we discuss elsewhere.

The figures shown for each trade conceal some fairly wide differences between types of firm within the trade. Thus in 1967–8, vehicle repairers' SET payments were 18.7 per cent of net profit + SET, while the figure for 'new car dealers' was

14.8 per cent and for other motor traders 11.7 per cent; the figure for shoe re-pairers whose turnover exceeded £100 000 p.a. was 20.6 per cent while for repairers with a turnover between £5000 and £100 000 it was 15.7 per cent.

Table IV.3   *SET as a Percentage of Net Profit + SET*

Trade	1967–8	1968–9
Hotels	12.8	13.7
Restaurants	11.5	13.6
Managed Public Houses	10.7	11.5
Motor Traders	14.1	n.a.
Hairdressers	13.9	16.3
Shoe Repairers	17.7	21.4
Unweighted mean of above	13.3	15.2[a]

(a) Assuming 15.0 per cent for motor traders.

Having shown the size of SET payments in 1967–8 and 1968–9 in relation to turnover, payroll expenses and net profits, we turn to the question of how the near-distribution trades were affected by other developments between the pre-SET year and 1968–9. We are chiefly concerned here to see what were the main cost changes, and what was the behaviour of profits, prices, output and labour productivity over the period.

Table IV.4 shows the change over the period in net profit as a percentage of turnover.

Table IV.4   *Net Profit[a] as a Percentage of Turnover*

Trade	1965–6	1966–7	1967–8	1968–9	% change 1968–9 cf. 1965–6
Hotels	12.1	12.4	13.0	13.6	+12.4
Restaurants	11.2	n.a.	11.9	11.6	+3.6
Managed Public Houses	6.4	n.a.	6.5	6.6	+3.1
Motor Traders	3.5	3.1	3.3	n.a.	−5.7[b]
Hairdressers	23.6	n.a.	20.9	21.0	−11.0
Shoe Repairers	13.7	13.5	12.3	11.4	−16.8
Unweighted mean of above	11.8	n.a.	11.3	11.3[c]	−4.2

(a) Before payment of rent, interest, and direct taxation.
(b) 1967–8 compared with 1965–6
(c) Assuming 3.4 per cent for motor traders.

Over the near-distribution field as a whole the profit ratio moved rather little, but there were important differences between trades. Hotels generally increased their profitability quite significantly, whilst at the other end of the scale shoe repairers suffered a fairly sharp fall.

For an understanding of these changes, one can examine the changes over the period in the different types of expenses, again expressed as a percentage of turnover in each year. In all of the trades, payroll expenses excluding SET were reduced as a proportion of turnover over the period. Between 1965–6 and 1967–8 this reduction was largest in the shoe repairers and vehicle repairers sectors, where SET had been high in relation to net profit. In the following year, hotels and hairdressers both recorded quite sharp relative reductions in payroll expenses.

Table IV.5   *Payroll, Including and Excluding SET, as a Percentage of Turnover*

Trade		1965–6	1966–7	1967–8	1968–9	% change, 1968–9 cf. 1965–6
Hotels	(a)	25.8	26.9	27.3	26.7	+3.5
	(b)	25.8	25.6	25.4	24.5	−5.0
Restaurants	(a)	24.9	n.a.	26.2	26.5	+6.4
	(b)	24.9	n.a.	24.6	24.7	−0.8
Managed Public Houses	(a)	12.0	n.a.	12.6	12.5	+4.2
	(b)	12.0	n.a.	11.9	11.6	−2.5
Motor Traders	(a)	8.2	8.7	8.6	n.a.	+4.9 (c)
	(b)	8.2	8.3	8.1	n.a.	−1.2
Hairdressers	(a)	47.6	n.a.	50.4	49.7	+4.4
	(b)	47.6	n.a.	47.0	45.7	−4.0
Shoe Repairers	(a)	42.9	43.0	43.2	42.8	−0.2
	(b)	42.9	41.6	40.6	39.7	−7.5
Unweighted mean of above	(a)	26.9	n.a.	28.2	27.8 (d)	+3.3
	(b)	26.9	n.a.	26.3	25.7 (d)	−4.5

(a) Includes SET
(b) Excludes SET
(c) 1967–8 compared with 1965–6
(d) Assuming for motor traders that payroll excluding SET amounted to 8.0 per cent of turnover.

When SET is added to payroll expenses, however, only shoe repairers were able to prevent the total increasing as a proportion of turnover over the whole period, perhaps again partly because of their partial diversification to shoe retailing, where less labour is required per £ of turnover than in repairing.

It is worth noting that between 1967–8 and 1968–9, four of the five trades for which information is available were able — whether by price increase or increased efficiency — to reduce the payroll + SET expense per £100 of turnover. This happened despite the increase in SET rates between the two years, which has been discussed above.

Apart from payroll and SET, the other items of expenses which our enquiries distinguished are the cost of goods for resale and materials used, rates, and other expenses. The difference between the cost of goods for resale and the relevant turnover can be regarded as the 'gross margin' on the goods sold. In some of the near-distribution trades, this concept has little operational significance, and we do not therefore show the ratio in the same way as we have shown the payroll/turnover ratios. In the catering trades, our surveys allowed us to calculate gross margins on the sale of food, drink and tobacco, and these margins are shown in Table IV.6. It will be seen that they generally increased between 1965–6 and 1968–9, and that the increase was usually greatest in the case of food, where the service content is largest.

The cost of goods for resale (including materials used in repair work) is an important element in the expenses of firms in the motor trades. Table IV.7 shows this cost as a percentage of total turnover in this sector; it increased slightly between 1965–6 and 1967–8

Table IV.6 *Percentage Gross Margins[a] in Catering*

Trade	1965–6	1966–7	1967–8	1968–9	% change 1968–9 cf. 1965–6
Hotels					
G.M. on Food	48.89	50.47	51.27	52.63	+7.65
G.M. on Liquor/Tobacco	41.20	41.43	41.08	41.78	+1.41
Restaurants					
G.M. on Food	54.53	n.a.	56.55	57.32	+5.12
G.M. on Liquor/Tobacco	34.87	n.a.	35.08	36.92	+5.86
Managed Public Houses					
G.M. on Liquor	28.42	n.a.	29.04	29.15	+2.56
G.M. on Tobacco	7.66	n.a.	8.33	8.37	+9.36
G.M. on Food	39.14	n.a.	39.57	43.48	+10.84
G.M. on Liquor/Tobacco	25.65	n.a.	26.24	26.38	+2.86

(a) Calculated as: $\dfrac{\text{Revenue from item} - \text{Cost of item}}{\text{Revenue from item}} \times 100$

Table IV.7 *Cost of Goods for Resale and Materials Used as a Percentage of Turnover in the Motor Trades*

1965–6	1966–7	1967–8	% change 1967–8 cf. 1965–6
83.7	84.1	84.2	+0.6

The next table gives the ratios for expenditure on rates and other expenses (which exclude rent and interest) in each of the trades. Rates are shown separately since, although in total relatively unimportant, they have been increasing over the period, and also they are probably less amenable to control by the firm than expenditure on miscellaneous items such as electricity and postage.

The figures in the last column show that in most trades, rates increased quite sharply as a proportion of turnover, whilst other expenses, which are of course much more important, remained at approximately the same percentage over the period.

A Summary Picture of Changes

Tables IV.5 to IV.8 have recorded changes in the main elements of business expenses as a percentage of turnover, and shown broadly that the percentage for payroll tended to fall, though not enough to prevent payroll + SET from increasing; that rates, though quantitatively not very important, increased quite sharply; and that other expenses showed no marked trend. This helps to explain the movements recorded in Table IV.4 of net profit as a proportion of turnover. To complete this explanation, we bring the figures together in Table IV.9, but show them as changes in the proportion of turnover accounted for by each expense item (and by net profit) instead of as percentage changes. This effectively combines the information given in previous tables about the size of each item and how quickly it altered, relative as before to turnover.

Table IV.8   *Rates and Other Expenses (Except Rent and Interest) as a Percentage of Turnover*

Trade		1965–6	1966–7	1967–8	1968–9	% change 1968–9 cf. 1965–6
Hotels	rates	1.97	2.04	2.07	2.05	+4.1
	other	22.3	22.2	21.8	22.7	+1.8
Restaurants	rates	1.66	n.a.	1.78	1.82	+9.6
	other	15.5	n.a.	14.8	15.3	−1.3
Managed	rates	1.78	n.a.	1.80	1.78	+0.2
Public Houses	other	6.2	n.a.	6.4	6.7	+8.1
Motor Traders	rates } other	4.5	4.1	3.9	n.a.	−13.3[a]
Hairdressers	rates	2.37	n.a.	2.52	2.66	+12.2
	other	26.4	n.a.	26.3	26.7	+1.1
Shoe Repairers	rates	1.74	1.93	2.09	2.15	+23.6 [b]
	other	14.7	14.4	14.2	14.5	−1.4
Unweighted mean of above	rates } other	16.5	n.a.	16.3	16.7[c]	+1.0

(a) 1967–8 compared with 1965–6.
(b) This rise may have been partly due to the concentration of multiple organisations on 'prime sites'.
(c) Assuming 3.7 per cent for motor traders in 1968–9.

The comparison is given both between 1965–6 and 1967–8 (Table IV.9) and between 1965–6 and 1968–9 (Table IV.10). It will be remembered that the 1967–8 ratios themselves were summarised in Table III.3, and a row has been added at the bottom of each table giving the mean 1965/6 ratio for the trades concerned.

Both Table IV.9 and Table IV.10 show that each section of the catering trade recorded a rise in profit per £100 of turnover, or at least no fall. This satisfactory result was essentially due to the fall in cost of goods sold per £100 of turnover − i.e. to an increase in gross margins. On payroll and expense items the catering trades did not, on the whole, do particularly well in comparison with other trades.

Table IV.9   *Percentage Point Movement in Ratios between 1965–6 and 1967–8*
(Each item is expressed as a percentage of turnover for the year in question)

Trade	SET	Payroll (excluding SET)	Cost of goods sold	Rates	Other expenses	Net Profit [a]
Hotels	+1.9	−0.4	−2.0	+0.1	−0.4	+0.8
Restaurants	+1.6	−0.3	−1.4	+0.1	−0.7	+0.7
Managed Public Houses	+0.7	−0.1	−0.9	+0.0	+0.2	+0.0
Motor Traders	+0.5	−0.1	+0.5	−0.6		−0.2
Hairdressers	+3.4	−0.6	n.a.	+0.2	−0.1[b]	−2.8
Shoe Repairers	+2.6	−2.3	+1.3	+0.4	−0.5	−1.5
Unweighted mean of above	+1.8	−0.6	−0.5	−0.2		−0.5
Mean ratio in 1965/6	*0*	*26.9*	*44.8*	*16.5*		*11.8*

(a) Before charging rent, interest or direct taxes.
(b) Includes cost of goods sold.

Table IV.10 *Percentage Point Movement in Ratios between 1965–6 and 1968–9*
(Each item is expressed as a percentage of turnover for the year in question)

Trade	SET	Payroll (excluding SET)	Cost of goods sold	Rates	Other expenses	Net Profit [a]
Hotels	+2.2	−1.3	−2.8	+0.1	+0.4	+1.4
Restaurants	+1.8	−0.2	−2.1	+0.2	−0.2	+0.5
Managed Public Houses	+0.9	−0.4	−1.2	+0.0	+0.5	+0.2
Hairdressers	+4.1	−1.9	n.a.	+0.3	+0.3 [b]	−2.7
Shoe Repairers	+3.1	−3.2	+2.2	+0.4	−0.2	−2.3
Unweighted mean of above[c]	+2.4	−1.4	−0.8	+0.2	+0.2	−0.6
Mean ratio in 1965/6	*0*	*30.6*	*37.1*	*1.9*	*17.0*	*13.4*

(a) Before charging rent, interest or direct taxes.
(b) Includes cost of goods sold.
(c) N.B. Motor Traders are omitted from this table.

In all trades, the largest increase in costs per £100 of turnover over either period was the imposition of SET,[1] and the other expenses, taken together, were reduced per £100 of turnover. In other words, in none of the trades were net profits per £100 of turnover reduced by as much as the SET payment.

This was not of course true for every firm, and it is therefore interesting to consider how diverse experience was within each trade with regard to the changes in net profit ratios. For simplicity, we show in Table IV.11 the upper and lower quartiles of the changes in this ratio between 1965–6 and 1967–8. One quarter of the firms in each trade showed movements more favourable than the higher figure, and one quarter showed movements less favourable than the lower figure. The first column gives the average net profit/turnover ratio for 1965–6 as an indication of the base with which the movements may be compared.

Table IV.11 *Inter-firm Diversity of Movements in Net Profit per £100 of Turnover, 1965–6 to 1967–8*

Trade	Average net profit/ turnover ratio for trade in 1965–6	Movements in ratio for firms, 1965–6 to 1967–8	
		Upper Quartile	Lower Quartile
	per cent	percentage points	percentage points
Hotels	12.1	+4.6	−2.5
Restaurants	11.2	+3.7	−3.0
Managed Public Houses	6.4	+1.3	−2.0
Motor Trades	3.5	+2.2	−2.4
Hairdressers	23.6	+2.0	−6.8
Shoe Repairers	13.7	+0.5	−4.1

1 This is not to say that SET was the largest increase in absolute terms, or per unit of constant price turnover, as Chapter 6 makes clear. For example, for every £100 of constant price turnover a typical hotel paid for goods for resale £37.8 in 1965–6 and £41.2 in 1968–9; this rise was bigger than SET in 1968–9 (£2.6), but because prices rose by almost 18 per cent over the period the cost of goods sold per unit of current price turnover showed a substantial fall.

It can be seen that there was considerable diversity of experience within trades in this respect, and that even in the catering trades, where the profit ratios of the average firm improved over the period, there was a substantial proportion of firms whose profit percentage fell. On the other hand, more than a quarter of the hairdressers improved their profit margins quite substantially, despite the average fall for the trade being almost 3 percentage points, and the same was true for rather more than a quarter of the shoe repairers. The diversity of movements between the two quartiles is least for public houses, and greatest for hairdressers.

V

Near-Distribution — The Historical Record: Prices and Productivity

In the previous chapter, we drew on the results of our surveys to give the main facts about changes over the SET period in different elements of cost and in net profit in near-distribution. To establish the historical record for prices in these sectors, we have used the methods described in Appendix F, based on official data. Table V.1 shows the price series used in deflating the turnover series from our enquiries.

Table V.1   *Price Indices used for Deflating Turnover, 1965—6 = 100*

Trade	1965—6	1966—7	1967—8	1968—9
Hotels	100	105.9	110.8	117.6
Restaurants	100	105.6	110.6	117.0
Managed Public Houses	100	104.1	105.2	110.8
Motor Traders	100	100.4	105.4	109.6
Hairdressers	100	n.a.	114.2	120.6
Shoe Repairers	100	106.3	111.6	117.4
Unweighted mean of above	100	n.a.	109.9	115.5

Note The definitions of the years varies from trade to trade. See Appendix B.

It can be seen that price increases over the period were substantial. Tables V.3 and V.4 show the amount of the price increase for each year which was, in a purely statistical sense, due to each of the factors listed. What this means is perhaps best explained by taking one of the trades (restaurants) as an example, to show how the figures were derived, and this is done in Table V.2

Table V.2   *Statistical Explanation of Price Increases, 1965—6 to 1967—8, for Restaurants*

Item	Cost per £100 of turnover, measured at 1965/6 prices		
	1965—6	1967—8	Difference
SET	0	1.7	+1.7
Payroll (excluding SET)	24.9	27.2	+2.4
Cost of goods for sale	46.7	50.2	+3.4
Rates	1.7	2.0	+0.3
Other expenses	15.5	16.4	+0.9
Net Profit	11.2	13.1	+1.9
Total[a]	100.0	110.6	+10.6

(a) This row measures the movements in price

21

The figures in the first column in Table V.2 are the accounting ratios for 1965–6 Those in the second column were obtained by taking the accounting ratios for 1967/8 (per £100 of turnover), and multiplying them by the price index for the trade, so that they show the amounts corresponding with *£100 of turnover at 1965/6 prices.* The differences between the figures in these two columns is, in total, equal to the price increase between 1965–6 and 1967–8: this *difference* and its analysis are shown for each trade as a row in Table V.3 (covering a two year movement) and Table V.4 (covering 3 years).

Table V.3   *Statistical Explanation of Price Increases, 1965–6 to 1967–8*

(Percentage points)

Trade	% price increase 1965–6 to 1967–8	Amount of increase due to[a] increase in each item per £100 of constant price turnover					
		SET	Payroll (excl. SET)	Cost of goods	Rates	Other expenses	Net Profit[b]
Hotels	11.8	2.1	2.6	2.2	0.3	2.2	2.4
Restaurants	10.6	1.7	2.4	3.4	0.3	0.9	1.9
Managed Public Houses	5.2	0.7	0.6	2.9	0.1	0.6	0.4
Motor Traders	5.4	0.6	0.3	5.0	n.a.[c]	−0.5	−0.1
Hairdressers	14.2	3.8	6.1	n.a.[c]	0.5	3.6	0.2
Shoe Repairers[d]	11.5	3.0	3.8	2.0	0.7	1.7	0.4
Unweighted Average of above	9.8	2.0	2.6	2.6	0.3	1.4	0.9

(a) In the sense explained in the text.
(b) Including rent, interest and direct taxes.
(c) Included with 'other expenses'.
(d) The data for shoe repairers has been adjusted to take account of diversification and its effect on the ratio via the increase in goods sold as a proportion of turnover.

Table V.4   *Statistical Explanation of Price Increases, 1965–6 to 1968–9*

Trade	% price increase 1965–6 to 1968–9	Amount of increase due to[a] increase in items per £100 of constant price turnover					
		SET	Payroll (excl. SET)	Cost of goods	Rates	Other expenses	Net[b] Profit
Hotels	17.6	2.5	3.0	3.3	0.4	4.4	3.8
Restaurants	17.0	2.1	4.0	5.7	0.5	2.4	2.4
Managed Public Houses	10.8	1.0	0.9	6.7	0.2	1.2	0.9
Hairdressers	20.6	4.9	7.5	n.a.[c]	0.8	5.7	1.6
Shoe Repairers[d]	17.4	3.8	5.8	3.6	0.9	3.1	0.2
Unweighted mean of above[e]	16.7	2.9	4.2	3.9	0.6	3.4	1.8

(a), (b), (c), (d) See notes to Table V.3
(e) It should be noted that motor traders are not included in this table.

22

The tables show how much smaller — generally about one-fifth — price increases over the periods shown would have been in the absence of SET if nothing else had been different. In fact SET probably led to increases in efficiency and reductions of profits in some businesses, so that the tax would not be fully passed on in increased prices: and it is also possible that in some cases the price increase attributable to SET was more than the amount of the tax, either to compensate for expected falls in the volume of turnover or because prices are determined by the addition of a constant percentage markup to estimated costs, which might include SET; in such cases SET would lead to increased profits.

Judgement on the over-all effect of SET on prices must therefore be deferred, but the tables do allow us to see the order of magnitude of different cost increases in a relevant aspect, and to see how big — or how small — the price increases due to the tax would be on various assumptions about the proportion which was passed on. Thus the next table shows the actual price increases, and the increase which would have been recorded in the absence of SET on each of the following assumptions

   (a) that the tax was completely absorbed;
   (b) that it was half passed on and half absorbed;
   (c) that it was entirely passed on;
   (d) that it was passed on with 20 per cent margin.

Of course, if the tax were completely absorbed, it would make no difference to prices, so that the figures in the first two columns are identical.

Table V.5   *Hypothetical Price Increases, 1965–6 to 1967–8*

					(Percentages)
Trade	Actual price increases	Increase which would have been recorded in absence of SET, on assumptions explained in text.			
		(a) 100% absorbed	(b) 50% passed on	(c) 100% passed on	(d) 120% passed on
Hotels	11.8	11.8	10.8	9.7	9.3
Restaurants	10.6	10.6	9.8	8.9	8.6
Managed Public Houses	5.2	5.2	4.8	4.5	4.4
Motor Traders	5.4	5.4	5.1	4.8	4.7
Hairdressers	14.2	14.2	12.4	10.4	9.8
Shoe Repairers	11.5	11.5	10.0	8.5	7.9
Unweighted mean of above	9.8	9.8	8.8	7.8	7.4

The figures in the previous three tables underline that SET was only one among several factors tending to increase prices, and not particularly important in quantitative terms. Taking the average of the industries, SET accounted statistically (i.e. on the assumption that it was passed on 100 per cent) for 20.4 per cent of the price increase between 1965–6 and 1967–8 (Table V.3) and 17.4 per cent of the increase between 1965–6 and 1968–9 (Table V.4). Increases in the cost of goods sold and payroll (excluding SET) were generally the major factors, each accounting for 26.5 per cent of the increase to 1967–8. If we assume that SET was passed on completely, then the average price increase over this period in the absence of SET would only have been 2.0 percentage points lower at 7.8 per cent, and even in the case of hairdressers, where SET was quantitatively most important, the increase over this period would only have been reduced by 3.8 percentage points.

Productivity

The contribution of payroll expenses to increased prices results from the combined effects of increased wages etc. and changes in productivity. The record of productivity changes is also of course of interest in its own right and our estimates covering the period since 1965–6 are given in the next table as indices with that year as base. To prepare these, estimates of current-price turnover were deflated for price increases, and the resulting constant-price turnover series divided by a series representing the numbers engaged in the trade: this labour series was obtained by deflating the payroll expenditure of the firms in the sample by an index of average earnings (plus employers' N.I. contributions). This method of estimating labour input has the consequence of, in principle, making allowance for changes in the amount of paid overtime or in the average grade of employee – i.e., in the proportion of highly paid employees (full or part-time). The alternative source for estimates of labour input from our sample are figures given by the respondents for the number of different types of employee at different specified dates. In the case of retailing, covered by our First Report, we were faced with corresponding alternatives, and after detailed investigation of the reliability of each with the help of the firms providing the data, we concluded that deflated payroll was strongly to be preferred.[1] We have maintained that preference for the near-distribution trades, and the figures in Table V.6 are based on that procedure.

Table V.6   *Indices of Movements in Productivity, 1965–6 = 100*

Trade	1965–6	1966–7	1967–8	1968–9
Hotels	100	101.5	103.0	109.7
Restaurants	100	n.a.	104.1	105.2
Managed Public Houses	100	n.a.	104.5	108.3
Motor Traders	100	99.0	106.2	n.a.
Hairdressers	100	n.a.	99.4	104.6
Shoe Repairers[b]	100	102.3	103.2	105.1
Unweighted Average of above	100	n.a.	103.4	107.0[a]

(a) Assuming motor traders to be 109.0
(b) With a turnover in the pre-SET year of more than £5000.

These estimates are inevitably very tentative, and it would be desirable to compare them with estimates based on aggregative data. Not much is available, but Table V.7 gives the most meaningful comparisons which we could achieve. It was necessary to combine our three catering sections, as nothing is available for any subdivisions of MLH 884 (1958 SIC) on the aggregate labour side: our surveys do not, of course, cover the whole of that field, so that this is an extreme example of the general point that we have not covered parts of the relevant MLH.

1   First Report, pages 64/5.

24

Table V.7   *Comparison of Estimates for Movements in Productivity*

Year[a]	Catering		Motor Trades		Hairdressing		Shoe Repairing	
	DAE[b]	Official[c]	DAE	Official[c]	DAE	Official[c]	DAE[d]	Official[c]
1965	100.0	100.0	100.0	100.0	100.0	100.0	100.01	100.0
1966	n.a.	101.1	99.0	98.1	n.a.	104.5	102.3	104.7
1967	103.5	100.8	106.2	105.6	99.4	102.4	103.2	104.3
1968	108.0	104.3	n.a.	108.9	104.6	103.0	105.1	105.1
1969	n.a.	100.5	n.a.	109.4	n.a.	107.6	n.a.	113.2

(a) The years given refer to calendar years for the official data and the years 1965–6, 1968–9 etc. for the DAE enquires.

(b) The series given in Table V.6 weighted together by estimated net output in 1963.

(c) The estimates are not officially prepared but based on official statistics. See Appendix E.

(d) Does not include shoe repairers with a turnover of £5000 or less in their pre–SET year.

This table can best be left to speak for itself. The main conclusion is obviously that measurements of this kind are subject to a considerable margin of error when the data are so inadequate.

VI
Effects of SET in Near-Distribution

Previous chapters have set out the historical record of changes in costs, prices, profits and productivity in the near-distributive trades over the years 1965/6 to 1968/9. This historical record was based largely on the results of our own surveys, because the existing data were so scanty and ill-suited for our purpose, though Chapter V ended with an attempt to compare our results for movements in productivity with those derived from existing aggregative statistics: it is obvious that our figures are always subject to a margin of error which is considerable in relation to the sort of effects which SET might be expected to produce.

If one is to assess what part of these changes was due to SET, one has to form a view as to what would have happened to the item in question if the tax had not been imposed. The main basis for this view can only be a consideration of the historical record in the period *before* SET was introduced, and on this our surveys can contribute nothing. Unfortunately, the existing information is even scantier and less reliable for the pre-SET period than it is for recent years, apart from some benchmark figures for isolated years when a census of some kind was taken. There is also the danger that if one attempts to establish relationships between the different variables for the pre-SET period in terms of the definitions and concepts used in the aggregative statistics, then they may not be reliable when applied to figures on a rather different basis derived from our surveys.

In these circumstances, we reluctantly concluded that it is not possible to produce separate estimates of the effects of SET for each trade: the most that we could hope to achieve was to combine the information over a large field, in the hope of producing some generalised statements about the service sector as a whole, or setting some limits to the proable range within which the answer would **lie**. The methods which we apply usually produce what looks like an 'answer' for individual trades or items, but we recognise that these are subject to substantial errors on account of the weaknesses of both the basic data and the methodology, so that they should *not* be regarded as estimates for that trade or item. We hope, however, that these errors are not caused by any consistent bias, which would tend to make the apparent answers all either too high or too low: we therefore treat this body of statistics as one which can be studied 'as a whole' in order to arrive at general conclusions.

In order to apply this method, it is obviously desirable to bring together data from as much of the SET field as possible, so as to provide more scope for errors to average out when one considers the whole set of figures. Moreover, for the important fields of prices and productivity, the pre-SET information had necessarily to be taken from sources other than our own surveys, and we therefore felt it best to use those sources also for the post-SET period, regarding our own surveys primarily as a broad check on the results so obtained. Consequently, we do not present any separate assessment of the effects of SET on prices or productivity in the near-distributive trades, but rather draw on the conclusions from Part IV, which considers the services sector (other than distribution) as a single whole. We see no reason why the general conclusions so arrived at should not apply, in a general way, to the field of near-distribution, but obviously the general result so obtained cannot be expected to hold good in each separate trade.

In the field of profits, however, we have not been able to achieve anything for the wider field, because there are no usable data for either the pre-SET or the post-SET period, whilst we do have some limited information from our surveys for near-distribution.

The object of this chapter is, therefore, firstly to extract what guidance one can get about the effects of SET on profits in the near-distributive fields (again confining ourselves to conclusions about the field as a whole, rather than about separate trades); and then to examine how far the generalised rules about prices, productivity and profits give a consistent picture when applied to the field of near-distribution as a whole, as derived from our surveys.

Profitability

As in the case of retailing, our basic assumption for the service trades under consideration is that there was no significant trend in the ratio of profits to turnover during the pre-SET period; this seems to be in broad accordance with the very sketchy aggregate data available, and it is also plausible *a priori*.

In the case of retailing, we managed to establish a system of making an allowance for the cyclical factors prevailing in any year, by applying rather devious econometric methods to the Blue Book figures for the pre-SET years. The application of the allowances there led to the 'expectation' that, in the absence of SET, the profit/turnover ratio in 1967/8 and 1968/9 would not have differed much from that in the basic year 1965/6, and for the two years together, the 'expected' change in the ratio from the basic figure was absolutely negligible. (See First Report, page 112). As an econometric analysis seemed to be impossible for the service trades, we made the simplest assumption of all for dealing with cyclical factors: we decided that no allowance for them was needed for the kind of broad conclusions which we might attempt, so that our assumption was that, in the absence SET, the profit/turnover ratio would have remained at the pre-SET level. In applying this 'expectation' to the figures for post-SET years, however, we thought it right to subtract the amount paid in SET from the turnover before calculating the expected profitability.

With the aid of this assumption, the analysis ran as follows. For 1967/8, Table IV.4 shows that the mean ratio of profit to turnover for the six trades was 11.3 per cent, and Table IV.1 gives the mean for SET as a percentage of turnover as 1.8 per cent. Expressing the profit as a percentage of turnover minus SET therefore, we get a figure of 11.5 per cent, which had to be compared with 11.8 per cent in the basic year (1965/6). It appears, therefore, that there was a small fall in the profit ratio below what would have been expected in the absence of SET: this fall might of course be a 'chance' result, or it might be attributed to errors in the figures or in the methodology, but it is equally plausible to assert that these factors might have caused an understatement of the reduction.

For 1968/9 we have no figure for the motor trades, and the analysis must therefore be done in terms of the mean for the other five trades. Applying the same method as was used for 1967/8, we find that the mean of the ratios for profit to turnover minus SET in 1968/9 was 13.2 per cent for these five trades, whilst the basic year ratio was 13.4 per cent. Thus we again find a small reduction below 'expectation'.

It will be apparent from the above exposition that our evidence on the effects of SET on profitability is scanty, and any conclusion from it must necessarily be treated both as tentative and as applying only 'in a general way', and not as applying to each separate trade. (Correspondingly, it would be quite unreasonable to apply our simple method to each trade separately, and so arrive — for example — at the conclusion that the effect of SET had been to raise the profit/turnover ratio for hotels.) It is, however, plausible on *a priori* grounds to expect that SET would slightly reduce the profits/turnover ratio in the affected trades in the early years after its imposition, and the results of our investigation are in conformity with that expectation.

It is perhaps right to add that anyone who believed for other reasons that the effects of SET on the profits/turnover ratio would be negligible is unlikely to regard the outcome of our analysis — given its admitted limitations — as providing much reason for him to change his views.

Prices and Productivity

Chapter XII describes two fundamentally independent methods which we adopted for assessing the effects of SET on the prices of services falling within the ambit of the tax. As explained above, neither the data nor the methodology were reliable enough to justify us in making any statement about the effects on the prices of individual services, and our object was to bring together the price series for all the items which seemed at all relevant to our investigations, with a view to arriving at a general conclusion. Some of these series come from trades outside the field of near-distribution, but there is no reason to suppose that the general conclusion would be less applicable in that field than elsewhere.

The main conclusions from the analysis in Chapter XII are given on pages 98 and 99. For our present purposes, however, it is probably sufficient to quote the main conclusions which were that the introduction of SET had led to an 'abnormal' rise in prices (over and above what would have been expected in its absence) which was about equal to the proportion which SET represented of the immediately preceding prices, or perhaps a little less; and that the same was also true of the two increases of SET, in 1968 and 1969.

It is, however, important to emphasise that these conclusions relate to the prices of what might be called 'services proper', rather than to distribution, construction or other 'services' where the cost of the thing sold is made up largely of goods bought from other businesses (e.g. alcoholic drink sold by public houses, or cars sold by motor traders).

On *productivity* Chapter XIII shows that the statistical problems are even more acute than for the analysis of the effects on prices; it is even more necessary to confine one's conclusion to statements about the field as a whole, and to make them in a very tentative form. Nevertheless, the statistics since 1965 do seem to suggest that there was some 'abnormal' increase in physical productivity per person engaged (measured on a full-time equivalent basis, and including self-employed) over and above what was to be expected in the absence of the tax. Moreover, it seems likely — although the evidence on this point is purely impressionistic — that this would be the outcome even if one could make a reasonable allowance for changes in the quality of the services rendered.

We naturally found it disappointing not to be able to put any quantitative figure on this gain in productivity, or even to be *sure* of its existence: however, this seems to be the position which one must expect to find at the end of research in a field as difficult statistically as the present one, especially as the enquiry had to be brought to an end without our having launched any special investigations over a large part of the field. We throughly expected, in fact, to find ourselves in a position of similar uncertainty when we started our analysis of the distributive trades, but in that field the statistics from all sorts of different sources (and dealing with different aspects, including margins) fitted together in a remarkably consistent way.

Consistency Test

The object of quoting the above results from later chapters is to enable us to use the results of our surveys in the near-distributive field, so as to see whether the independent conclusions reached about profits, prices and productivity are, collectively, consistent with the movement in our sample's accounting ratios between 1965/6 and 1968/9.

This consistency test is of the same broad type as the ones we used in the First Report (pages 114—118), but had to be adapted to apply to trades where the concept 'gross margin' has no meaning, and where in consequence one is considering the movement in the *price* of the thing sold, rather than in the gross margin. It is perhaps worth repeating that even if the consistency test shows a remarkable degree of agreement, nevertheless this does not prove that our conclusions are correct; the agreement might reflect compensating errors in two or more of the conclusions, and there is no way from the test of assessing how large such errors might be. In brief, the use of a consistency test of this kind is a method of subjecting one's results to an ordeal in which one may lose, but cannot win.

Before looking at the figures, one other preliminary point should perhaps be made. We have chosen to apply the test to the year 1968/9, although we have no figures for the motor trade for that year, and so have to work with the mean ratio for the other five trades. The *positive* reason for this choice of year is that it seemed desirable to take the year which was as late as possible, when the rate of SET was higher; *negatively*, however, it also seemed quite sensible to omit the motor trades, because the 'conclusion' about prices (which is very important) rests on a consideration of 'pure service items', and a large part of the business of the motor trade is concerned with selling cars or petrol. We considered omitting public houses from the exercise also, for similar reasons, but we decided that the reasons were not as powerful in this case and that it would be better to retain five trades for the test.

The basic material for the consistency test is shown in Table VI.1, and was obtained by the following procedure:-

The first column is simply the unweighted mean of the ratios for the five trades in 1965/6, as derived from our survey.

The second column is based on the corresponding ratios for 1968/9, but all the figures have been multiplied by 1.167, which is the unweighted mean of the price indices for the five trades: in this way they are converted from being the amount 'per £100 of turnover' to being the amount for every £100 of turnover *at 1965/6 prices.*

The third column shows what we would have 'expected' the figures to be in 1968/9, per £100 of turnover at 1965/6 prices, in the absence of SET. It is derived from the second column by using our 'conclusions' about the effects of SET on prices productivity and profits 'in reverse' : in more detail, the items emerged as follows:

(a) The figure for SET is naturally zero.

(b) The figure for payroll reflects our conclusion that SET led to a modest gain in productivity; *for the purpose of this exercise* the gain is put at 2 per cent, although we do not regard that as more than an illustrative interpretation.

(c) The profit figure is found by taking the 1965/6 percentage (13.4 per cent) and applying it to the 1968/9 turnover, minus SET.

(d) The turnover itself is based on our conclusion that prices are raised by rather less than the amount paid in SET; *for the purpose of this exercise,* we have interpreted that as meaning that four-fifths of SET is passed on in higher prices, and reduced the figure from the second column accordingly.

(e) The item for other expenses is treated in the table simply as a residual; the essence of the exercise is to consider whether this residual bears a plausible relationship to the 'actual' figure 1968/9 — and this is examined below.

The final column represents simply the difference between the actual figure for 1968/9 and what was 'expected'. It can be thought of as reflecting the effects of SET, measured per £100 of turnover at 1965/6 prices. Since both the columns from which it was derived were balanced, it is inevitable that the sum of the four items above the line will equal the effect on prices; the essence of the exercise can be regarded as a consideration of whether the figure in brackets for 'other expenses' is a reasonable one or not.

What, then, should one expect the effect of SET on 'other expenses' to be? A reasonable first approximation would clearly be to assume that it would be negligible, as we did in our First Report for distribution: from this point of view, it is at least re-assuring to find a figure of only 0.4, on an item for which the 'actual' figure was 64.8.

If one seeks to think of ways in which SET might have had some impact on this category of expenses, two possiblities seem to be worth considering. First, the service trades buy some services from outside — e.g. hotels pay for laundry services — and our conclusion about the effects of SET would lead us to expect the cost of these services to be increased. Secondly, the 'squeeze on profits' might have led traders to economise on various forms of 'other expenditures', possibly at the cost of some fall in the quality of the service rendered (e.g. through using less expensive foodstuffs in preparing hotel meals). It is possible, however, that some of the attempts to economise on labour would lead to a rise in other expenses, e.g. through the purchase of ready-mixed footstuffs, instead of buying the basic articles and having them prepared in the kitchen.

We obtained a little information of a qualitative kind on the second type of development, either through questions on the forms or in the course of interviews. The

Table VI.1 *Consistency Test for Results of Analysis*
(All figures are in current prices, and show the size (in £) of the specified item 'per £100 of turnover at 1965/6 prices'.)

Item	1965/6	1968/9		
		Actual	'Expected'	Actual minus 'expected'
SET	0	2.8	0	2.8
Payroll, excl. SET	30.6	34.1	34.8	−0.7
Other expenses	56.0	64.8	(64.4)	(+0.4)
Profit	13.4	15.0	15.3	−0.3
Turnover	100.0	116.7	114.5	+2.2

Note Derived from DAE surveys for 5 trades, by methods described in the text. Assumes a 2 per cent gain in productivity and 80 per cent passing-on of SET in higher prices.

only conclusion which we could draw, however, was that the developments of this kind were rather small, and that some would operate to raise 'other expenses' whilst others would reduce them. It would be presumptuous to say that one could base any sort of quantitative estimate on this information, but we would expect it to be small, and we would be rather uncertain even about its sign.

So far as the 'indirect' costs of SET to our five trades are concerned, we do of course know that the item is positive, and it seems unlikely that it could be higher than about 0.2 in the final column. This can be seen from the fact that, if one eliminates Local Authority rates and 'cost of goods sold' from the 'other expenses' item, then the figure for other expense in column two of Table VI.1 is reduced to rather under 20. Moreover this has to cover a great number of things which are not affected by SET — e.g. postage, telephones, electricity, and many types of goods which are used in the various businesses, for purposes other than 're-sale'. Admittedly, the goods would often have been handled by distributors who would have to pay SET, but our First Report came to the conclusion that the effects of SET (when taken together with the effects of ending re-sale price maintenance, which could not be separated) was to leave the gross margin of distributors at much the same level as was to be 'expected'. Consequently, we are only concerned with the 'services proper', such as laundry, professional services (e.g. accountancy) and business services generally. It would almost certainly be a gross exaggeration to put the cost of these as high as £10 per £100 of turnover at 1965/6 prices, and the price of such services might be taken as being raised by SET to the extent of 2 per cent. Hence it would seem unlikely that this factor could contribute more than +0.2 to the final column at the outside.

Conclusions from the Consistency Test
The upshot from our review of Table VI.1 seems, therefore, to be that the residual item is rather higher than one would have put down if asked to make an assessment of what should appear there, but the evidence is clearly rather weak, and the size of the apparent discrepancy is a good deal smaller than one would have been prepared to find in view of the uncertain statistical basis for all our three conclusions. In particular, of course, one must remember that in order to carry out the exercise we had

to make a quantitative interpretation of the very broad conclusions that prices probably rose by 'rather less' than the direct cost of SET, and that there was probably a modest gain in productivity. It is perhaps worth noting that the size of the residual would be reduced if we put the gain in productivity at less than the presumed 2 per cent, or if we assumed that more than 80 per cent of the cost of SET was passed on in higher prices; there would clearly be no difficulty in 'interpreting' our broad conclusions in such a way as to make the residual for the effect on 'other expenses' come to any figure which we would regard as at all plausible.

At the risk of appearing to attach too much importance to this rather weak test, we thought it worthwhile to see what results would emerge if we left the assumptions about profits and prices unchanged, and experimented with different assumptions about productivity — since this conclusion rests on such weak statistical evidence. The two experiments which we made both seem to be of some interest.

First, we tried the experiment of seeing what would happen if we assumed that there was no gain in productivity at all. In terms of Table VI.1 the result is, of course that the final column shows zero opposite payroll, and the figure for 'other expenses' becomes —0.3. Such a figure might appear fairly plausible in itself, since it is at least small; it has, however, a somewhat strange implication when taken with the assumption that there was no gain in productivity. For it means that the firms liable to SET were able to effect a reduction in their expenses other than payroll, whilst being unable to secure any saving in labour employed. Such a result is of course *possible*, but the direct incentive given by SET would be towards effecting a saving in labour, rather than in other expenses, since it was labour which was made more expensive

The second experiment was to see what would happen if the saving in labour were put at 5 per cent, so as to be roughly in line with what was found in distribution (though we must not forget that the ending of re-sale price maintenance was responsible for an unknown proportion of that saving). The result in Table VI.1 would then be to raise the saving on payroll (excluding SET) from 0.7 to 1.7, and the residual item for other expenses would go up from 0.4 to 1.4 to preserve the balance. Such a result is perhaps *conceivable,* if one believes that the firms liable to SET secured the economy in man-power mainly by replacing labour by purchased input (on the lines mentioned above, with the use of more expensive prepared foods in place of employing kitchen staff to work on basic foodstuffs). But it is not too easy to think of many good examples of this kind, and certainly we did not get any hint of changes of this kind being made on the sort of scale which these figures would imply. Nor did we get the slightest suggestion of manpower being saved on this sort of scale at the cost of increased depreciation allowances on new machinery.

It seems more reasonable to infer from this second experiment that an assumption of a productivity gain as high as 5 per cent would imply a rather paradoxical picture of the behaviour of the entrepreneurs: for it implies that they were very successful at reducing the amount of labour which they needed for a given output, but allowed their other expenses to rise quite substantially, even though they were suffering a loss of profits. It would, of course, be possible to escape from this dilemma by revising the conclusions on prices or profits : thus the figure for other expenses could be left as it is in Table VI.1, if the effect of SET on prices were reduced from £2.2 to £1.2. This would, however, mean that one was assuming that only 40 per cent of the cost of SET was passed on in higher prices, and we regard that as highly improbable in view of the evidence about prices given in Chapter XII.

On the whole, therefore, we feel that the consistency test provides some good reason for doubting whether the gain in productivity could have been as large as 5 per cent, at least so far as the near-distributive trades are concerned. The arbitrary figure which we originally took 'for purposes of illustration' (i.e. a gain of 2 per cent in a year which, on average, was centred rather more than two years after the introduction of the tax) gave a much more plausible picture, though the plausibility would have been slightly increased if the gain had been put rather lower.

It is, perhaps, fitting to end this chapter by noting one other point. Anyone who believed that the effects of SET would be to raise prices by the full equivalent of the tax, whilst having no impact on productivity at all, would find the consistency test giving him no reason to change his views. An opponent who wished to cast doubt on such a theory must either rely on the statistical evidence presented in Chapters XII and XIII, taken separately, or resort to *a priori* reasoning.[1]

---

1 For my own part, I started without any preconceived views about the effects of SET on prices and productivity, and the results which emerged from Chapters XII and XIII seemed perfectly plausible: I therefore regard them as my best estimate of the true position and the fact that they 'passed the consistency test', as set out in this chapter, added a little to the strength of my belief. But obviously one cannot *rule out* the belief set out above.

VII
Further Effects of SET on Near-Distribution

The preceding chapter considered the effects of SET (and other abnormal new factors) upon prices, productivity and profits. These effects were studied in a purely statistical sense, however, and it is the object of the present chapter to examine how businessmen reacted to the tax to achieve, for example, the abnormal productivity gains indicated. We also look at some of the wider aspects of the tax as it affected businesses in the near-distributive trades.

Premliminary Observations

As a preliminary to this discussion we feel it necessary to reiterate two general points made in our First Report, which are equally relevant to near-distribution.

The first of these concerns the nature of the information contained in this chapter. In the main it is drawn from our own enquiries amongst businesses in the near-distributive trades and represents the post-SET historical record. There are in general no statistical devices available for disentangling the 'effects' of SET, from changes caused by other factors. We can, however, consider this historical record in the light of the comments and views of the businessmen who participated in our enquiries. As with the distributive trades, our over-all impression was that although similar decisions might well have been taken in the absence of SET, nevertheless processes were often accelerated as a result of the introduction of the tax.

Secondly the changes which had taken place since the introduction of SET were not perhaps as great as one might have expected on purely theoretical grounds. In this respect experience was again similar to that found in our study of distribution. The superficially surprising degree of inertia which emerged is probably explained by the fact that SET was not a single disturbing force introduced into an otherwise static situation, but rather one of a continuous stream of changes which affected the conditions under which businesses were operating: moreover other changes were often more important. Adjustments to SET had to be part of a continuing process of adjustments to events of many kinds, and it is probably for this reason that SET often appeared to do no more than accelerate processes already under way rather than lead radically new policy changes. Businesses were already faced with the problems of constantly rising costs, especially the costs of labour, and SET merely produced three upward jerks in these.

We have divided our discussion of the effects of SET on near-distribution into several main categories: quality of service; methods of working and investment; composition of employment and other aspects of employment policy; pricing policy; and changes in numbers of outlets and in scale of operation. We felt that such an approach would be more useful than a trade-by-trade analysis.

There is obviously a certain amount of overlap between the categories; for example, if a motor trader ceases to offer a warranty with his used-car sales, does this class as a reduction in quality of service or an increase in prices? In some instances, our division of material between headings is inevitably somewhat arbitrary.

It should also be noted that we have by no means reproduced all our findings in full as this would have resulted in an enormous and rather unproductive use of available space. We have concentrated our analysis upon those changes which we feel have occured on a significant scale.

Quality of Service, Methods of Working and Investment

An appropriate way to start this study is with an examination of changes in quality of service, methods of working and investment; for it will be remembered that in the preceding chapter we were unable to quantify the extent to which there had been any changes in quality of service and what would be the resulting quantitative implications for our estimates of SET upon productivity and prices.

We have not attempted to separate rigidly changes in quality of service, methods of working and investment since there is a considerable overlap between them. Investment may result in changed methods of working, or vice versa, and may lead in turn either to an improvement or a deterioration in the quality of service offered.

The Catering Sector

In the catering sector — hotels, restaurants and managed public houses — experience varied with regard to changes in quality of service and methods of working. Some firms claimed that since the introduction of SET they had improved the service they offered (for example, to attract more customers), whilst others said that they had been forced to reduce their standard of service in the interests of economy. In addition some businesses claimed to have achieved reductions in expenses without any accompanying reduction in the standard of service offered. The results of our enquiries are summarised in Table VII.1

Table VII.1 *Changes in Quality of Service Offered in Catering Since the Introduction of SET* (Percentage of questionnaires reporting each result[a])

Changes made	Hotels		Restaurants		Managed Public Houses
	Chains	Independents	Chains	Independents	
(i) Reductions in service in the interests of economy	9	19	40	33	12
(ii) Improvements in service or changes in the character of the business designed to attract more customers	33	72	34	50	62
(iii) Reductions in expenses with little or no effect on service	n.a.	n.a.	42	55	38
No. of questionnaires analysed	*95*	*58*	*50*	*60*	*130*

(a) Some establishments made changes in two or more of the above categories

Table VII.2 *Methods by which Catering Establishments Effected Changes in Quality of Service and Methods of Working*

Numbers of establishments achieving	Hotels	Restaurants	Managed Public Houses
(i) *Reductions in standard of service offered by means of:-*			
Reduction in menus	7	16	–
Reduction in staff numbers	4	3	3
Introduction of convenience foods	–	27	–
Stricter portion control	–	8	–
Removal or reduction in music	–	2	10
(ii) *Improved standards of service by means of:-*			
Redecoration, modernisation or extension of facilities or rooms	56	32	74
Introduction of better menus or catering facilities	36	8	5
Extension or provision of other amenities	12	–	6
Extension or provision of conference facilities	5	–	–
Increased staff numbers	2	–	–
Improved music or entertainment facilities	–	13	10
Introduction of alcoholic licence	–	2	–
Introduction of speedier service	–	2	–
Increased range of drinks served	–	–	17
(iii) *Reduction in expenses with little or no effect on standard of service by means of:-*			
Introduction of general economy measures	n.a.	15	–
Better staffing arrangements	n.a.	6	5
Better buying and delivery arrangements	n.a.	33	–
Introduction of convenience foods or better cooking arrangements	n.a.	21	–
Reduction in wastage (of food etc.)	n.a.	12	–
Increased automation	n.a.	3	13
Introduction of stock control	n.a.	–	9
Better management or management control	n.a.	7	–
Introduction of contract cleaning or reduction of laundering expenses	n.a.	–	18
Number of questionnaires analysed	*153*	*110*	*130*

More firms claimed improvements rather than reductions in the quality of service offered, but one should perhaps treat this conclusion with caution since a firm may be reluctant to admit to a fall in the standard of service offered. An increase in quality of service is however by no means incompatible with what one might have expected as a result of the introduction of SET, since firms may have felt it necessary to attract more business to cover the added costs of the tax. (Nevertheless it may have been the general rise in living standards and increased competition from overseas package holidays rather than the introduction of SET which induced businesses to compete for more trade.)

The over-all changes indicated in Table VII.1 were achieved in a wide variety of ways, which we have attempted to summarise in Table VII.2. The most important changes were as follows. Reductions in standards of service largely took the form of restrictions in menus, size of portions and types of food provided in the case of hotels and restaurants, and reductions in entertainment facilities in the case of public houses. There were some instances of reduction in staffing but this is discussed more fully later in the chapter.

Improvements in standards of service in the main took the form of redecoration, restyling, refurnishing of premises or improvements in menus, catering or bar facilities. There was also some improvement in entertainment facilities.

Hotels were not asked about economy measures introduced which had little or no effect on standards of service. Restaurants achieved such economies mostly through better buying, delivery and cooking arrangements and a reduction in food wastage. Public houses seemed to have effected such ecomomies on a much smaller scale, generally through introduction of stock control, increased automation or reductions in cleaning costs. Again there were cases of economies achieved through better staffing arrangements.

Although hotels were not specifically asked about such reductions in expenses general comments made by these businesses suggested improvements in management control, increased automation and better buying arrangements (e.g. improved discounts or use of cash and carry facilities).

It is of interest to note that a number of hotels and restaurants complained about lack of adequate tax allowances on investment. They claimed that this factor together with the squeeze on profits that had taken place as a result of rising costs (including SET) had had an adverse effect upon the level of investment.[1] Several hotels also said that reduced profit margins had forced them to cut back on renewals and repairs. It should, however, be noted that SET was not generally singled out as being the factor primarily responsible for this.

Firms were also asked about their advertising policies and the times of the year (or hours of the day) during which they were open. There seemed to have been a tendency to try to attract more trade rather than to cut back on advertising or on periods of opening, as is shown in Table VIII.3.

Table VIII.3 *Changes Made Since 1965 in Advertising Policy and in the Period or Hours during which the Establishment is Open*

Trades		Number of questionnaires analysed	Advertising		Period of Opening	
			More	Less	More	Less
Hotels	Chains	95	29	1	0	0
	Independents	58	21	7	5	2
Restaurants		110	17	16	10	13
Managed Public Houses		130	6	2	n.a.	n.a.

---

1 One group of hotels also suggested that the introduction of SET had depressed stock market share quotations and expectations and made raising of finance more difficult.

It is perhaps worth noting the point made by one hotel group — namely that it was not necessarily an economic proposition to close a hotel for part of the year (e.g. during the off-peak period), if only because of loss of staff continuity. Bars often had to be kept open for local trade and even with the hotel closed, many overheads still had to be met.

Finally we asked restaurants and hotels about utilisation of space; for example, whether since 1965 there had been any increase in the average number of beds per room or in the number of seats in existing restaurant facilities.

There had in fact been no signicant change in the average number of beds per room, but independent hotels and both independent and chain restaurants had achieved some increases in seating capacity in existing restaurant facilities. These increases were on average fairly marginal. There had also been an increase in self-service facilities as against waiter service in ten per cent of the restaurants in our enquiry, but this was probably designed to economise on staff rather than achieve a higher utilisation of space.

Trades Other than Catering

The experience of the remaining trades — shoe repairing, hairdressing and the motor trades — can be dealt with more quickly for, in general, the changes that occured were far fewer.

Hairdressers did not report many changes in quality of service offered, methods of working or investment. This is perhaps hardly surprising since the scope for such changes must be very limited. Whilst three-quarters of the hairdressers returning questionnaires claimed to have taken steps to reduce costs and increase efficiency since the introduction of SET, most of these steps consisted of a pruning of labour requirements. There were some instances of increased bulk buying and closer stock control but the scope for savings here cannot have been large.

The main changes that occured in shoe repairing — a move towards more retailing and while-you-wait services — were largely a continuation of earlier trends. The rapid decline that had been taking place in the industry as a result of cheaper ('throw-away' footwear accompanied by rising repair costs had forced a large number of repairers to look towards retailing as a future livelihood. Changing methods of shoe construction, fashions and type of repair work done had all contributed to the growth of the heel-bar and while-you-wait service. In the majority of cases repairers claimed that where they had increased the latter service, it was to match that offered by their competitors

It could be argued that SET was a further addition to repair costs, forcing businesses to become more competitive and look to alternative lines of business. However whilst it may have led to an acceleration of the trends described above, its introduction certainly does not seem to have produced any radical new policy changes.

There were also some instances of increased mechanisation and better buying terms, mainly amongst the larger repairers, but the scope for this is not very great. Where increased mechanisation had taken place larger repairers often claimed that this was to effect labour economies or to offset labour shortages; whilst the smaller repairers seemed more concerned in matching the service offered by their competitors.

The general impression was that repairers faced considerable problems resulting from the decline in the industry and that SET was just one more cost that added to the ever increasing unit overheads.

38

The numbers of shoe repairers making changes in the type of service offered or in methods of working are recorded in Table VII.4

Table VII.4   *Numbers of Shoe Repairers Making Changes in Service Offered or Methods of Working since the Introduction of SET*

Changes made	Independent Repairers[a]	Large Repairers[b]	Total All Repairers
(i) Increasing while-you-wait services	10	9	19
(ii) Increasing or extending range of non-repair activities[c]	44	21	65
(iii) Increasing the extent to which machinery is used in the repair workshop	17	16	33
(iv) Obtaining better terms from suppliers	9	7	16
Total number in sample	105	31	136

(a) These include *all* members of the St. Crispins Boot Trades Association who completed the questionnaire section of our forms. They represent the small independent repairer, many of whom pay little or no SET since they are largely self-employed.

(b) These include all members of the National Association of Shoe Repair Factories who completed the questionnaire section of our forms.

(c) For the firms who could supply us with a breakdown of turnover between repair and non-repair activities, repair receipts fell from 87.9% of turnover in 1965/6 to 81.7% in 1968/9.

What is most evident from the table is that the larger repairers appear to have adapted themselves to changing conditions far more than the smaller repairers. This is probably a reflection of availability of resources as much as ability and probably only to a minor extent due to the heavier SET burden that they have to bear.

Motor traders can be conveniently divided into three categories for the purposes of this chapter — large motor traders, small motor traders and vehicle repairers. We collected information about standard of service, methods of working etc. from large motor traders and vehicle repairers.

Of the 48 large motor traders completing our forms 11 had *reduced* their hours of opening for petrol sales and 8 had reduced them for repairs: only 2 had *increased* opening hours for petrol and only 1 for repairs. Vehicle repairers presented a slightly different picture. On hours for vehicle recovering (comparing 1969 and 1966), of the 34 firms surveyed, 7 had increased them, 3 had decreased them, 21 had made no change whilst 3 firms did not recover crashed vehicles.

However their behaviour was more consistent with regard to credit facilities offered. Of the large motor traders 1 had increased its credit facilities whilst 26 had reduced them; the corresponding figures for vehicle repairers were 2 and 21 respectively. These changes are quite consistent with what one would have expected given the rising cost of credit, but higher administrative costs resulting from SET may have been a contributory cause.

The other ways in which firms attempted to reduce costs are summarised in Table VII.5.

The vehicle repairers were also questioned about the services provided by firms that sold to them. 16 firms replied that the service had changed over the past three years and had deteriorated, the main complaints being less frequent deliveries, no orders accepted under £5, fewer skilled storemen and delays in obtaining supplies: all these changes would increase the expenses of the repairers involved.

Table VII.5 *Number of Large Motor Traders and Vehicle Repairers Making Changes in Methods of Operation since the Introduction of SET*

Changes made	Large Motor Traders (48 firms)	Vehicle Repairers (34 firms)
(i) Increasing the use of (or buying) additional specialised equipment	32	16
(ii) Carrying out deliberate reorganisation of layout of operations	27	8
(iii) Starting to use the services of a computer	11	n.a.
(iv) Narrowing the range of goods normally stocked in any department	12	8
(v) Reducing cost of goods		
(a) by increasing size of orders	18	} n.a.
(b) by other methods	8	
(vi) Introducing labour incentive payment schemes	12	3

Composition of Employment and Employment Policy

Our enquiries gathered a great deal of data on the composition of the labour force in each trade, aimed at seeing whether important changes had been made, and we also asked a number of questions about the employment policy followed by respondents. Underlying these enquiries was the fact the SET had added a varying percentage to the cost of employing different types of labour, and that this might have produced important results.

Part-time Workers

Our results for the composition of the labour force in each trade are given in full in the table in Appendix C. Study of this table showed that there had been remarkably few changes of any importance, though one can see the influence of the discrimination against part-timers in the first year of SET, when the full rate of tax was payable on part-timers without any refund. It seems sufficient to give here a comparison between our earliest ('pre-SET') and latest figures for the percentage of the total labour force in each trade which was provided by part-time workers of all kinds: this is shown in Table VII.6, and it is important to remember that part-timers have been converted to a full-time equivalent (F.T.E.) before the percentage is calculated.

Three reasons probably limited the size of the changes and particularly the smallness of the increases: difficulty in using part-time labour on many jobs; lack of suitable recruits; and the costs involved in making changes, especially when the conditions which seemed to favour them might be changed by a further change in SET regulations.

Since part-time work is so important in the case of public houses and restaurants, our questionnaire asked whether the respondents had attempted to secure more part-time workers for whom they did not have to pay National Insurance (and so SET — essentially 'double-jobbers'): we got positive responses from 15% of the restaurants and 40% of the public houses.

Elderly Workers

We did not collect statistics for the number of elderly workers employed, but we did ask firms whether they had made any changes in the employment of elderly

Table VII.6   *Part-time Employment as a Percentage of Total F.T.E. Employment*[a]

Trade		Month	Pre-SET %	Latest Available[b] %
Hotels[c]	I	November	11.5	11.4
	II	July	11.0	12.0
Restaurants[c]	I	November	17.9	19.4
	II	July	18.0	19.3
Managed Public Houses		April	57.2	55.0*
Large Motor Traders		April	2.2	2.3
Vehicle Repairers		April	1.5	1.6
Hairdressers		August, 1966 and End 1969	2.9	3.9*
Shoe Repairers		April	5.0	5.6*

(a) See Appendix C for full tabulation of composition of employment.

(b) 1968 excepted where indicated * when 1969.

(c) See Appendix C for explanation of which firms are included in the two groups I and II.

workers after the introduction of partial refunds for them. As many of our respondents had only a small labour force, their reactions in this matter were liable to depend largely on chance factors, such as the availability of suitable people who were known to them. The answers which we obtained are summarised in Table VII.7.

Table VII.7   *Employment of Elderly Workers*

Trade		Total number of firms in group	Firms increasing numbers of elderly workers employed after the introduction of refunds on such workers.	
			Number	% of total
Hotels	Independent	58	5	8.6
	Chains	95	4	4.2
Restaurants	Independent	60	6	10.0
	Chains	50	1	2.0
Managed Public Houses		130	2	1.5
Large Motor Traders		48	4	8.3
Vehicle Repairers		34	2	5.9
Hairdressers		n.a.	n.a.	n.a.
Shoe Repairers	Small firms	105	2	1.9
	Larger firms	31	5	16.1

Changes in Policy

Especially in the case of the motor trade, we put a number of questions about employment policies, the results of which are summarised in Table VII.8. Amongst the large motor traders one can generally assume that the absence of a reply meant that the policy listed was *not* followed — very probably in some cases because the opportunity did not arise (e.g. in the case of elderly workers). The questions were concentrated primarily on the effects of the increase in SET in 1968, rather than its initial introduction, because this was a recent event about which the respondents were better able to give accurate answers.

Table VII.8 *Employment Policy in Motor Trade*
(Numbers of firms making specified changes in employment policy)

Changes made	Large Motor Traders (48 firms)		Vehicle Repairers (34 firms)	
	Yes	No	Yes	No
(1) *Did the changes in SET rates in September 1968 lead you to make or to plan to make any of the changes set out below?*				
(i) Tighter assessment of labour requirements	32	16	28	6
(ii) A change in your employment policies such as	30	18	–	–
(a) greater use of part-time workers	9	9	2	32
(b) greater use of elderly workers	4	14	2	32
(c) greater use of women or juveniles	6	12	4	30
(d) greater use of apprentices	11	7	13[(a)]	21
(e) greater use of skilled staff	14	4	17	17
(2) *Did the introduction of SET in 1966 cause you to make*				
(i) a tighter assessment of labour requirements?	36	12	n.a.	n.a.
(ii) any other changes in your employment policies[(b)]	15	33	n.a.	n.a.

(a) The employment figures for 7 of these firms show no change in the number or proportion of apprentices employed.

(b) The most frequent type of change seemed to be a re-examination of the use of administrative staff with some reductions. Other replies spoke of fewer part-timers (4), fewer elderly employees (1), more women (2), more juveniles (2), less seasonal staff (2).

The main impression that we derive from this table is again the comparatively small impact which SET had on the *policies* of the firms, quite apart from the smallness of the actual changes. The 1968 concessions on part-time and elderly workers, for example, seem to have produced little in the way of conscious reaction.

In other trades a few respondents reported general changes in staffing policy and opening hours in a general attempt to economise on labour. One hotel group was training its staff to do a number of different jobs in its hotels so as to cut down the amount of 'idle' man-hours spent during the course of the day. There were also efforts to introduce labour-saving equipment amongst a number of firms, but the scope for this seemed limited in the majority of instances. Some firms also reported changes in the organisation of their businesses (discussed in the preceding section of this chapter) in an attempt to increase productivity. Several restaurants had, for example, moved towards self-service catering so as to cut down on staff numbers, whilst one brewery group said that it had transferred some of its 'loss-making' managed public houses to a tenanted (self-employed) basis, thereby avoiding some SET costs and increasing the publican's incentive.

It is also of interest to note that several firms claimed that SET had forced them to hold down their wage levels. However this is to some extent conterbalanced by the pressures that recruitment difficulties must put on wages.[1]

---

1 This point is discussed in Chapter XIV, which considers the SET sector as a whole.

All in all it appeared that the introduction of SET had acted as a mild spur to increased labour efficiency. Firms seemed to be more aware of the need to economise on labour wherever possible, but in practice the already existing man-power shortages made the scope for such economies small. No really radical changes of policy seemed to have occured, but some already existing trends may have received a slight impetus, as with other changes in methods of operation.

Pricing Policy
Our previous chapter on the effects of SET anticipated the results of Chapter XII on prices, which arrived at the conclusion that in the majority of services a substantial proportion of the cost of SET had been passed forward to the customer in the form of higher prices.

The Catering Trades
In the catering sector price increases took a number of forms. In the case of hotels and restaurants these included higher service charges, cover charges, surcharges, higher tariffs or meal charges. In some instances hotels had covered the cost of SET by increasing the cost of minor items such as morning tea or coffee.

Hotels and restaurants had also met with customer resistance to the principle of 'SET surcharges' and had subsequently abolished them, raising prices instead.

A problem that confronted hotels was the timing of the introduction of SET. In many cases tariffs for the season had already been fixed and bookings taken. Hotels felt reluctant to put surcharges on the bills of customers already booked with them and this created budgeting problems. However a few hotels seemed to overcome their moral scruples in the face of imminent declines in their profit margins.

A large number of hotels and restaurants also claimed that SET had led to increases in the cost of bought-in services which somehow had to be absorbed. 24 hotels said that there had been such increases; whilst 16 restaurants claimed that their suppliers had used SET as an excuse for price increases and 2 that maintenance contracts had risen because of the introduction of the tax.

Public houses perhaps had less scope for passing forward the cost of SET since public bar prices were subject to government control. However it did not appear to be uncommon for both tenanted and managed public houses to have increased the differential between their saloon bar price and that in the public bar. In some instances a larger proportion of a house's accommodation had been devoted to lounge bar facilities. Other houses had introduced meals or entertainments, possibly in an attempt to boost trade to cover the cost of SET or merely as a means whereby the tax could be passed straight on to the customer. We did find instances where there had been fairly substantial price increases on meals already provided by public houses and one brewery group said that it had increased entertainment charges in an attempt to cover the cost of SET. It is perhaps of interest to note that two brewery groups claimed that they could not increase the prices of drinks further because this would lead to diminishing returns. It may be however that the ending of resale price maintenance in off-licences and consequent price-cutting had acted as a special restraint on price increases for drinks.

Taken as a whole the information on pricing policy obtained from the catering businesses in our enquiry did suggest that SET had been a positive factor in leading to price increases. We obtained the impression that at least some firms had attempted to absorb part of the cost of SET when it was introduced; but when inflation led to price increases for other reasons a considerable proportion of the tax had been passed forward to the consumer — in so far as one can distinguish between the various increases in cost which lead to higher prices on such occasions.

Shoe Repairers

The evidence available from our own enquiries about shoe repairers' pricing policy is more limited. In the case of shoe repairers we collected price data from the firms approached in our enquiries, and found this to be broadly in agreement with the D.E. price series. What was of interest was the somewhat greater price increases made by large as against small repairers. For example between April 1965 and July 1969 repairers with turnover of more than £100 000 per annum increased prices for various specified items on average by 31.9%; whilst those with turnover of under £5000 increased prices by only 24.6%, and the intermediate group increased prices by 29%.

It could be argued that the different rates of price increase reflected the relative burden of SET on these firms, since self-employed labour becomes more important as the firm's size class is lowered. However this conclusion should be treated with care. The price data may be inaccurate (since firms were asked to remember what prices they had charged as long ago as April, 1965) and it is also equally possible that the larger repairers (often occupying prime sites) were faced with generally more rapidly rising costs than the small repairers.

There also seemed to be a fairly widespread introduction of minimum charges for minor repair jobs during the post-SET period; but whether this could in any way be attributed to SET is a different matter.

Motor Traders

The scope for price increases and the ways in which they can be effected vary throughout the different sections of the motor trades. Appendix D (Notes on the Trades) discusses pricing and margins in the motor trades — i.e. on new vehicles, used vehicles, petrol, spares and repairs. Against this background we have examined what changes occured in pricing policy during the post-SET period.

We asked firms a number of questions about their pricing policy and the over-all impression created by their answers was one of attempts to raise margins, although there were some instances of reductions in margins presumably designed to attract more trade.

The changes that occured in the pricing policy of the large motor traders with regard to sales of new or used vehicles are summarised in Table VII.9. The recession in vehicle sales which occured at the end of the 1960's may have led to some of the price concessions, which were presumably designed to attract more custom.

The majority of firms adhered to manufacturers' recommended prices on their petrol sales: these led to a fall in gross margin as a percentage of sales, because prices rose and margins remained stable in cash terms. However since February 1966, 5 firms (out of 48) had at least on some occasions sold petrol at other than recommended prices and 11 firms had given trading stamps. The average values of stamps and price discounts and the number of firms making such offers are given in Table VII.10 for each of the years 1966 to 1969.

44

Table VII.9   *Summary of Changes in Pricing Policy of Large Motor Traders*
(Numbers of firms making specified changes)

Comparing March 1969 with February, 1966 have you:	More/ greater/ better	Less smaller/ worse	No change
On new vehicle sales:			
(i) changed the value of free items (seat belts, underseal, petrol, road tax, delivery charges etc.) which you are normally prepared to give in addition to those provided by the manufacturers' warranty?	5	12	31
(ii) changed your *policy* on the size of cash discounts (off recommended prices) which you are normally prepared to give on sales where no part exchange is involved?	11	13	24
(iii) changed your *policy* on the size of excess allowances (in comparison with Glass's guide) which you are normally prepared to give on trade-in sales?	7	10	31
On used vehicle sales:			
(i) changed your *policy* as to the size of cash discounts (below advertised or asking prices) which you are normally prepared to allow on retail used vehicle sales where no part-exchange is involved?	8	6	34
(ii) changed the value of free items (petrol, seat belts, road tax etc.) which you are normally prepared to give on retail used vehicle sales?	1	7	40
(iii) altered your *policy* as to the amount which (in comparison with Glass's Guide) you are prepared to give on part exchanges in your used vehicle sales?	8	12	28
(iv) altered the terms of offer, the coverage or the interpretation of your guarantees on retail used vehicles?	9	10	29

Table VII.10 *Numbers of Large Motor Traders (out of 48) Selling Petrol at other than Recommended Prices and/or Giving Trading Stamps*

Year	Number of firms pricing petrol at other than recommended prices	Average amount by which petrol prices were above or below recommended prices (per gallon)	Number of firms giving trading stamps	Average cost to firm (per gallon)
1966	2	$-\frac{3}{4}$ d	3	1.04d
1967	3	$-\frac{1}{6}$ d	6	1.24d
1968	4	$-\frac{1}{16}$ d	8	1.45d
1969	4	$+\frac{9}{16}$ d	9	1.50d

Note Of these firms many have either moved from cash discounts to stamps (or vice versa) or have raised petrol prices to cover the cost of stamps

Finally charge-out rates (or rates per man-hour) normally charged on repairs rose on average (for the firms in our enquiry) from £1.28 (25s.7d) in 1965/66 to £1.53 (30s.8d) in 1967/8.

Gross margins of the smaller motor traders declined between 1965/6 and 1967/8, partly no doubt because of the declining percentage margin on petrol and partly because their suppliers were taking a bigger part of the available margin on spare parts. We have no direct evidence as to changes in charge-out rates or petrol selling practices for the period 1965/6 to 1967/8. However for 1968/9, the questionnaire replies summarised below may be of some interest.

Table VII.11 *Summary of Questionnaire Data for Small Motor Traders*

	1968	1969
Firms included in the financial analysis		
Charge-out rate (average, all firms)	21s. 3d.	25s. 2d.
Average value of stamps given with one gallon of petrol (4 firms)	1.15d.	1.275d.
Reduction in petrol prices from recommended prices (1 firm)	¾d.	½d.
Firms with insufficient data to be included in the financial analysis		
Charge-out rate (average, all firms)	23s. 4d.	27s. 3d.
Average value of stamps given with one gallon of petrol (6 firms)	1.54d.	1.71d.
Average difference between selling price and recommended price (5 firms)	0.8d.	0.9d.

Vehicle Repairers

In the case of vehicle repairers we have fewer indications still of the factors that affected percentage gross margins, which in fact fell over the period under study.

One factor that would have been likely to widen margins would have been the increase in charge-out rates over the period concerned – from an average of £1.20 to £1.35. Another factor likely to increase margins would have been the decline in 'wholesale' sales (i.e. work done for the trade) as a proportion of total sales of the firms concerned. Fifteen firms gave us details of the proportions of such sales and their figures revealed a fall in the average amount of business done on wholesale terms from 45.6% in 1965/6 to 40.1% in 1967/8. Similarly the fact that 10 of the 34 firms questioned reported reducing their normal discounts 'to the trade', while only one firm increased them, would suggest a widening of margins.

Against this we can only set the increased cost of goods subject to SET surcharges (all firms but 5 reported being subjected to these and one of the remainder had paid a surcharge previously but had seen it dropped by the supplier concerned and re-placed by higher prices), increased pressure from insurance companies to keep down the costs of repairs, and competition from firms which escaped the payment of SET because they used self-employed labour or were mainly engaged on vehicle-building.

Number of Establishments

We conclude this chapter with some brief notes on changes in the number of estab-lishments in shoe repairing and hairdressing for which we obtained some information through enquiries to Trade Associations and multiple firms. There is also some official data from censuses, but this does not extend beyond 1966.

Shoe Repairing

In the case of shoe repairing both the Census of Distribution and the Trade Association membership data pointed to a continuous decline in number of shoe repair establishments and organisations over the pre-SET period. In 1950 the Census of Distribution recorded 18 467 shoe repair establishments; in 1961, 11 154; and in 1966, 8769. What was most noticeable was the growth in both the numbers and turnover of the multiple organisations. In 1950 they operated 3.2% of total establishments; in 1961 8.1%; and in 1966 14.3%. Their share of total turnover rose from 8.2% in 1950 to 33.6% in 1966.

The data collected in our own enquiries would suggest a continuation of these trends. Membership figures from the St. Crispin's Boot and Shoe Traders Association suggest a decline of some 30% in the number of small independent repairers between the end of 1965 and end of 1969 − a slight acceleration in the annual rate of decline over the pre-SET period 1961 to 1966 as indicated by the Census of Distribution. Data from the local Shoe Repair Trade Associations also suggests a slight acceleration in the rate of decline in numbers of independent shoe repair establishments in the post-SET period.

The larger repairers (members of the National Association of Shoe Repair Factories) were asked about the number of outlets they operated and about any changes they had made in their policy towards closures, acquisitions, opening of new branches etc. The 31 firms completing our questionnaires operated just over 1100 establishments at the time of our enquiry (August, 1969) and just over 1200 at the beginning of 1966. They had, in fact closed or sold 321 establishments, acquired 31 and opened 178 during that period. There was thus a net decline of 112 establishments between the beginning of 1966 and August 1969 − a net decline of 9.2% or approximately 2½% per annum.

Since we wanted to compare post-SET changes with pre-SET changes, the 31 firms were asked how the figures that they gave for closures/acquisitions etc. since the beginning of 1966 compared with those for the previous three years. Their answers pointed to some acceleration of the concentration process, the number giving various replies being as follows:

	Greater	Smaller	No change	No answer
(a) Closures and sales:	9	1	16	5
(b) Acquisitions:	5	2	18	6
(c) Premises opened:	6	9	13	3

These larger repairers seemed to have followed a process of rationalisation, acquiring or opening profitable prime site establishments, whilst cutting back on smaller, less profitable outlets in poor locations.

Since the rates of change were so large before the introduction of SET, it would clearly be wrong to assert that the small acceleration is a measure of the effects of the tax, especially as the exemption for self-employed workers would in itself help to keep the very small businesses in operation. But SET may have played a part in the contraction of the medium-sized and larger businesses.

Hairdressing

The information about hairdressers is less extensive. Local branches of the National Hairdressers Federation were asked about numbers of members in 1967, 1968 and 1969. Total membership fell on average by just over 3½% between 1967 and 1969, and the answers on these associations' forms suggested that in general changes in their membership numbers broadly reflected the position in the trade as a whole. This decline is a reversal of the previously increasing trend, as shown by the censuses; but again no firm conclusions can be drawn as to the effects of SET upon numbers of hairdressers in business.

Conclusion

This chapter has necessarily looked at a wide range of different aspects of the businesses falling within the field of near-distribution. The main conclusion is the one set out at the beginning of the chapter: even if one regards changes in practice as effects of SET unless there is clear reason to think that they would have taken place anyhow, the effects of SET on business practices seem to have been rather small. The probable explanation is partly that SET was merely one of a continuous stream of factors raising costs, and not a particularly large one at that.

PART III. DISTRIBUTION AND CONSTRUCTION

VIII
Productivity in Distribution

This chapter has two objectives: first, to carry forward to 1970 the analysis of the distributive trades given in the First Report, which ended with 1968 or 1968/9; and secondly, to consider at greater length the case for attributing a substantial part of the abnormal rise in productivity which has taken place in the SET period to other abnormal new factors besides the introduction (and raising) of SET and the progressive ending of resale price maintenance.

Difficulties in Updating

As regards the 'up-dating' process, we must start by saying with regret that it can only be applied to the *productivity* analysis, and not to the analysis of gross and net margins: this is particularly unfortunate in that the latter lent so much support to the whole set of results becuase, though independently obtained, they all fitted together so unexpectedly well.[1] The reason for this regrettable absence is simply that the financial part of the analysis depended fundamentally on our sample survey, and there are no substitute data available which fill even part of the gap. For the productivity analysis, on the other hand, we worked basically from official statistics for the volume of output and numbers engaged in various categories: our own survey provided an independent check on the movement in productivity in both retailing and wholesaling, which showed surprisingly close agreement in each case,[2] but we did not actually use those figures in the calculations — and of course they are not available for the later years as a check.

One general point may also be made here to avoid repetition. The techniques adopted for measuring the effect of 'abnormal new factors' in the SET period are bound to become more precarious, the longer the period over which they are carried. They consist in establishing 'statistical rules', on the basis of the pre-SET period, which tell us what level of productivity was to be 'expected', in the absence of abnormal new factors, in each year. These 'rules' are not simply a crude extrapolation of past productivity figures — though they do include, as a very important element, just such an extrapolation: they allow also for the 'cyclical' factors in ways which differed between retailing and wholesaling (and also between the various approaches which we adopted to get independent checks on the retailing results).[3]

---

1 See First Report, Chapter XIII, and especially pages 114–118.

2 See First Report, pages 67 and 70.

3 See First Report, page 99 (and also pp. 95/97).

But whilst they do make a reasonable allowance for the 'squeeze' on demand they cannot allow for 'changes in structure', and the longer the period, the greater the chance of such a change occuring. The fact that the movements in productivity are so largely explained by a time-trend makes the danger particularly acute, and also makes it difficult to use other evidence to assess (for example) whether something abnormal had happened which might change the trend.

Nevertheless, the case for carrying the analysis forward in time is very strong, even though the figures are subject to increasing error.[1] In the first place, even if SET had not been raised (and RPM ended on more goods) there was some presumption that the effects on productivity would have been rather greater in the long run than in the first two or three years:[2] at the least, one would like to see whether this appeared to be true or not. On top of this, the 'causal factors' *were* made more powerful, by increasing SET (even when expressed as a percentage of wages) and by ending RPM on more goods: one would like *some* guidance as to the effect of this — even if its reliability were declining, and even though we can offer no means of distinguishing this factor from the first one. It *might* be, for example, that the figures pointed to no further abnormal gain in productivity after 1968, in which case the most plausible 'explanation' would be that the SET/RPM combination gave an upward 'jolt' to the normal rise in productivity, which was soon complete and could not be repeated by a larger application of the same medicine.[3]

One last point is worth adding. In so far as the results for later years are exposed to the risk of errors through new factors, there is no presumption that these will operate in one direction rather than the other: thus an apparent further gain in productivity which emerges from the calculations is (so far as one can tell) just as likely to be an under-estimate as an over-estimate.

Productivity in Retailing

The First Report used a large number of methods for estimating the effects of SET/RPM on productivity — some done before the circulation of a draft to commentators, and some after the comments received had persuaded us that we should try using a wider range of possible ways of setting up the 'pre-SET rules'. The result — which is rather unusual in such circumstances — was that all the various methods showed a marked positive effect on productivity, and the figures obtained by the one method described in detail in the draft report seemed to reflect quite reasonably the conclusion which we would have drawn from all the investigations taken together. As speedy publication was important, therefore, we left the draft as it stood, but made it very plain that the case for taking figures of that broad size did not rest simply on the one equation which had been fully described.

With the extension of the investigations to cover 1969 and 1970 it still appears that the results of the equation which was described in the First Report reasonably

---

1 They are however 'best estimates': the error is equally likely to be in either direction.

2 As will be seen in the next chapter, however, there is no real evidence that SET/RPM was 'concentrating retail trade on a smaller number of shops, in which the staff would be more fully employed', even when the statistics are extended to cover 1970.

3 As it turns out, this is *not* what the figures suggest.

reflect the outcome which we would infer from the whole body of our research. We have therefore set out the results of that approach in detail, so that they can be seen as a continuance of the original Report; we have however added in a later section two tables showing the results from a selection of different equations, along with the results obtained by applying similar equations to manufacturing.

The Basic Data

First, it is useful to set out the basic data used in the analysis, and this is done in Table VIII.1 for the years 1965–1970. The figures for 1965–1968 are unchanged; there were various problems in getting 1969 and 1970 figures for the full-time equivalent of the number engaged in retailing (including self-employed) on a basis comparable with the one used in the First Report, but we think that the methods adopted avoid any serious non-comparabilities.

Table VIII.1 *Basic Data for Analysis of Productivity in Retailing*

Year	Index numbers, 1954 = 100			Unfilled vacancies (%)
	Output	Employment	Productivity	
1965	139.7	107.0	130.6	1.64
1966	141.7	105.9	133.8	1.58
1967	143.8	103.9	138.4	1.07
1968	147.1	101.4	145.2	1.17
1969	145.9	99.2	147.1	1.23
1970	148.5	95.5	155.7	1.13

Note 'Output'　　 = specially weighted series for volume of sales, produced by Board of Trade. See *First Report*, p.294.

　　　 'Employment' = full-time equivalent of numbers engaged, including self-employed. See *First Report*, Appendix D.

The main feature of the additional figures which are now available is the actual *fall* in the output figure (based on the volume of sales) which took place between 1968 and 1969. This reflected the taxation and other measures adopted by the Government in 1969, with the object of holding down internal demand and encouraging exports.

The number of people in retailing continued to fall on a full-time equivalent basis, throughout the extra two years, and ended at a level significantly below the 1954 starting-point for the series. This reduction sufficed to give some rise in productivity, even in 1969, but it was less than the pre-SET trend of 2.4% a year. By contrast, the rise between 1969 and 1970, at 5.8%, was exceptionally great, although the rise in output was again sub-normal.

Saving in Manpower

The First Report described in full the method of using the basic equation to compute what movement in numbers engaged was to be 'expected' between one year and the next, in the absence of abnormal new factors (see pages 90–92); by comparing this with the actual movement one gets a measure of the extra manpower 'saved' in that year through the operation of abnormal new factors, which has to be added to any 'saving' already secured up to the earlier year. The results of these calculations are shown in Table VIII.2, which is simply an extension of Table XI.1 in the First Report: to avoid any possible risk of confusion we have, however, referred to the 'ANF effect', instead of using the term 'SET effect', with a note to say that it was shorthand for 'the effect of abnormal new factors'.

Table VIII.2 *'ANF Effect' in Terms of Manpower Saved for Retailing*

Year	% saving in manpower compared with number expected on experience of pre-SET period, *minus* 'ANF Effect' up to the previous year	Manpower engaged as a % of pre-SET 'expectations'	% saving in manpower compared with number expected on pre-SET experience
1966	1.64	98.36	1.64
1967	1.56	96.84	3.16
1968	1.87	95.03	4.97
1969	−0.39	95.40	4.60
1970	2.67	92.85	7.15

Note 'ANF Effect' means the effect of SET, the progressive ending of RPM and any other abnormal new factors operating in the period.

It will be seen that between 1968 and 1969 the abnormal new factors apparently had a small *negative* effect on manpower saving, but between 1969 and 1970 the effect was strongly positive. As was stressed in the First Report, it is quite impossible to expect this kind of exercise to give year-by-year results which are accurate enough to justify fine conclusions, and much more attention should be devoted to the cumulative total than to its allocation between years. The negative figure for 1969 may well reflect the fact that the equation makes inadequate allowance for the effect on productivity of an actual fall in the volume of sales – or, to put the point more directly, exaggerates the extent to which employment can be expected to fall under such circumstances.[1]

The important lesson from Table VIII.2 is undoubtedly that the cumulative saving of manpower comes out a good deal larger in 1970 than it was in 1968.

Productivity

The picture in terms of productivity follows automatically from the calculation of the 'expected' change in employment: with output given, the percentage gain in productivity (compared with what was expected) is the manpower saving, divided by the actual employment. Table VIII.3 (like Table XI.2 in the First Report) gives the figures in terms of productivity, both year by year and as a cumulative effect: as before, it is more important to consider the cumulative figures, which are markedly higher for 1970 than for 1968.

One further point is perhaps worth making. Table VIII.3 shows the rise in productivity 'expected' between 1965 and 1970 as 10.6%, whereas a straight extrapolation from 1965 of the pre-SET trend of 2.4% a year would give a rise of about

1 A further possibility is, of course, that the result reflects errors in the data, which are subject to a considerable margin of uncertainty. But errors in the data might equally well tell either way, whilst the explanation in the text would be expected to lead to an *exaggeration* of the expected fall in employment.

12.6%. If that figure had been used as a standard of what was to be 'expected', the cumulative ANF effect in 1970 would have come out at about 5.4%, instead of 7.7%. The difference reflects the fact that as sales rose much more slowly in this period than in 1954–1965, one had to expect a slower growth in productivity. It is, however, striking that if one had used the simplest approach of all – the assumption that productivity would rise from the 1965 level at the old rate – one would still find a large ANF effect.

Tabel VIII.3 *'ANF Effect' in Productivity Terms for Retailing*

Years compared	Actual % rise in productivity	Expected % rise in productivity on pre-SET experience	'ANF Effect' gained between the two years compared, as a % of expected level in end year	Cumulative 'ANF Effect' (%)[(a)]
1965 and 1966	2.5	0.8	1.7	1.7
1966 and 1967	3.4	1.8	1.6	3.3
1967 and 1968	4.9	3.0	1.9	5.2
1968 and 1969	1.3	1.7	−0.4	4.8
1969 and 1970	5.8	2.9	2.7	7.7
1965 and 1970	19.2	10.6	7.7	–

(a) Gain in productivity in the terminal year named in column one, as a percentage of productivity which would have been expected on pre-SET rules.

The Labour Market Approach

To conclude the up-dating of the First Report figures, it is worth mentioning the rather simple approach embodied in Figure XI.2 of that Report (page 86): this showed how, in the pre-SET period, the deviation of any year's productivity figure from trend could be largely explained by the level of unfilled vacancies in that year, but also showed that the points for 1967 and (still more) 1968 were far above the regression line.

If points for 1969 and 1970 are inserted on that chart, the 1969 one is less striking than that for 1968 (in line with what we have been seeing above). That for 1970 is, however, off the picture altogether:[1] its distance from the regression line implies that abnormal new factors were raising productivity by about 7.6% above what was expected. Once again, this simple approach agreed closely with the more elaborate one.

Productivity in Wholesaling

Only one, rather simple method was used in the First Report for estimating the ANF effect in the case of wholesaling, essentially because the weakness of the data did not seem to justify more elaborate research which seemed certain to give similar results. From the pre-SET period it was found that productivity in any year could

1 The actual coordinates are:		1969	1970
	% Deviation of Productivity from Trend	3.8	7.3
	% of Unfilled Vacancies	1.23	1.13

be predicted with fair accuracy by taking a logarithmic trend to give a rise of 1.4% a year, and adding (or subtracting) a cyclical correction based on the deviation of output in that year from its centred four-year moving average. The validity of this pre-SET rule was illustrated in Figure XII.2 on page 103 of the First Report, which gave a scatter diagram of *percentage deviations of productivity from trend* against *percentage deviations of output from moving average:* up to 1965 all the points were close to a straight line, but those for 1966, 1967 and 1968 were all well above it, by progressively increasing amounts.

If the basic data for 1969 and 1970 are added to the series given on page 300 of the First Report we get the picture given in Table VIII.4.

Table VIII.4 *Basic Data for Analysis of Productivity in Non-Industrial Wholesaling* (Index Numbers, 1963 = 100)

Year	Output	Employment	Productivity
1965	105.8	100.9	104.9
1966	107.7	99.6	108.1
1967	108.4	97.6	111.1
1968	112.0	96.9	115.6
1969	114.2	94.9	120.3
1970	116.1	94.4	123.0

For sources and definitions, see *First Report*, p.299.

From these data, and some estimates for the later years of the 4-year moving average for output, it was possible to calculate the coordinates of the points for 1969 and 1970 on Figure XII.2 of the First Report. Both were 'off the picture', the actual coordinates being:

	1969	1970
% deviation of productivity from trend	+9.2	+10.1
% deviation of output from moving average	+0.4	+0.3

This implies, of course, that the ANF effect was much bigger in each of these years than in earlier ones, and the results are conveniently summed up in terms of figures in Table VIII.5

Table VIII.5 *'ANF Effect' in Productivity Terms for Non-Industrial Wholesaling*

Year	Index Numbers, 1963 = 100		% deviation of actual from expected productivity
	Actual Productivity	Expected Productivity	
1965	104.9	105.0	−0.1
1966	108.1	106.0	2.0
1967	111.1	105.1	5.7
1968	115.6	109.1	6.0
1969	120.3	110.7[a]	8.6
1970	123.0	111.9[a]	9.9

(a) Partially estimated, since the 4-year average for output is not yet known. (The figures for 1967 and 1968 have been slightly revised, because it now is known).

On the face of it, the ANF effect in 1970 had become greater for wholesaling than it was for retailing. We are, however, a bit dubious about drawing such a conclusion, because the output series for wholesalers is to some extent derived from indirect evidence, and may not allow sufficiently for the tendency of retailers to buy more goods direct from manufacturers — a tendency which SET has encouraged. There is also the important point that cash-and-carry wholesaling has been increasing, so that the wholesaler is offering less service.

The more important point is simply that the analysis for wholesaling agrees with that for retailing in showing a substantial increase in the cumulative ANF effect between 1968 and 1970. We return to this at the end of the chapter.

General Factors versus SET/RPM

In the First Report the logical case for attributing the ANF effect basically to a combination of SET and the ending of RPM, rather than to some other and unspecified abnormal new factor, was summarised on pages 99–100. It rested essentially on the point of *timing:* the movement of productivity in the years prior to the appearance of the SET/RPM combination followed certain statistical rules, but from that time onwards productivity rose further and further above the expected level, by a margin many times greater than had been seen in any previous year. Moreover alternative ways of defining the 'rules' all led to broadly the same result.

Such 'circumstantial evidence' clearly cannot rule out the possibility that some other explanation might account for part, or even the whole of the ANF effect. Econometricians know to their cost that there may be departures from well-established statistical rules which rest on a sound economic analysis, without its being possible to name the factors which are responsible: one's faith in the conclusion must inevitably depend, in the last resort, on a subjective assessment of what seems likely, based on such diverse factors as a review of other possible abnormal new factors which would not be reflected in the cyclical elements of the 'rules' (this is why we added RPM to SET as a single factor); one's *a priori* assessment of the power of the explanatory factor; and one's assessment of the likelihood of a coincidence of a third abnormal new factor appearing at much the same time as the introduction of SET and the weakening of RPM. In logic one can say only that the statistical results, which are now extended to 1970, are all consistent with the hypothesis that SET/RPM was a powerful factor raising productivity: an enthusiast for that hypothesis might reasonably add that, unless evidence is produced to the contrary, he considers that the figures found for the ANF effect are just as likely to be underestimates (caused by the coincidence of some new *adverse* factor — perhaps greatly intensified demarcation rules) as over-estimates.

The First Report did however include a footnote on p.99 which qualified the statement that the timing point 'would make the idea of an unspecified " other factor" seem very implausible', which read as follows:

> There is, however, the argument that productivity in manufacturing seems to have accelerated its growth, relatively to what was to be expected on previous rules, at much the same time — the evidence for which has become much more convincing since the preparation of the new index of production.
>
> On this we can say very little, since a proper assessment of the position in manufacturing would require research on a scale which is beyond our

powers. We did do a very simplified analysis, which suggested that there was indeed a break from the previous rules in the course of the 1960's, but that it was not as clear-cut in its timing as in distribution: a more elaborate set of 'rules' — involving the stock and age of capital in use, for example — might show that there was really no break at all, or that it was more clear-cut than the one which we found.

It seems right to mention this point, but its relevance to the results of the analysis of distribution requires a belief in a powerful *common* factor, which explained the acceleration both in manufacturing and in distribution — e.g. a general wave of productivity drives in all types of enterprise, inspired by the advent of a new Government. The fact (if it is a fact) that departures from the old rules took place at much the same time in the two sectors is perfectly compatible with attributing the one in distribution to the SET—RPM combination and the manufacturing one to some different 'new factor'.

This section considers, rather briefly, the results of further work done on this subject. This work was initiated by J.D. Whitley and G.D.N. Worswick of the National Institute of Economic and Social Research, and most of the results were published in three issues of the National Institute Economic Review.[1] I should perhaps start, however, by saying that the work does not seem to me to alter the position much from the one which was described in the above footnote, since its main characteristics are:

(a) The evidence for an abnormal acceleration in the growth of productivity in manufacturing is strengthened — but it still rests on the application of rules of the kind developed for retailing, and takes no heed (for example) of the stock and age of capital in use, so that we cannot know whether a better set of 'rules' would explain away the apparent 'break', or alternatively show a bigger departure from the expected figures.

(b) No real examination has been made as to the timing of any 'break' (and there are some suggestions that it started earlier and was less clear-cut).

(c) No convincing 'common factor' has been suggested.

(d) The analysis has only been carried out for *one* industry other than retailing, so that the case for a common factor does not rest on evidence of similar results appearing in a whole row of industries outside the SET field — e.g. manufacturing, mining, agriculture, transport.

Clearly this list does not prove that further analysis of the non-SET sector would fail to build up a more powerful argument for attributing a large part of the ANF effect to factors other than SET/RPM. For the present, however, my own attitude is summed up in three paragraphs which are almost identical with the ones which I suggested that the National Institute Review should include as a footnote in its final article, to represent my position:

I assume for the purpose of this note that one is satisfied about the existence of an abnormal productivity gain in manufacturing, which comes at the relevant time. I would then regard this as relevant to an assessment of the productivity gain caused in retailing by SET/RPM in the sense that it

---

1 May 1971, page 36; August 1971, page 62; November 1971, page 72. The second article was a Reply by W.B. Reddaway.

would constitute a *warning* that part of that gain might be attributable to the factor(s) which had produced the rise in manufacturing, since these might also apply in retailing: one would need to identify these factor(s) or at least to have a list of 'possibles', to look for evidence as to whether they would be likely to operate in retailing, and finally to assess what sort of effect they might produce there.

It is obvious that such a procedure *might* lead to the conclusion that the effect in retailing would probably be about as big as in manufacturing, in which case it would be correct to subtract the recorded abnormal gain in manufacturing from the abnormal gain in retailing to arrive at the SET/RPM effect. For my part, however, I find such a conclusion highly improbable, since I am unable to think of any common factor which is likely to have contributed substantially to the abnormal gain in manufacturing, and which would operate with equal effectiveness in retailing. Thus the factor to which the May article attached most importance ('shake-out') seems to me to have been quite a plausible explanation for manufacturing, but (as stated in my Reply) to have been unlikely to have had more than a minor impact (if any) on retailing, since our enquiry did not reveal any retention of excessive labour there, which was not needed for the current level of trading, in the expectation of an expansion.

Since the present Rejoinder does not name the alleged common factors, one cannot even make economic speculations about their likely impact in retailing. The assumption about 'equal effects in retailing' seems to rest on the assumption that the whole of the productivity gain in manufacturing should be regarded as caused by a factor which would produce equal productivity gains in all industries (including retailing), and I cannot regard such a hypothesis as probable in the absence of some statistical evidence in its favour. The minimum requirement would seem to be a demonstration that at least one other industry had secured abnormal productivity gains roughly equal to those in manufacturing at much the same time.

Those readers who are not interested in the details of the reasons for these conclusions can pass from this point to the concluding section of the chapter on page 63 without losing the thread of the argument.

Productivity Gains in Manufacturing and Retailing
Having started, like the Red Queen, with the conclusion to the story, let us see something of what lies behind it — whilst still leaving it to those who are interested in the controversy as it developed to read the three articles.

Whitley and Worswick based the whole of their first article on the assumption that the First Report had relied wholly on the use of the equation which it had described in full, and they applied the same procedures to manufacturing. They obtained a similarity between the residuals for manufacturing and distribution which remains remarkable even when the errors in their figures for 1970 are corrected.[1] Expressed in the form of cumulative productivity gains, the (corrected) year-by-year figures

---

1 The authors have agreed that the corrections were needed.

show the following percentages:

	1966	1967	1968	1969	1970
Manufacturing	1.3	3.9	5.5	5.2	5.7
Retailing	1.7	3.3	5.2	4.9	7.5

It is entirely reasonable to regard this set of figures as constituting a very strong 'warning', in the sense used above: it would certainly seem very rash to regard the similarities as a string of coincidences – though in their final article Whitley and Worswick emphasized that it was not part of their argument that the abnormal gains should be equal, and that they had not intended to imply this.

The above figures are, however, derived entirely from the use of *one* of the equations developed for the retailing analysis. It is not, of course, really legitimate to apply to manufacturing *any* equation developed for retailing – and the one described in the First Report was formulated very specifically for retailing; but if the procedure is admitted at all it should be applied to all the equations. The results of doing this for a representative selection of equations (including the original one) are shown in Table VIII.6, using as a test the cumulative gains to 1968 and 1970: the economic logic of the equations is described under the table and the mathematical formulae and parameters, etc, are set out in Appendix C.

Table VIII.6 *Productivity Gains in Retailing and Manufacturing: Equations fitted over the Period 1954–65*

Ref. No. of Equation	(Percentages) Cumulative gain to 1968		Cumulative gain to 1970	
	Retailing	Manufacturing	Retailing	Manufacturing
(1)	5.2	5.5	7.5	5.7
(2)	4.7	3.1	8.7	3.5
(3)	2.9	1.1	5.9	0.3
(4)	4.7	5.3	6.8	3.6

Notes on Table VIII.6

Full details of the equations and the computation are given in Appendix C.

Equation (1) is the one described in the First Report.

Equation (2) ($\Delta E = a + b_1 (\Delta O_t - \overline{\Delta O}) + b_2 (\Delta O_{t-1} - \overline{\Delta O})$) reflects an alternative way of arriving at the expected change in employment between one year and the next. As in the first equation, the intial term is a constant, which reflects mainly the combined effect of the 'normal' (or average) growth in output, *less* the normal growth in productivity. The other two terms reflect the fact that the growth of output in any particular year may have been above or below the average, *plus* a corresponding term for the preceding year (to reflect the idea that the adjustment of employment may lag behind the adjustment in output). As this equation works on year-to-year changes, the expected levels of employment in years after 1965 have to be built up by a cumulative computation, starting with 1966, but we escape the complication which arose with the basic equation of computing D for each year. The gain in productivity is then found by using these 'expected' employment figures, in contrast with the actual ones.

Equation (3) is the same as equation (2), except that it recognises the possibility that the annual productivity gain was increasing during the reference period – the point which was discussed on pages 96–97 of the First Report. It does this by including a term in '*t*', which may be thought of as modifying the constant term so as to allow for any acceleration in the upward movement of productivity. For making projections this 't' term is stabilised at the value reached in the last year – i.e. we then assume a constant productivity trend at the (highest) value reached at the end of the reference period

The third alternative equation (log productivity $= a + b_1 t + b_2 (V - \Delta)$) goes directly to the level of productivity in any year, by relating it to a (compound) trend term, together with a 'cyclical' factor represented by the deviation of the vacancies percentage from its average (which can reflect both 'the state of trade' on the output side and 'the difficulty of securing labour'). This equation has the great statistical convenience, for exploratory analysis, that one can read off the answer for any particular year without going through a cumulative projection.

The figures in this table can largely be left to speak for themselves. Thus the switch from the original equation to equation (2) makes little net difference in the case of retailing – with the 1968 figure somewhat reduced, but the 1970 figure raised; on the other hand, the manufacturing figures for both years are reduced quite substantially. Equation (3), which allows for a rising trend in the productivity gain during the reference period, lowers the results for retailing (a point which we consider further below), but produces much bigger reductions in those for manufacturing. Equation (4) does not make much difference in 1968, but in 1970 it reduces the gain for manufacturing quite substantially.

In brief, Table VIII.6 makes one think that perhaps the similarities between retailing and manufacturing shown by the original equation really *were* a string of coincidences. Moreover it also shows that for manufacturing one must be a good deal more careful over deciding whether one equation is to be preferred to another than one could be for retailing, where the answers were mostly in the same street: for manufacturing the 1970 figure is only 0.3% on equation (3), which is the kind of figure that could easily arise if the true answer were zero.

A Shorter Reference Period

Besides examining the results from different equations, the First Report analysis also considered what would happen if we omitted 1965 from the reference period. The logical reason for this was that in 1965 the RPM factor was already becoming of some importance, and we really ought to have adopted this procedure from the start, since the very first internal working-paper of the Enquiry recognised the RPM problem: our objective in including 1965 was to lengthen the reference period, which is obviously desirable in itself, but we should have resisted that temptation. Mercifully the inclusion of results based on the shorter reference period if anything strengthened our feeling that the figures published in the First Report were a fair representation of *all* our investigations taken together.

If the same four equations are used with a shorter reference period, the results obtained for retailing and manufacturing are as given in Table VIII.7.

So far as retailing is concerned the figures in this table are all rather higher than in the previous one: in the case of the first three equations this is mainly because they include the productivity gain between 1964 and 1965, which must be attributed to the RPM factor, as SET had not been invented. Equation (3), which gave a rather low figure on the previous basis, now comes more into line as equation (7): it is noteworthy that it gives exactly the same figure for 1968 as the one from the original equation which was published. Most of the figures for manufacturing are also raised, and the proportionate spread of the results is again much bigger than that for retailing in each year.

Table VIII.7 *Productivity Gains in Retailing and Manufacturing: Equations fitted over the Period 1954–64*

| Ref. No. of Equation[a] | (Percentages) | | | |
| | Cumulative gain to 1968 | | Cumulative gain to 1970 | |
	Retailing	Manufacturing	Retailing	Manufacturing
(5)	6.3	6.9	8.9	7.6
(6)	6.9	4.2	11.5	5.0
(7)	5.2	2.4	9.0	2.0
(8)	5.1	5.2	7.3	3.4

(a) Details of the equations are given in Appendix C. (They are the same as in Table VIII.6, but use a different reference period).

What, then, should one infer from this collection of results? Whitley and Worswick in their Rejoinder, chose to take an average of the results from each of these two tables, and produced the following summary table (Table VIII.8).

Table VIII.8 *Cumulative Productivity Gains in Retailing and Manufacturing*

| | | | | (Percentages) | |
				Retailing	Manufac-turing
To 1968	..	..	A	4.4	3.8
			B	5.9	4.7
To 1970	..	..	A	7.2	3.3
			B	9.2	4.5

A = average of equations (1), (2), (3) and (4)
B = average of equations (5), (6), (7) and (8).

It will be seen that for 1968 the manufacturing figures are of the same order as for retailing, but rather smaller in each case, whilst for 1970 they are rather under one-half of the retail figures.

This is in itself quite a long way from the close agreement suggested by the original comparison on page 57/8, but there is a strong case for considering which of the equations should be given most weight – and there is no reason for choosing the same one for each industry, since the object is to get the *best* computations in each case, and there is no reason to suppose that this will come from the same equation. So far as retailing is concerned the matter is not very important, because the results all give broadly the same picture, but for manufacturing the range is rather large, with equation (3) – and its counterpart equation (7) – giving particularly low results.

The data for the statistical tests are given in the table in Appendix C. To my mind, the crucial test should be based on the standard error of the residuals, since one is concerned with the margin of error which is to be expected when applying the equation to calculate expected productivity. For the first three equations, which are all predicting the same thing, a simple comparison of the figures in the SE column gives the ranking and it is noteworthy that for manufacturing equations (3) and (7) have the lowest SE of these three; a further calculation shows that equations (4) and (8) are also liable to give worse results than these two. On statistical grounds, therefore, one should prefer (for manufacturing) the equations which show the lowest gains.

Since this form of the equation also seems to have at least as good an *economic* justification for manufacturing as any of the others, one is perhaps entitled to say that in using a simple average of the results, Whitley and Worswick were taking a view of the data which was a bit over-favourable to their argument.

Problems of the Common Factor

The exact size of the abnormal productivity gain in manufacturing is not, in my view, as important as the two over-riding questions which have to be tackled before one can make any inferences about distribution. These are, to repeat:

(a) Is there any positive reason to suppose that there was a common factor operating in manufacturing and retailing?

(b) If reasons can be given in favour of (a), is there any way of assessing whether it would produce equal *effects* in the two industries?

It is important to realise that *both* of these questions need to be tackled: there might well have been a clear-cut 'common factor' which would affect all industries — say the complete abolition of all restrictive practices by labour, to take an imaginary example — but it would be quite wrong to infer that the abnormal productivity gain in manufacturing was a rough guide to the result which this factor probably produced in retailing. One might well say that the impact on retailing would be much smaller, perhaps negligible, because restrictive labour practices hardly affected productivity there.

This point is important to the controversy because Whitley and Worswick do not claim to have named at all definitively the common factor(s) which are supposed to have been operating, and so have not considered the second question at all, or even admitted its existence. Thus they say on page 74 of the November article:

> One possible interpretation of the statistical results above is that the cumulative productivity gain for manufacturing represents the influence of common factors and that the remaining differences between the retailing and manufacturing effects is available for SET/RPM. We are not putting this forward as an exact interpretation of the results.

Despite the disclaimer in the second sentence, the reader might well draw the inference that they regarded this interpretation as *approximately* correct, and I wish therefore to emphasize that it depends *entirely* on the unstated assumption that the (unnamed) common factors would have a roughly equal effect in the two industries. On seeing the draft of their Rejoinder I suggested that this point be made explicit by adding, after 'common factors', the words 'which produce equally large effects in all other industries (including retailing)', but this suggestion was not accepted.

There is a similar omission in the acknowledgement at the end of that discussion, which reads

We acknowledge, however, that even if the existence of the abnormal gain in manufacturing is accepted this does not necessarily establish a common factor or factors; it could simply be that there were by chance other factors working in manufacturing at the same time as SET/RPM in retailing.

No action was taken on my suggestion that the first part of this should end with '. . . . establish *the existence of* a common factor or factors, *or that they operate equally powerfully in other industries*'; (suggested additions in italics).

My emphasis on this point reflects much more than a mere insistence on the niceties of logical inference, and a desire that the reader should be fully informed about the issues in question when making his own subjective judgment. On that generalised basis one *might* even argue that the common factors would be equally likely to have a *bigger* impact in retailing than in manufacturing as they are to have a *smaller* one, so that if one were satisfied that there must have been a common factor (even though it is unspecified), then one could treat the difference between the retailing and manufacturing effects as a 'best estimate' for SET/RPM.

The real point is that all attempts which I have heard about to 'explain' the abnormal productivity gain in manufacturing attribute it to factors which seem to me unlikely to have any significant effect in retailing. This is obviously true of explanations which rest on the growing intensity of international competition 'forcing' manufacturers to raise productivity in order to retain and expand their business. It also seems to be true of the 'shake-out' explanations, so far as I understand that analysis, and on this point the information collected in our Enquiry can throw some light. I doubt whether this information does much more than confirm what I thought to be common knowledge, but the point is nevertheless worth making since Whitley and Worswick seemed to treat 'shake-out' as the most plausible candidate for the role of common factor, and did not discuss the likely size of its impact on retailing.

As I understand it, the background to the shake-out explanation is the belief that before the 'squeeze' measures of 1966 many employers tended to keep on workers during periods of recession, as an insurance policy to ensure that they would have them when the inflow of orders accelerated with the next spurt of demand. This policy was sometimes held to apply only to *skilled* workers, but sometimes extended to all grades. On a limited view this meant that labour was 'hoarded' during the recessions, but fully utilised at the peaks of demand. On a more extended view, however, it is sometimes argued that even in active periods firms sought to build up their labour force in anticipation of further expansion, so that there was always some excess labour somewhere: given the uncertainties of future orders and the time taken to build up a labour force in the face of 'normal wastage' it is logically quite possible that there would always be some excess labour employed somewhere in the system, as a result either of 'over-insurance' against the risk of labour shortage, or of plain misjudgments.

The shake-out hypothesis is, then, that the squeeze of 1966 both weakened the belief of employers in the future growth of demand, so that there was less case for insuring against it by carrying more labour than was needed for immediate purposes, and also left them with inadequate profit margins to be able to afford this luxury on the old scale. Hence they had good reason to reduce the surpluses – not necessarily by redundancies (though these were made less painful at much the same time by the introduction of the Government redundancy provision), but largely by reducing recruitment below the level of natural wastage.

As an explanation of the abnormal rise in productivity in manufacturing, this seems to me plausible — although I would claim no expertise on the subject. But in relation to retailing it seems to me to come up against the abundant evidence that even before the 1966 squeeze retailers were finding it very hard to recruit as much labour as they wanted to hire, merely to do the current level of business. If the typical employer had no hoard of labour which he was treating as an insurance against future expansion, the shake-out process could produce little or no result, even if he became completely convinced that there would be no expansion — though there might be isolated cases where a surplus existed.

Our questionnaire to retailers included no question directly related to this point, but we were absolutely showered with statements about it, either in the 'general comments' section, or in the course of our interviews. Such statements may not, of course, have been wholly unbiassed: many of our informants clearly considered it important to establish that 'there was no justification for introducing SET to make us more economical with labour and so divert it to manufacturing, because we had already been forced by recruitment difficulties to introduce all reasonable economies'. But the statements mostly carried conviction about the general position, even if they may have been a bit exaggerated, and they were sometimes accompanied by supporting evidence. One multiple concern, for example, was at great pains to show that the increase in employment which took place between 1966 and 1967 reflected the branches' success in recruiting more nearly up to their authorised labour force (thanks to the general recession) and was *not* a reflection of laxer standards: this was particularly convincing evidence of the recruitment difficulties which had prevailed in the earlier years, because the labour force was in fact increased when it became possible to do so, *in spite of* the added cost imposed by SET[1].

Conclusions

It is time to summarise the main conclusions from this chapter.

An extension of the calculations in the First Report to cover the years 1969 and 1970 shows a substantial increase in the abnormal productivity gain between 1968 and 1970, both for retailing and for wholesaling; the combined 'saving' of manpower in 1970 was of the order of 200 000 people, on a full-time-equivalent basis.

Any calculation of this kind is bound to be exposed to increasing statistical uncertainty, the longer the period over which it is carried: but it would be very surprising if this could explain the whole increase in the abnormal productivity gain between 1968 and 1970, and formally one can argue that the increase is just as likely to be under-stated as over-stated. All the methods of calculating what level of productivity was to be 'expected' in retailing in the absence of abnormal new factors agree in showing a substantial rise in the abnormal gain.

In the nature of the case, there is no way of assigning the abnormal productivity gain to any particular abnormal new factor. The First Report considered that it

---

1 Since the above was written, my attention has been drawn to an article by R.D. Sleeper in *Oxford Economic Papers* for July 1972 which produces strong arguments in favour of the view that there was little or no scope for 'shake-out' to operate in distribution.

should be essentially assigned to the combination of SET (including its increase) and the progressive ending of resale price maintenance, fundamentally because the break from the old 'statistical rules' came just at the time which one would expect on that hypothesis, and the progressive growth in the gain was also what one would expect. The further growth up to 1970 is also what one would expect, but it is not possible to divide this between the effects of the rise in SET and ending of RPM on more goods on the one hand, and the delayed effects which one would have expected from the initial actions even without such intensification.

The First Report recognised the formal possibility of the gain being partly due to a common factor causing an abnormal gain in both manufacturing and retailing. It is possible that the gain in manufacturing would not appear 'abnormal', if a satisfactory analysis of it were made, instead of using equations designed for retailing; but in any case this line of argument cannot be regarded as providing much more than a formal possibility unless a plausible common factor can be suggested, and its probable effectiveness assessed.

The work done on this question between the two Reports suggests:

(a) That the procedures used for retailing point to a smaller productivity gain in manufacturing than in retailing; the timing of the break has not really been tested, but appears to be somewhat different in the two industries;

(b) That the most plausible common factor suggested — the so-called 'shakeout' — would be unlikely to have much effect in retailing.

It must inevitably be a matter of subjective judgment in these circumstances to decide how much of the gain in manufacturing one thinks should be attributed to unspecified common factors (rather than to something peculiar to manufacturing) and how much effect those factors would produce in retailing.

Whilst recognising that this *could* be an important factor I see little reason to attach much weight to it unless further evidence in support of it is produced.

IX
SET and the Number of Shops

In our First Report we took a preliminary look at the possible effect of SET on what is loosely called 'the number of shops', but should really be interpreted as 'the total retailing capacity in use' (since there has for many years been a progressive tendency for the number of shops to decline, whilst their capacity to do business has been increased because one larger shop has replaced a number of small ones).

There were two reasons for studying the effect of SET on the retailing capacity in use: firstly, it is of some interest in itself, as reflecting (for example) the effect of SET on one aspect of the consumers' freedom of choice; and secondly, it has sometimes been argued that the effect of SET in producing an increase in productivity would be secured largely through its effect in reducing what the protagonists of this view describe as 'the number of shops'.

The First Report also looked at what had been happening to the amount of new building of shops which was being put in hand. These figures were not scrutinized as a means of arriving at the movement in the retailing capacity in use, because the new construction schemes would frequently have no effect on available capacity for some years, owing to the time involved in getting plans passed and buildings erected; moreover capacity would also be influenced by transfers of buildings into or out of retailing. The object was rather to see what light the building statistics (and above all the figures for orders placed) threw on the consequence of the profit squeeze in retailing produced by SET. This part of the investigation was, however, inevitably a hazardous one, because of the disturbing effects of two important factors which were not consequences of SET: the building controls, which were intensified in 1966, and the slow growth of the volume of retailing which reflected the general economic position in the years 1966 to 1970. Moreover, as the new building consisted to a considerable extent of long-range developments in the centres of cities, the scale of new orders is much influenced by long-term views about the profitability of retailing, as well as the current level of profitability and the supply-demand position for shops at the time (which reflects the scale of *past* building, *inter alia*).

At the time when the First Report was written, the amount of post-SET data available was very limited, and our conclusions were therefore very tentative on both matters. This chapter brings up to a later date the statistics previously used, and reconsiders our first tentative answers – but in fact comes to much the same conclusion.

Growth of Retailing Capacity
Our method of approach is to arrive first at movements in 'retailing capacity' *available*, including vacant shops, and then to make an assessment of the effects of

changes in vacancies. The primary sources are all derived from the work of keeping up to date the rating lists.

First of all, Table IX.1 brings up to date the figures for the number and rateable value of 'shops' previously given in Table XIV.8 of the First Report.

Table IX.1   *Rateable values for England and Wales*

1st April	Shops assessed with private dwelling accommodation		Shops (including banks in shopping areas) and cafes		Total shops, banks in shopping areas and cafes	
	Number	£ m.	Number	£ m.	Number	£ m.
1958	325 628	20.2	347 384	52.7	673 012	72.9
1959	321 197	19.9	353 195	54.6	674 392	74.5
1960	317 518	19.8	356 555	55.9	674 073	75.7
1961	313 833	19.7	359 997	57.5	673 830	77.2
1962	309 168	19.5	362 384	59.1	671 552	78.6
1963 (31st Mar.)	303 616	19.3	365 902	60.8	669 518	80.1
1963 (1st Apr.)	294 257	44.3	374 671	165.5	668 928	209.8
1964	290 202	43.8	374 615	165.5	664 817	209.3
1965	284 881	43.2	376 055	166.8	660 936	210.0
1966	279 079	42.5	379 060	169.3	658 139	211.8
1967	272 878	41.9	381 859	172.4	654 737	214.3
1968	266 011	41.2	385 291	175.4	651 302	216.6
1969	259 110	40.5	387 782	179.2	646 892	219.7
1970	251 992	39.8	389 269	182.6	641 261	222.4

Source: Reports of Commissioners of Inland Revenue.

Note A new rating list came into force on 1st April, 1963.

The statistics for *numbers* are not much use as a guide to 'capacity', because the average size of shop has been rising, and one cannot assume that the speed of this rise has been uniform. The valuation figures are a much better guide, apart from the discontinuity in 1963, when a new valuation was introduced: effectively the figures in each section are 'constant price' series, except that the initial figures in the second section (primarily 1963, but to a declining extent 1964 and 1965) are biassed upwards slightly, because they do not reflect the reductions in valuation which were subsequently obtained by the ratepayer on appeal.

The main lesson to be learned from Table IX.1 is that the total valuation of 'shops' continued to rise after the introduction of SET, with little sign of any discontinuity compared with the preceding years: from 1966 to 1970 the rate of growth was about 1.2% per annum, and deviations from this were relatively small. This is distinctly *higher* than the rate shown for 1963 to1966, or indeed for any year in that period, but the valuation point mentioned above could well account for this. The rate is somewhat lower than the one for 1958 to 1963 (abour 1.8%), but that relates to a period some years earlier, and one can hardly expect a constant rate of growth for more than a decade. Our main conclusion must therefore be that the statistics suggest a remarkably stable pattern of development.

Floor-space Figures

The First Report also gave (in Table XIV.7) some figures in terms of square feet for the change in floor space during each of the 3 years prior to 31st March 1967, with separate figures for 'additions' and 'reductions': these figures were also derived from the work of maintaining the valuation lists, and correspond with the central column of Table IX.1 above (i.e. excluding shops assessed with dwelling accommodation).

These figures are brought up to date in Table IX.2, but it will be apparent that there is a discontinuity between the figures for the year to March 1967 and the subsequent years. This discontinuity undoubtedly arose out of the floor-space 'census' which was taken in respect of March 1967, even though no formal change in procedures was adopted as a result: we had to devote a great deal of work to disentangling the statistics (although the approach which we finally adopted is quite simple, if a bit impressionistic) before we could draw any conclusions.

Table IX.2   *Changes in Floor-space for England and Wales*
(Figures are in million square feet, and cover shops, restaurants and banks in shopping areas)

Year ended 31 March	Additions	Reductions	Net change
1964–5	13.2	5.3	+7.9
1965–6	13.8	4.9	+8.9
1966–7	13.4	5.9	+7.5
1967–8	23.4	12.1	+11.3
1968–9	23.6	13.3	+10.3
1969–70	23.3	12.8	+10.5

Note The total floor-space on 1st April 1967 was 556 m.sq.ft.

Source: Commissioners of Inland Revenue.

Our first important clue was that, although the 'net change' figures for 'shops' showed an obvious discontinuity, nevertheless there was nothing obviously wrong if we considered the three main use-categories together, as one can see from Table IX.3

Table IX.3   *Net Increase in Floor-space for 3 Main Use-Categories*
(England and Wales, m. sq.ft.)

Year ended 31 March	Shops etc.	Offices etc.	Industrial premises etc.	Total – 3 categories
1964–5	7.9	7.7	33.5	49.2
1965–6	8.9	9.2	35.2	53.3
1966–7	7.5	8.5	31.5	47.5
1967–8	11.3	14.5	28.7	54.5

Note No figures for the remaining category (warehouses etc.) are yet available, and the only series available after 1967/8 is for shops etc.

Source: Inland Revenue Statistics.

From this we concluded that the main reason for the statistical discontinuity was that the floor-space figures before March 1967 had largely omitted transfers between uses which did not involve extensions or other developments, such as would necessitate a visit to the premises by the valuation officer. These were *supposed* to be included, but had been missed until the census of floor-space drew the officers' attention to the matter.

The next problem was to estimate how much should be added to the pre-discontinuity figures for shops etc. to allow for the net inward transfers which had been missed. Here we relied primarily on the fact that the rateable value figures were reasonably continuous, and on enquiries which revealed that they should reflect use-transfers as well as new building, extensions and demolitions. For the three-year period after the discontinuity the increase in floor-space amounted to 32.1 m. sq.ft., and the increase in rateable value to £10.2 m., giving an average of 3.15 sq.ft. per £1 million added to rateable value. We did not think it safe to apply this to any year before 1966/7, because of the valuation problems mentioned above, but for that year it gave a net increase in floor-space of 10.0 m. sq.ft., implying an inward transfer of 2.5 m. sq.ft.

If this figure is taken as broadly representative of the inward transfers which were missed in the pre-discontinuity years,[1] and added to the final column of Table IX.2, then we arrive at much the same conclusion as before: the available 'capacity' — this time measured in terms of floor-space for shops etc. without dwellings attached — showed a rather steady upward trend, with increases fairly consistently about 2% a year.

Vacancies and Capacity in Use

The statistics considered so far relate to capacity 'available', and we need to make an allowance for possible changes in vacancies. We could find no statistical series for these, but we again sought the advice of a leading firm of surveyors, valuers and auctioneers, who gave us the benefit of their experience for the whole period covered by our rating statistics and right up to March 1971. This information — which covered most parts of the country — was very valuable for its qualitative character (discussed in the last section of this chapter) as well as for its direct relevance to the assessment of vacancies.

Inevitably, there is no single answer about the behaviour of vacancies, which has varied between different towns in the country and between prime positions and those in less favoured areas.[2] The general trend was however that the shop property market had continued to move in the direction of owners finding it more difficult to find satisfactory tenants — or, more strictly, to find them *quickly* — except in the case of favourable positions in town centres. Rent reductions had sometimes been necessary to secure a tenant, and the general tendency for rents to rise rapidly had

---

1 We applied other tests as well, which gave similar results. Thus we projected a figure for shops etc. for 1967/8 on the 'old' basis, by assuming the same percentage rise above the average for the 3 previous years as was shown for the final column of Table IX.3 (i.e. the 3 categories taken together); this gave 8.8 m. sq.ft., which was 2.5 m. sq.ft. less than the 'new basis' figure.

2 For this reason we must stress that the responsibility for our attempts to draw general conclusions rests wholly with us.

become less marked: in some cases seven- or fourteen-year leases had been renewed in 1970 at the end of their term at rents which might well represent a decline when one allowed for the fall in the value of money. It had however become more general for leases to provide for frequent rent reviews to prevent owners from losing seriously in real terms during the period of the lease.

Besides this direct information from people engaged in the property market, we also had the evidence of the building statistics discussed below – above all the placing of new orders – which gave indirect evidence that vacancies were not high enough to prove a deterrent to new building.

Our tentative conclusion was that vacancies must have increased, so that the rise in 'capacity in use' would be less than that shown by the rating statistics. Nevertheless it seemed highly improbable that it could have turned that increase (of nearly 5% for rateable value between March 1966 and March 1970) into a decline: an increase in vacancies equivalent to 5% of the total retailing capacity would be a truly major event, such as would create a renter's market in which talk of rent *increases* would disappear. The sort of figure which we had in mind was an increase in capacity-in-use of about 2 or 3% over the 4 years.

The Effects of SET on Capacity-in-Use

The increase in capacity-in-use between 1966 and 1970 was almost certainly less than the increase over the previous four years, which may be guestimated on the basis of the valuation figures at about 6 or 7%. The decrease must not, however, be regarded as measuring the effects of SET (or even of SET plus the progressive elimination of RPM), because other factors changed markedly: in particular, the volume of trade grew much less rapidly over this period, and one must allow for that in assessing what would have happened to the capacity of shops in the absence of SET and other abnormal new factors,[1] just as we had to do when assessing how many workers would have been needed.

We have not attempted a formal analysis of the influence of growth in the volume of sales on the capacity-in-use of shops: since some of the effects would be slow in appearing, it would clearly be extremely difficult, and it would have to rest on changes in *sustained* rates of growth, rather than annual changes. In broad terms, however, there can be no doubt that the factor would be important: we should have directed more attention to it in the First Report – notably in our 'tentative conclusions' on page 144.

It is convenient to examine the matter by using four-yearly growth rates, rather than annual ones, both because that is the period for which we have a post-SET estimate of capacity-in-use, and also to emphasize the longer-term nature of the effects. On that basis, the period up to 1966 showed a fairly steady growth in sales volume of rather over 10% per four years, but in 1970 the volume was only 4% above 1966. This is a much bigger fall in the growth-rate than that given above for

---

1 It may be helpful to remind the reader that 'abnormal new factors' are those which could not be allowed for econometrically: the slower rate of increase in the volume of trade (which is attributed to the disinflationary policy as such, not to the choice of SET as one of the instruments in that policy) was allowed for. To quote the First Report (page 99): 'our method automatically allows for the basic upward trend in productivity and for all factors which affect retailing through the level of demand or the general state of the labour market.'

capacity-in-use. If one could assess the causal connection, one would of course expect a drop in the four-yearly sales growth of 6 percentage points to reduce the capacity-growth by less than 6 points, especially when one remembers the inevitable lags; but it would be very difficult to argue convincingly against the view that the slower growth of sales volume is sufficient to account for the slower growth of retailing capacity-in-use.

Putting the matter the other way round, the statistics do not provide any convincing evidence that SET as such, even with the aid of the RPM changes, had any effect on the growth of the capacity used in retailing. One may hold that belief on *a priori* grounds, and the statistics are not strong enough to refute it; but one's faith is held *in spite of* the statistics, not because of them.

The 'Number of Shops' Theory about Productivity Increases

What, then, are we to say about the theory that the gain in output per worker in retailing was largely obtained because the introduction of SET (and the ending of RPM) tended to reduce the number of shops and so increase the sales of the remaining shops, which would be able to handle the increased trade without a proportionate increase in their labour force (and perhaps without any increase at all)?

Stated in this way, the theory is of course a drastic simplification of the real world, and it is couched essentially in terms of comparative statics: it needs to be interpreted with a liberal addition of *ceteris paribus* clauses, so as to fit into a world in which (for example) productivity normally shows an upward trend, and the average shop size is getting progressively bigger. The theory then becomes one in which:

    (a) the number of shops in the later years is smaller than it would otherwise have been (allowing for the normal rise in average size, as well as the change in the total volume of trade);

    (b) each of the remaining shops has a higher level of trade than it otherwise would have had;

    (c) the number of workers per shop is not increased above what it would have been — or at least not increased proportionately to the gain in trade under (b).

In brief, we have to replace simple comparisons with the base year by measures of the 'effects' of SET and other abnormal new factors.

So far this chapter has been examining the validity of point (a) in the above list, and one might argue that the doubts which were cast on it should conclude the investigation. The statistics are however sufficiently uncertain to justify considering the remaining steps of the argument, on the assumption that there was some small SET effect on the 'number' of shops.[1]

Even if one grants this point, however, the theory encounters further — and more formidable — difficulties. For if the *only* way in which SET/RPM affects productivity is through its effect on the 'number' of shops, this necessarily implies that the effect on the number of shops will be at least as great as the effect on the number

1   In the discussion which follows I will follow the tradition of the theoretical model by assuming that shops are all of equal size, so that we can refer to 'number' as a measure of the capacity in use: this makes the argument rather easier to follow, without affecting its substance.

of workers, and probably greater. In terms of the static model, if the number of shops was reduced by x per cent, then the best that could happen was that the remainder would do the increased amount of trade which each received with the same number of workers per shop: if they had to take on extra workers, the reduction in the total labour force would be *less* than x per cent.

Now whatever view one may take of the statistics on capacity, they certainly do not point to an 'SET/RPM effect' on capacity which is anywhere near as big as the effect on the number of workers (discussed in Chapter VIII), let alone exceeding it. Consequently there must have been some other route by which the bulk of the productivity gain was secured: it was not, in the main, a case of 'more sales per (standard-size) shop, without a corresponding increase in the shop's labour force', but rather a case of 'fewer workers per shop' (or, rather, 'per unit of retailing capacity').

To avoid misunderstanding one should say explicitly that the 'number of shops' factor may nevertheless have made a *modest contribution* to the improvement of productivity, and it is one which might logically be expected to grow with the passage of time. As is so often the case, an elegant static model — in which 'time' simply does not feature — seems to be a very poor guide to what happens within a time-period which is short enough to be relevant for policy-making purposes.[1]

New Orders for Shops

Our second question relates to the effect of SET and other abnormal new factors on the building of additional shops, which is of interest both in itself and as a reflection of the reduction in profitability which followed from SET and the ending of RPM.

We now have, of course, more statistics than at the time of the First Report, and Table IX.4 brings the figures for 'orders placed' down to the end of 1970.

Table IX.4   *New Orders for Shops[a] in Great Britain*

Year	New orders for shops by private sector (£m. at current prices)	New orders for shops by private sector (£m. at 1963 prices)	New orders for shops by private sector as percentage of total private orders for new non-housing work
1964	106	104	12.3
1965	100	94	12.3
1966	84	76	10.7
1967	77	68	10.3
1968	95	81	11.5
1969	106	86	11.3
1970	118	90	11.4

Source: Department of the Environment: Monthly Bulletin of Construction Statistics. Deflation to constant prices by Index of the Cost of New Construction.

(a) Where a contractor receives an order for a mixed development he is asked to classify the whole to whichever type of building describes the greatest part of the scheme.

1   Alternatively, one may look at the matter in a less sophisticated way which does not rely on econometric methods to calculate 'effects'. In the pre-SET period the volume of sales was rising rather faster than the rateable value (on a constant valuation basis) of the shops in use. In the post-SET period both growth rates fell, but the fall for the sales volume was probably greater. There was no new tendency for trade to be 'concentrated' at a speed that was not already happening before, such as could explain a sudden spurt in productivity.

In the First Report we also gave figures for gross fixed capital formation by retailers, but in view of the fact that these do not cover the large amount of developments done by property companies and the like we decided not to repeat this table: even if it were complete it would give a more delayed picture of the reactions of potential shop-owners, since the order figures reflect an earlier stage in the development process.

Even with these later figures, however, it is very difficult to draw any firm conclusions. The first major difficulty is the operation of building controls, which started to operate under the Building Control Act 1966 at much the same time as SET was introduced, then underwent various changes in both formal limits and intensity of restriction, and were suspended indefinitely with effect from November 1968. We devoted a lot of effort to trying to allow for these − partly by considering the position in the Development Areas, where they did not apply − but the difficulty of allowing for all the various lags left us with no more than general support for the broad views expressed below.

The second difficulty is, once more, the fact that the volume of retail trade was growing a good deal more slowly in the years 1966−1970 than it had been before, and this was bound to affect the incentive for new building of shops. One cannot escape from this by saying that developers would ignore such 'temporary' factors in favour of 'a long-term view' without providing an explanation of how that view would be formed.

Finally, in making comparisons between pre-SET and post-SET we have to remember that the figure for 1964 was an abnormal peak (as explained in the First Report).

On a broad view, our conclusion from Table IX.4 (and from various analyses and enquiries which we made, and which all seemed to point the same way) were that the introduction of SET and the ending of RPM probably had very little effect on the amount of shop-building. The low figures for the volume of orders in 1966−1968 seem explicable in terms of building controls and the general squeeze, and the fact that the recovery in 1969 and 1970 did not restore the 1964−5 level is explicable in terms of the slow growth in retail sales and the peakiness of 1964. There does not seem to be any need to invoke 'special' SET/RPM effects, although one certainly cannot rule them out.

It is interesting − though highly speculative − to elaborate the picture by bringing in the qualitative information which we obtained from our property experts, and in particular their stress on the combination of a keen demand for shops in favoured sites and for supermarkets with a 'slower' market for shops in general. It would be plausible on *a priori* grounds to argue that SET and the ending of RPM strengthened a tendency which was already in existence towards the development of new types of shop: the relatively high level of new building (given the slow rise in sales) would then be attributable largely to technological change, of a kind which is not always included in theoretical models. We have found nothing in our empirical investigations which seems to be in conflict with this explanation.

X
Construction

With considerable regret, we have to report that our hopes of achieving a proper statistical study of the effects of SET on construction were largely frustrated. In Chapter XVI we deal at some length with the important anomalies which the workings of the tax created in this industry: even this part of our study was however much affected by the truncation of our programme which followed the change of Government, since this meant that we made no systematic enquiries of firms operating in the industry, either on that subject or on any other. For our main task, however — that of analysing in statistical terms the effects of SET on prices, productivity and margins in construction — we can offer nothing more than the few tentative scraps contained in the final section of this chapter, in spite of having devoted considerable resources to this industry.

Reasons for Paucity of Results
As these resources were largely paid for out of a grant received from the Government, we feel under an obligation to explain the reasons for the smallness of the results achieved. As will be seen, the reasons overlap somewhat, and the *combination* of various adverse factors made the problems much more formidable than any one by itself might suggest.

Difficulties of Research on Construction
In the first place, it is obvious that there are very acute problems (outlined below) which confront any analysis of this kind in the field of construction. For that reason, when the original proposal for the SET enquiry was first mooted, I asked that our terms of reference should be confined to the service industries — a big enough task in itself — and so leave out the special case of construction. The final agreement to make the formal terms cover the whole field was reached on the understanding that the order in which the trades would be tackled would be at the discretion of the Department of Applied Economics, as an automatic consequence of the Department's freedom to settle all matters about the conduct of an enquiry which was to be strictly impartial. We intended to learn from experience how the job could best be tackled, and leave construction to a point when we would (hopefully) have found ways of overcoming some of the formidable difficulties.

A brief list of the difficulties which we foresaw was as follows:

(a) In the construction field it is very difficult to measure *prices* with sufficient accuracy to permit the kind of fine comparisons which are needed for this sort of analysis. This is because there are no quoted prices of the ordinary kind for most types of construction work, since each job is different: at best, a firm will assess the particular job in hand and quote a price, but frequently this price will be subject to variation clauses and contingency provisos.

Because of this, most so-called 'price' index numbers are not really based on prices charged by the builders at all, but are based on the prices of their inputs — i.e. labour and materials. Sometimes the labour element includes an allowance for changes in productivity, but that allowance is almost inevitably very uncertain, and over a period of more than a year or two this problem can clearly cause serious inaccuracies. Contrariwise, over short periods the absence of any measure of the *gross profit* element means that any study of the effect of SET on prices can take no account of its impact on profit margins if it is based on this type of index. Indeed, the whole analysis becomes circular in its nature: the 'substitute price index' cannot be constructed without making an *assumption* about how SET affects prices, both through its effect on productivity (and so on the labour-cost element) and through its effect on profit margins.

(b) Further complications in the 'price' field arise out of the need for different measures for different purposes, and above all out of the *timing* problems: these would apply even if one had had a genuine 'price' index. Thus most prices are fixed in advance of the performance of the work, and (at least in the absence of variation clauses) work done in one period should be valued on the basis of prices fixed at varying dates in the past. The same price index will not serve *both* to measure the prices currently being quoted for future work *and* to deflate the value of work currently being done, if one wants to get a constant price series.

The whole problem is further complicated when one has a mixture of 'firm' prices and of prices quoted with variation clauses of different types.

(c) In the output field, the collection of good figures (even in value terms) is very difficult for reasons which are common to the SET field — notably the large number of firms, including many small ones with high birth- and death-rates. There are however also serious problems arising out of *sub-contracting,* which hardly arise elsewhere: one must neither miss the output of the sub-contractor nor count it twice.

(d) If one wants a *volume* of output, the 'normal' way is *via* a value series and a price deflator, so that all the above problems are super-imposed — with the addition that one needs different deflators for different types of product (e.g. repairs, new building, civil engineering), and that a shift towards the use of more highly fabricated materials may make movements in gross output a poor guide to movements in net output.

This list of 'special' problems in construction is far from exhaustive, and of course it has to be seen as an *addition* to the problems found in other parts of the SET field. On the 'credit' side was the fact that far more statistics already existed in relation to construction than in relation to most service industries: these were however known to display serious inconsistencies amongst themselves, and also to rest in some cases on dubious principles, so that their existence did not really encourage us to put construction high in our time-table.

Why We Moved Construction up the Queue

In view of the above, it is necessary to explain why we decided to tackle construction as the next step after the completion of our analysis of distribution and the allied trades, on which we began work because this fitted well with other research projects in the Department. Essentially, the answer is to be found in the actions of the Ministry of Public Buildings and Works (as it then was), although it would have been open to us to insist rigidly on our right to make an independent decision. When the Chancellor of the Exchequer announced the setting-up of our enquiry in March 1968, the Minister of Public Buildings and Works indicated publicly that we would be covering construction at a rather early date. As this statement, and various Parliamentary Questions about the size of our staff in relation to the vastness of the job, were causing the Treasury some embarrassment, we had various discussions with them about the position. We made it clear that we could not tackle more trades simultaneously unless it was possible to recruit a senior and experienced research-worker to take the main responsibility for (say) construction, within the general framework of the over-all enquiry; we also agreed that it was very much better to keep any enquiry into construction within the framework of the over-all enquiry, rather than having it done separately by a different agency, which might adopt a completely different approach and produce results which could not be combined with those for other trades. The Treasury approached M.P.B.W. about the possible recruitment or secondment of a senior person who was knowledgeable about construction, but this eventually led to nothing.

The Department of Applied Economics was, understandably, approached by representatives of many trades at the beginning of our enquiry, all wishing to set out their own special problems, and usually wanting to be covered early in our enquiry. Naturally enough, in view of the actions of the Minister of Public Buildings and Works, we got embarrassing enquiries from Trade Associations in the construction industry, and these led eventually to a meeting with representatives of some of them, at which I explained the reason why we could not start serious work on construction forthwith. This led to our acquiring some very useful background information.

In the course of 1969 we had to make an advance decision about which trades should be investigated when our work on distribution and near-distribution was completed, since this affected staff-recruitment and the nature of the preparatory work which had to be done before a new trade could be approached (and which can often be done in the intervals which arise on the survey of a trade already under investigation, whilst replies are being awaited). We decided that, in all the circumstances, it would be right to tackle construction next, provided that we could recruit somebody with a good knowledge of its statistics (and this condition was met by our recruiting John Sugden). We undertook this with some trepidation, in view of the problems discussed above, but there was the considerable incentive that construction was much the biggest of the remaining trades, having about one-fifth of the total number of employees in the SET sector: if it could be added to the list of trades completed, then we would have covered over 70% of the total number of employees.

Our plan was to start by getting a really thorough understanding of the statistics which existed, including their weak spots, since without this we could not decide what we needed to seek from special enquiries to the trade: nor could we usefully start to design these.

Review of Existing Statistics

We had hoped that, with the whole-hearted assistance of M.P.B.W., we would get through this preliminary study quite quickly, but unfortunately it took much longer than we had expected, largely because many queries arose. The basic statistics were assembled quickly, but the investigation of their real meaning and their statistical limitations involved a review of the procedures followed by M.P.B.W. and the various checks which had been attempted (or could be), and this proved a very time-consuming process.

For the purpose of estimating the effect of SET a very high degree of accuracy was needed, or at least a knowledge of the probable direction and possible size of the errors: the principal results of our investigations are set out in Appendix H, which came to the conclusion that the main statistics, as collected and analysed by M.P.B.W., were in many respects ill-suited to our requirements, and also subject to a margin of statistical error which made them a poor starting-point. This stage in our investigations was reached just as the new Government came to power, and we did not therefore start work on designing plans for systematic trade enquiries.

As an illustration of our problems with M.P.B.W. statistics, we might take briefly the assessment of productivity movements on new construction. This was done *via* quarterly returns of the value of output and numbers employed, both of which are subject to the statistical weaknesses explained in Appendix H. A crucial element however was the so-called 'index of the cost of new construction', which was used to deflate the series for the *value* of output, so as to get a series at constant prices. We clearly had to get a good idea of how reliable this index was, especially as it was constructed by very round-about methods.

In brief, at the relevant times[1] this index was prepared by combining an index of material prices (published by the Board of Trade) with a calculated series for 'labour cost per unit of output': overhead costs and profits did not appear in the calculation, so that the use of the index for deflating a value series implied an assumption that in combination they always represented a constant proportion of the price. The 'labour costs per unit of output' were estimated from movements in earnings, plus employers' share of National Insurance etc., together with a 'productivity corrector' supplied by M.P.B.W.

The adjustment for productivity changes was derived by M.P.B.W. from the quarterly returns which it collects from a sample of the trade (see Appendix H). It rests on the assumption that movements in output, in real terms, can be taken as proportional to movements in the 'volume' (i.e. value at constant prices) of the materials used by the firms. This value of materials was not asked for on the returns, and was therefore calculated by substracting from the value of new construction, shown in the output section, a fixed percentage to cover 'overheads plus profits', and then further subtracting the labour costs as estimated from the number of workers shown on the form as engaged on work of new construction. The residual figure was then regarded as the value of the materials used, and was deflated by the Board of Trade's index of material prices. Movements in productivity were then found by combining movements between one period and another in this 'materials

---

1 In 1972 a changed system was announced, with which we are not concerned here.

used' series (assumed to reflect output movements) with movements in the number of workers.

The result of following this procedure was to produce a cost index which — in spite of various smoothing devices incorporated in the calculation — seemed on occasions to move in an implausible manner. Consequently adjustments had been made to the figures for various quarters, in the light of the Ministry's general impression of what was happening in the trade. These adjustments may well have made the index more accurate, but their existence left us with an uneasy feeling that we needed a lot of information before we could use the series in any way: this meant that the productivity series derived from it was open to similar doubts, quite apart from its other shortcomings (described in Appendix H).

Our Reduced Programme

When the change of Government led to the truncation of our enquiry, it was obvious that there could be no question of our carrying out a trade survey. The question at issue was therefore whether we should attempt to do as full a job as possible on the basis of the existing statistics, or whether we should simply decide that such an attempt might well yield no results of any value, and that the limited resources which still remained to us should be devoted to other things. Somewhat reluctantly we decided for a minimum programme in the field of construction, and this decision had the following effects:

(a) *Prices* We completely abandoned any attempt to make use of the index of new construction costs in our study of prices: its conceptual basis made it totally unsuitable for our purposes, quite apart from any question of its accuracy for any other purpose. On the other hand we decided to see whether we could reach any tentative results by using the index of tender prices for Local Authority houses, which was at least based on the *prices* at which the houses were to be built, rather than on the costs of labour and materials.

(b) *Productivity* We abandoned any attempts to study productivity: these would have had to be based on figures for the value of output (in the accuracy of which we had little faith — see Appendix H), deflated by some price index, and related to labour statistics which seemed to us not to cover the same ground as the recorded output and to have been much affected by the growth of self-employment (see Appendix H). As the Government seemed to be about to undertake an overhaul of the figures and obviously had much better facilities for doing so we did not wish to put in a lot of work on attempts to make them more suitable for our use.

(c) *Profits or Margins* As there were no published statistics which we could use this section automatically fell out of the programme when it became impossible to conduct a trade survey.

One question did remain. Chapter XIII gives the results of our attempts to use available statistics to study productivity in the trades other than distribution (covered in the First Report) and construction, and there can be no doubt that for many of these trades the statistics are worse than they are for construction. Was it right to abandon construction completely, or should it have been treated like the other trades

Our decision in favour of complete abandonment rested mainly on one simple point. Chapter XIII categorically says that no conclusions of any kind should be drawn about any individual trade: it recognises the limitations both of the statistics and of the methods used, but expresses the hope that by considering all the figures together, one can draw some very tentative conclusions about the effect of SET in these service trades *as a group*. Since construction is not a service trade and the effect of SET might be very different, we did not think it right to regard it as part of the group.

Two subsidiary 'pragmatic' reasons were firstly that, just because there are a lot of statistics on construction, it was not at all clear which ones were really the best to include in the group analysis, or how far they should be adjusted; and secondly that if we showed any figures for construction, they would be likely to be quoted without any reference to the accompanying cautions, in a way that might not apply to other trades. We were very much aware of the doubts about the statistics which had been expressed to us in general terms by trade representatives, and we had no time or resources to learn their views in detail.

How Big is SET in Construction?

After this lengthy explanation of why our results are so meagre in this field, it is time to see what they are.

We can usefully start with a quick review of how large a tax SET was at various dates in the construction industry. Comparisons will be made where appropriate with similar measures of its 'size' in near-distribution, given in Chapter III.

First, in the straightforward case of a full-time adult employee, SET adds a rather smaller percentage to the other direct costs of employing a man, as represented by his earnings and the employer's share of the National Insurance stamp: this is because average earnings are higher in construction than they are in near-distribution. For adult male operatives, the comparative percentages of SET to other direct labour costs at two relevant dates are roughly as follows:

	Construction	Near-Distribution
October 1966	5.7	6.9
October 1969	9.3	11.0

Next, one must take into account the fact that in construction refunds are obtained for a substantial number of employees through the working of the 'split establishment and other rules, whereby they can be treated as engaged in manufacturing. These rules are discussed at some length in Chapter XVI, and the methods used to estimate their quantitative importance are set out in Appendix G (which covers other trades besides construction). One clearly wants a figure for the average addition to costs caused by SET, which takes account of this factor.

The question then arises as to whether one should also allow for the refunds paid to Local Authorities in respect of their maintenance etc. employees, since these are included in the Standard Industrial Classification under 'Construction'. This seems however to be mixing up two different objectives by paying too much heed to a formal industry classification, and we preferred to evade the problem by calculating a figure relevant to private employers only.

For the private sector, then, the effect of the reclassification factor is to reduce the average SET cost of an adult male full-time operative by about one-tenth – i.e. broadly to reduce the figure of 9.3% given above to an average of about 8.35%.

Finally, it is useful to see how large (or perhaps one should say 'how small') a percentage SET is of the value of the industry's gross output (which can also be thought of as its turnover, free from duplication). Again, it seems more meaningful to confine our attention to the private sector, since so much of the output of the Public Sector is exempt. Even so, we must expect the figure to be a fairly small one, because of a combination of two main factors:

(a) Materials represent about half of the value of the output: we allow nothing for any tax 'embodied' in them, although a little is incurred in the process of distribution;

(b) A good deal of work in construction is done by self-employed people and employers, who do not pay SET: this is of course particularly true in small-scale repair work, but it has also developed a good deal on large construction sites through the system of labour-only sub-contracting.[1]

What the figures show is that private sector output in 1970 was about £4188 million, and our calculation of the net SET payments by private employers (after allowing for refunds, in the way set out in Appendix G) represented 2.7% of this.

A separate calculation showed that the proportion for new work only was not very different: presumably this results from a counter-balancing of two factors – repair work has a higher labour content, but more of it is provided by self-employed workers.

The Effects of SET on Prices

Our tentative attempt to assess the effect of SET on actual prices had to be confined to Local Authority houses, for which there is an index of tender prices which seemed to us likely to be reliable enough to provide a chance of our obtaining meaningful results. Unfortunately this series only started in 1964: it is published on a half-yearly basis in Housing and Construction Statistics.

This is not the place to describe the construction of the index of tender prices, which is set out in Housing Statistics No. 10, published by HMSO. For present purposes it can be thought of as measuring, at least approximately, changes in the tender price for a house of constant quality. The great majority of the tenders are on a fixed-price basis, without variation clauses: in some ways it would have been preferable for our purposes to have a series based wholly on quotation *with* a variation clause to cover changes in wage-rates and material prices, since this would largely eliminate the 'speculative' element in this respect (which can change substantially), but we had no option in the matter. We made some hazardous calculations to see whether the decline in the proportion of tenders with a variation clause would give the series a significant upward bias (looked upon as a series for fixed-price contracts), since contracts with a variation clause tend to be at a lower price, and a reduction in their proportion would raise the calculated average. It appeared however that the

---

1 If the sub-contractor employs wage-earners, the latter are of course liable to SET (but there is some doubt about how much of this is actually paid – see Chapter XV). It is however possible for the workers to be 'partners', and so count as self-employed and escape liability.

effect was negligible, partly because the proportion was always small, and partly because in later years the differential was presumably larger, as an off-set to the proportion being smaller.[1]

The logic behind our approach is to assume that the tender price at any time will be the sum of the following:

(a) costs with today's wage-rates and material prices;
(b) allowance for expected rise in costs caused by rising wage-rates and material prices (as estimated by the tenderer);
(c) allowance for gross profits.

SET may affect the outcome in three main ways:

(1) it is itself a cost;
(2) it may stimulate increased productivity, and so reduce costs;
(3) it may lead to a change in the profit margin.

Our method can only hope to throw light on the combined effect of all three factors, at least in the first instance.

As a guide to the movement in 'normal' costs, we constructed a simple index which combined the price index for house-building materials with an index of assumed labour cost; the latter was in turn based simply on the movements in hourly earnings *plus* employer's share of National Insurance (but *not* SET), assuming a uniform rise in productivity of 2% a year. The resulting series is set against the series for tender prices in Table X.1, which also shows the percentage by which the price index exceeds the cost index.

Variations in this last percentage naturally reflect a combination of several factors, and attempts to draw deductions from them need to take account of the whole table, rather than concentrating on the figure for a particular period. As a contribution to the process of interpretation, the table includes a column showing our rough estimate of the cost of SET as a percentage of the tender prices, as it might have been made by the contractor when preparing his tender. The table also includes two columns dealing with cost escalation, which reflect the recent experience which the contractor making the tender would know about at the time when he submitted it: the first reflects the percentage addition to the tender price which a variation clause might have permitted if embodied in a contract made a year earlier, and the second the average of that and the corresponding figure for two years earlier.

If life were really simple, the pre-SET figures for the two indices in each period would always be very similar, and we could assume that the 'normal' cost index was a reliable guide to the movement in tender prices which one could have 'expected' in the absence of SET, unless there were some obvious reason for expecting a disturbing factor – e.g. a changed allowance for expected inflation or the inclusion in the tender price of a changed profit margin. For post-SET periods one would then compare the observed difference with the percentages which SET represented of the tender price.

With such a short series, and in the enforced absence of an elaborate study of the industry's experience, our own tentative conclusions are as follows:

(1) The figures for the pre-SET period are consistent with the assumption that

---

1 Rather fortunately, the Government ruled that a 'firm' price may be adjusted to cover changes in SET, so that we do not have to worry about the builders' speculations on that score.

the 'normal' cost index is a reasonable guide to what was to be expected for tender prices in the absence of SET, if one also considers the effect of 'the state of the market': the rather slower rise in the tender price index seems to be in conformity with the lower margins expected in 1965–6 after the boom of 1964.

(2) The sudden rise in the tender price index relatively to the cost index in the second half of 1966, when SET had been announced, is consistent with the view that SET was immediately passed on at least in part. Moreover we do not have to rely on a single period's figure: with one trifling exception, the tender price index is always above the cost index from that time onwards – although of course other factors are relevant too.

Table X.1   *Tender Prices and 'Normal Costs' for a Local Authority House*

(1)	(2)	(3)	(4)	(5)	(6)	(7)
Half-year	Tender price index (1964=100)	'Normal cost' index[a]	% excess of price index over normal cost index	Estimated cost of SET as % of tender price[b]	Effect of cost escalation (%)[c]	
					Latest year	Average of 2 latest years
1964 – I	(98)	98.9	–0.9	0	3.6	
II	(102)	100.5	+1.5	0	3.4	
1965 – I	105.0	103.8	+1.2	0	3.9	3.7
II	105.2	105.5	–0.3	0	3.2	3.3
1966 – I	107.2	108.9	–1.6	0	4.0	3.9
II	110.3	109.2	+1.0	2.1	2.8	3.0
1967 – I	111.8	108.7	+2.9	2.0	1.6	2.8
II	114.3	111.5	+2.5	1.9	3.8	3.3
1968 – I	118.5	116.5	+1.7	1.8	5.5	4.1
– II	120.7	117.5	+2.7	2.5	4.3	4.1
1969 – I	122.1	119.8	+1.9	2.6	2.1	3.8
– II	125.3	122.5	+2.3	3.1	2.1	3.2
1970 – I	130.8	130.9	–0.1	3.0	7.5	4.8
II	136.5	133.9	+1.9	2.8	10.4	6.2

(a) Based on house building materials and labour cost (assuming 2% p.a. rise in output per head, and *not* including SET). Computed with 1964=100, but scaled to equate the average for the pre-SET period to that for the tender price index.

(b) Based on the value of output of L.A. houses and the number of workers engaged, as reported by M.P.B.W., with allowance for A.P.T.C. workers and for 'reclassification' of some workers under manufacturing. Rates for SET taken as they were at the time of tender, or at later rate if already enacted. Lag of two months assumed between submission of tender and inclusion in statistics as 'accepted'.

The calculation was checked against a simple one based on SET in relation to earnings, with reassuring results.

(c) It is assumed that the escalation clause allows 39% of the tender price to be raised in proportion to the rise in standard wage rates and 45% of the tender price to be raised in proportion to the index of building material prices, and that the relevant interval between the tender date and the average date of expenditure is one year. The 'latest year' column reflects the 12 months up to the midle of the half year in question: the final column is the average of the latest figure and the one for a year earlier.

(3) A comparison between the cost of SET (column 5) and the 'excess' of the tender price index over the normal cost index (column 4) is tantalisingly difficult to interpret. Broadly speaking, the excess of the former over the latter in any period reflects a combination of
    (a) expected gains in productivity as a result of SET or other abnormal factors;
    (b) the poorness of the market in that period, compared with 1964–1966 I;
    (c) any *reduction* in fears about future costs, compared with the base;
    (d) Errors which under-state prices or exaggerate normal costs.

The strength of the market in 1967 may well explain why prices seem to have been raised by more than the cost of SET at the time. The growing fear of cost inflation in the later periods might well have been expected to raise tender prices relatively to normal costs even though the market was then rather poor: the cost escalation figures in columns (6) and (7) are all recording what *had* happened up to the date of tender, and contractors may well have predicted a more rapid rise. If this is so, then it is difficult to make sense of the later figures without assuming that abnormal productivity gains were helping to keep down tender prices, since the excess of that index over the normal costs index is consistently *less* than the cost of SET.

This whole exercise shows how desperately difficult it is to arrive at conclusions in quantitative terms without really good statistics. SET is a small factor in relation to the tender price — only about 3% at its peak. Plain price effects are therefore bound to be hard to estimate, when other factors are also changing: one ought to be getting a different answer for each rate of tax, but the best one can really say is that prices were raised. The fact that the price effect was probably rather less, on the whole, than the cost of SET (when allowance is made for other factors) suggests a productivity effect, but we cannot quantify it. The fineness of calculation required is almost ludicrous: since labour costs are only about 40% of price, if one attributed one percentage point of the price-cost difference discussed above to productivity gain, this would imply a 2½% gain in productivity.

XI
Some Background Figures

Ideally, the final Part of the Final Report on the effects of SET ought to be drawing together the results obtained for each of the various industries or groups of industries, and adding an analysis of the effects of the tax taken as a whole. Owing to the truncation of our research following the change of Government, there are no analyses for a large number of trades which have to pay SET without refund, and it is also the case that the different circumstances applying in distribution and construction make their results in some respects very difficult to aggregate with the results for other parts of the field. In consequence, this final Part is something of a hybrid. On the one hand, it uses data which were already available to give a very broad idea of the effects of SET on prices and productivity for the field outside the industries of distribution and construction: the data are not good enough to enable one to say anything separately about individual trades, but they are probably better than nothing as a guide to the over-all effect in that area. On the other hand, we also give some analyses for the SET field as a whole, including distribution and construction – but these are inevitably tentative in character.

This particular chapter is intended to give some of the background for the more detailed analyses which follow, covering the whole SET sector. It gives various measures of the size of the field, and also shows various movements through time, with comparative figures for the economy as a whole; and it gives a crude measure of the size of the tax in comparison with total taxation.

The size of the SET field is indeed very large, whether it is measured in terms of the number of people liable to the tax without refund, or of the output of the industries in which they are engaged. The net yield of the tax (i.e. the gross receipts, payable in respect of all employees *less* the refunds to those engaged in manufacturing etc.) was, however, always rather modest, even when the tax was at its highest – although it undoubtedly represented a very welcome *marginal* addition to taxation from the viewpoint of the Government: the net yield never exceeded 4% of the total revenue from taxation. In effect, therefore, it should be thought of as applying over a very large area, but at a relatively low rate: there are logical difficulties about saying what rate of purchase tax would have been needed to collect the same revenue from the SET sector as was collected by SET, but on the most reasonable interpretation it would have been lower than the lowest rate actually applied as part of purchase tax.

Employment and Output
Table XI.1 shows the number of employees in the industries in which most employees are liable to SET without refund: the figures are not the exact numbers on whom

83

the tax was paid (see note under the table), but in round figures there were about 7.5 million people liable in 1968 which represented about 33% of the total number of employees in Great Britain at that date. Variations in this proportion are discussed in Chapter XIV: the object here is merely to give an impression of the size of the field.

Table XI.1   *Number of Employees in SET Sector*[a]

1958 SIC		No. of Employees, G.B. June 1968 (Thousands)
Orders		
XVII	Construction	1506
XX	Distributive Trades	2774
XXI	Insurance, Banking and Finance	665
XXIII	Miscellaneous Services	2100
Minimum List Headings		
709	Miscellaneous Transport Services and Storage	81
871	Accountancy Services	91
873	Legal Services	110
879	Other professional and scientific services	190
	Total	7157
	Total number of Employees in G.B.	22 645

Source: Department of Employment.

(a) The SIC classifications shown are those in which it seems likely that the majority of the employees are liable to SET without refund. There are undoubtedly substantial numbers of employees who are liable in other SIC categories (e.g. educational or medical services); these categories have been omitted because refunds are probably obtained for the majority of employees in those industries on the grounds that the employer is a Local Authority or a charity, or because the tax is paid by the Government and therefore cannot be counted as a net addition to the yield. On the other hand, a minority of the employees included in the table are exempted for one reason or another − e.g. through the working of the split-establishment rule, or because the employing Body is a charity.

The formidable size of the field can also be seen from the contribution made by SET paying industries to the national product. Again, this cannot be calculated exactly from available statistics, but Table XI.2 combines the four Blue Book categories in which the majority of employees were liable to SET without refund, and the resulting total is, on the 'swings and roundabouts' argument, probably about right as a measure of the output of establishments paying SET without refund.

It will be seen from the table that the SET field represents about one-third of the total economy on this basis also. The percentage increased somewhat between 1960 and 1964, but was broadly stable thereafter. This approximate stability during the SET period does not mean that the value of output in each of the four sections was rising at the same rate as GDP: both insurance, banking and finance and miscellaneous services show rising percentages, but those for construction and the distributive trade show declines.

Table XI.2 *Contribution of SET-Paying Industries(a) to GDP at Factor Cost*

Trades	1960 £m	1960 %	1961 %	1962 %	1963 %	1964 %	1965 %	1966 %	1967 %	1968 %	1969 %	1970 %	1970 £m
G.D.P.	22 583	100.00	100.00	100.00	100.00	100.00	100.00	100.00	100.00	100.00	100.00	100.00	42 307
Construction	1363	6.04	6.20	6.43	6.45	6.96	7.12	7.05	6.95	6.93	6.84	6.24	2640
Distributive Trades	2756	12.20	11.89	11.94	11.85	11.73	11.54	11.47	10.92	11.00	10.90	10.69	4524
Insurance, Banking, Finance	681	3.02	3.20	3.39	3.42	3.30	3.17	3.11	3.13	3.42	3.49	3.67	1552
Miscellaneous Services	3545	11.27	12.09	12.07	12.41	12.40	12.35	12.60	13.05	13.13	13.63	13.90	5879
Total SET field	7345	32.52	33.37	33.83	34.12	34.39	34.18	34.22	34.05	34.48	34.85	34.50	14 595

(a) The figures relate to those Blue Book categories in which the majority of the employees were liable to SET without refund. Some of this output was produced by firms which obtained refunds, but some output included in other categories bore the tax.

Source: 1971 Blue Book, Table 17.

Notes 1. The value of the GDP in the Blue Book is shown *after* making a deduction to allow for stock appreciation, but no such deduction is possible for the individual industries. Hence all the percentages are slightly too high, and the over-statement increases throughout the period: if stock appreciation were added back to the GDP the percentages for 1960 and 1970 for the SET field would be reduced by about 0.2 percentage points and 0.8 percentage points respectively.

2. The industry definitions in this table are not the same as in Table XI.1.

3. The total figures may not equal the sum of the components because of rounding errors.

Table XI.3 Output *Output(a) and Gross Profits, etc.(b) by Industry, 1960-1970*

Trades			1960	1961	1962	1963	1964	1965	1966	1967	1968	1969	1970
Construction	Output	£m	1363	1497	1623	1727	2018	2205	2305	2401	2540	2637	2640
	Gross profits etc.	£m	311	339	358	417	506	552	573	609	667	714	682
	as % of output		22.82	22.65	22.06	24.15	25.07	25.03	24.86	25.36	26.26	27.08	25.83
Distributive Trades	Output	£m	2756	2872	3012	3174	3400	3574	3752	3773	4028	4205	4524
	Gross profits etc.	£m	1157	1175	1196	1270	1395	1454	1469	1449	1541	1604	1640
	as % of output		41.98	40.91	39.71	40.01	41.03	40.68	39.15	38.40	38.26	38.15	36.25
Insurance, Banking, Finance	Output(c)	£m	1474	1625	1739	1853	2026	2234	2381	2545	2905	3221	3718
	Gross profits etc. (c)	£m	947	1055	1116	1167	1271	1421	1536	1615	1878	2082	2406
	as % of output		64.25	64.92	64.17	62.98	62.73	63.61	64.51	63.46	65.65	64.64	64.71
Miscellaneous Services	Output	£m	2545	2920	3047	3325	3593	3824	4122	4511	4810	5257	5879
	Gross profits etc.	£m	843	867	842	952	994	1085	1119	1204	1283	1355	1428
	as % of output		33.12	29.69	27.63	28.63	27.66	28.37	27.15	26.69	26.67	25.78	24.29
All Industries	Output	£m	22 882	24 244	25 334	27 003	29 350	31 513	33 042	34 566	36 239	39 566	43 339
	Gross profits etc.	£m	7708	7837	8028	8813	9648	10 252	10 296	10 880	11 934	12 384	12 852
	as % of output		33.69	32.33	31.69	32.64	32.87	32.53	31.16	31.48	32.93	31.30	29.65

Source: 1971, Blue Book. Table 17.

(a) Output means gross value added in the industry, before providing for depreciation and stock appreciation.

(b) Gross profits etc. include other trading income, and are taken before providing for depreciation and stock appreciation, or for direct taxes: as this applies to the all-industries figures, the output figure is *not* the GDP (and also excludes the residual error).

(c) Including rent and net interest.

Share of Profits in Value Added

The Blue Book figures also provide a very crude guide to movements in the share of profits as a percentage of value added, both for industry groups and for all industries taken together. The most relevant figures are given in Table XI.3, but the reader is particularly warned to be careful about understanding the definitions before drawing any conclusions. The main points are given under the table, but these notes do not attempt to deal with the special statistical problems arising on insurance, banking and finance; a fuller account is of course available in the Blue Book and in the explanatory publications of the Central Statistical Office. In order to secure at least formal comparability between the all-industries figures and those for the four SET sectors, stock appreciation has been added back to the all-industries figures for both 'output' (i.e. gross value added) and for gross profits etc. In view of the statistical problems arising on insurance, banking and finance (in which the profits percentage is much higher than elsewhere) no row is given for the four SET sectors taken together, but some comments are made on it in the text.

Taken as they stand, the figures for the four SET sectors present a very mixed picture for the movement in the profits percentage during the SET period. Both construction and insurance, banking and finance show, if anything, an upward movement in this percentage, though with marked wobbles; on the other hand distribution and miscellaneous services show a fairly clear downward trend. If we could allow for stock appreciation, the outcome would certainly be less favourable from the viewpoint of the profit-recipients, with construction and distribution being most affected because of the high level of their stocks (including work in progress). The over-all outcome for the SET sector, for what that is worth, is that the profit percentage shows a marked downward trend even on the figures as they stand, and that this would be increased if stock appreciation could be eliminated.[1]

It is, however, very important to set this falling trend in the profits percentage for the SET sector against the background of the position for the economy as a whole. Taking the position before allowance is made for stock appreciation, the 'all-industries' figures in Table XI.3 show a downward trend in the SET period, from 32.5% in 1965 to 29.7% in 1970: this is the 'background' for the mixed picture shown for the four SET sectors, and represents a sharper rate of decline than one gets for a combination of those four. If one subtracts stock appreciation from the national total for output and profits, and so produces a more meaningful percentage, the fall for the national percentage is from about 32% in 1965 to about 28% in 1970, and that is again a sharper decline than one would get for the SET sector as a whole, if stock appreciation were allocated between the two sectors on any sensible basis.

This comparison between the movements in the SET sector and those for the country as a whole provide, therefore, a very clear warning against attributing the fall in the profit percentage in the SET sector simply to the existence of SET. One must, however, also avoid the opposite danger of saying that as the fall in the profit percentage was greater in other industries, therefore SET cannot have had any part

---

1   In terms of plain money, however, profits certainly rose during this period — by about 37% over the five years from 1965 to 1970, before allowing for stock appreciation, and by about 30% if the national total for stock appreciation in each year is allocated *pro rata* to gross profits.

in producing a fall within its own sector. Far too many other factors have influenced the percentage for any naive deductions of this type to be at all justified.

Revenue from SET

It is useful to start a review of the revenue from SET by giving the rate charged for a full-time adult male in various periods. The figures are:-

From 5th September 1966	25s.
From 2nd September 1968	37s. 6d.
From 7th July 1969	48s.
From 5th July 1971	24s.

Details of the rates of tax on other categories of employee are set out in Appendix I. Apart from the increases (and then reduction) in the standard rates, illustrated by the above figures, the main change was the introduction of refunds of part of the tax for part-time employees and the elderly one year after the tax had been introduced.

Table XI.4 gives figures for the net yield of SET to the Exchequer in each fiscal year from 1966–7 to 1970–71. The way in which SET was collected, as a 'supplement' to the National Insurance contribution for employees, means that these figures are by no means ideal for our purpose – a subject to which we return in Chapter XVII. The basic figures in the official revenue returns give the *gross* yield from SET, whilst the refunds and (in the earlier years) the premiums paid to manufacturing employers etc. are recorded on the expenditure side of the accounts. For the purpose of our table, these outgoings have been subtracted from the gross revenue to show the net amount of cash received by the Exchequer in the financial year. This does not, however, represent the amounts paid by the industries which have to bear the burden of the tax, partly because the amounts paid out in premiums have been subtracted as well as the refunds, but mainly because of the problem of time lags. It was inevitable, for example, that the figure for 1966–7 would be much too high as a measure of the burden on the SET sector, because the payment of refunds to manufacturers etc. could not start until some time after the in-payment on their employees, so that the figure of £258 million is considerably too high for our purpose. Similarly, in 1968–9 and in 1969–70 the raising of the rates meant that there was again an over-statement of the burden on the SET sector, because the tax had been collected at the higher rate for more months in each of these years than the period for which the refunds had been correspondingly raised. From this point of view, the years 1967–8 and 1970–71 are the ones which are least affected by the time-lag problem, but even in these the net yield was affected by changes in the speed with which refunds were made, so that 1967–8 (for example) had its figure reduced by a speeding-up of the payment of refunds.

It will be clear from the above description that Table XI.4 should be looked at primarily from the point of view of the Exchequer, rather than as giving a measurement of the burden on the SET sector. It would, of course, have been possible to get nearer to the latter concept by not subtracting the premiums paid to manufacturers etc., but this would have left the major problem of time-lags unaffected, and it seemed better in this chapter to give figures which are directly relevant for one purpose – i.e. measuring the impact on the Exchequer's net cash receipts. Even from that point of view, of course, an economist might well argue that one should not

Table XI.4   *Net Yield[a] of SET to the Exchequer*

	1966–7	1967–8	1968–9	1969–70	1970–71
Net Yield (£m.)	258	325	438	527	501
As % of total tax revenue, *less SET refunds etc.*	*2.86*	*3.24*	*3.66*	*3.94*	*3.62*

Source: Financial Statements.

(a) See text for description of the meaning of this term. The figures for 1966–7, 1968–9 and 1969–70 are substantially raised by the time-lag between payments by manufacturers etc. and refunds.

treat an in-payment which will be refunded in a few months on the same basis as a true tax, but that is a convention of Government accounting which lies right outside our terms of reference.

The table also shows for each year what percentage the net yield from SET represented of the total revenue from taxation — with, for consistency, the latter being also reduced by the out-payments for SET refunds etc. The figure for 1970–71 is perhaps the best guide, since it is least affected by statistical problems of time-lag etc., and it shows that the net yield of SET was rather under 4% of total tax revenue. One must, of course, remember that in 1970–71 SET was being collected at its peak rate throughout the whole year.

XII
Prices

(N.B. This chapter does not apply to distribution or construction)

The greatest obstacle to a proper study of the effects of SET on prices is, as always in our investigation, the scanty and unreliable nature of the data, which is discussed in more detail in Appendix F. This is particularly serious when one is seeking to assess these effects by looking for a fine difference between the price movement which *did* take place (the historical record) and that which one would have *expected* in the absence of SET.

Methodological Problems

It is useful to start the analysis by a brief sketch of the problems involved in setting up these 'expected' price movements. The trouble is, of course, that 'other things do not remain equal': we cannot just observe the price movement between some date before the introduction of SET and some date after it, and regard that movement as representing the 'effects' of SET. Broadly speaking, the prices in question may also be influenced by any or all of the following types of factor during the period studied:

(a) The general decline in the value of money, which has continued throughout the post-war years, but which has proceeded at varying speeds in different years.

(b) Special cost factors affecting particular trades — e.g. a wage increase (or absence thereof) at a pace different from the general increase covered under (a).

(c) Seasonal factors (e.g. the inclusion in the period of a date when it is conventional to change a price which is then held stable for a year or a season).

(d) Cyclical factors applying with unusual strength to the trade in question.

(e) Purely random factors — with which we may include the important item of errors in the recording of price changes (since we can do nothing about either except hope to 'average them out' by combining results in which they can be expected to operate independently).

For each price series which we used we attempted to arrive at a set of 'expected' price movements to compare with the recorded movements for the various periods: in form, therefore, there is a figure which might be regarded as a first approximation to an estimate of the 'SET effect' for each item and each period. We would not, however, regard it as legitimate to deduce anything about individual items, or to make comparisons between them, on the basis of these figures. Rather, we regard the figures as providing a body of data from which one can try to draw general conclusions about the effects of SET on prices of the services produced by the trades which pay it: the simplest way — but not the only one — is to take an average of the recorded price movements and of the expected movements, and hope that the errors in each set of figures will average out.

With this objective in mind we have sought to include all the price series for services in the SET field which passed our not-very-exacting tests of quality and availability over the period needed for the method being used,[1] in the hope that they would have no common bias. The series inevitably relate to *items* (e.g. 'man's haircut') rather than trades (e.g. hairdressing). This in contrast to the series given in Chapter V for each trade in near-distribution, which we used for the deflation of turnover: these are not suitable for our present purpose — they had necessarily to include some very weak data to cover the whole trade, and they included some series (e.g. for alcoholic drink sold in public houses) where the influence of the wholesale price of the drink would be bound to dominate other factors.

The Short-term Method of Analysis

Our first method of approach was basically simple. To assess the effects of introducing SET we took the movement in prices for each item over the three-month interval between July 1966 and October 1966, and we compared it with the average movement between July and October for that item in each of the years 1961 to 1965. As the prices are recorded in the middle of the month, and the tax was introduced at the beginning of September, this seemed to minimise the risk of getting anticipatory increases into the pre-SET figure, and to allow time for any 'quick' adjustments to get into the post-SET figure.[2]

So far as the comparative figure for each series is concerned (which represents what would have been expected in the absence of SET), the use of the average of previous July–October movements is a broad way of allowing for seasonal factors and for the decline in the value of money (at the average rate for 1961–1965); it does little or nothing, however, to allow for the other potential disturbances listed above. One might argue that over such a short period as three months these are likely to have a relatively small influence, but this has to be considered against the background that SET itself typically added only about 2½% to costs, and the trade *might* have had (say) a big wage-increase in the period.[3] If one considers all the trades together, however, the use of the previous average movement is implicitly allowing for the influence of these factors to be, on average, of 'average' importance, and that should not be too bad an assumption.

Table XII.1 starts, then, by setting out for each item the 'benchmark' figure for the percentage increase in price recorded between July and October — i.e. the average of such increases recorded in the five years 1961 to 1965. It then shows, for each of the years 1966 to 1970, the extent to which the price increase between July and October was 'abnormal' — i.e. the difference between the percentage increase

1   See Appendix F, first section.

2   We discuss these points more fully later.

3   In 1966 this was in fact forbidden by the 'freeze', but we use the same method for assessing the effects of the increases in SET in 1968 and 1969.

actually recorded and the benchmark figure.[1]

As the table shows, the 'benchmark' increases are all relatively small, with an average of 1%: the advantage of the short-term approach is of course that the influence of factors other than SET is held down to a fairly low level by considering only a three-month interval. We shall also see, in Table XII.2, that the average was in the range 0.8 to 1.2 for each of the five years, which increases one's confidence in it as a measure of the so-called 'normal' movement.

All the items except car maintenance charges[2] showed price increases for July—October 1966 which were above their benchmark level — strong evidence that for these 'service' items (as opposed to the case of distribution, where the trader's price relates to goods) there was a strong tendency to raise the price promptly when SET was introduced.

In 1967, on the other hand, when SET was not changed, we find that some items showed increases greater than their benchmark, and some were below it, and the average 'abnormal' movement for the 10 items came to 0.0. It is, of course, a coincidence that this average should be so precisely zero, but it is nevertheless reassuring that it was small: one expects to find some sizeable abnormal movements for individual items in any short period.

In both 1968 and 1969, when SET was increased, we again find a predominance of positive figures for the abnormal movements, with the average being about +1%. One item shows a zero figure for both years — dance-hall admission charges, which are normally changed only at the end of the year; no item showed a negative 'abnormal movement' if we take 1968 and 1969 together.

The above four years, therefore, produce results which conform very closely to the ones which one would expect if one believed that, in general, SET on services is passed forward speedily. It is of course natural that the mean increase should be much smaller in 1968 than in 1966, because the 1968 increase in SET was only half as great as the initial levy when expressed as a cash sum (and still smaller as a percentage addition to costs, which had risen meanwhile); similarly the 1969 increase was rather smaller than the 1968 one, even in cash terms.

What, then, should one say of the fact that 1970 shows a preponderance of positive figures, although SET was not increased? Should this shake one's faith in the method?

The answer, fortunately, is a firm negative, but it does provide a warning of how careful one has to be in exercises of this kind, and it also points to the link between this method and our second one.

Quite simply, the 'benchmark' which we have used is the average of the July—

1 For 1969 the percentage increase in price from mid-June to mid-September was taken instead so as to cover the July, 1969 increase in SET. A check on the available data indicated that the average increase in prices for the period mid-June to mid-September for the years 1961 to 1965 inclusive were very similar to those for the period mid-July to mid-October. We therefore felt justified in comparing the increase in price from mid-June to mid-September, 1969 in Tables XII.1 and XII.2 with the average increase for mid-July to mid-October, 1961 to 1965, since this much simplified the presentation of the tables.

2 It is doubtful whether we should have included this item in the list. The quotation is in fact the amount used by a repairer to arrive at the 'labour charge' for a repair job, being sometimes applied to a 'standard' number of hours for that type of repair, and sometimes to the actual number of man-hours used on that occasion. It is not normally varied unless wages change.

Table XII.1 *Price Increases Between Mid-July and Mid-October*
(All figures are percentage movements)

Item	Average increase for 1961 to 1965	'Abnormal' price increase[a]				
		1966*	1967	1968*	1969*[b]	1970[c]
Dry-cleaning	+ 0.9	+ 5.4	− 2.4	+ 4.4	− 0.2	− 0.9
Laundering	+ 1.4	+ 4.0	− 0.7	0	+ 2.6	+ 1.6
Hairdressing:						
man's haircut	+ 1.5	+ 3.1	− 0.1	+ 0.5	+ 1.0	+ 0.3
woman's shampoo & set	+ 0.8	+ 3.5	0	+ 1.5	+ 0.7	− 0.1
Shoe repairing:						
man's sole & heel	+ 0.5	+ 1.3	+ 0.4	+ 0.3	+ 1.1	+ 1.0
woman's heel repair	+ 1.8	+ 2.1	− 0.3	− 0.4	+ 0.8	+ 0.6
Watch cleaning	+ 1.4	+ 1.7	+ 0.1	+ 0.7	+ 0.5	+ 0.4
Mean of above items[d]	+ 1.2	+ 3.0	− 0.4	+ 1.0	+ 0.9	+ 0.4
Cinema admission charges	+ 1.2	+ 1.8	+ 3.1	+ 2.6	+ 0.6	+ 1.7
Dance-hall admission charges	0	+ 2.4	0	0	0	0
Car maintenance charges	+ 0.4	− 0.4	− 0.4	+ 0.3	+ 1.6	+ 2.0
Mean of all items	+ 1.0	+ 2.5	0	+ 1.0	+ 0.9	+ 0.7

Source: All price movements shown are based on Department of Employment price indices.

*Years in which SET was increased.

(a) Increase for year in question *less* average increase for 1961 to 1965.
(b) For 1969 the deviations shown are the deviations of the percentage increases in prices from mid-June to mid-September from the average increases from mid-July to mid-October for 1961 to 1965.
(c) The special circumstances of 1970 are discussed in the text.
(d) These are the items for which a long-term approach is possible − see Table XII.3.

October price movements in the years 1961 to 1965, and the main purpose which this served was to allow for the general decline in the value of money. In 1970 this decline was obviously a good deal more rapid than in earlier years, and such an acceleration would naturally show itself as a preponderance of positive items in our 1970 column. The average abnormal movement of + 0.7% in three months − equivalent to 2.8% a year − seems quite reasonable as a reflection of the 'abnormality' of 1970 price-increases.[1]

1 As a rough guide, the index of retail prices (excluding food and housing) showed the following percentage increases between July and October:
    1961−1965 Average 1.2
    1966   1.3
    1967   0.9
    1968   1.2
    1969   1.1
    1970   2.1
It appears that from this independent test that the 1961−65 average was a good guide to use for what to 'expect' in each of the three years when SET changed, but perhaps a bit high in 1967. What stands out a mile is that 1970 prices in general were rising more rapidly than in 1961−65; this test suggests an 'abnormal' rise of 0.9% in the three months, against the 0.7% shown for services in Table XII.1.

Table XII.1 showed the figures for individual items, partly to emphasize the point that the method does not work for each individual item in each individual year: it is clearly *not* right to say that the effect on dry-cleaning prices of the increase in SET was to raise them by 4.4% in 1968 (i.e. by much more than the added cost) and to reduce them by 0.2% in 1969. One has to combine the figures for a fair number of items and/or years before one can draw any conclusions.

Table XII.2 therefore concentrates on giving a summary picture. It shows first the mean increase recorded for the items considered for each year from 1961 to 1970. The second row then gives the 'abnormal' element in that movement for each year; we have already discussed these figures, but the comparision with the first row shows readily that the abnormal element was a substantial part of the whole in the years when SET was increased or introduced. Finally, rows (3) and (4) allocate the ten items according as their price increase in the year was above or below the benchmark for that item.

The picture which emerges is that in all three years when SET was introduced or increased, the average price increase between July and October significantly exceeded the benchmark — and indeed, as we shall see later, the excess was of the same order as the effect of the SET change on the average trader's costs. Moreover this excess was always a *general* phenomenon, with 8 or 9 of the items appearing in row (3): it is not explained by one or two freak movements.

On the other hand 1967 shows the average price increase equal to the benchmark figure, with the items fairly evenly divided between the two rows (6 against 4). Admittedly 1970 seems to disturb the picture, but this is readily explained by the abnormally rapid general decline in the value of money in that year.

There remains however one big query: do these results perhaps *exaggerate* the effects of SET, because traders do not like making price-changes frequently and regarded the introduction or increase of SET as a suitable occasion for making the price increase a bit larger than would be justified by SET alone, so as also to cover other increases in cost which had already occurred or were expected? Or do the results perhaps *under-state* the effects of SET, because the price increases due to SET were held back until that factor could be combined with other cost increases to give a single 'worth-while' change in price, instead of a series of changes of 2% or so? The very shortness of the interval considered, and the use of prices at one date, expose us to the risk of getting distorted results if price increases are concentrated in either of these ways.

These points are to some extent covered by our longer-term approach, which compares annual averages of price quotations taken at least two years apart. Such an approach clearly, however, requires a more elaborate method of allowing for changes in other factors: we cannot simply subtract the average price increase shown in earlier years, thereby assuming *inter alia* that variations in the speed of the secular fall in the value of money will be sufficiently small to be ignored. Indeed we found this to be unsafe in 1970, even when measuring price changes over a three-month interval.

The Longer-Term Approach

On this approach our basic calculation rests on a comparison between the average level of prices in the last pre-SET year (taken as August 1965 to July 1966, to avoid

Table XII.2 Summary of July–October Movements in Prices

	Average 1961–1965 inclusive	Pre-SET years					Post-SET years				
		1961	1962	1963	1964	1965	1966*	1967	1968*	1969*	1970
(1) Mean increase in prices for items considered	+ 1.0	+ 1.2	+ 1.2	+ 0.8	+ 1.0	+ 1.0	+ 3.5	+ 1.0	+ 2.0	+ 1.9	+ 1.7
(2) Difference between row (1) and its 1961–1965 average	0	+ 0.1	+ 0.2	− 0.2	− 0.1	0	+ 2.5	0	+ 1.0	+ 0.9	+ 0.7
(3) Number of items showing increase above their 1961–1965 average(a)	—	4½	5½	3½	5	6	9	4	8	8½	7½
(4) Number of items showing increase below their 1961–1965 average(a)	—	5½	4½	6½	5	4	1	6	2	1½	2½

* Years in which SET was increased.

(a) Items for which the increase was equal to the 1961–1965 average have been counted as ½ in both row (3) and row (4).

95

the risk of anticipatory rises in August 1966) and the corresponding twelve months four years later (i.e. August 1969 to July 1970, for all of which SET was at its peak rate). We experimented with a great many other approaches, using data for a series of separate years, but came firmly to the conclusion that this relatively simple approach was both the most logical and the most practicable in view of the data available.

A subsidiary calculation was also made, which proved more successful than we had expected. This took the same base year, but considered only a two-year interval, ending with the twelve months to July 1968. The terminal period was thus convenien the last year in which SET operated at its original 25s. rate.

The crucial assumption underlying our calculation of the price movement to be expected in the absence of SET was also essentially simple: we took the movement in the cost to the employer of a week's labour (including his share of the National Insurance contribution) as the basic guide to the movement in prices which was to be expected in any period. This reflected both the decline in the value of money and any special factors which might affect the trade in question through changes in the relation of its wage-level to those elsewhere. We assumed that any effect which SET might have had on the movement of wages in the trades affected was negligible — a matter on which Chapter XIV provides confirmatory evidence.

Taking the matter in more detail, we expected to find that in pre-SET years the rise in prices would be rather less than the rise in earnings (plus National Insurance), because of *inter alia,* improving productivity: over a four-year period we also hoped that the influence of other factors would be relatively unimportant and the productivity factor fairly stable, so that the four-year 'price-relative' for prices in any trade would be a fairly constant fraction of the corresponding relative for earnings. The chance of getting this result was of course much higher with essentially 'service' items, in which the cost of labour is a large part of the price; in a broad way, moreover, the earnings relative (reduced by the factor reflecting its average ratio to the price-relative) also provides some guide to the expected movement in other cost items, because it reflects changes in the value of money, and it is variations in the speed with which this declined which are liable to cause most trouble.

As is shown in Appendix F, the three different methods which we used for arriving at the pre-SET ratio of the price-relative to the earnings-relative gave somewhat different results for individual items, but each method gave much the same average (0.96 to two decimal places) for the seven items covered by our analysis — these being the only ones for which we had statistics covering a long enough period. We decided to take the average of the three methods in making the calculations for each item.

The method of estimating the SET effect for each item was, then, to calculate the 'expected' price-relative in the absence of SET, for the period 1965–6 to 1969–70, by multiplying the recorded earnings relative for that period by this pre-SET ratio, and to see how much greater the *actual* price-relative was: this we call the estimated 'SET effect', but of course this expression is really a short-hand term for the effects of all abnormal new factors, and — much more important — the estimate is once more subject to serious errors, both in the data and in the methodology. We do not attach any importance to the results for individual items, but we hope that the errors largely average out when one takes the mean for the 7 items.

The Results

Table XII.3 shows the 'SET effect' as calculated for each item, both for 1969–70 and for 1967–8; it also gives an estimate for each item of the 'SET cost' – i.e. how much SET represented as a percentage of the price (less SET) in that year. Attention should however be directed primarily to the final row, which gives the average for the seven items.[1]

It will be seen that both in 1967–8 and in 1969–70 the average 'SET effect' is closely similar to the 'SET cost', but rather smaller. It would clearly be pushing the results too hard to be more specific than this: the figures for the individual items are a warning against assuming the results to give more than a broad indication of what seems probable. On the whole, however, it seems reasonable to say that a result of this kind is inherently plausible, and that the figures which have emerged do nothing to upset one's faith in it, especially as the same broad picture emerges for each of the two years.

Table XII.3   *Comparison of 'SET Effect' and 'SET Cost' in 1967–68 and 1969–70*
(All figures are percentages)

Item	1967–68		1969–70	
	SET effect[a]	SET cost[b]	SET effect[a]	SET cost[b]
Dry-cleaning	3.1	3¼	8.6	5¾
Laundering	0.9	3½	− 1.2	6¼
Hairdressing:				
man's haircut	4.3 ⎫	3½	2.8 ⎫	6¼
woman's shampoo and set	4.5 ⎭		5.1 ⎭	
Shoe repairing:				
man's sole and heel repair	3.2 ⎫	3	7.2 ⎫	5½
woman's heel repair	2.6 ⎭		4.3 ⎭	
Watch cleaning	2.5	3¾	4.2	6¾
Average of all items	3.0	3¼	4.4	6

(a) SET effect on prices as estimated from our long-term analysis; these figures are NOT reliable for individual items. See Appendix F for further details.

(b) Estimate of SET cost as a percentage of 'turnover, less SET'.

In a rather different way it is also reassuring to find that the results of the long-term approach are in reasonable conformity with those of the short-term approach. This is brought out in Table XII.4, which attempts a comparison of the two methods. Naturally, there are some considerable discrepancies on individual items, because both methods are exposed to substantial risks of error both in data and methodology, and these are fundamentally independent. But when the results for the seven items are averaged, 'the effect of SET at 25 shillings' comes to 3.0% for both methods, and the two estimates for 'the effect of SET at 48 shillings' are very close at 4.9% and 4.4%. One might perhaps feel tempted to say that the difference between these last two figures points to some tendency for traders to 'concentrate' their price increases at a time when SET is increased, by covering other cost increases (past or future) as

---

1 Appendix F gives the results obtained by various alternative methods of approach which we tried.

well: but this seems to be over-straining the results of a very imprecise pair of calculations, and we are more impressed by the closeness of the agreement. This is what one would expect if one believed that the abnormal increase in prices which took place at the time when SET was introduced or increased was a fair estimate of the true effect of SET on prices.

Conclusions

It is perhaps wise to end this chapter with a summary statement of what one can learn from it.

First, the chapter is concerned solely with the price of genuine services, and not with distribution or construction or other cases where the cost of the thing sold is made up largely of goods bought from other businesses.

Next, the statistical data and the methods of assessing what would have happened in the absence of SET are both too weak to avoid the risk of serious errors in the figures for individual items: consequently we can say nothing about differences between what happened on individual items, whilst recognising that there may well have been genuine differences. The most that we can do is to make a general statement about what the 'average' or 'typical' outcome probably was.

Beyond any reasonable doubt, the outcome on each occasion when SET was introduced or increased was to produce a quick rise in prices, over and above what would otherwise have been expected. Anyone who wished to deny this can get no support from the statistics, and must indeed explain away a great deal.

Table XII.4   *Comparison of Short-Term and Long-Term Estimates of the 'SET Effect'*
(All figures show the abnormal price increase as a percentage of what we expected prices to be in the absence of SET)

Item	SET at 25s.		SET at 48s.	
	Short-term method[a]	Long-term method[b]	Short-term method[c]	Long-term method[d]
Dry-cleaning	5.4	3.1	9.6	8.6
Laundering	4.0	0.9	6.6	− 1.2
Hairdressing				
man's haircut	3.1	4.3	4.6	2.8
woman's shampoo and set	3.5	4.5	5.7	5.1
Shoe repairing				
man's sole & heel repair	1.3	3.2	2.7	7.2
woman's heel repair	2.1	2.6	2.5	4.3
Watch cleaning	1.7	2.5	2.9	4.2
Average, all items	3.0	3.0	4.9	4.4

(a) 1966 short-term effect.
(b) 1967−8 c.f. 1965−6.
(c) Sum of three short-term effects: 1966, 1968 and 1969.
(d) 1969−70 c.f. 1965−6.

On average, this 'abnormal' (quick) rise in prices appears to have been about equal to the proportion which SET represented of the immediately preceding price, or perhaps a little less.

The 'quick' rise in prices *might* have represented a concentration into those few weeks of increases which would otherwise have taken place gradually over succeeding months. The longer-term analysis which we made to test this, however, suggests that if there was any effect of this kind, it was very small.

This last point may be put in another way. Our longer-term analysis suggests that in 1969–70, when SET was at its peak rate of 48s. for a man, prices of the affected services were on average about 4½% higher than would have been expected in the absence of SET, and this figure was a little less than the proportion which SET represented of those expected prices. The same was also true for prices in 1967–8, when SET for a man was 25s., and its effect was to raise the price of affected services by about 3% on the average.

XIII
Productivity

(*N.B. This chapter does not apply to construction or distribution*)

In some respects the problems involved in trying to assess the effects of SET on productivity in the true service trades are similar to those which arose in the case of prices, but even more acute. In principle it should be possible to assess the effects of SET upon productivity for each trade in each of the separate years, by the sort of methods used in our First Report: one needs to measure the movement in output and employment compared with some base period, calculate an index of productivity and compare that index with the level which would have been expected in the light of pre-SET experience. Alternatively, if one assumes, as a first approximation, that SET had little effect on the level of the trade's output, then what is required is essentially to 'predict' what the level of employment would have been in the year in question if the pre-SET relationships had continued.

Unfortunately, this again requires *both* a high degree of accuracy in the measurement of the actual movements in output, employment and productivity ('the historic record') *and* considerable success in the econometric handling of the pre-SET data to establish reliable relationships (which may simply not exist, or be extremely unstable). The position is, of course, made a great deal worse by the fact that one is looking for a small difference between two large items, so that a very high standard of accuracy is required (unless one can plausibly assume that there is a common error in each of the two figures). Thus, Chapter VI ended with a comparison between the estimates of productivity movements derived from our surveys in the near-distributive trades and those derived from official statistics, and the degree of agreement was not as bad as we had expected in such a difficult field: the two sets of statistics gave a broadly similar picture of the historical record. The differences between the figures for individual trades in individual years were, however, big enough to produce radically different estimates of the 'effects' of SET, if they were compared in turn with an econometric estimate of what was to be 'expected' — quite apart from any errors there might be in that estimate.

Chapter II has already explained in broad terms how scanty and unreliable the available statistics are in the SET trades, particularly on output, and the matter is discussed in more detail in Appendix E. We were sorely tempted to give up the struggle, and say that it is impossible to come to any conclusion at all from such inadequate data. We could not, however, assess how much one might learn from attempting to use the available information except by actually making the attempt, and we do feel that the results of our efforts at least provide some limited guidance as to which of various possible views are *more likely* to be correct.

As in the case of prices, we proceeded as if we were trying to arrive at results for each trade separately, but the 'answers' which emerged are certainly not to be regarded as usable estimates for that trade. Rather, we looked at them collectively and considered what general inferences one might draw for the field as a whole by making the assumption that the errors in the statistics used (and in the econometric methods applied) will tend to average out when one considers all the figures together; we also considered whether one can set some limits to the probable range of the various answers, or regard one general view as more probable than another.

We have in fact made a great many attempts to apply alternative methods to the ones described or sketched in this chapter, which it would be tedious to reproduce in detail. Further particulars of some of our procedures are given in Appendix E, which also gives more detailed statistics from which readers may like to attempt other approaches.

It is perhaps worth concluding this introductory section by making the familiar point that we are concerned throughout only with estimates of *movements through time,* so that a series which would obviously be inadequate as a measure of (say) the output of legal services (because it is obviously incomplete), may nevertheless give a reasonable guide to the movements between years which are not very far apart; moreover even if that is not true − as it probably is not in that case − one can at least hope that consistent procedures of this kind applied to a number of trades will not be seriously biased in the direction of always tending to give too high (or too low) results. Furthermore, in so far as we derive the *expected* level of productivity by assuming the same trend as in previous years, an output series which does tend to have an upward bias will have relatively little influence on the answer, if the bias is the same in the two periods.

The Historical Record

Table XIII.1 gives, in its first three columns, a summarised version of the 'historical record' for all the SET trades for which we were able to secure statistics for both output and employment over the period since 1960: in some cases, trades had to be combined because one or other series was not available.[1] A much fuller version is available in Appendix E, which also describes the nature and source of the figures, which are based on official data; but for our analysis we only need index numbers for output, employment and productivity, showing the movement between 1965 (taken as 100) and 1969.

It is apparent from the table that the results for some trades are a bit difficult to believe: thus in the case of accountancy, productivity is shown as having risen by 21% within four years, whilst for the entertainment item it is shown as having fallen by 8%. It is not perhaps surprising that one gets such an outcome, however, when one realises that the official estimate of the movement in the real output of accountancy rests solely on the numbers of tax assessments of various kinds, whilst that for entertainment takes no account of the advertising revenue received by the television contractors. The quality of the statistics is a good deal worse than it was in our investigation of prices, even though its nominal coverage is much greater.

When confronted with data of an obviously unreliable kind, in which one hopes that the errors will be unbiased, the best procedure seemed to be to take a median

---

1 The table does not cover distribution or construction, in which special factors apply, and which are discussed elsewhere.

Table XIII.1 *Output, Numbers Engaged and Productivity in 1969*
(Indices: 1965 = 100)

Trade	(1) Output in real terms	(2) Numbers engaged (FTE)	(3) Productivity	(4) 'Trend' productivity[a]	(5) Difference (3) minus (4), as % of trend productivity
Insurance, banking finance	123.1	108.3	113.8	101.3	12.3
Accountancy	121.3	100.0	121.4	103.5	17.3
Legal services	116.1	101.9	113.9	103.8	9.7
Cinemas, broad-casting, enter-tainment & other sport	90.8	98.7	92.0	93.0	− 1.1
Betting	98.5	96.5	102.0	98.1	4.0
Catering	98.1	97.6	100.6	100.4	0.2
Dry-cleaning	85.0	73.8	115.2	113.3	1.7
Motor trades	107.8	98.5	109.4	112.0	− 2.3
Shoe repairing	65.5	57.8	113.2	95.1	19.0
Hairdressing	99.5	92.4	107.6	107.7	− 0.1
Medians (1969)	99.0	98.0	111.3	102.4	2.9
Medians (1968)	102.0	98.7	106.6	101.7	4.0

(a) Assuming same rate of rise as between 1960 and 1965.

of the figures in each column to arrive at an over-all view for the field as a whole. This has the consequence for example that if one is sceptical about the enormous rise shown for accountancy, then one can console oneself by reflecting that one is giving accountancy no more influence on the over-all figure than it would have had if the figure were reduced to (say) 12%, or any other figure which is higher than the median. Correspondingly, it would make no difference to the answer if one raised the low figure for entertainment, so long as it was not put higher than the median.[1]

Table XIII.1 shows, then, a median rise in output per head of 11% between 1965 and 1969. In itself this provides no real basis for judging what effect SET may have had on productivity, but in a very broad sense we felt that such a rise in a period of only four years was higher than we would have expected in service trades: we would, for example, have expected the 'normal' rise to be rather less in these trades than in retailing, for which the pre-SET rise in four years averaged about 10%. Moreover, as we see below, the conditions in 1965−1969 were unfavourable to the growth of productivity in one important respect: output was growing abnormally slowly, as a result of the slow growth in demand. On the other hand the introduction of computers was opening up important labour-saving possibilities in some trades.

As a bit of a check on the impressions obtained from the 1965−1969 movement, Table XIII.1 also shows (at the bottom) the medians for 1965−1968. The rise of 6.6% over that three-year period is not so impressive as the four-year gain, but still seems fairly high for service trades. And perhaps one should add that our own surveys give some broad support to the estimates of productivity movements for this period, so far as near-distribution is concerned.

1 One technical point should perhaps be mentioned: although for each trade the productivity index is derived by dividing the output index by the employment index, this is not true for the row of medians.

Trend Productivity

In the hope of providing a more scientific standard of what gain in productivity one should have 'expected' in the absence of SET, we tried a great many econometric experiments. None, however, proved anything like as satisfactory as the ones which we used in our First Report on Distribution. The most probable explanation for this lack of success is the very poor quality of the available statistics, but it is also quite possible that no simple 'explanation' of productivity movements exists: if, for example, the various relationships keep changing, no econometric procedure can hope to find a collection of 'pre-SET rules' which would explain what happened.

There was also a further difficulty about the traditional type of equation-fitting. In a number of trades (e.g. laundries) the pre-SET period was essentially one of rising output, and relationships which gave a reasonably good 'fit' under such circumstances did not seem applicable to a period of persistently falling output. It seemed to emerge, for example, that when output rose by rather more (or less) than the average amount during the 'expanding' period the effect on numbers engaged was rather small, because the 'unusual' movement in output was largely met by a greater (or smaller) effort on the part of the existing staff, possibly including some overtime (or short time). But if one then gets a row of decreases in output in succession, these changes no longer appear 'unusual', and radical changes in the industry's structure become essential: the labour force *must* be contracted, on pain of enormous losses, and some establishments will be closed. As the research team came to put it, 'one has moved into another economic world, and the old rules are no guide'.

In these circumstances we felt that the best general guide to what was to be expected was the simplest — i.e. a plain figure for the past rise in productivity in each trade: this had, of course, to be measured by the very imperfect statistics available, but at least their nature was the same for each trade in the reference period as in the post-SET period. Such a guide enables one to calculate a set of figures for the differences in the speed of productivity gain, which are obviously unreliable as a measure of the SET effect on a trade by trade basis, but which one can then review to see whether any general conclusions seem to emerge. Such a review need not be confined to such devices as taking a median but can consider in a broad way in which direction important disturbing factors might be expected to influence the outcome.

The fourth column of Table XIII.1 gives, therefore, the productivity index which would have been found in 1969 if productivity had risen between 1965 and 1969 at the same rate as it did between 1960 and 1965; and the final column expresses the differences between the actual index and this trend productivity index as a percentage of the latter. For each trade, this final column gives something which might be regarded as a measure of the effect of abnormal new factors on productivity — but in view of the poor quality of the statistics and the crudity of the procedure it would be absurd to use these figures separately in that way. The apparent gains of 19% for shoe-repairing and 17% for accountancy are clearly wrong.

Taking the ten figures as a group, however, they do suggest that there was some new factor tending to raise productivity. Thus 7 out of the 10 trades show a positive outcome, the 3 negative figures are all small, and the largest of these (— 2.3% for motor trades) is readily explicable in terms of the low level of new car sales in 1969, relative to trend. In view of the hazardous nature of the statistics, one should clearly not attach any importance to the very large size of some of the positive figures, beyond noting that they are above the median: the median for the ten is in fact + 2.9%, and might be considered a conservative way of summarising the outcome.

We do not attach much importance to the actual figure which is reached in this way, except as a *very* broad order of magnitude, but it does seem to support the view – which is in any case plausible on *a priori* grounds – that SET had some positive effect on output per head.

For what it is worth, the corresponding figure for 1968 is + 2.8%, but the statistics are much too rough to deduce anything about whether the effect had been mainly secured by 1968 or was still growing.

Possible Refinements and Checks

Although we decided that more elaborate econometric methods were really inapplicable, it is perhaps worth while to consider the main ideas which they would have embodied, and to see in each case whether they would tend to raise or lower the figure arrived at by our simple approach. We can also consider some alternative ways of applying our basic approach, and we start with some of these.

Alternative assessment of 'trend productivity'

We assessed 'trend productivity' for 1969 by simply taking the (cumulative) rate of increase shown between 1960 and 1965, and assuming that rate to apply between 1965 and 1969. Alternatively, we might have fitted a logarithmic trend to the figures for all the years from 1960 to 1965, and projected that.

This alternative method would have made quite a difference to some of the 'trend' productivity figures for individual trades, but its effect on the median would have been negligible – a change from 102.4 to 102.2. Good arguments could be advanced in favour of either method, given that 1960 and 1965 were broadly similar years: our choice of the 'end-years' method rested partly on its easier intelligibility, and partly on the fact that the other happened to increase the differences between actual productivity and trend productivity for individual trades at both ends of the spectrum.

Did 1965 give a biassed standard?

The fitting of these trends to the data for 1960–1965 had one convenient by-product because we were able to see whether productivity in each trade was above or below 'trend' in 1965. As we compared the actual productivity in 1969 with that in 1965 to see what happened after SET had been introduced, this would be setting a *stiff* standard if 1965 had been a 'good' year, but a *lax* one if it had been a 'poor' year.

In point of fact 5 trades showed 1965 productivity as above the 1960–1965 trend, and 5 showed it as below, so that the test seems to have been a fair one, so far as the whole group is concerned. For what it is worth, the median was slightly above trend, so that if anything the test was a little on the stiff side.

Attempts to improve individual series

In a number of industries we were particularly unhappy about the suitability of the output series for our purpose and we tried our hand at using the available material to construct alternatives. In the end we decided however to leave the CSO basis, apart from a few corrections of inconsistencies, as giving our main calculation, since there was a clear danger that our selection of cases for investigation would be biassed, through being linked with the nature of the answers which they yielded: we did not have time or resources to tackle the job comprehensively.

It is, however, perhaps worth noting that the effect of adopting the two alternative series on which we did most work[1] would have been to leave unchanged the apparent productivity effect for the group of trades since the median remained at 2.9%.

General upward bias in output series?

We considered two reasons why there might be a general upward bias in the output series:

(a) There might be a general worsening of the *quality* of the service rendered, stimulated by the increased cost of labour which SET brought, and possibly taking the form of making the customer put up with a less pleasant 'machine-made' output (e.g. computerised bank statements which are not available on demand at the local branch), or choose between a long wait and a shift in his purchases to off-peak periods.

(b) Increased *specialisation* between industries may lead to a general exaggeration of the output (and so productivity) series, because these take no heed of the increase in purchased inputs. Thus the use of prepared foods by a restaurant in place of raw ingredients would save labour without affecting the recorded (gross) output, and so exaggerate the rise in productivity — quite apart from any argument about the quality of the meal.

On neither of these did our survey of near-distribution suggest that the factor had been of much quantitative importance, but the evidence was necessarily thin and impressionistic. There is, however, not much scope for service trades to 'escape SET' by getting jobs done by *untaxed* specialists — e.g. a hotel which ceased washing its own sheets and sent them out to a laundry would still be paying indirectly.

The rapid gain in productivity for insurance, banking, and finance, in 1965–1969 is in very marked contrast to its previous slow rise, and we felt tempted to attribute a good part of it to the spread and better use of computers: in part this leads to a worse service to customers, but in large part it is a genuine economy. In any case it would need an enormous reduction in the output index to have any effect on our answer for the group of trades, because this rests on the *median,* and the figure for banking etc. is well above it.

The very high output and productivity index for accountancy might be partly explained by a tendency for customers who were not liable to SET to do more of the work themselves, rather than giving it to professional accountants. This is because the output indicator rests simply on the number of tax returns made, and takes no heed of the extent to which the profession had been involved, or of the ratio of their 'tax' work to non-tax work. The trouble here is clearly the general weakness of this indicator — if the output estimate had been based on the (deflated) revenue of the profession there would have been no problem: but again our use of the median means that only an enormous reduction in the output index would affect our answer.

1   The two cases in question are *cinemas, broadcasting etc.* and *insurance banking and finance,* and there is a certain 'balance' in their selection, as the output (and productivity) indices for the former 'looked low' and for the latter 'looked high'. Appendix E gives a brief account of our approach and the results obtained.

Downward bias in the labour figures?

It is possible that the amount of double-jobbing may have increased since 1965 (e.g. in public-houses), thereby exaggerating the gain in productivity, (since the Department of Employment figures do not include double-jobbers). It would be plausible to argue that SET would encourage the use of such labour, on which the secondary employer would pay no insurance contribution and so no SET. However, the information which we collected for near-distribution (which is one of the most 'promising' areas) did not suggest that this was of much quantitative importance when converted into full-time-equivalent labour.

It is also possible that SET may have stimulated the evasion of National Insurance – a subject which we discuss in Chapter XV. On this the important point arises however that our calculation of the 'productivity effect' depends on the increase in evasion being *more rapid* in 1965–1969 than in 1960–1965: an equally rapid increase in both periods means an equal exaggeration in the productivity gain, and leaves our answer unaffected. The very uncertain outcome of our investigation does not give any real support to the belief that such an acceleration happened on a scale which would be quantitatively important.

Output and productivity

Finally, we came to the economic question whether, apart from SET, one would have expected a faster or slower rise in productivity in 1965–1969 than between 1960 and 1965.

The normal presumption is that productivity will grow faster in periods when output grows faster. So far as that test is concerned, the answer is decisively that we would have expected a *slower* growth in productivity in 1965–1969: the median change in output for the ten industries in 1960–1965 was $+ 3.3\%$ a year, whilst in 1965–1969 it was $- 0.2\%$ a year. Taken over a four-year period, this gives a difference in output growth of nearly 15%: those who have faith in Verdoorn's law can make their own estimates of how much lower the 'expected' productivity index for 1969 should be than the one derived from a simple projection of the 1960–1965 movement.

A second factor points the same way. Service industries are said to increase their 'recorded' productivity faster when the labour market is tight, because they cannot then recruit all the workers they desire, on the basis of the demand for the services which they sell, and yet they manage to meet the demand – perhaps by skimping on quality, perhaps by more intensive work and over-time.

The labour market was undoubedly less 'tight' in 1969 than in 1965, so that this factor would be slowing down the rise in recorded productivity between 1965 and 1969: on the other hand there was not much difference between 1960 and 1965, so that there was no corresponding bias. In so far as one feels that the intervening years were relevant, they also tell in the same direction.

Conclusions

The statistical data in the field are so unreliable that it would be presumptuous to claim a high degree of confidence for any conclusions about productivity movements, let alone for the effect of any particular factor on them. Certainly we would not wish to say anything about any particular trade.

Nevertheless the figures in Table XIII.1 do make it plausible to believe that, over the field as a whole, there was some acceleration of productivity growth after 1965. Moreover the possible refinements which we have examined seem to us to suggest, on the whole, that these crude figures are more likely to understate the effects of abnormal new factors than to exaggerate them.

To pass from there to a judgement of the effects of SET requires an assessment of the possible existence and strength of other abnormal new factors. This can only be based on the crudest of impressions, because one has to compare two sets of dynamic forces without being able to measure either: thus the computer was undoubtedly having an important effect on productivity in banking during 1965 to 1969, but there were technological advances in the earlier period also. The most that can be said is that our use of the median minimised the disturbing influence of this particular factor.

It would have been easy to resign from the struggle at this point, and say that no answer is possible (which is not, of course, the same thing as saying that the effect should be assumed to be zero or negligible). I feel however, bound to record that our efforts leave me with the rather strong impression that SET probably did have some upward effect on productivity in the services covered (as well as in distribution); but I do not feel able to put a figure on it.[1]

---

1 To avoid misunderstanding, I want to say explicitly that the gain of 2% over a two-year period used in Chapter VI was taken for purposes of illustration only: it rested on general presumptions and the need for a computationally convenient figure, rather than the detailed results of our statistical analysis.

XIV
The Labour Market

Employment in the SET Sector
One of the ideas associated with the introduction of SET was that it would divert workers from jobs in industries liable to the tax, and 'make more labour available for the expansion of manufacturing industry'.[1]

Different reasons for change
There are a number of ways in which SET could have affected the labour market, apart from its general deflationary effect (which as we explained at the start of this Report is not under examination). Firstly, it might have led to increases in productivity in the sectors on which it fell as a net burden. Quite independently of what might happen to output, this would be reflected in fewer recruitments by those industries to replace natural wastage, and possibly in more redundancies: an increase in labour productivity might also involve the substitution of part-time employees for full-timers. Secondly, SET might have led to a deterioration of service in the affected sectors, so that less manpower was required per shirt washed or other unit of output: in practice, this would often be statistically indistinguishable from an increase in labour productivity. A third possible effect is that the tax might have led to a reduction in the output of firms in the trades affected, because price increases due to the tax caused customers to switch part of their expenditure to other industries: they might, for example, have switched from buying the services of laundries to buying washing machines, and this would reduce the demand for labour to work in laundries. Finally, if the tax led to some businesses or sections of businesses being closed, this might have meant that some customers were unable to buy the service in question ('no laundry near enough') and this artificial reduction in demand would have reduced the total labour employed in that industry: even with service industries, however, this 'non-availability' factor would probably not be very large.

These four ways in which the use of SET rather than some other tax might have diverted labour from the service trades have very different welfare implications. A straight gain in productivity is a clear benefit, giving the community the same output with less labour absorbed – unless, of course, the 'freed' labour is wasted because there is a corresponding fall in total employment.[2] By way of contrast, the other

1 At first, the premium paid to employers in manufacturing industry was an additional factor which might have led to a transfer of workers.

2 This outcome is most improbable on our assumption about the general policy of demand management pursued by the Government; the point is discussed further below.

three factors release labour from the service trades, but at the cost of reducing the quantity and/or quality of the services provided to the community. In so far as the services affected by SET were previously 'too cheap' because they were less heavily taxed than other services or goods, there is a case (discussed in Chapter II of our First Report) for regarding the change as an improvement, but it is at best a small matter. Otherwise, the benefits secured by this kind of transfer must be sought in the differential advantages which some economists believe to arise from an expansion of manufacturing (and other trades not affected by SET) to a size greater than would be possible in a free (but imperfect) market, at the expense of a reduction in the output of services affected by SET. We regard it as outside our terms of reference to enter into this debate, which turns crucially on an assessment of what would happen in manufacturing.

Lines of approach

It has often been suggested to us that we should examine the effects of SET on the allocation of labour between services and manufacturing etc. by looking at the actual movement of workers between industries; we have on occasions been asked 'did you find a single instance of a worker being transferred from services to manufacture as a result of SET?'

This approach seems, however, to be an extremely unpromising one, on two quite different grounds. In the first place, it seems to misconceive the basic way in which one would expect the tax to produce a reallocation of the labour force, which is primarily through *reduced recruitment* to the service trades — whether of new entrants to the labour market or of people transfering from other activities. Since natural wastage in the SET sector is probably of the order of 3% *per month*, a substantial reduction in the number of its workers could obviously be secured quite quickly by reducing recruitment without a single extra worker being transferred to the rest of the economy. A study of workers moving from the SET sector to manufacturing would by itself be of little or no value, even if the statistics were perfect.

The second difficulty is on purely statistical grounds. If one is to work from data about movements into or out of particular industries, one needs to have statistics not only for the period after the tax was introduced, but also for earlier periods, since these are needed to provide a basis for estimating what would have happened in the absence of the tax. Moreover, the statistics would have to cover all new entries into a particular industry, whether from another industry, from non-employment (including juveniles, and married women returning to the labour market), from the unemployed, or from abroad; and the same would be true of departures from the industries. Furthermore the statistics would have to cover self-employed as well as employees, since some of the important differences in the movement might be in that sector.

We are aware that the Department of Employment have recently started to publish some statistics for the numbers of employees (but not self-employed) whose National Insurance cards show that the industry to which they are classified has changed between one year and the next, but these and other statistics do not go very far towards meeting the exacting statistical requirements needed for the use of this approach. As there are also very awkward problems of principle about the establishment of figures for the 'alternative position' we decided not to embark on a path which we felt convinced would lead to no useful result.[1]

Two other lines of approach seem possible. The first is to attempt an assessment of the effect of SET on productivity, so as to see how much higher it was than one would have expected with an alternative tax: this indicates how much lower the the number of people engaged would be, for any specified level of output, and needs to be coupled with an assessment of how the output would compare with that expected in the alternative position, if one is to arrive at the effect on numbers engaged.

The second method is to look at the history of the numbers engaged in the SET sector, both before and after the tax, as a proportion of *total* numbers engaged in the country, or − as we consider more relevant − as a proportion of the total *excluding* certain industries where the number depends essentially on Government expenditure (i.e. public administration and defence, education and medical services, but *not* the nationalised industries). If the pre-SET history suggests some plausible 'rules' for predicting what the proportion would have been in (say) 1969, then one can calculate the number which one would have 'expected' to find in the SET sector, and contrast it with the actual numbers.

The first of these two methods has been attempted elsewhere in our Reports, so far as the productivity part is concerned: we revert to it after we have examined the second, and it is useful to start this examination with a brief consideration of the logic underlying it.

First, by calculating the 'expected' number in the SET sector from the actual total for numbers engaged, we are automatically assuming that Government macro-economic policy would have produced the same level of employment with the alternative tax arrangement. It makes no difference if we first subtract the number in public administration, etc., except that we are also assuming that this would not be affected to a significant extent.

Secondly, the idea of using pre-SET experience to predict the percentage can in principle be made as elaborate as one likes: it might, for example, be found that this percentage had an upward trend, but also rose (or fell) in years of slack trade, and one would then need to allow for the actual state of trade in 1969 when making a prediction, as well as for the passage of time. One might, of course, find that there was no sort of regularity on which to base a prediction, in which case the method would fail.

Why, then, should one expect any sort of regularity? Fundamentally, movements in this percentage reflect the combined effect of two factors:

(a) the shift in the composition of the 'bill of goods (and services)' demanded by all spenders of money combined (including businesses and foreign importers) between the products of the SET sector and those of the rest of the British economy;

(b) the differential growth of output per head in the two sectors.

These composite factors are things in which one might hope to find some continuity of development, and both lead one to expect a percentage which rises through time.

---

1 An attempt to distinguish between the inter-industry flow before and after the introduction of SET was made by R.D. Sleeper in the Bulletin of the Oxford University, Institute of Economics and Statistics, Nov. 1970.

We sought to reduce the impact of one element which might well disturb the movement in the bill of goods by eliminating the numbers in industries which are dominated
by Government expenditure decisions: clearly these are influenced by forces quite
different from those which decide the allocation of demand between the SET sector
and the rest of the economy, and we found that they did in fact show very different
movements from either of these. Even with this adjustment, however, there was
clearly no guarantee of getting more than a rough indication (if that) of the differences
between the 'expectation' for 1969 and the actual outcome.

One should perhaps add that if the labour in the SET sector is found to be below
the expected level (as it was), this approach provides no way of saying how far this
was due to a diversion of demand from its products, and how far to productivity being
higher than was to be expected in the absence of SET and/or other abnormal new
factors.

The Labour Statistics

Table XIV.1 shows numbers engaged in the SET sector and in all industries for the
relevant years, in terms of full-time-equivalents (including self-employed). The most
important column is the last one, which shows the SET sector as a percentage of the
labour force excluding the three 'public policy' categories. This figure rises progressively
during the pre-SET period from 36.9% in June 1954 to 40.7% in June 1966, just before
the introduction of the tax, which gives an average rise of 0.32 percentage points a
year; the increases do not seem to conform to any obvious cyclical pattern, though one
might perhaps argue that they are rather larger in the depressed years (e.g. 1959, 1962
and 1963) – but 1958 shows a subnormal rise.

Since 1966 movements in the proportion have been small and include a fall in 1969,
so that the net rise in three years from 1966 to 1969 was only from 40.7% to 40.8%.
A rise at the previous average rate would have brought the figure to 41.65% – and if
anything one might have expected the rise to be above average in a period of poor trade.
Alternatively one might look at the matter from a slightly different angle and say that
the table shows no three-year interval in the pre-SET period where the rise was anything
like as small as 0.1 percentage points – the smallest being 0.6 percentage points between
1954 and 1957.

It seems fair to conclude, therefore, that the percentage of the labour force in the
SET sector was definitely lower than one would have expected from pre-SET experience. Our basic assumption is that the total number of people at work would have
been the same if some other tax had been used, and we also assume the same number
in the three 'public policy' categories, so this clearly implies that the *number* in the
SET sector was also smaller than expected. As an order of magnitude, the difference
might be put at 150,000 to 200,000 workers, or about 2% of the numbers that would
have been 'expected' in the absence of SET or some other abnormal new factor.

The Productivity Approach

For the SET sector as a whole (including distribution and construction) we do not have
anything which can be regarded as a real estimate of the difference between actual
productivity and what was to be 'expected'. To show the principles of the method,
however, and to give some idea of the numbers involved, we take an illustrative
'productivity gain' of 3% for 1969.

111

Table XIV.1 *FTE Numbers Engaged*

| Year[a] | FTE Numbers Engaged (000's) | | | SET sector as a % of: | |
	SET sector	Total all industries and services	Total all industries and services excepting Public Administration etc.[b]	Total FTE numbers engaged	Total FTE numbers engaged except Public Administration etc.[b]
1954	7098	21 887	19 241	32.4	36.9
1955	7207	22 142	19 516	32.6	36.9
1956	7311	22 317	19 655	32.8	37.2
1957	7369	22 340	19 672	33.0	37.5
1958	7301	22 136	19 440	33.0	37.6
1959	7451	22 211	19 493	33.6	38.2
1960	7584	22 625	19 877	33.5	38.2
1961	7671	22 859	20 053	33.6	38.3
1962	7829	22 928	20 045	34.1	39.1
1963	7934	22 898	19 935	34.7	39.8
1964	8101	23 075	20 121	35.1	40.3
1965	8157	23 178	20 167	35.2	40.4
1966	8181	23 220	20 102	35.2	40.7
Post-SET					
1967	7986	22 813	19 579	35.0	40.8
1968	7909	22 555	19 285	35.1	41.0
1969	7833	22 490	19 198	34.8	40.8

(a) All figures relate to June so the 1966 figure is pre-SET.
(b) Public Administration etc., covers MLH (1958 SIC) 872 (Educational Services), 874 (Medical and Dental Services), and Order XXIV (Public Administration and Defence) — i.e. those sections mainly supported from public funds.

Sources: See Appendix C.

This means that, in the alternative position, the number of workers needed to produce the output of the SET sector which actually was produced would have been 3% greater — an increase of some 235 000.

However, in the alternative position the output of the SET sector would not have been the same, for two conflicting reasons:

(a) We have assumed that the total number engaged in all industry is unchanged. Hence, with a lower level of productivity in one large sector (the SET sector) the total national output of goods and services would have been smaller, and the resultant lower real income would have meant a smaller demand for SET output.

(b) On the other hand, we have seen in Chapter XII that SET led to higher prices for services proper, and this is likely to have diverted some demand from these services to other things: in the alternative position, therefore, the proportion of these services in the total national output would have been rather higher.

It may be useful to attempt some quantification of these two factors. We again assume that the number of people in the three 'public policy' industries is unaffected.

In round figures, then, the alternative position would show output of the whole economy (other than the three 'public policy' industries) as reduced by perhaps 1%: the productivity gain of 3% affects about 40% of the number of workers, but the value of output per head in the SET sector is somewhat below average. If we were correcting for that factor alone, we might then argue that the output of the SET sector would, in the absence of the abnormal productivity gain, have been about 1% lower, and the extra employment there would have been 2% instead of 3%.

So far as the 'switching' of demand is concerned, we can do no more than express our conviction that this is a very small factor, for the following reasons:

(a) In the large part of the sector represented by distribution, the question does not arise — or perhaps one should say that, if anything, it arises in an inverted form. For distributive services are bought in conjunction with goods, so that if the main effect of SET were to produce a switch of consumer demand from services to goods, this would imply an *increase* in the volume of goods distributed. Admittedly, of course, there might be a smaller amount of distributive 'service' associated with each unit of goods distributed, and indeed this probably happened to some extent. But the statistical method of measuring the output of the distributive trades uses the volume of goods as its indicator, so that this type of development has already been brought into the picture as an improvement in productivity. It would be quite wrong to calculate the extra labour needed in the alternative position by counting *both* the effect of lower productivity (computed in this way) *and* the extra amount of 'service' per unit of goods.[1]

(b) In the field of construction the effect of any small rise in price in causing a switch of demand can hardly be large, because there is no close substitute which is untaxed.[2]

(c) With services proper, for which we attempted some estimates of the price effect in Chapter XII, there must have been some diversion of demand. We considered the possibility of making a quantitative estimate of it, using the preliminary results of work being done on another project in the Department of Applied Economics, but concluded that one could not really get further than saying that it would be very small. To give an idea of what that means — but not as a statistical estimate — we might add that we imply that a typical service, for which the price-rise caused by SET in 1969 was (say) 4% might suffer an output loss of perhaps 1% on that account.

The reasons why this answer is so small can be summarised thus:

(i) The price rise caused by SET was much smaller than many people imagine — even though Chapter XII concluded that it was not much less than the equivalent of the cost of SET.

(ii) We are not concerned with what economists call the 'income effect' of price rises — i.e. the reduction in the quantity sold caused by people's real purchasing-power being reduced. The 'alternative position' is one in which there is an alternative tax.

1 This is not the place to revert to the question whether (for example) a switch from counterservice to self-service should be regarded as reducing the output of the distributive trade. See First Report, pages 74–75 and 126–132.

2 The logic of the problem requires the inclusion of self-employed building workers and their output within 'the SET sector', even though they pay no SET: increased activities of the 'do-it-yourself' brigade, however, constitute a diversion of demand.

(iii) The 'substitution' or switching effect produced by the tax was much reduced by its wide incidence. Because SET applied over such a wide field, the effect of a price rise for any particular service was mitigated by the fact that prices had also risen for others.

For the SET sector as a whole, therefore, we have a small switch effect applying to part only of the field, and we reckon this correction to the original calculation to be insufficient to off-set the first one. The broad conclusion to the whole assessment is, therefore that if the productivity gain is put at 3% then the alternative position would show an addition to the labour in the SET sector of somewhere between 2% and 3%.

As this is a purely contingent calculation, it cannot be said to confirm or refute the result derived in the previous section, which put the figure at about 2%. But we derived a certain amount of reassurance from the fact that assumptions chosen independently as reasonable illustrative figures led to results which were in reasonable harmony.

Self-Employment

The analysis in this chapter has been entirely concerned with the total number of people engaged in the SET sector, including not only employees, but also the self-employed. Although SET was not payable in respect of the self-employed, this is the meaningful concept for any consideration of productivity or man-power absorption: there is no virtue in raising 'output per employee' in an industry if that has been achieved by increasing the number of self-employed.

It is however a matter of some academic interest to see what light the official statistics throw on the extent to which the introduction of a discriminatory tax led to an increase in the proportion of people classified as self-employed. It does not tell the whole story, so far as tax-avoidance is concerned, because it does not cover the increased use of double-jobbers, or the artificial creation of 'separate units' which could qualify for refunds as 'manufacturing' (e.g. on building sites), or other anomalous ways of avoiding SET (discussed in Chapter XVI); and of course it does not cover *tax-evasion* at all (whether through non-payment of insurance stamps, or illegitimate claims for refunds). But it does illustrate one part of the consequences of yielding to 'administrative convenience' by choosing a tax basis which is not in conformity with the economic objective.

Table XIV.2 gives a simple time series for the numbers involved. The percentage of self-employed was persistently falling from 1954 to 1966, as a reflection of the well-known tendency for companies to displace unincorporated units and for operations to be done on a larger scale. With the advent of SET this movement was put into reverse.

Unemployment and Regional Effects

This section discusses two somewhat allied matters, which clearly aroused considerable interest, but on which the basic nature of the problem enables us to say very little. We understand why people are concerned about these matters, but on our definition of the problem (to investigate the effects of *alternative* taxes) they largely disappear 'by assumption': this is because we assume that the Government will pursue

Table XIV.2 *Self-Employed as % of Numbers Engaged in SET Sector*[a]

Years (June)	Employees in employment (000's)	Self-employed (including employers) (000's)	Self-employed as % of total
1954	6415	1171	15.44
1955	6538	1187	15.36
1956	6670	1176	14.99
1957	6741	1172	14.81
1958	6703	1146	14.60
1959	6854	1168	14.56
1960	7003	1183	14.46
1961	7132	1171	14.10
1962	7344	1157	13.61
1963	7459	1176	13.62
1964	7654	1172	13.28
1965	7790	1132	12.69
1966	7856	1132	12.59
Post-SET			
1967	7566	1209	13.77
1968	7518	1204	13.80
1969	7433	1235	14.25

(a) MLH 500 709, 810, 820, 831–2, 860, 871, 873, 879, 881–9, 891, 899

Sources: See Appendix C.

a macro-economic policy which yields the same level of total employment in each case.

The first point raises the whole question of unemployment. In its simplest form it asserts that the introduction of SET led to some firms reducing their staff, or closing altogether, and says that the people concerned would be quite unsuitable for work in manufacturing, or were too far from any factory where they might find work. 'Hence the tax may raise productivity, but the labour "saved" is simply unemployed'.

As we see from Table XIV.3, the introduction of SET was followed by some increase in the number of people recorded as unemployed in the SET sector, and it may be that this view of SET as a cause of unemployment largely reflects that historical fact. If so, the main fallacy in the argument is easily revealed: there was also a rise in unemployment in the rest of the economy, which was about equally steep. The rise in the SET sector does not reflect anything specifically connected with SET, but simply the general policy of disinflation which the Government was pursuing. That policy was not aimed at 'creating unemployment' for its own sake, but rather at reducing the pressure on the labour market, so as to prevent desirable forms of expansion from being frustated by difficulty in securing labour.

It is obviously outside our terms of reference to consider whether this policy was a wise one, or whether it was skilfully executed. What the figures clearly show is that the increase in recorded unemployment was *not* concentrated in the SET sector, as one might imagine from the type of argument set out above.[1] SET was part of the

1 We consider in the next chapter whether there was an increase in *unrecorded* unemployment: the changes in activity rates (i.e. the percentage of people in various classes who seek gainful work) do not point to any substantial involuntary retirement of women from the labour market 'because SET deprived them of job opportunities for which they were suitable'.

Table XIV.3 *Unemployment 1965–69*[a]

	1965	1966	1967	1968	1969
Total numbers unemployed (000's)	276	261	500	517	499
SET Trades	110	103	198	212	195
of which: Construction	39	37	85	95	88
Other SET trades	71	66	113	117	107
Numbers unemployed in the SET trades as % of total unemployment	39.9	39.5	39.6	41.0	39.1
of which: Construction	14.1	14.2	17.0	18.4	17.6
Other SET trades	25.7	25.3	22.6	22.6	21.4

(a) The figures given are for June in each year: 1966 is therefore in the pre-SET period.
Source: Ministry of Labour Gazette.

Government's general disinflationary policy, which increased the level of unemployment; but that increase must be attributed to the general policy, and not to the choice of instrument.

In case this conclusion may seem strange, it is perhaps helpful to explain why we fully expected to find this result, even though the issue was complicated by SET being introduced at a time when the Government's *general* policy was disinflationary. The reason is – once again – that the process of reducing the proportion of the labour force engaged in the SET trades was bound to be secured mainly by incomplete replacement of wastage. In so far as the reduction in the number of jobs in the SET sector led to people being unemployed, who might otherwise have been at work, these might fall in any of the following categories (or others):

School-leavers and others not previously in the labour market.

People from other sectors seeking jobs in the SET sector.

People from SET firms who were seeking to move to other jobs within the sector.

Of these three, only the last would be classified as unemployed 'in the SET sector', and they would be indistinguishable from others who had left a job in the SET sector, and were unsuccessfully seeking one in (say) manufacturing.

In brief, given the large amount of *gross* movement of labour, there is little connection between any specific cause of a widespread nature (e.g. contraction of employment in the SET sector) and the industrial classification of the resulting unemployed. It is not really meaningful to ask whether the introduction of SET led to some people losing a job 'to no good purpose', and if so how many: there doubtless were some cases of this kind, but in a complex world it is impossible to define the category.

Regional Effects

The second point concerned the regional impact of SET. In its simplest aspect, it rested on the argument that SET was designed to increase jobs in manufacturing at the expense of service trades, and that this ignored the 'fact' (sic) that the service trades are concentrated in Development Areas, where there is not much manufacturing to provide alternative employment.

1 If the introduction of SET had been accompanied by a reduction in some other tax (so as to leave the demand for labour essentially unchanged on a historical basis), the question at issue would have been simply to see whether there was some small amount of extra frictional unemployment in the SET sector.

In that simple form, the argument basically fails because its central point is a caricature of the true facts, which are given in Table XIV.4.

Table XIV.4 *Employment in SET Orders*[a] *as Percentage of Total Employment in June 1966* (A Regional Analysis for Great Britain)

Description of Regions	% in SET sector
Almost wholly Development Areas:	
Scotland, Wales, Northern	31.5
Partly Development Areas:	
South-West, North-West	31.0
Other Regions	32.8
Whole Country	32.2

(a) SET Orders are XVII, XX, XXI, XXIII on 1958 SIC.
Source: Abstract of Regional Statistics.

The percentage of employees in the SET Orders is clearly very similar in the three groups of regions — and indeed slightly *lower* in the Development Areas. This reflects, in part, the large amount of service employment in London — which is still large, even when the exempt services are excluded.

In spite of these inconvenient facts, it is still possible to develop a 'regional' argument on the following lines. 'The pure logic of SET envisages the tax as destroying jobs in service trades, whilst the Government's macro-economic policy expands the general level of demand (e.g. though a cut in some other tax), and so produces an off-setting increase in job opportunities. If this expansion were evenly spread throughout the country — i.e. if it were proportional to present employment in each of the Regional groups — the net outcome would be neutral between them. But it is likely to go largely to the regions which are expanding anyhow, so that the Development Areas will lose'.

This argument is essentially outside our terms of reference: it is equally arguable that the Government would take advantage of the need for an expansionary policy 'to off-set SET' by introducing something with a deliberate bias in favour of the Development Areas. The regional employment premium might be quoted in support of this possibility.

Wages and Salaries

When SET was introduced, the view was expressed in various quarters that it would have a depressing effect on wages and salaries in the SET sector — i.e. lead to these rising less rapidly than was otherwise to be expected. Very broadly, this possibility can be examined by comparing what happened in SET trades with what happened elsewhere in the economy, and the best available data are provided in Table XIV.5 for manual workers and XIV.6 for clerical, etc., staff.

The data themselves are far from ideal, because earnings figures are so scanty in the service trades. (We investigated the data on wage-rates, but concluded that they would be of little value as a guide to what was actually paid). Consequently we felt that any attempts at elaborate analyses to establish 'what was to be expected in the absence of SET' would inevitably fail: a straight comparison between the movements in the post-SET period for trades affected by SET and those outside seems as good

Table XIV.5 *Growth-rates for Average Earnings of Manual Workers*
(All figures are compound growth rates)

			Construction	Certain Miscellaneous Services[a]	Manu-facturing	All Industries
			%	%	%	%
Male (21+)	Weekly Earnings	Post-SET[b] (Pre-SET)[c]	5.25 (7.04)	5.61 (6.35)	5.46 (5.97)	5.58 (6.28)
	Hourly Earnings	Post-SET[b] (Pre-SET)[c]	5.94 (7.36)	6.00 (7.06)	5.70 (6.64)	5.82 (6.85)
Female (18+)	Weekly Earnings	Post-SET[b] (Pre-SET)[c]	6.00 (5.44)	5.19 (5.60)	5.61 (5.34)	5.58 (5.36)
	Hourly Earnings	Post-SET[b] (Pre-SET)[c]	4.98 (6.40)	5.37 (6.43)	5.88 (6.51)	5.88 (6.53)

(a) 'Certain Miscellaneous Services' is composed of laundries, dry-cleaning, motor repairers and garages, and repair of boots and shoes.

(b) Post-SET: 1965–6 to 1968–9 (average of October and April surveys).

(c) Pre-SET: 1959–60 to 1965–6 (average of October and April surveys).

Source: Derived from Table 48, 'Historical Abstract of Labour Statistics' and D.E. Gazettes. For details see Appendix C.

Table XIV.6 *Growth-rates for Average Weekly Earnings of Administrative, Technical and Clerical Staff*
(All figures are compound growth rates)

		Banking & Insurance %	Construction %	All manufacturing %	National & Local Government[a] %
Male	Post-SET[b] (Pre-SET)[c]	4.72 (4.89)	6.77 (6.17)	6.00 (5.78)	5.58 (6.09)
Female	Post-SET[b] (Pre-SET)[c]	4.72 (6.14)	7.37 (5.50)	6.54 (5.46)	4.77 (6.03)

(a) Great Britain only.

(b) Post-SET: October 1965 to October 1969.

(c) Pre-SET: October 1959 to October 1965.

Source: Derived from Table 53, 'Historical Abstract of Labour Statistics' and D.E. Gazettes.

as anything else, but it can be supplemented by looking at the comparative movements over the previous six-year period.

Given the weakness in both the statistics and the methodology, it is clearly necessary to look at all the figures as a group, rather than attempt to arrive at separate conclusions for males and females or for individual trades. On this basis the SET figures are sometimes above and sometimes below the various yardsticks which might be deemed relevant, and the inclusion of pre-SET trends in the picture still leaves the same conclusion. This is the sort of outcome which one would expect to find if SET had in fact had no effect; but strictly one should only say that the statistics provide no evidence that it did have an effect of any quantitative importance.

Obviously such a conclusion is perfectly consistent with the existence of individual cases where SET had a depressing effect. The general conclusion is, however, in accord with the qualitative results of our enquiries both in distribution and in near-distribution: many respondents emphasized the fact that they had great difficulty in recruiting the staff which they wanted, both before and after the introduction of SET.

XV
Activity Rates

For two quite different reasons, we devoted a fair amount of energy to the study of 'activity rates' — i.e. the percentage of the population in various age-and-sex groups who are seeking gainful employment, whether or not they find it (including the self-employed). The results of our investigations were not as clear-cut as we had hoped, on account of various statistical difficulties explained below: but they do nevertheless seem to be worth recording, together with a brief indication of the difficulties.

Very briefly, then, the two questions on which we were seeking some guidance were as follows:

(a) We were concerned to get an indication of the extent (if any) to which people had been led to retire from the labour force because they were unable to find jobs in the SET sector, and so did not appear in the unemployment figures, although they would have liked to work in the SET sector.

(b) It seemed possible that SET might have led to errors in the official estimates of the number of people who are at work in the SET sectors, by increasing the number of people who failed to maintain National Insurance contributions even though they were in fact working (whether as employees or as self-employed persons): this would, of course, lead to an over-estimate of the effect of SET on productivity.

In order to study these questions we had the figures for activity rates, portrayed in Figure XV.1. In calculating each of these rates the *numerator* was the number of people in a certain age-and-sex group who were estimated by the Department to be 'in the labour market' — the main source of information being the card-counts; whilst the *denominator* was the total number of people in that age-and-sex group, as estimated from the Census of Population and statistics for subsequent births, deaths and migration.

The two factors under study would both tend to lower the numerator — the first by producing a genuine reduction in the size of the labour force, and the second by causing it to be under-estimated. By studying *different* groups, however, we hoped to get some light on each of the factors taken separately, since past experience would lead one to expect different types of development.

The position was however complicated by the possibility (which seems to have been real) that there might be errors in the *denominator*: a surprisingly low activity rate for males aged 25–54 in 1970, for example, might equally well reflect evasion of National Insurance, or over-estimation of the total number of men in the country, or a mixture of the two. The reader is particularly warned that the Figure XV.1 does not reflect any changes which may be needed in the light of the 1971 Census of Population.

Abnormal Withdrawals from the Labour Force?

The logical case for thinking that there might have been withdrawals from the Labour market as a result of SET runs roughly as follows:

(a) SET led to a reduction in the number of jobs available in that sector.

(b) Some people might be prepared to offer themselves for jobs in SET trades, but not in others — perhaps because the only jobs for which they were suitable (and/or which were available in their locality) were in SET trades.

(c) Some of the people coming under (b) would be amongst the unlucky ones who could not find jobs because of (a).

(d) Some of the people coming under (c) would opt not to remain in National Insurance under Class I (employees) or Class II (self-employed), and so disappear from the active population. They might, for example, decide to take the old age pension (which is strictly speaking a *retirement* pension) if they were old enough, or they might — if they were married women — decide to rely simply on their husband's insurance.

On the statistical plane, one obvious difficulty is that withdrawals of this kind have to be separated from withdrawals which might have been expected anyhow in the years after 1966, as a result of the general disinflationary policy and the increased difficulty of obtaining jobs. One would need, as usual, to have a fairly reliable indicator of 'what would have happened in the alternative position'. in which the same demand for labour in general had been reached by some alternative means.

Moreover the difficulty is not confined to the need to allow for varying states of the labour market: particularly on the women's side, the percentage of women seeking work can be significantly influenced by changes in the proportion of the female population who are married, or have a family in certain age-groups, or are of a certain age themselves. Changes in the proportion of people continuing their education beyond the school-leaving age are also relevant for both sexes.

In the hope of minimising these difficulties we decided that — for the purpose of assessing 'abnormal withdrawals' — the most useful category to consider was that for females aged 40 to 54. Over a period of a few years the demographic factors are not likely to vary very much, and neither pensions nor the pursuit of further education can distort the picture. Moreover if SET is likely to create special difficulties for any class, it must surely be for this one.

From Figure XV.1 it appears that the activity rate for females aged 40—54 had been showing a progressive upward movement in the years from 1954 to 1966 (which rates as pre-SET, since the figures relate to June), with pauses in 1958 and 1963. Its subsequent movements might be said, broadly, to reflect a continuance of the same pattern: there is again a pause between 1966 and 1967 (which might well reflect the *general* slackening of the demand for labour), followed by a further upward trend.

It would not be right to say that this series proves the idea of 'SET leading to abnormal withdrawals from the labour force' to be a complete myth: the statistics are liable to error, other factors may have intervened, and one might argue that the rise between 1966 and 1970 is if anything less than the previous trend would have suggested (though this last point is very dubious if one allows for the state of the labour market, and an upward trend of this kind commonly falls as the proportion at work reaches this sort of level). What one *can* say, however, is that the graph

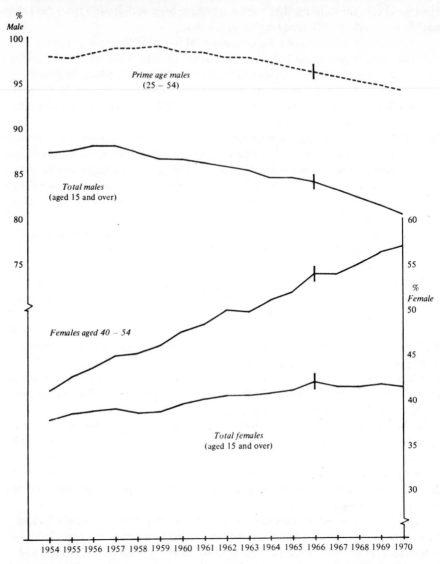

Figure XV.1 *Activity Rates 1954 – 1970*

% Male

Prime age males (25 – 54)

Total males (aged 15 and over)

Females aged 40 – 54

% Female

Total females (aged 15 and over)

1954 1955 1956 1957 1958 1959 1960 1961 1962 1963 1964 1965 1966 1967 1968 1969 1970

N.B. The figures used to prepare this chart do not reflect any revisions which may be needed in the light of the 1971 Census.

122

provides no support for the idea that this effect was of any quantitative importance: those who believe in it must rest their faith on something else, and explain away the statistics.[1]

The result should not be regarded as in any way surprising. There may well have been individual cases of married women losing a job 'because of SET' and withdrawing from the labour market: but consideration of the four factors listed above as underlying the logic of the case led us to expect that the quantitative outcome would probably be very small.

Thus we have seen in Chapter XIV that the number of jobs available in the SET sector was not cut in half, as some discussions might suggest, but reduced by perhaps 2% below what it otherwise would have been. Moreover this result was bound to be produced mainly by reduced recruitment, so that SET produced few dismissals (which are perhaps more likely to lead to a person withdrawing from the labour market than refusals to take people on). Furthermore, many of the people who failed to get a job in the SET sector would be mobile — and we are assuming that the *total* demand for labour would be the same in the alternative position. And lastly, if SET did lead to some additional unemployment, we would expect a good proportion of the people concerned to register as unemployed.[2]

Evasion of National Insurance

The chart on activity rates provided the *prima facie* case for investigating the possibility of errors in the labour force statistics, caused by evasion of National Insurance. For *this* purpose, the most useful line was the one for 'prime-age males' (i.e. males aged between 25 and 54), which showed a significant fall in the activity rate between 1966 and 1970. Such a fall is inherently surprising, since one would expect that almost all men between 25 and 54 would be in the labour force, either as employees, or as self-employed, or as unemployed people registered with the Department of Employment: the only prime-age males who are genuinely outside the working population are the 'leisure class', the chronically sick, students who do not take employment part-time or in the vacation, and any unemployed who decide not to register with an employment office (and thereby forgo any claim to insurance benefit). It seemed to us very unlikely that any of these groups would be both large enough, and subject to sufficient change, to produce a decline in the activity rate on the sort of scale shown in the chart, which raised the gap between the working population and the total from some 300 000 in 1966 to over 500 000 in 1970. Consequently, there seemed to be a *prima facie* case for making investigations, but of course these would have to cover both the numerator and the denominator of the activity rate calculation: as explained above, the explanation might be *either* that the estimate of the working population of prime-age males in 1970 was too low, *or* that the estimate or the total population in that category was too high (or a bit of both).

---

1   If they also believe that SET led to *evasion* by women who were really working this task is even more difficult.

2   Just as we were going to press, preliminary figures from the Census of Population were released which suggested that the rise in the activity rate was steeper than is shown in the Figure. This weakens even further the case for believing in a loss of workers from the labour market as a result of SET.

The need to examine the accuracy of the figures for the total population of prime-age males was, indeed, underlined by the preliminary results of the 1971 Census of Population, which showed that the previous estimates of the population had been too high. At the time of preparing this Report, however, the revised figures for the population divided by age had not been made available, and we have therefore had to leave the chart on the basis of the statistics which were previously available, based on the estimates of the Registrar-General: it did not seem sensible to embark on highly speculative calculations for figures which should be available on the Census basis by the time that the Report is published.

We feel it to be useful, however, to record the results of our investigations into the figures for the working population, since it is by no means certain that the whole matter will be explained by changes in the figures for the total population of prime-age males.[1]

SET and National Insurance

The official estimates of the working population are based chiefly on counts of the number of N.I. cards exchanged. Employers are required to maintain the contributions of their employees by stamping the N.I. card, and to exchange the cards as the year's contributions are completed. Even where the employment amounts to only a few hours a week a small contribution is supposed to be paid to cover the risk of industrial injuries. Self-employed people are also normally expected to maintain N.I. contributions, and to exchange their cards each year. Married women who are self-employed however have the option of relying on their husband's contributions, and self-employed men over 70 years old and self-employed women over 65 years old are also exempt. Statistics of the numbers of unemployed are obtained from the records of the local employment exchanges, with which the unemployed must register if they wish to be paid unemployment benefit.

As SET is collected by means of an addition to the cost of the N.I. stamp for employees, it created an incentive for some employers to change workers from employee to self-employed status; it has been suggested that such changes may have been fairly common in some industries, particularly where unincorporated small firms can call their workers 'partners'. In itself, this *ought* not to cause any error in the estimates of the working population, since the reduction in the number of employees should be balanced by an increase in the number of self-employed (but the statistics for these are much less reliable). However, some workers giving up employee status may have failed to maintain N.I. contributions as self-employed. This would mean that the estimates of the total working population might be deficient since 1966, when the latest information not based on N.I. contributions was taken in the sample Census of Population. Estimates of the self-employed since 1966 were derived by starting from the 1966 Census figure and adding on the changes shown by the card counts for self-employed since 1966. If the number of self-employed workers not maintaining N.I. contributions rose, there would be some understatement of the working population.

1   When the detailed Census figures do become available, it will of course be possible to make much more detailed checks than the ones reflected in activity rates. Thus the Censuses will show the movement between 1966 and 1971 in the number of people in each age-and-sex group who were (a) employees in employment (b) self-employed (c) unemployed, and these movements can be compared with those estimated by the Department of Employment.

It is also clearly possible that some employers evaded N.I. contributions for employees, with their knowledge and agreement. This may have been particularly common where the employment was temporary – e.g. 'casual' jobs, and students' vacation jobs – and of course the incentive for this type of evasion was greatly increased by SET.

A proper assessment of the possible quantitative importance of these types of evasion calls for a much more thorough review of the forces operating against them than we could possibly attempt. As we understand it, there are two main forces:

(a) Since entitlement to various benefits depends on the individual's N.I. contribution record, there is a greater incentive to pay these contributions than to pay taxes; and in principle this incentive will be particularly strong for employees, since part of their entitlement comes from payments made by the employer. To some extent, therefore, the N.I. scheme can be regarded as 'self-policing'. However, the incentive to make N.I. contributions is probably not felt strongly by many of the people concerned. For some temporary workers, such as students in vacations, the advantages of making contributions may be small and long-deferred, and others may well prefer a higher net income at the present time to better claims for N.I. benefits in the event of their illness, unemployment, etc. The size of the total stamp for an adult male in 1970 was £4.23, including £2.40 for SET (which clearly brings no benefit to either employer or employee): there is plenty of scope for mutually advantageous bargains between employer and employee at the expense of the insurance fund and the revenue.

(b) The D.H.S.S. make routine checks on the contribution records of individuals, and if no card is exchanged for somebody before he reaches retirement age they will normally initiate enquiries. We are obviously in no position to make a judgment about the thoroughness with which such enquiries are pursued, but it is difficult to see what the D.H.S.S. could in practice do if the person could not be traced.

A further point is that although routine enquiries may be started where contributions cease, there is no corresponding automatic way of discovering that people who have joined the labour force (e.g. immigrants from Ireland) have been issued with a card.

We did not think it our job, as outside investigators, to attempt an appraisal of the D.H.S.S. methods for dealing with these problems, nor to discover whether any record is kept of the number of their enquiries which fail to yield a satisfactory explanation.

The Phelps Brown Inquiry

Some details of checks made by D.H.S.S. on the level of evasion of National Insurance contributions in the Construction industry were published, however, by the Phelps Brown Committee.[1]

In early 1967 checks were made on 529 construction sites in the South West, North Midlands and East and West Ridings. These sites were found to include 13 700 operatives, of whom 11% were self-employed. Among these self-employed,

---

1 Report of the Committee of Inquiry under Professor E.H. Phelps Brown into Certain Matters concerning Labour in Building and Civil Engineering – Cmnd. 3714, H.M.S.O., pp. 147–8.

5–6% (i.e. about 0.6% of the total operatives) were found to be 'not in compliance', in the strict sense that they had contribution arrears extending beyond the current contribution year. A number of self-employed workers (equivalent to 3.7% of the self-employed who were counted, and many of them Irish), were *known* to have 'disappeared' during the survey.

A second survey was held in the South East and North West, with broadly similar results. 9% were fond to be self-employed, 5–6% of these were not in compliance. 60 men (5% of the self-employed) were known to have disappeared during the survey as the proportion of self-employed discovered seemed low for a survey which included the South East, Phelps Brown wondered if there were not more that got away. In more than one area visited, sales of insurance stamps by post offices increased greatly at the time of the survey.

It seems very unlikely that many of the workers found to be 'not in compliance' would be included in the D.H.S.S. 2% sample card-count totals as they would most probably lack a contribution in the latest period. A partially-stamped card surrendered promptly would be counted by the Department of Employment card count. But most of those found to be in 'non-compliance' would either have no card at all, or be still in possession of an expired card.

The main use of these statistics, so far as we are concerned, is to emphasize that inclusion in the National Insurance statistics is far from automatic. Moreover we must remember that these enquiries were largely into the operations of relatively big firms: the proportion of small firms and self-employed workers is much higher in the jobbing and repairing sections of the building industry, and it is in these that the scope for evasion of National Insurance might be expected to be most prevalent.

Other Indications

The D.H.S.S. is continuously sending inspectors to firms of one kind or another, to check whether their records suggest that irregularities are being committed: the difference is that these inspections do not normally include a check on all the people working on the site, but are concentrated on the paper records. We were told that D.H.S.S. had increased the number of these visits in the construction industry in the years after the Phelps Brown Inquiry, and rather over one-quarter had shown one or more irregularities: the proportion of 'successes' in this sense had fallen slightly, but this is what one would have expected with an increasing number of visits, because inspectors choose the firms to visit with an eye to the likelihood of finding something, so that diminishing returns are likely to appear.

The discovery of an irregularity does not normally lead to a prosecution, but rather to the payment of arrears and a warning: before a prosecution is decided upon, the case must be reported to the D.H.S.S. regional offices. We were informed that prosecutions had been 'considered' in this way on an increasing scale from 1966 onwards in relation to the construction industry: the number of cases where a prosecution for an offence in connection with an employee was 'considered' was equal to 1.1% of the number of employers in the building industry in 1966, and rose to 1.7% in 1969 and 1970; whilst for offences on Class II (self-employed cases) the cases considered rose from 1.5% of the number of self-employed in 1966 to 2.2% in 1969 and 1970.

For the country as a whole, there are published statistics of the number of cases in which a prosecution is launched for failure to pay National Insurance contributions, and also for the number of cases in which civil proceedings are taken to recover unpaid contributions. Table XV.1 gives the two series for each year from 1965 to 1970, but it is important to note that the figures for civil proceedings do not include cases where the Inland Revenue is seeking unpaid taxes in the same suit.

Table XV.1 *Legal Action in Relation to Unpaid National Insurance Contributions*

Year	Number of prosecutions for failure to pay contributions	Number[a] of civil proceedings to recover unpaid contributions
1965	3688	5592
1966	3787	5791
1967	4561	5978
1968	5630	6673
1969	7177	8094
1970	8760	6374

(a) Excluding proceedings brought by the Inland Revenue to recover both taxes and contributions.

Source: D.H.S.S. Reports.

The numbers involved are small, but they do serve like the proverbial straw to show which way the wind was blowing: more action was being taken to enforce payment of contributions, and it seems likely that this reflected more attempts at evasion as well as more supervision. We cannot, however, make any direct assessment of the evasion which was not detected — which is what we really want to measure.

One other matter is worth mentioning, which seems to point the other way, so far as employees are concerned. If there was to be collusion between an employer and an employee not to make National Insurance payments (i.e. not to have a card) the incentive to defraud the Government was probably strongest in the case of those married women who opt not to pay normal insurance contributions and to rely on their husband's insurance. In such cases the employee was only liable to pay a few pence to cover industrial injuries, but a card was still supposed to be maintained, and the employer still had to pay his full contribution *plus* the SET charge. Consequently there was a substantial amount to be 'saved' by not buying stamps and not returning the card, and nothing to lose except the provision against industrial injuries. Moreover if the employer could make a plausible show of putting the married woman nominally onto a self-employed basis (through a contract *for* service, or a nominal partnership), then there was no legal obligation for her to have a card.

The actual statistics do not, however, provide a very convincing support for the thesis that SET led to evasion or avoidance of insurance contributions by married women employees on any big scale. Table XV.2 shows that the number of married women paying National Insurance had been rising in the years up to 1966, both as an absolute figure and as a percentage of married women aged 15–64: this reflected the social tendency whereby it became progressively more acceptable for married women to seek gainful employment, *plus,* in most years, an active demand for labour. In 1967 there was a bit of a pause in this upward movement, which might be attributed to the slackening of the labour market; but the later years show a

Table XV.2 *Participation by Married Women, G.B. 1961–69*
(Millions)

Year	(1) Population of married women aged 15–64(a)	(2) Total number of these in respect of whom National Insurance was paid(b)	(3) Number for whom employer only contributes	(4) Number themselves contributing	(5) (2) as % of (1)	(6) (3) as % of (1)
1961	11.81	4.26	3.04	1.16	36.0	25.7
1962	11.91	4.31	3.11	1.14	36.2	26.1
1963	11.93	4.33	3.15	1.12	36.3	26.4
1964	11.98	4.49	3.30	1.14	37.5	27.5
1965	12.04	4.63	3.44	1.14	38.5	28.6
1966	12.09	4.75	3.57	1.13	39.3	29.5
1967	12.13	4.74	3.55	1.14	39.2	29.3
1968	12.17	4.86	3.68	1.13	40.0	30.2
1969	12.20	4.97	3.77	1.16	40.8	30.9

(a) These figures do not incorporate any revisions which may be needed in the light of the 1971 Census.
(b) Including a small number who returned cards as self-employed or non-employed.

Source: D.H.S.S. Annual Reports and Annual Abstract of Statistics.

resumption of the upward trend, in spite of the prolonged period of relatively slack labour market.

As the knowledge about SET and avoidance might well have become more wide-spread with the passage of time, and as the level of SET was raised and the incentive to avoid it thereby increased, this rather points to the avoidance factor being rather small. Moreover this conclusion is reinforced by considering separately the figures for married women who do, and do not, pay the full employee contribution. It is the latter class for whom SET gave a great incentive to avoidance, but Table XV.2 shows that it is in that class that the number paying increased.[1]

Tentative Conclusions

This partial review of the evidence cannot possibly be decisive, because we cannot know the size of the problem until we get the full data from the Census. This may show that our suspicions about a growth in evasion — based on the implausibility of the apparent growth in the number of prime-age males who seemed to have no card in Class 1 or Class 2 — was nothing but a false alarm, resting entirely on faulty population estimates. Our enquiries are however certainly consistent with the *possibility* of avoidance of insurance on a scale which is decidely serious for the numerous statisticians who regard the card-count as the foundation of our current labour statistics. Proportionately the problem seems likely to be greatest on the self-employed, but in absolute terms the error may be greater for employees. From the point of view of this Report, the main consequence would be that productivity gains have been exaggerated (except to the extent that the under-estimate of the active population is matched by an under-estimate of the number unemployed).

As explained above, the testing process made possible by the Census will be much more direct and detailed than our approach *via* activity rates. The numbers of employees in employment, self-employed, unemployed and 'non-active' will be available for each age-and-sex group: all these except the last can be compared with the DE estimates, and the same thing can be done for *movements* between 1966 and 1971. The process will in no sense be confined to 'prime-age males'.

Nevertheless there is a certain special value in maintaining the test *via* the activity-rate for prime-age males, because this is the figure for which one has strong *a priori* reasons for expecting the rate to be at a certain level — i.e. a little short of 100 per cent. In most other classes there is some degree of uncertainty as to how a fair number of people *ought* to answer the Census question which determines their 'activity status' e.g. a married woman who sometimes takes paid work (or helps in a family business) may or may not record herself solely as a housewife, a student may or may not record his vacation job, an elderly person on a pension may or may not record his intermittent activities in the labour market (rather than say simply that he retired); even if the instructions give an unambiguous direction, they may not be observed. For prime-age males these ambiguities are reduced to a minimum, though there may be some difficulties (e.g. over the disabled or chronic sick).

It would seem wise, therefore, to combine the Census results with the statistics for births deaths and migration to produce as authoritative a series as possible for

1 It may be however that the Census will show that the true growth in this class was even bigger, and partly hidden by increased evasion.

the total number of prime-age males in each year,[1] and to combine these with DE estimates of the active population (based essentially on the card-counts, and including the unemployed) to get a revised series of DE activity rates. If these still show a falling trend which is in conflict with reasonable expectations (and, probably, with the activity rates shown by the Census itself, which we expect will be roughly stable — but even in this field the ambiguities may cause some disturbance) then the evidence for increased evasion would be particularly strong. It will also be possible to see *how this probably developed through time,* in a way which is impossible if one merely compares Census years: the relevance of this to the SET analysis is obvious.

If the revised DE activity rates, based on the card-counts, do show an implausible falling trend, it would be quite understandable if this started before the introduction of SET. There were already incentives to avoid paying stamps, which had been growing with the rise in the cost of the stamp and the increasing recognition that unemployment was not the sort of hazard that it was before 1939; moreover income-tax dodgers may have thought it better to do the job thoroughly and dodge insurance contributions also.

1 In view of the uncertainty about the 1966 sample Census, the whole period 1961–1971 should be considered.

XVI
Anomalies Caused by SET

In our First Report we devoted three chapters, (pages 156–186 and 196–206) to a discussion of various kinds of anomaly created by SET in the distributive trades, giving a quantitative assessment of their importance where possible, on the basis of information collected in the course of our enquiry and/or published statistics. We envisaged that our Final Report would contain a wider-ranging discussion, covering the whole field of SET, when we had completed our investigation; the change of Government and consequent truncation of our work has however made this impossible. It nevertheless seems useful to present a brief over-all survey on the basis of the information gathered in our investigations of distribution and near-distribution, and a miscellaneous collection of unsolicited material which was sent to us by people operating in other trades.

As we emphasised repeatedly in the First Report (see especially page 7 and page 156) *all* taxes create some anomalies, and this is particularly true of any tax which is 'selective' (as most indirect taxes are); one must certainly not, therefore, condemn SET simply because it created anomalies. It is necessary, for any practical decisions, to compare the anomalies caused by the SET with those caused by possible alternative taxes and also, of course, to bring into the assessment other consequences – e.g. productivity effects and the cost of collection. Our reports are inevitably concerned only with the SET side of the comparison, but this is of some use even by itself – if only because it might point to ways of reducing the anomalies arising under SET.

The Principle of Selectivity
It may be useful to start by repeating the point made in our First Report that SET is not to be automatically regarded as an anomaly *in toto* simply because it is 'selective'; most indirect taxes are selective, and are not thereby automatically regarded as anomalous. Those who are more concerned about the uniformity of taxes than I am should not be considering SET in isolation, but rather asking whether the system of indirect taxation *as a whole* was made more, or less, uneven by the introduction of SET. This matter was discussed in the First Report (pages 12–15) and the conclusion was reached that the effect was probably of little quantitative importance, but certainly not that SET had made matters worse.

On detailed points, the need to consider other taxes as well as SET is clearly important, as we shall see below when we discuss the fact that SET often falls on repairs and servicing, but not on the production of new goods.

Main Sources of Anomalies
There are two main ways in which SET created anomalies, which are distinct in logic, but which overlap in practice (especially in the building industry) so that they

131

are best discussed together. They can be set out briefly as follows:

    (a) *Border-Line Problems*: whenever any tax is confined to part of the economy there are always problems over the exact definition of the boundary, and consequential anomalies between activities which are classed administratively as being on opposite sides of the dividing line.

    (b) *The Establishment Principle*: SET differs from most indirect taxes in that its general rule is that effective liability is determined on an *establishment* basis, for the whole establishment, rather than applying to those parts of the output which are regarded as within the scope of the tax, and not to the rest. It is as if a chemical factory producing toilet preparations and industrial fine chemicals would *either* have to pay purchase tax on all its output, if toilet preparations were the greater element (subject to the possibility of applying the 'split establishment' rule) *or* be totally exempt, if fine chemicals were the greater.

Manufacturers' Distributive Organisations

In the distributive trades, the inter-action of the above two factors (coupled with the rule whereby a manufacturer's distributive establishment was normally classified to the same MLH as the owner's manufacturing business) created very serious anomali in competition between wholesalers and manufacturers' distributive establishments; this was made worse insofar as the latter were allowed to handle a large amount of goods bought from other producers, so long as more than half of the employees were engaged on handling goods produced by the firm itself.[1]

Perhaps we should also repeat that these anomalies tend to produce unfortunate consequences of at least three kinds. They create two sorts of *inequity* – firstly as between people engaged in different kinds of business, and secondly to consumers who buy goods which have been taxed more heavily (e.g. people in country areas, whose retailers necessarily rely to a greater extent on wholesalers); and they also create *inefficiency,* insofar as they encourage the use of methods which will involve the payment of less taxation, even if those methods may be more costly apart from the tax element.

Repairs and Servicing

The First Report dealt briefly with an apparent anomaly in the treatment of repairs and servicing for SET purposes (see in particular pages 205–6). When SET was introduced, the original principle was that repairs and servicing were to be liable to SET, unless the Standard Industrial Classification specifically recorded a particular type under a 'manufacturing' heading (as it did, for example, in the case of ship-repairing). This simple rule might seem to be 'anomalous', since it implies that repairs are taxed but not the production of new goods with which the repairers compete; for many items, however, this argument would be an illustration of the danger of considering only one tax at a time, since the new goods are subject to purchase tax, which is usually a heavier burden than the SET paid on repairs.

The above rule did, however, mean that real anomalies could easily arise out of the establishment principle; manufacturers could do repairs as a substantial side-line

---

1 See First Report, Chapter XVI, and especially the table of page 159.

without being taxed, whilst specialist repairers, or repair and servicing done by distributors, would be liable to SET.

As a result of Tribunal decisions, the Department of Employment and Productivity changed its practice somewhat, and thereby possibly reduced the problem arising out of mixed establishments. It was, of course, bound to follow the SIC where this said something specific about a given type of repair — whether by making it a separate heading in the services sector (e.g. shoe repairing), or by naming it as part of the activities of a business which would be taxable (e.g. repairing motor vehicles or buildings) or of a business which would escape (e.g. repairing ships or aircraft). But where the SIC was silent, the practice seems to be to regard as 'manufacturing' those types of repair which are largely done by manufacturers, and consequently to pay refunds to specialist repairers doing that kind of work; distributors who have a repair department mainly engaged in this type of work might be able to get these classified as a split establishment, but such cases are probably rare.

On the other hand, repairs of a type which are seldom done by manufacturers were regarded as ineligible for refund, although they would still escape if done as a side-line by a business which was otherwise exempt (e.g. a road haulier). In practice, these repairs were virtually all mentioned specifically in the description of an MLH which was not eligible for refund.

Such treatment was probably the best way of making the law workable, and in a number of cases it does produce 'rough justice' in the sense that new goods are liable to purchase tax (and of course to SET in course of their distribution), whilst repairs come under SET. Inevitably, however, it leaves a lot of loose ends. Thus goods vehicles and agricultural tractors are exempt from purchase tax, although repairs to them come under SET — but this SET is refunded when the work is done by the repair staff of the owner if his business is exempt (e.g. if he is a haulier, a manufacturer or a farmer), and is also refunded if a vehicle is sent back for repair at the factory, or fitted with an engine which was reconditioned there.

We attempted to obtain direct evidence on one aspect of this anomaly in the motor trade, where motor vehicle builders, who may do some body repair work, are eligible for refunds of SET if the normal qualifying rules are met, whilst specialist body repairers pay the tax without refund. A questionnaire designed to investigate the importance of this problem was sent to a random sample of members of the Vehicle Builders' and Repairers' Association, excluding those entered in the list as builders. Only a very small proportion of firms stated that they were meeting serious competition from firms whom they believed to be receiving SET refunds, and of this small proportion a number emphasised competition from self-employed repairers. The major form of competition mentioned was price competition both in body building and in repair work. However, corroborative evidence from the financial returns of these same firms did not suggest any significant difference in the movement in their gross margin from that of the sample as a whole. Thus the returns from the trade do not suggest that this anomaly was serious. This view is supported by the fact that there are approximately 700 vehicle builders who could do repair work as an ancillary activity as compared with 1300 repairers (although the number of self-employed repairers is unknown) so that the small number of anomalies revealed in our sample is remarkable. When we discussed this subject with one vehicle builder, he explained that repairs and building called for different techniques and workshop organisations, and that he did not contemplate complicating his business with the introduction of repair work. If this attitude is shared by other vehicle builders, the smallness of the anomaly detected in our results is understandable.

'Do It Yourself' by Exempt Businesses

The establishment principle inevitably gave a stimulus to manufacturers and others who could claim refund on their SET to do many kinds of work themselves, which would be liable to SET if done by a specialist. They needed, of course, to make sure that they did not lose their 'refund' status by over-doing this, but in most cases there was no risk of raising the proportion of non-qualifying workers at the establishment above the 50% limit.

The types of activity likely to be affected in this way are mostly carried on by firms in trades which we have not covered in our investigation; before describing some which we studied during our investigation of near-distribution, however, it may be useful to emphasise the width of the problem by mentioning some examples which were brought to our attention by 'unsolicited' communications. We have of course no means of assessing the quantitative importance of the matter in these cases, but the following are examples of circumstances where there seems to be a *prima facie* case for the existence of anomalous diversion:

(a) A leading security organisation complained that its night-watchmen etc. were liable to SET, even when they were guarding a factory or other building where the occupant could obtain refunds, which would also be obtainable if he employed his own night-watchmen.

(b) Industrial consultants complained that they were prejudiced by the refund obtainable if a manufacturer took an efficiency expert on to his own staff, instead of calling them in.

(c) An accountant complained that 'more of the job' was now done by direct employees of exempt bodies (including Local Authorities, as well as manufacturers etc.).

(d) Direct mail firms complained that exempt businesses (and charities) were sending out their own circulars, instead of putting work out to specialists.

(e) Building firms complained of unfair competition from the maintenance squads of factories or Local Authorities.

These 'do-it-yourself' cases merge easily into the more general case of firms in the refund category carrying on, or developing, side-line activities in the taxable field which still allow them to claim refund on all their employees under the establishment principle. Anybody who has had any connection with SET is likely to have been told of at least one restaurant run by a bakery, which therefore obtained refunds because it was part of a 'manufacturing' business; in consequence it was able to compete unfairly with legitimate restaurants, on which the prosperity of the district's tourist trade apparently depended. As a further illustration of the variety of these things, we might also mention the complaint that yachting agencies were having to meet unfair competition from boat-builders, who did a hiring business on the side.

Industrial Catering

Within the field of near-distribution one particular case seemed likely to produce important anomalies from the 'do-it-yourself' bias produced by SET, and we therefore made considerable efforts to assess its importance in both quantitative and qualitative terms. This was the case of Industrial Catering, under which the contractors agree to provide a catering service on the premises of major employers for their staff — usually in return for a fixed fee, with the client meeting all the cost and taking all the proceeds of the operation. Whatever the financial arrangements, SET is payable on employees on the payroll of industrial caterers, even if they work full-time on the premises of a client who receives full refund for his own employees (as in the case of a factory, or a local authority office). There is in consequence an incentive to the client to stop using a contractor, and to run his own catering service.

A second possible anomaly arises in this field, because some organisations which contract to provide industrial catering services can obtain refunds on their staff. This applies automatically if the employer is a Local Authority and it also applies to food manufacturers who do this as a side-line activity of their factory. In this latter case the workers can clearly be treated as working 'from the factory' rather than from a catering establishment where the business is that of 'outside' catering to places which keep changing (e.g. weddings, receptions): industrial catering can also be covered if the main cooking and preparation is done at the factory, and the 'outside' workers organised from it. This ability to obtain refunds applies even where the client is not able to obtain refunds for his own staff (e.g. in an ordinary office).

We sought information which would be relevant to a quantitative assessment of both types of anomaly by means of a questionnaire which we drew up in close consultation with the Industrial Staff Canteens Division of the Caterers' Association. In spite of the support of that Association there was a poor response to our initial questionnaire, with only six out of twenty six firms replying. We therefore drew up a second, simplified questionnaire, again in consultation with the Association, and sent it to those who had not replied to the first one; this version did not seek all the information which we would have liked to assess the effects of these anomalies, but it did give the industrial caterers a relatively simple way of indicating their broad nature and extent. In the event, four more caterers replied, so that the response was still rather poor.

Competition with Exempt Caterers

To take the second type of anomaly first, our initial questionnaire asked industrial caterers to state the number of their contracts which had been terminated between 1966 and 1969 because they had been displaced by competitors who obtained refunds of SET. Although four of the six respondents had, between them, lost 54 contracts during this period, none claimed that any of them were terminated for this reason.

Our second questionnaire asked much less about contracts lost for other reasons, but did ask the respondent whether he could name any cases where one of his contracts had, since 1966, been diverted to an organisation which received SET refunds on its own staff. Of the four respondents, one replied affirmatively, and marked the square on the form which implied an estimate that between 0 and 5 per cent of his contracts had been lost in this way. In addition, he produced convincing evidence that one long-standing contract with a college for which the Inner London Education Authority was responsible had been lost to the I.L.E.A.'s Catering Service, which escaped SET.

We also asked on both questionnaires whether the respondent had been up against significant competition from outside contractors not paying SET. Only two of the ten respondents replied affirmatively, one stating that there was competition from a food manufacturer, and the other stating that he had been at a serious, continuing risk of losing a large contract to Birmingham Corporation, which had lower costs because it did not pay SET.

Our conclusion from this evidence is that Industrial Caterers very understandably felt a grievance that they had to compete with rivals who had an unfair advantage, which the Government could perfectly well have eliminated. On the other hand, the number of rivals who had this advantage was small, and they were mostly not making great efforts to expand their activities, so that the quantitative effect of the anomaly was not great.

Competition with Self-Suppliers

We hoped to assess the importance of the first kind of anomaly by making use of the fact that it did not arise where a caterer was operating on the premises of a client who could not reclaim SET on his own staff, so that we would be able to compare what had happened in such cases with what had happened in factories, etc.

In our first questionnaire we asked how many contracts had been terminated between 1966 and 1969 because clients had taken over the catering themselves, and for a division of these cases between clients who could – or could not – obtain refunds on their own staff. Only one of the six respondents stated that he had lost contracts for this reason, and in his case the proportion of contracts lost was the same, whether the client could obtain refunds or not.

In our second questionnaire one of the four respondents said that he had lost contracts between 1966 and 1969 in cases where a client receiving full SET refunds had taken over the catering; he named three actual cases, in accordance with the questionnaire's request, and estimated that in all he had lost more than twenty contracts in this way. He also stated that this represented a higher proportion of his initial contracts than had been lost in respect of clients *not* receiving SET refunds, although a number of these had also taken over the catering themselves. One should, however, take into consideration that the four respondents between them had 635 contracts, so that whilst the evidence pointed fairly clearly to the existence of a significant anomaly, one should not exaggerate its importance.

We were also anxious to test whether the industrial caterers had suffered through potential new contracts not being received, because clients receiving SET refunds would undertake their own catering. We therefore asked in our first questionnaire for the number of new contracts gained since 1966, classified according to whether or not the client received SET refund. The four firms which produced relevant statistics, however, showed no tendency for the proportion of new contracts from clients who could obtain refunds to be less than had prevailed in their initial set of contracts. In our second questionnaire we invited firms to produce any evidence which they could along these lines, without demanding further statistics, but none was offered.

On the whole, therefore, we felt that in spite of considerable efforts on our part to discover evidence about a shift to self-catering by firms which could obtain refunds, the amount which had emerged was relatively small, and this conclusion was

136

strengthened by the fact that a majority of the businesses approached did not respond to either of our questionnaires.

One important reason for this somewhat negative result did, however, emerge rather clearly from our investigation. Since the client normally has to meet the cost of paying for the caterer's workers (as explained above), it is quite possible to produce this result by transferring them to the payroll of the client, and then sending him a smaller bill for expenses, since he will have paid for the workers directly. (In the same way, the client normally provides the premises without charging any rent to the caterer, and may provide other facilities such as heating etc.). If the staff is on the payroll of the client, and the latter is able to obtain refund for his staff, then he can obtain a refund for the catering workers as well; thus the 'SET anomaly' is virtually confined to the managerial and technical staff of the caterer, who are normally not transferred.

This practice rarely occurred before the introduction of SET, and had not been introduced on any scale since that introduction for clients who did not receive any SET refund on their own staff. It did, however, spread rapidly after 1966 in respect of clients who could obtain SET refund; our returns showed that of some 545 contracts which respondents had in respect of clients receiving SET refunds, there were 135 cases (25%) in which the transfer had occurred.

We asked whether this practice had any disadvantages, either to the caterer or to the client. Five caterers said that there was some loss of control and discipline over staff, and that there was also a greater risk to them of losing contracts because the client could more easily take over the catering. Two caterers said that there were no disadvantages to them, and three did not answer.

All the people replying agreed that there were disadvantages from the client's view-point, and it was clear that many clients had been unwilling to agree to a transfer. Thus a factory often had a higher rate of pay and better fringe conditions for unskilled female labour than applied in catering, and trade unions were said to demand the factory rate of pay if a transfer occurred — which might easily outweigh the gain from avoiding SET.

Construction

We have no doubt that the construction industry in its many aspects is the part of the SET field in which much the most serious anomalies have arisen. We intended to make a thorough study of these in the course of our investigations of that industry, and had made some preliminary enquiries before the change of Government led to our investigation being truncated; we would have wished to follow these up by making enquiries of the employers themselves, but it is possible to give some broad indications on the basis of published information and our preliminary enquiry.

A number of factors combined to make the construction industry play such a major role in the matter of anomalies, and the anomalies are in consequence of very varying kinds. A rough list of the main factors (some of which overlap) might run as follows:

(a) *Self-Supply*. It has always been normal practice for many companies and other Bodies to have a maintenance team of their own, which will deal with minor maintenance work on their premises, which might otherwise be put out to building repair firms. If these potential customers of the building repair firms are able to claim SET refunds, they naturally have an added incentive to do jobs themselves, and to take on more elaborate jobs than was previously normal, so as to avoid SET. There never was, of course, any uniform division between jobs which the client does for himself and those which he puts out, since some clients (notably the bigger ones) are likely to have a bigger and more versatile maintenance team which can undertake more elaborate jobs; but whatever the size of the client's business, SET gave him an incentive to extend his operations to bigger jobs, including minor works of construction or alteration. This is a clear-cut anomaly, but one which would be extremely difficult to handle by amending the SET legislation.

(b) *Prefabrication of Building Components.* Builders have traditionally varied the extent to which they buy their 'materials' or 'components' in a highly fabricated form, or alternatively as plain timber, metals etc. If they follow the former course, the fabrication undertaken by the supplier will normally attract refunds of SET, because it is typically a manufacturing process done in a factory. On the other hand, the builder who buys crude materials will not obtain any refunds, unless he can persuade the Department of Employment to recognise a part of his activities as being done in a separate establishment engaged in 'manufacturing' (see below). As this is by no means always possible, and is often difficult and costly to arrange, there is an artificial incentive towards the use of highly fabricated materials.

(c) *Split Establishments.* In all the trades which have to pay SET without refund, there is an incentive to the company to split off any part of its activities which might plausibly qualify as 'manufacturing' (or some other exempt industry), and get it recognised as a 'split establishment' (or possibly a *separate* establishment). In most trades, however, there is not much which they do which would be exempt if separated off, and this procedure has largely been applied to *side-line* activities rather than to a part of the main process. With construction, however, the position is so different in degree as virtually to produce a difference in kind; construction is essentially a work of *production*, rather than a service, so that there is great scope for separating off parts of the activity and treating them as 'fabricating things for use by the erection department'. The workers involved would then qualify for refund because they were engaged in a manufacturing establishment, devoted to the production of (e.g.) builders' wood-work or pre-cast concrete blocks.

The rules and practices governing this process are discussed in more detail in the annex to this chapter. As an example of the difficulty of drawing an inevitably artificial line between 'manufacturing' (exempt) and 'erection' (taxable), things which are transported from one part of the building site to another (or brought from the builder's workshop) can qualify as manufactured products (if the other conditions are met), whereas a system which produced concrete walls by casting them *in situ* was part of the erection process, and no refunds could be obtained. As it was put to us by several knowledgeable people, 'the creation of artificial "split establishments" has been a major activity for the managers of many large building firms.'

(d) *Competition with exempt companies.* As with all activities which come under SET, construction work provided openings for manufacturers and other exempt

138

companies to develop side-line operations in respect of which they could obtain refunds, although they were competing with construction firms which had to bear the burden of SET. This problem might not seem particularly important in the case of construction, because one does not readily think of manufacturers going in for building work. Its importance does, however, become much more understandable if one thinks of 'installation' of equipment going into a building or civil engineering project, whether this be in course of erection or already in existence: an extreme case arose with the manufacturers of prefabricated buildings, which they could either deliver for erection by building firms, or erect themselves with their own employees. In total, this 'installation' work provided quite a large field for competition between building firms proper and manufacturers of the equipment, and this was sometimes extended to servicing and repair activities. Where the manufacturer was able to claim refunds in respect of his staff, on the grounds that they were 'based on the factory', he clearly secured an unjustified advantage against the builder, who could obtain no refunds.

This matter is discussed further in the annex to this chapter, which deals with some of the legal problems determining whether refunds could be obtained by the manufacturer. In a sense, this is the inverse of the 'split establishment' problem, since the manufacturer had to show that the work of erecting the prefabricated buildings, for example, did *not* constitute a separate establishment.

(e) *Border-line between construction and manufacture.* The divisions between the various trades and industries used in the Standard Industrial Classification are inevitably imprecise, and were not intended to serve as a basis for the legal determination of whether a tax was due or not in a particular establishment. In the service field the importance of this factor was kept down by the fact that the 'neighbouring' classifications were normally *both* liable to SET, so that it did not matter whether an establishment was allocated to one heading or the other. In the case of construction, however, there was a substantial 'problem area', in which it was not at all obvious whether particular types of activity should be assigned to construction (including civil engineering), and so have to bear the burden of SET, or to one of the manufacturing headings — notably MLH 341, Industrial Plant and Steelwork.

This is not the place to discuss the legal issues involved. There were, however, a series of cases in which the employers persuaded the Courts to rule that activities which had traditionally been regarded, for statistical purposes, as coming under construction in MLH 500 should be regarded for refund purposes as belonging to MLH 341. The one thing which can be said by an economist is that the resulting position did not correspond with any logical economic principle. The Department of Employment naturally tried to adjust its practice in the light of the decisions which were reached, but it seems probable that further appeals to the Courts would have pushed the boundary further in the refund direction, it they had been made. To a layman, it seems that the fixing of the boundary in this large area must be an unending task, since circumstances can vary in so many subtle ways, and there is no real principle to which one can appeal.

(f) *Quantitative assessment of last three factors.* The last three factors all produce the result that refunds were paid in respect of workers who, for ordinary statistical purposes, were regarded as being in construction. It would, of course, be most valuable to have a separate assessment of the number of workers involved in each category, but we found no way of assessing this from the available statistics, and we did not undertake a trade enquiry. We did, however, devise a statistical method of gaining a rough appreciation of the extent of 'reclassification' produced by the three factors taken together, which is described in Appendix G (since we used it to deal with reclassifications out of other industries as well as building, notably distribution). In essence, this operation consisted in a review of the various 'manufacturing' activities to which the building workers were likely to have been reclassified for SET refund purposes, which measured the excess of refunds actually paid under those classifications over the amount which would have been expected on the basis of the number of workers recorded in the ordinary Department of Employment statistics. The only reservation which one needs to make is that some of these 'transferred' workers might have come from some other industry in the SET sector rather than from construction – e.g. some might have been reclassified from builders' merchants.

Table XVI.1 *Reclassification of Employees from MLH 500 for SET Refunds, 1970*

Recipient Industry (and SIC number)	No. of Employees in Employment ('000)		
	In Normal Statistics	For Refund Purposes	Surplus
336 Construction and earth-moving equipment	44.3	64.1	19.8
337 Mechanical handling equipment	70.0	72.1	2.1
341 Industrial plant and steelwork	188.0	246.7	58.7
469 Building materials n.e.s.	120.4	141.5	21.1
471 Timber	108.0	125.0	17.0
474 Shop and office fitting	36.2	37.8	1.6
Total of above			120.3

For definitions, see Appendix G.

The results of this comparison are given in Table XVI.1 from which it will be seen that about 120,000 workers appear to have been transferred. It should be emphasised that this method of calculation does not reflect any tendency for builders to have bought more prefabricated products from genuine factories; insofar as this was done, the ordinary employment statistics would be raised in the same way as the refund statistics, so that the 'surplus' would not be affected. One of the more unfortunate consequences of the anomaly created by SET may, indeed, have been to stimulate the production of pre-cast parts of buildings in factories, which then created traffic congestion because very awkward loads had to be transported to the building site. This type of anomaly is *additional* to what appears in Table XVI.1

(g) *Self-Employment and Labour-Only Sub-Contractors.* The fact that self-employed workers were exempt from SET obviously gave an artificial stimulus to people to set up as one-man businesses doing repair work, and to small firms to avoid SET by making their few employees into nominal 'partners'.

SET also gave an artificial incentive to the system whereby firms which were engaged on construction of substantial buildings or civil engineering projects put out various bits of the work to 'sub-contractors', who might be single self-employed workers, or groups of 'partners' in an independent firm, or perhaps labour-only sub-contractors, who *ought* to have paid National Insurance and SET on their employees, but who sometimes escaped the vigilance of the Government departments.

(h) *Exemption for Local Authorities.* A special case of unfair competition between ordinary building firms and employers who were exempt from SET arose in connection with the exemption which was given to the direct-labour squads of Local Authorities. At first it was proposed that this should be quite general, applying to major construction work as well as to maintenance work and minor bits of construction, but the protest of the building employers led to the rule that Local Authority employees engaged on work of major construction should not receive SET refunds. This still, however, left the position that Local Authorities had an artificial incentive to get the large amount of maintenance work needed by their own housing estates and buildings done by direct labour, instead of putting it out to contractors.

We had a considerable discussion and correspondence with the Ministry of Housing and Local Government (as it then was) about this anomaly, which we regarded as a great deal more serious than their representatives did; the main points are set out in the Annex to this Chapter. We also discuss below the general position of Local Authority employees in the wider context of SET as a whole.

As we said at the beginning of this section the truncation of our work made it impossible for us to arrive at a really complete view of the working of SET in the construction sector. Nevertheless, it seems clear from the work which we did that the anomalies created in this sector were quite disproportionately large, and some of them would have been remarkably difficult to remedy, because the line between 'manufacture of building materials and components' and 'erection' is such an arbitrary one. Although it is outside our terms of reference to attempt any sort of judgement on the matter we feel bound to ask the question whether it was really wise to include construction within the ambit of SET, even though its exclusion would inevitably (given the 'establishment principle') have meant also the exclusion of building repairs.[1]

Competition with the Public Sector
Broadly speaking the Public Sector (including the nationalised industries) are exempt from SET, except in a few special cases where refunds are specifically excluded (e.g. railway hotels) because they would clearly make competition unfair. This was intended (we understand) to be part of a 'package deal' whereby Local Authorities, for example, would have advantages in some directions but not secure benefits (e.g. investment grants) in others. Such a package deal may, however, be reasonably

1 This question raises, of course, much wider questions than the 'anomaly' problem. See First Report, Chapter II.

'fair' to the Local Authority, which can take an all-in view of the arrangements as a whole, but may nevertheless be quite unfair to a specific firm in (say) the industrial catering trade; the latter derives no 'compensation' from the fact that Local Authorities in the developing areas do not qualify for investment grants, to set against the fact that the Inner London Education Authority does not pay SET on its catering staff.

We mentioned in our First Report (page 186) various types of unfair competition which arose in relation to the distributive trades, but recorded that after the anomaly of the show-rooms operated by Electricity and Gas Boards had been put right in September 1969, the remaining anomalies did not seem to be of great quantitative importance.

Outside the distributive trades, the major anomaly seems to be the exemption from SET of the direct labour squads doing maintenance work etc., where the number of workers involved is clearly large, but we have also met anomalies, which could be important in particular cases, in the field of catering. There may well be other anomalies in trades which we have not investigated.

It seems to us, therefore, that more consideration should have been given to the alternative procedure of having no exemptions from SET for any workers on the grounds that they were employed by a Local Authority. It would have then been open to the Government to arrange a genuine 'package deal' between itself and the Local Authorities, in which nobody else would have been indirectly prejudiced; the obvious form which this could have taken would have been an increase in the general grants made by the Central Government to Local Authorities, by an amount roughly equal to the amount collected in SET in respect of Local Authority employees. Apart from anything else, this would have been 'good public relations', since all the arguments about encouraging the economical use of labour are applicable to employees of Local Authorities, as well as in private service trades.

Such an arrangement would, of course, still have left it open to Local Authorities which carried on activities which qualify for refund (e.g. transport or water supply) to obtain such refunds on the strength of the *industrial* classification of their employees, rather than their status as working for Local Authorities.

If this approach had been adopted, it would of course have been necessary to consider whether some additional Minimum List Headings in the Standard Industrial Classification should be added to those in respect of which refunds can be obtained. Educational Services (MLH 872) and Medical and Dental Services (MLH 874) provide examples of cases which would perhaps have to be considered; at present, refunds are obtained in respect of the great bulk of the employees in each of these headings, because the employer is *either* in the Public Sector *or* a charity, but no refunds are available for a minority of employees. Sometimes the payment of the tax is 'allowed for' as part of some other Government operation (e.g. the fixing of payments to general practitioners and dentists under the National Health service), but in other cases there is no off-set except the ability of the employer to pass on the burden of the tax to his customers (e.g. in private schools or nursing homes).

Self-Employed Workers

In our First Report we stressed our belief that the logical presumption in favour of including self-employed workers within the scope of the tax outweighed the administrative difficulties of achieving this (see pages 177 to 181). We do not feel it necessary to go over the general ground again, but we think it right to report the results of our enquiries within the field of near-distribution, in which the number of self-employed workers is large — especially in shoe repairing and hairdressing.

Shoe Repairing

In shoe repairing we had two main sources of information. We included in our questionnaire to members of the National Association of Shoe Repair Factories a question asking whether they had been losing business to self-employed repairers since the introduction of SET. Of the thirty-one completed questionnaires which we received, six showed no answer to this question, whilst fourteen said that they *had* been losing business to self-employed repairers, and eleven said that the tax had made no difference. The large proportion of firms saying that they had lost business may, of course, reflect their self-interest, but the result is in accordance with reasonable expectations — even though the larger repairers who belong to the N.A.S.R.F. have been holding their own, thanks to the decline of small businesses with employees.

We also asked local Trade Associations of repairers whether they thought that there had been an increase in the proportion of the local repair trade which was handled by self-employed repairers. Of the twenty-four replies, only two said that they thought the proportion had increased whilst eleven thought that there had been a decrease; nine said that they thought there had been no significant change, and two replied that they could not answer the question.

Hairdressing

The hairdressers participating in our enquiries were asked whether, since the introduction of SET in September 1966, there had been any increase in the tendency for employees to leave their business and set up on their own. They were asked to deal separately with cases where the employee had set up a regular business in a salon, and also with those who had started doing hairdressing at home. Most of the 185 firms completing the questionnaire gave an answer to this question, and about 20% of those who replied said that there had been an increased tendency for employees to set up in their own salon, and about 25% said that there had been an increase in employees starting to work from home.

The questionnaire also asked about the effect that competition from hairdressers not paying SET had had on the business of the respondent. Ignoring the very small proportion who did not answer the question, only 22% said that there had been no effect, whilst 54% said that there had been *some* effect, and 24% that the effect had been serious. As might be expected, three-quarters of those who claimed that they had been affected said that they had suffered a loss of business, whilst one-half said that they had been forced to hold down their prices below the level which they would otherwise have charged.

We also obtained information from branches of the National Hairdressers Federation. Of the thirty-three branches which replied, eleven claimed that SET exemptions for self-employed had led to important changes in the hairdressing trade in their area; seven of the eleven said that there had been an increase in rented chairs operated by self-employed workers within a salon run by a larger business, and about the same said that there had been an increase in home hairdressing.

Other Trades

We did not put direct questions on this subject in the other trades, but some information arose incidentally from replies to other questions. Thus a question to vehicle repairers about competition from competitors who did not pay SET (which was primarily aimed at finding out about competition from vehicle builders, mentioned above) produced a number of replies which emphasised competition from the self-employed workers operating on their own.

We should perhaps also mention complaints which reached us as part of our 'unsolicited' mail. The most important of these was from a leading firm of driving instructors, which complained bitterly of competition from self-employed drivers who did not pay SET – and added the point that such unqualified people were liable to lower the safety standards which were so important.

It is clearly very difficult to collect reliable evidence about the effects of exempting self-employed workers; on the one hand, the evidence from traders who pay the tax is liable to be biased, but on the other hand many of the firms with which we were concerned were run by somebody who was himself escaping SET because he was not an employee, and who was unwilling to make statements which might lead to his having to pay the tax. The same tended to be true of Trade Association secretaries, who might well feel that their typical member would be more concerned to retain the exemption for himself and his partners than to get the tax paid by self-employed rivals.

Basis of the Tax

Our First Report made the point (on pages 182–3) that if there were to be a selective tax on workers engaged in a particular group of industries, then the basis of it should be their *earnings*, rather than having it expressed as so much a head (even if different rates were fixed for different age-and-sex categories and for part-time workers). In brief, a selective payroll tax (or, better still, a selective 'earnings' tax) would be more logical than a selective employment tax based on numbers of people.

We collected no further evidence on this matter, but we did receive further complaints about one particular issue which is related to it, and that is the treatment of apprentices. Professional Bodies and Trade Associations representing accountants, lawyers, surveyors, builders and hairdressers all stated in various ways that SET was having a serious effect on the recruitment of apprentices.

One way of setting out the argument is to say that SET has made employers scrutinise their labour requirements very closely, and that they have concluded that the work obtained from an apprentice (after allowing for the diversion of effort for teaching him) was not 'good value' as compared with that obtained from a person of the same age, in respect of whom the same SET would be payable; alternatively, the number of apprentices might be reduced, and an adult worker recruited if necessary. It was said that SET implied that an apprentice contributed half the output of a full-time man, and that this was simply untrue.

We have not been able to test this assertion about reduction in the number of apprentices in any way, but if the SET payment were related to earnings, then employers would have no incentive to discriminate against them which is not already implicit in the existing level of wages.

144

A system of relating SET to wages paid, rather than expressing it per head, would also make some contribution to helping with a problem which was mentioned to us in various forms – i.e. the problem of securing employment for 'handicapped' workers. This was sometimes raised in relation to elderly workers, who have become a bit slow but whom employers would like to retain on humanitarian grounds; in some cases, it is essential to pay them full wages (if only to avoid trouble with the trade unions), so that a change in the SET regulations would not help, but in other cases they can be put on to a somewhat shorter working week, or moved to a job which carries a lower rate of pay, and in that case the change would be of some assistance.

Another form of the problem about which fears were expressed concerned the difficulty of finding employment opportunities for educationally sub-normal or handicapped children. We referred to this in our First Report; on the basis of enquiries directed to the Cambridgeshire County Council, we recorded our preliminary impression that in fact there was no evidence that SET had affected placements in the service trades for handicapped boys and girls. We later made a second enquiry of the Department of Employment's Central Youth Employment Executive, which produced the same reply. Obviously, this is a very difficult matter on which to make any judgement, and of course if handicapped workers are paid the full wage, then a change in the system for assessing SET would make no difference (except to the extent that it would bear less heavily on the lower-paid grades of labour, whatever the reason for their lower pay). For what it is worth, however, our conclusion is that this problem does not seem to be of any quantitative importance.

Alleged Impossibility of Passing on SET

At various times in our enquiry, we have received a considerable number of complaints from Associations or individual firms that it is very unfair to apply SET to them, because it is 'impossible' for them to pass it on to their customers. In some cases this meant no more than a claim that market conditions made it difficult to pass on SET – an argument which would apply equally to any other rise in costs, whether due to Government action (e.g. local rates) or to the decision of the people concerned to raise the wages of their workers. On such points there is nothing which we can say in general terms.

In a number of cases, however, the argument was that the selling price of their services was determined 'externally', either by Government action (as in the case of various charges made by solicitors) or by a convention, sometimes of an international kind, whereby (for example) a fixed percentage discount was to be allowed to travel agents supplying tickets for journeys by air. Whilst we naturally sympathise with any serious problems which may emerge in this way, and which may persist as a result of the difficulty of altering 'bureaucratic' regulations, it is clear that complaints are being sent to the wrong address when the people concerned try to secure exemption from SET on the grounds that it 'cannot' be met out of the revenue which comes from externally fixed charges. As we have seen both in distribution and in near-distribution, and as is indeed clear for all trades, SET is very far from being the only reason why costs rise, and is indeed normally a comparatively small one. The system by which the 'externally fixed charges' are reviewed must therefore incorporate some methods of securing adjustment to take account of changing

145

circumstances, and indeed in many cases that method is largely the 'automatic' one of expressing the payment to the solicitor or the travel agencies or the architect as a percentage of the value of something which itself rises in price through the years. Naturally, this 'percentage system' may not produce an ideal answer − in many cases (as with conveyancing fees) we would say that it produced too *high* a charge, even when SET is adding to costs. But if the 'automatic' adjustments do not work out properly, then there is a need for some system for reviewing the charge, which would take account of SET simply as *one* of the factors which had influenced costs. To expect a special exemption of some service from SET on the grounds that the price of that service is externally determined would be quite unjustified, if the service was of a kind which would 'naturally' be included within the scope of the tax; one cannot allow the tail to wag the dog.

'Near-Charities'

A tax on employment in service occupations (other than those specifically excluded) has the great virtue as a revenue-raiser that it automatically catches a lot of services which would be almost impossible to cover in other ways.[1] Inevitably, however, it suffers from the corresponding disadvantage that it catches a number of activities which the Government might not wish to tax, if it were administratively possible to exempt them without creating endless anomalies. In the event, the Government decided to exempt charities as such, which had the great administrative convenience that it could be linked to a criterion which was already in operation and which was frequently recognised by inclusion in one of the registers of charities. The definition of charity has, however, been a very difficult problem for centuries, and this 'administrative' solution meant giving exemption to many activities which some people would consider quite undesirable, and the continued taxation of others which many − and especially their organisers − regarded as far more worthy.

As might be expected, we received a large amount of unsolicited correspondence on the theme that some particular activity was of great social value, frequently supported by the argument that it was non-profit-making; our correspondents varied in size from village tennis clubs to the Automobile Association, and we had to get the Government departments concerned to agree that they would not send on to us any letters which they received which were essentially concerned with the political decision about what activities should be regarded as sufficiently 'worthy' or 'special' to deserve exemption. A particular example which led us to adopt the shorthand name of 'near-charities' for this type of case was an organisation which existed to collect money for distribution to other charities, and which apparently could not be registered as a charity itself.

On all this we can only say that the problem is obviously a real one, but that it lies outside our terms of reference. An economist has no special ability for defining socially desirable ends which might be exempted from SET: he can only emphasise that any tax must have an administratively workable definition, which will make sense not only in a particular chosen case, but when applied generally.

1   See First Report, pages 15−16.

Hotels in Rural Development Areas

Finally, we turn to an 'anomaly' which was deliberately created in 1968, by the exemption from SET of hotels in Rural Development Areas. This deliberate act of policy inevitably created genuine anomalies between hotels situated just outside an R.D.A., which continued to pay SET, and those just inside, but we did not feel able to make such fine comparisons as that. We did, however, attempt a comparison of the experience of hotels in R.D.A.'s and broadly similar hotels outside those areas, which we thought might throw some light on the effects of this change: some people have suggested that it might throw light on the effects of removing SET generally, but on this we are extremely sceptical.

As from the first contribution week beginning on or after 2nd September 1968, hotels or similar establishments situated in Rural Development Areas were allowed to receive repayment of SET in respect of all their employees. For the purposes of the Act, a hotel was defined as one containing '... not less than four rooms which at all times during the contribution week .... were available for use as sleeping accommodation by guests ...'.

We first considered whether we could learn anything much from a comparison between the hotels in our sample which were situated in R.D.A.'s, and the rest of the sample. We did not, however, feel that much could be learnt from such a comparison, since the two groups were in many ways dissimilar — with the ones in the rest of the sample including, for example, many hotels in the centres of towns. Our analysis was, therefore, based mainly on a separate investigation of prices obtained from the Official Guides of the British Travel Association, relating to 15 hotels in R.D.A.'s and a matched list of 15 apparently similar hotels in other areas. In each case we used the minimum charge quoted for bed and breakfast in the various annual editions of the Guide to give an indication of price movements between the various years: as these prices are the ones which are announced in advance at the beginning of the year, the '1966' figure had to be regarded as having been fixed before SET was announced, and similarly the '1968' price was fixed before any announcement about the changes in SET introduced during that year (which included a general increase of one-half and an exemption from the tax for hotels in Rural Development Areas, with both of these changes becoming effective in September).

Table XVI.2 *Price Indices of Hotels in Rural Development Areas and of Matched Sample Elsewhere*

Year	Price Indices (1965 = 100)[a]		% Rise on Previous Year	
	R.D.A.'s	Matched Sample	R.D.A.'s	Matched Sample
1965	100.0	100.0	–	–
1966	103.7	103.1	3.7	3.1
1967	108.8	112.1	4.9	8.7
1968	114.7	118.1	5.4	5.4
1969	122.3	127.2	6.6	7.7
1970	126.1	138.6	3.1	9.0

(a) The indices were calculated as the mean of indices for the hotels in each sample.

Source: British Travel Association Guides to Hotels and Restaurants in Britain.

The results of this analysis of prices are shown in Table XVI.2. One clearly cannot expect that the matched sample would show exactly the same movement for years when the experience on SET was similar, but it provides a rough control: thus the price increase between 1965 and 1966 was slightly smaller outside the R.D.A.'s, but the movement between 1966 and 1967 (which reflects the introduction of SET in both areas) was greater outside the R.D.A.'s. It is perhaps reassuring from the statistical viewpoint that the movement between 1967 and 1968 (i.e. the last movement for which conditions were comparable in the two areas) was the same in both areas, so that the difference in movement between 1966 and 1967 is probably irrelevant to a consideration of the effects of the differential SET treatment, which applied first to the movement between 1968 and 1969.

It will be seen that hotels in the R.D.A.'s did, on average, make a smaller increase in their prices between 1968 and 1969 than those outside (6.6%, against 7.7%): this difference was clearly not large enough to reflect the fact that in the R.D.A.'s SET had been abolished, whilst elsewhere it had been increased by one-half, but in view of the limitations of the statistical technique one should not attempt to draw fine conclusions from a single year's outcome (e.g. that the hotels in the R.D.A.'s were more anxious to secure an immediate increase in profits, rather than to cut prices with a view to attracting more business). It is wiser to consider the price movement between 1969 and 1970 as well, when the R.D.A. sample showed a very much smaller price increase than the matched one (3.1% against 9.0%): this difference was far greater than could be explained by the 'differential' factor – i.e. that the hotels outside the R.D.A.'s had a second increase in SET, which became effective in July 1969, which naturally did not affect the hotels in the R.D.A.'s because they were obtaining full refunds. On a two-year comparison between 1968 and 1970, the difference between the rise in price shown by the R.D.A. sample and the greater one shown elsewhere is considerably more than could be explained arithmetically by the fact that SET had been abolished for the R.D.A. sample, and twice increased for the other hotels. One cannot, in view of the statistical limitations of the technique, make any dogmatic statement such as that the favoured group not only passed on the effect of the exemption, but also secured economies through better utilisation and passed those on in lower prices also: but the evidence is at least *consistent* with the hypothesis that the effect of removing the tax was to produce a corresponding fall in price, even though it cannot *prove* this.

Other effects which the removal of SET in the R.D.A.'s *might* have had on businesses are: a fall in productivity; an increase in profits; an effect on other aspects of the 'commercial policy' of the business, such as a change in the quality of service offered, or perhaps an increase in investment. On these the guidebooks naturally gave us no data, so we had to see whether any light could be obtained from our own survey, despite the fact that it ended with the year 1968–9.

On this very weak basis we did get some slight support for the suggestion that the removal of SET would initially increase profits, but in view of the practice of fixing a price quotation for a whole year this should probably be regarded as a special case. Since even in the R.D.A.'s the 1969 tariff was higher than that for 1968, it would have been a very paradoxical policy to make a reduction when SET refunds were introduced in September 1968, especially in view of the difficulty of publicising that reduction. Our analysis is also much complicated by the fact that each hotel in our sample made its return for its own financial year, so that '1968–9' has a different meaning for each of them, and can never be regarded as a post-exemption year.

For what they are worth, the 1968–9 returns for the R.D.A. hotels in our sample showed a payment of SET amounting to 1.39% of sales on the average, and our attempt to calculate what the payment would have been in the absence of exemption (allowing for the seasonal problem and the increased rate of SET) gave a figure of the order of 1.97%. The difference, 0.58% of sales, is a very rough measure of the benefit to the R.D.A. hotels which exemption brought within the financial years which we classified as 1968–9. This may perhaps be set against the fact that between 1967–8 and 1968–9 profits as a percentage of sales increased by 0.81 percentage points for the hotels in the R.D.A.'s, and by 0.58 percentage points for those in the rest of our sample (but we must emphasise that this is *not* a case of a matched sample). The most that can be said is that the larger increase in the profit percentage obtained within the R.D.A.'s is consistent with the expectation that the initial effects of the remission, operating largely before the annual revision of tariffs, would be to raise profits.

Apart from that, the only faint suggestion which our returns gave us was that the R.D.A. hotels increased their advertising expenditure in 1968–9 (in comparison with earlier years) more frequently than was normal throughout the sample. This also seems a plausible reaction to expect from the exemption.

On the longer-term consequences, including any effects on productivity, our surveys can unfortunately throw no light at all.

Annex to Chapter XVI

Some Special Points on Construction

This annex deals in rather more detail with some of the points covered broadly in the main chapter.

Installation Work Done by Manufacturers

The first problem might be described as 'the split establishment in reverse', or 'what can a manufacturer regard as *not* being an establishment?' It has been important where manufacturers of pre-frabricated buildings deliver them in sectional form to the building-site, and employ workers themselves to assemble the parts into a whole, and in various analogous cases.

If the work of assembly on the site had been done by a builder, there would be no doubt about the matter: this is 'erection', and SET would be payable without any refund.

At the other extreme, if workers from the factory had arrived with the sections, assembled them in a day and returned to the factory, then there would have been no doubt that they were part of the factory staff, and eligible for refund. It would be *anomalous* that the genuine builders were put at a competitive disadvantage, but this would simply be a case where the establishment principle created an anomaly: the *legal* position would be clear, because the manufacturing firm would clearly have only one establishment – the factory.

The legal problem was then to decide under what circumstances (if any) the work on the building site constituted a separate 'establishment', which could be regarded as engaged in the erection of buildings, and therefore not eligible for refunds.

The original position taken by the Department of Employment was that if employees were organised to work on a site for more than a very short period, then that constituted an 'establishment', and it did not matter if they were engaged on the erection of pre-fabricated sections made elsewhere by the same firm (doubtless with the aid of nuts and bolts etc. made by other firms and possibly other components such as radiators).

This position, which was inevitably a bit ill-defined at its edges, was eroded by litigation, and a new set of principles had to be evolved on the basis of the case involving Vic Hallam.[1] As manufacturers of pre-fabricated buildings this firm employed some 900 people at their factory in Nottinghamshire and a further 250 men were involved in the erection of these buildings all over the country. One site was taken as a test case, which had minimal facilities, whilst over-all control of both permanent

---

1 See Secretary of State for Employment and Productivity versus Vic Hallam Ltd. (1970) 5ITR 108.

and temporary staff remained at the factory. Although it was agreed that the firm might continue to work at the site for a substantial period, it was nevertheless held that it did not constitute a separate establishment for SET, so that the firm was entitled to refund in respect of employment on the sites as well as in the factory, because the employees were working 'from the factory'.

The Department of Employment did not appeal from the Queens Bench Divisional Court in this case, but used its circumstances (e.g. the extent of facilities on the site, the place from which the workers were controlled, the length of time for which the firm was likely to operate on the site) as benchmarks for what it would in future allow as 'not constituting a separate establishment', where the operations on site consisted primarily in assembling things made in the firm's own factory. An attempt was made to erode this position further by firms manufacturing steam-raising boilers, electricity generating equipment etc., who claimed refund in respect of employees of construction departments, even though these employees might be recruited locally to operate on a particular site for a substantial period, and might be engaged in maintenance rather than installation. These firms were successful in the lower courts, but this decision was reversed by the House of Lords in January 1972.[1] Thus the principle emerged that there are some limits to what sort of construction site operated by a manufacturer can be held to be 'not an establishment', but these limits are hard to define, and it is interesting to note that litigation on the matter was continued after the demise of SET had been announced.

Industrial building

SET was bound, on the whole, to encourage industrialised building methods as against traditional methods, because the former often involved doing more work in factories and less on the building site. On top of this, the detailed regulations gave further help: in some cases it was possible to create artificial 'split establishments' on the building site, in which 'manufacturing' operations could be done under conditions which enabled the firm to obtain refunds; and sometimes 'installation' work on the site could be done by employees based on the factory, who qualified for refunds. This might, perhaps, seem to have been in line with the long-standing policy whereby system building in general has been encouraged by the Government (e.g. through exhortation, formation of the National Building Agency, and tolerance in the application of cost limits by Government departments) — for which the justification is supposed to be the 'infant industry' argument about securing long-term benefits in exchange for short-term losses.

Nevertheless, this argument seems to us to be essentially fallacious. The effect of SET was to give a further encouragement to some types of industrialised building, but this did not apply to some which seem to be particularly desirable. Thus under the building system known as Wimpey No-fines, the walls are constructed in their intended positions by pouring concrete into moulds formed by shuttering, and this was held by the Court to be ineligible for refund because it was essentially a part of

---

1 See The Lord Advocate versus Babcock and Wilcox (Operations) Ltd., House of Lords, January 1972.

the construction process.[1] The firm did not appeal from this decision, which is not surprising, since the pouring of concrete *in situ* seems to be clearly part of the work of construction: but from the economic point of view the ruling was unfortunate, since the result of the system was much the same as would be achieved by pouring the concrete elsewhere on the site, and carrying the resulting panels to the spot where they would be erected by jointing them together — a system under which refunds can be claimed for the pouring department.

In some cases, therefore, one could reasonably argue that SET imposed a positive handicap on the systems of industrialised building which could not be manipulated to secure refunds, since (for example) bricks used in the traditional form of building are produced in a factory, where refunds are secured, whilst the pouring of concrete *in situ* attracts no refund. It is clearly inefficient to discourage what seems to be a particularly desirable form of industrialised building, and the fact that other systems receive an artificial and unintended stimulus adds to the amount of economic loss. One should also remember the 'waste' which is involved through the employment of management, accountants, tax consultants and lawyers in the otherwise unnecessary reorganisation of firms to secure SET refunds — not to mention all the costs involved for many parties in the accumulation of definitive case law.

Problems of Equity

As regards equity, the position which arose under SET seems to be highly unfortunate First, there are anomalies as between contractors and manufacturers: if a manufacturer of building components erects these himself, rather than selling them to contractors, then he may receive refund of SET in respect of work which would not attract refund if it were done by the contractor. Second, there are anomalies between contractors themselves: if prefabricated parts are *moved* from one part of a site to another, their manufacture by the contractor becomes eligible for refund, but this will not apply if the parts are 'constructed' *in situ*.

Thirdly, SET will indirectly cause anomalies between manufacturers themselves, as happens when some manufacturers supply metal windows ready-glazed, whilst others supply wooden windows for glazing on site.

It is difficult, however, to say how the lines could have been better drawn, within the basic principles of SET operated on an 'establishment' principle.

Local Authorities' Direct Labour Force

As explained in the main chapter, Local Authorities are allowed to obtain refunds of SET on their building workers, except where these are employed on work of major construction. This gives the Authorities an artificial incentive to get works of minor construction and of repair done by direct labour, instead of putting it out to contractors.

This possible conflict is not very acute in the important field of Local Authority housing maintenance, most of which was performed by direct labour even before SET, although the point of principle remains: we were also told by one of the employer organisations in the building trade that their members were interested in

---

1 See Report on Tribunals etc., edited by Angels, Volume 3 part 6.

performing the smallest housing repair jobs, and they quoted the example of one Local Authority which gave all its housing repair maintenance to contractors, to show that the 'interest' was not merely academic. In the case of repair and maintenance of other public buildings etc., however, there is a substantial element of rivalry, as may be seen from the fact that in April 1969 contractors employed 66100 operatives on this type of work, against 91700 employed by Local Authorities. On minor works of construction the potential conflict might well be similar to that in the field of maintenance of buildings other than houses.

We asked officials of the Ministry of Housing and Local Government whether they could offer any justification of this unequal treatment of Local Authority workers, and their replies can be summarised under the headings of

    i the unimportance in practice of the anomaly;

    ii compensating factors affecting competition between direct labour and contractors;

    iii administrative convenience.

When we asked for details, we concluded that the arguments under (ii) were really worthless. It was argued that Local Authorities in development areas were in the disadvantageous position of not qualifying for investment grants under the Industrial Development Act 1966, whereas contractors could qualify, and also that Local Authorities have a liability to bear a charge for superannuation, which contractors would not normally incur. It emerged, however, that contractors engaged in repair and maintenance would at most attract £4½ million per annum in investment grants, as against £28 million per annum paid in SET by contractors in respect of labour engaged in repair and maintenance work (the figure being for 1967/8, before the increase in SET). As regards superannuation, this is only one aspect of employees' remuneration, and we do not feel that it would be relevant to consider this one aspect without considering the whole lot: private firms may well, for example, pay higher wages to attract labour.

The argument for administrative convenience was that the non-refund of SET in respect of new construction work, and the refund in respect of repair work, accorded with Local Authority practice in the charging of work to capital or revenue account, and that the cessation of refund for maintenance staff would cause difficulties, insofar as workers whose remuneration was charged to revenue accounts would have to be divided between the building department and those for whom a refund could be obtained (because they were not building workers). It was later agreed, however, that the present practice already calls for a division of workers, but within the *capital* field, since SET is not refundable on major capital works, but is refundable for minor ones: Local Authorities do not, apparently, experience difficulty in dividing the expenditure and the tax into these two elements, so that it is hard to see how difficulties would arise if all people concerned with building and repairs were liable to the tax, and other workers were not.[1]

The arguments about the unimportance of the anomaly in practice had two main parts — the absence of complaint from the building trade, and an analysis of how

---

1 This point is, of course, quite separate from the more radical suggestion made in the main chapter for making *all* Local Authority workers liable, unless they were working in establishments which would qualify for refund on the basis of their industrial classification.

competition worked 'in practice'. As regards the former, we were later told that one of the main Trade Associations had in fact put their complaint into writing, but had not done so when SET was introduced, apparently for the 'human' reason that they had been primarily concerned with getting SET refunds disallowed on major construction contracts (where the issue seemed to be of greatest importance). They said that they had made oral representations in the course of the main discussions, and indicated that their members were in fact very interested in competing for repair work.

The analysis put forward by M.H.L.G. about the working of competition started from the point that in general Local Authorities which had established direct labour organisations would have done so for reasons of convenience, rather than comparative cost, which would therefore not be an important element in deciding on the allocation of work. It was added that Local Authorities are nevertheless expected to 'test the market' by inviting tenders from contractors for the purpose of comparison with direct labour costs, and that it would not seem unreasonable for an authority to include SET in its own costs for purposes of the comparison, even though it would be refunded. We felt considerable doubt whether the Councillors would be able to satisfy their auditors that it would be right to put out the job to private contractors if the actual cost to the rate-payers were thereby increased above what it would be with direct labour (because SET would then be recoverable) and we were told that M.H.L.G. had not issued any advice about the comparisons being made on a basis which ignored SET refunds. The reason given to us for the absence of a circular on this matter was that no such advice had been requested by Local Authorities, and the Ministry did not think that 'on a matter of minimal significance a general circular would be justified' (because convenience and the political composition of the Local Authority concerned would be more important factors in decisions between the use of contractors or direct labour than the niceties of cost comparisons).

In our view, it was quite unrealistic to expect that Local Authorities would ask for advice, when the object of the comparisons would be to see which course would be cheapest for the rate-payers; and we are doubtful whether a general circular would in fact have produced much result, because 'notional allowances' which had to be added to the costs *actually payable* would probably have been disregarded, or evaded by taking an optimistic view of the efficiency of the direct labour squad. We were not therefore at all impressed with this attempt to show that the anomaly in the law was of little importance: something which distorts the cost comparison substantially will normally be important, even though other factors influence the decision as well. We regard the payment of refunds in respect of Local Authority building workers as a serious breach of promises about 'fair competition between the public and private sectors under SET', even though its worst feature was removed by not allowing them where the workers were engaged on major works of new construction.

XVII
Some Macro-Economic Consequences of SET

This chapter examines various macro-economic consequences of SET, including especially the question 'who pays it'. This question has to be tackled in two different senses: thus we seek first to estimate the net amount which is paid by each industry or industry group, after deducting refunds; and secondly we calculate, on various assumptions, the 'incidence' of the tax on the various types of final user of the national product. This second calculation takes account of the passing-on of the tax by the employers who actually make the payments, and also by the purchasers of their product if that is not a part of final consumption or investment etc.

To illustrate the difference between these two questions, one could take the example of the tax which is paid by a chartered accountant in respect of his employees. For the first question we have only to estimate the amounts paid by people in each industry, and the amount which they get back in refund: this amount would therefore be included (less a deduction for any partial refunds on elderly or part-time employees) in the figure for the M.L.H. 'Accountancy Services' and in the Order which covers this, 'Professional and Scientific Services'. For the second question, however, our assumption might well be that the accountant passes on the tax in the form of higher charges to the firms whose books he had audited, and that these firms would in turn raise the prices for their products, and that this process would continue until a 'final user' was reached. We have then to estimate how much of the ultimate burden rests on the various types of final users.[1]

Industry Analysis: Logical Problems
The statistical problems involved in arriving at figures for the net payment of SET by each industry are inevitably rather formidable because of the system adopted for its collection. In effect, *all* employers pay the tax, as an addition to the National Insurance stamp, and there are no statistics recording the division of these payments by industries or industry groups; those employers who are entitled to refunds then have to make applications to one or other Government department, and for reasons discussed below it is not at all easy to derive an industrial analysis of these refunds from the records kept by the Government departments. In addition, however, there are formidable problems in the way of preparing useful statistics which arise out of the time-lags between payments made by the employers who are entitled to refunds, and their actual receipt of those refunds; not only is there bound to be such a

---

1 We do *not*, however, consider the further repercussions which might follow, if for example the rise in the cost of living led to higher wages, which would represent higher costs for all kinds of firms.

time-lag, but in practice it has varied in length (one continuing reason being the irregularity with which employers lodge claims), and this would have made it difficult to produce a meaningful series for different periods, even if the rate of the tax had remained constant. On top of this, the variations in the rates of SET levied have meant that whenever these were changed, the in-payments to the exchequer in the next quarter were at the new rates, whilst the refunds were still at the old rates.

Under these circumstances there are various objectives which one might have in seeking to arrive at figures for the industrial incidence of the tax. One might, for example, take a narrow 'cash' view of the matter, by saying that one wanted to see for each period what net payment was made by any industry, and that one would arrive at this on the simple principle of estimating the in-payments made in that period and subtracting the refunds, ignoring the fact that the refunds were related to an earlier period: on that basis, a large cash payment would be shown for the final quarter of 1966 for every industry, since payment of the refunds had not then started, and every employer was paying the tax; conversely manufacturing and other industries entitled to refunds would show negative figures for the third quarter of 1971, because the rate of tax had then been halved, whilst the refunds were still being made in respect of tax paid at the old rate.

At the other extreme, one might say that the objective should be to measure the amount of tax paid in any period which would not subsequently be repaid as a refund. One would not then be interested in estimating the tax paid by an industry which was certain to receive the whole of it back again and then subtracting the amount refunded, since the only result would be to get a small sum (either positive or negative) which reflected the errors in the statistics. One would, however, need to estimate by one means or another the amount paid in respect of those establishments belonging to an 'exempt' industry for which the employers were not entitled to any refund: this happens, for example, where a manufacturer has a geographically separate Head Office in which more than half of the workers are engaged in office duties. At the *measurement* level — as opposed to the conceptual level — it might be easiest to get at the figure by estimating the total payments to the exchequer made by these industries, and subtracting the actual refunds (provided that one could solve the problem of lags etc.); alternatively, it might be better to make an estimate of the number of people in such establishments which do not get refunds, and estimate their payments directly, without any reference to the refund statistics and without necessarily estimating the total payments made by the industry.

This second objective also requires, of course, that one estimates by one means or another the amount of refunds obtained by each industry (or industry group) which is basically in the SET sector. These refunds may be *partial*, and reflect the fact that the workers are elderly or part-timers; on the other hand the larger part of them consists in *full* refunds, which may arise on any of the following grounds:

(a) Certain types of establishment which are classified for statistical purposes to an MLH allocated by us to the SET sector, were made eligible for refund by legislation, or even for premium: this happens, for example, with the printing of cinematographic film, which is classified to the MLH 'cinemas, theatre, radio etc.'

(b) The 'split establishment' rule and other possibilities for reclassification enable employers in the SET sector to get refunds for many workers —

156

notably in building (see Chapter XVI) and in distribution (see First Report).

(c) The employer may be entitled to refund on grounds of his *status*, whether as a charity or as part of the Public Sector. The importance of this factor is so great in the case of educational services and of medical and dental services that we have treated these two MLH's as belonging to the non-SET sector, although there is no exemption for them on 'industrial' grounds (and in consequence we have the reverse problem of estimating the tax which is *not* refunded in these MLH's). But the factor is also important in relation to some parts of the SET sector — notably construction (for repair-workers employed by Local Authorities) and miscellaneous services (for employees of charitable organisations, other than those in universities etc.)

As in the case of head offices, there is in principle a choice between deriving figures for these refunds from the statistics of actual refunds paid (in which case one has to consider the 'lag' problem) or of estimating, from employment statistics etc., how much was paid in the period in question in respect of workers for whom a refund would subsequently be obtained.[1]

Of these two possible objectives we regarded the second as definitely the one which we should adopt. The apparently simple 'cash' figures are of very limited value for any economic purpose, and of course the amount paid varies so greatly from quarter to quarter, or from year to year, that no single computation of the industrial break-down is of much value except in relation to that particular period. It was difficult enough — given the scanty and ill-coordinated nature of the refund statistics — to arrive at a meaningful answer even for one period, and we were quite incapable of doing it for a whole series of periods.

In point of fact, however, our analysis for 1970 comes fairly close to the figures which would emerge on a 'cash' basis, so that people who are interested in that basis can treat them as approximations for what they want.

Industry Analysis: Statistical Procedures

The procedures which we used to overcome the great statistical problems involved in making our estimates are described in Appendix G. Very briefly, however, the main points in our strategy can be set out here.

Period Covered

Our basic calculations relate solely to the calendar year 1970, although we made a number of partial calculations for all sorts of other periods as part of the process of checking that our results were sensible.

There were two main reasons for choosing 1970 for our main effort. In the first place, no detailed industrial analysis of refunds paid was available for any earlier period, and this was indispensable for some of our calculations: in our attempts to produce corresponding figures for some other period for checking purposes, a number of important ones had to be guessed on the basis on the 1970 estimate.

---

1 In practice, as we see below, the limitations of the statistics do not give one much option.

In the second place, there was no change in the rate of the tax during 1970, and indeed it had been stable since July 1969. This did not mean that all the refunds paid in 1970 related to tax at the peak rate, since refunds are commonly claimed by employers with a considerable delay (e.g. by covering two or more quarters on one return); but it did mean that problems of this kind were of small quantitative importance.

Besides these two points, we understood that there was no major speeding up of repayment claims during 1970, and no wave of back claims based on Industrial Court decisions, so that we could hope that the refund statistics would broadly reflect one year's entitlement. Moreover, inspection of the quarterly series for aggregate in-payments of tax by employers and refunds paid by the Government did not suggest that there were any awkward disturbances affecting 1970.

Estimation of Payments by each Industry, and Checks

The first stage was to estimate the payments made by employers in Great Britain, industry by industry, using the ordinary labour statistics, and making allowance for the average number of people who did not pay in a particular week for one reason or another – e.g. because they were sick, or unemployed, or on strike, or earned less than the minimum amount needed to make them liable to SET. This was quite a complex process, since it was necessary to arrive at the age and sex composition of the people paying as well as estimating the number who would be liable to the tax, and it was therefore necessary to make as many checks as possible to see whether our results were reasonable, or whether we could detect any particular bias.

The first check was a very simple one. The total amount of payments made by employers is given in *Financial Statistics*, and fortunately this agreed well with the total of our own industry-by-industry estimates. The actual figures were:

Sum of our estimates   £2027 million

Total payments by employers   £2029 million

Whilst this check was satisfactory as far as it went, there was always the danger that it reflected compensating errors in our estimates, and we sought therefore to make what checks we could on the separate parts of our figures. It was possible to make a number of these, by treating the estimate which we had made of in-payments by various categories of employer in 1970 as the basis for an estimate of the refunds which might be 'expected' for the twelve months from April 1970 to March 1971. First we did this for the whole field, starting from the estimates for payments made by the whole non-SET sector, and making various adjustments so as to arrive at an estimate for the total refunds 'expected' in 1970/71. Here again the agreement was good, the 'expected' figure being £1497 million and the actual refunds £1,500 million (see page 252 of Appendix G).

Our next test related to manufacturing by itself, and the details which are given in Appendix G illustrate forcibly the difficulty of operating with refund statistics which do not mean what they seem to mean. Thus the Department of Employment figures for 'manufacturing' do not include refunds on many types of manufacturing establishment which are *also* eligible for refund because the employer belongs to the Public Sector (although they *do* cover the steel industry): on the other hand, they include the workers who have been reclassified to 'manufacturing' for refund purposes, although the ordinary labour statistics count them as in (say) building or distribution. However, our independently estimated figures for the various elements, set out in Appendix G, led to an estimate of £851 million for refunds in manufacturing (as defined by the DE) as compared with a 'control' figure of £848 million.

Finally, our estimate for agriculture, forestry and fishing agreed almost exactly with the actual refund figure.

Refunds and Net Burden

Having established what seemed to us reasonable figures for an industrial analysis of the in-payments by employers, our remaining task was divided into two main parts:

> For the *SET sector* we estimated the amount of these payments which would be likely to be repaid, industry by industry, and treated the difference between the (large) in-payments figures and the (relatively small) repayable part as measuring the net burden.

> For the *Non-SET sector* we estimated the amounts which would *not* be repayable for each industry (e.g. manufacturing head offices, employees of doctors and dentists), and arrived at the amount which would be eligible for refund by subtracting this small element from the large figures for in-payments.

The various devices which had to be adopted to secure these results are summarised in Appendix G, which also says something about some of the checks which were used, based partly on the figures which are available for other periods (though these figures are very deficient in industrial detail for the refunds, and are upset by changes in the lags between payments and refunds, as well as by changes in tax-rates).

The final outcome is given in Table XVII.1, which shows our estimates for the in-payments, refunds and net burden for the industry groups which are of main interest. These figures should be regarded as applying to 1970: the refund figures, however, are not the actual refunds *made* in 1970, but rather an estimate of the part of the 1970 payments which would be refunded after an interval.

At the foot of the table, figures are given for the aggregate payments by employers, derived from the sale of insurance stamps etc. in 1970, and for the total refunds paid by the Exchequer in 1970/71, which is probably the best 'control' figure for our refund estimates. It is, however, the column for the *net burden* which is really of most interest.[1]

Conventional Analysis of Incidence

The figures provided in Table XVII.1 enable us to calculate the incidence of SET on the various categories of final users, on any desired assumptions about the effects of the tax on prices and productivity. We started with the traditional assumption that the tax is passed on in full by each producer who pays it, without any addition of a 'mark-up', but also without any deduction at the expense of profits,

---

1 One small point is just worth noting. In 1970 manufacturers in the Development Areas were receiving, for part of the year, a premium on top of the refund of the tax which they had paid. We have *not* subtracted this from the payments made by manufacturers, preferring to regard it as a regional subsidy to the manufacturers, which merely used the SET machinery for distribution purposes.

Table XVII.1 *Estimates of In-Payments, Refunds and Net Burden of SET by Industry for G.B. 1970*

(£ million)

Industry (1968 SIC)	Estimated In-payments, Calendar Year 1970	Amount Refundable	Net Burden
'Mainly exempt industries'			
Agriculture, Forestry and Fishing I	36	36	–
Manufacturing III–XIX	851	844	7
'Other mainly exempt industries'[a]	545	542	3
SET Sector			
Construction XX	144	30	114
Distribution XXIII	205	21	184
Insurance, Banking and Finance XXIV	78	2	76
Accountancy, Legal and Other Professional and Scientific Services 871, 873, 879	26	1	25
Miscellaneous Services XXVI	131	21	110
Other Road Haulage and Miscellaneous Transport 704, 709	11	–	11
Total	2027	1497	530
Control Figures[b]	*2029*	*1500*	

(a) These are Mining and Quarrying; Gas, Electricity and Water; Transport and Communication (excluding 'other road haulage' and 'miscellaneous transport services'); Education Services, Medical and Dental Services, Religious Organisations, Research and Development Services; Public Administration and Defence.

(b) These are the total in-payments for 1970 and the total refunds for the year to 31 March 1971. See Appendix G for discussion of the (minor) disturbance to the refund figure caused by the postal strike.

or because of a gain in productivity; if the purchaser is using the service which he has bought to produce something else, then it is further assumed that this purchaser will pass on the extra amount which he pays for the service in his own price (e.g. in the case of a hotel which has had to pay a higher price for getting sheets washed by a laundry), and the process continues until a 'final user' is reached.

This assumption follows the traditional practice in relation to calculations of the incidence of indirect taxes, and so can serve as a standard of reference; in giving it, we do not imply that SET had no effect on productivity, nor yet on profits in the industries which paid it in the first instance. Those who are sceptical about either of these effects, at least in the long run, will consider that this is the assumption which they wanted to be used; it may also appeal to people who want to see how much tax is in some sense 'incorporated' in what they buy, even though they may recognise that the Government's action in imposing the tax has been mitigated by the producers' action in holding down prices. But its main purpose is as a starting-point for the analysis, rather than an end-point.

On this simplest of all assumptions, the amount by which the value of final goods and services is raised in value is simply equal to the net revenue from the tax, and we can make a reasonable allocation of where the tax will 'end up' with the aid of the input-output tables. The method is described in Appendix G, and the results are shown in Table XVII.2.

160

Table XVII.2 *Conventional Calculation of Price Effects of SET*   (£ million)

| Industry | Net SET burden, 1970[a] | Amount falling on each end-use | | | |
		Personal consumption	Government consumption	Invest-ment	Exports (goods and ser-vices)
Construction	115	22	7	84	2
Distribution	185	144	7	15	19
Other main services in SET sector	212	138	26	20	28
Other SET-payers[b]	21	11	3	2	5
Total	530	315	43	121	54
Value of Final Expenditure in 1970.	*31238*	*9055*	*9340*	*11182*
SET as % of above		*1.0*	*0.5*	*1.3*	*0.5*

(a) Figures for SET relate to U.K., in line with the expenditure figures; the total is taken from the Blue Book and the industry figures scaled up accordingly

(b) Miscellaneous transport etc. (MLH 704, 709) and taxable establishments in the non-SET sector (head offices etc.). See Table XVII.1.

Table XVII.2 also shows the value of the final expenditure at market prices in each of the categories in 1970, and this enables one to see how large an addition to prices SET would have made, if our assumptions about passing on had applied. Several interesting points arise:

(a) So far as consumption expenditure is concerned — which is the item which concerns most people — the effect of SET would, on our assumption, be to raise prices by about 1%. This is not, of course, a negligible result, but it is a good deal smaller than one might have thought from the agitation which was made about the effect of the tax on the cost of living.

(b) Perhaps the most striking result is the substantial proportion of the tax which falls on investment. Not only is the tax shown as raising prices by a somewhat bigger percentage for this item than for consumption, but such a result is a highly abnormal feature of the British tax system: the normal approach is to arrange indirect taxes in such a way that very little falls on either investment or exports.

The high amount of SET falling on capital formation reflects, or course, the fact that it is levied on construction. On the face of it, it might seem strange to impose a tax on building, when so many kinds are encouraged by special tax concessions or subsidies (e.g. factories, houses); but it is outside our terms of reference to consider whether that fact makes the policy anomalous, or perhaps provides its justification.

(c) The amount of SET shown statistically as falling on exports represents about 0.5% of their value. This is clearly a good deal higher than it would be with many types of indirect tax — e.g. tobacco duty or purchase tax or VAT — because exports are exempted from these taxes, whilst there is no system for giving rebates of SET. On the other hand, SET shows a lower amount falling on exports than would arise if an equal amount of revenue were collected by raising the employers' share of the National Insurance contribution, and the same may well be true for the duty on fuel oil. As always, a full judgement about the effects of SET must allow for the nature of the alternative tax, as well as considering other assumptions besides the conventional one used in this part of our analysis.

(d) Despite the fact that the Government and Local Authorities are effectively exempted from SET on their employees, a significant part of the tax nevertheless falls on Public Authorities' expenditure, through the things which they buy.

These statistics in Table XVII.2 inevitably relate to very broad categories of expenditure, and if we could make a comparable analysis for detailed categories some of the price increases would naturally look a good deal larger. Nevertheless, if we take an item like hairdressing, or some of the other services for which estimates were given in Table XII.3, the percentage addition represented by SET would only be some 6–7%, and this is probably as high a figure as one could find for any type of expenditure. In effect, this result emphasizes the fact that SET was a widespread tax, but not a heavy one, even when at its peak rate.

Finally, I must emphasize once again that the analysis in this section is concerned only with the effects of SET, without bringing in those of *alternative* taxes. It is, however a basic part of our whole approach that SET is regarded as an *alternative* to some other tax. The fact that Table XVII.2 shows rises in price for all categories does not mean that prices would be higher under SET than under this alternative tax: at least some of them might indeed be lower.

Effects of Productivity Gain

As soon as one departs from the simple assumption of the conventional incidence analysis, the logical problems which have to be tackled become a good deal more formidable. If, for example, one assumes that SET provoked a rise in productivity in a way that the alternative tax would not, then obviously the effect on prices will be reduced as compared with our first analysis, but the position cannot be properly examined unless one considers other effects as well. In particular our basic assumption about the Government managing its macro-economic policies in such a way as to produce the same level of employment in either situation means that we need to consider a number of macro-economic developments as well as a plain price rise. This problem may perhaps be most simply approached by looking first at a problem in the conventional incidence analysis which we have ignored.

One of the assumptions of the conventional type of analysis is that the use of the tax in question (SET in this case) has a negligible effect on the level of productivity, and so does not affect productive *potential*. It might nevertheless have an indirect effect on the level of *production* in various ways (e.g. through an effect on confidence leading to changes in investment), which would operate through the level of aggregate demand: in our analysis, however, we have 'assumed this away' by postulating that the Government would introduce alternative arrangements (which need not be entirely in the tax field, though that is what we have typically implied) to ensure the same level of employment.

One particular point does however call for some elaboration: the relatively high incidence of SET on exports, as compared with that of other taxes, might affect the balance of payments, and this might not only be important in itself, but have awkward repercussions on the maintenance of full employment. In relation to the rather formal and conventional analysis of the first section, however, we do no more than use this case as a means of putting the balance of payments formally onto the agenda, and noting that it will receive more elaborate treatment in later sections, where the issue is quantitatively more important.

Rise in Gross Domestic Product

If we assume that SET leads to a rise in productivity, which does not apply with the alternative tax, then our assumption of Government action to make the level of employment the same in the two positions necessarily implies that SET will bring a higher level of GDP. This rise in GDP implies in turn a number of interesting consequences, over and above any which follow from the impact of cost-changes, such as the following:

(a) With given tax-rates, all the old taxes will yield a higher revenue than they would if coupled with the alternative new tax.

(b) More imports will be needed as raw materials etc. to make production of the higher GDP possible, and the extra income will raise the demand for imports generally. The balance of payments will thus move in an adverse direction, unless the Government's macro-economic policy includes counter-acting measures.

The first step towards studying this sort of thing is clearly to get an idea of how large the extra GDP would be in real terms. This involves a series of assumptions, both in the logical field and in that of statistics, and our figures can serve as little more than illustrations.

(a) First, we define our objective as a study of the long-run effects, without being concerned about transitional problems: these transitional effects would logically have to be set against those of the alternative tax, and as we have not been given the job of making a comparison with any specific tax, we can say nothing on that score. For the long run we make the conventional assumption that the effects of the alternative tax on productivity are negligible.

(b) Next, we assume that the expansion of GDP made possible by SET is not inhibited by the effect which this expansion (like most others) tends to have on the balance of payments. This is a necessary assumption if we are to retain the basic premise that the level of employment is to be the same in the two situations: in logic it might imply that the balance of payments was still 'acceptable' to the Government with a higher level of imports (possibly because otherwise the reserves would have grown unnecessarily fast — a possibility which happens to be very plausible in relation to 1970); or it might imply that some special action directed at the balance of payments was included in the macro-economic measures taken to ensure that the level of employment was unchanged (e.g. a scheme of export promotion or import restriction).

When we move on to assess further consequences, we take the second of these two assumptions; this makes the analysis rather easier, since the gain in GDP is simply shared out between the categories of internal usage, without adding a further component derived from the adverse effect on the balance of payments. Imports rise, but exports are assumed to rise equally, through some policy measure.

(c) We deliberately take a rather low, and very conventionalised, assumption about the effects of SET on productivity. This may seem cowardly, but our information on this subject is in fact very sketchy. Even in the case of distribution, where the statistical analysis worked best, we could not eliminate the effects of the progressive elimination of resale price maintenance, which we believe to be important: for the other trades (including construction) we cannot say much more than that the evidence for the existence of a positive productivity effect seemed to make this the most plausible hypothesis.

We therefore take for our illustrative calculation the assumption that SET at the 1970 rate would have as its long run effect a gain of productivity in distribution of 3% (compared with what would have happened with the alternative tax) and a gain in all the other trades of 2%.

The effects of taking other assumptions can be derived from Table XVII.3, discussed below.

(d) The next question is what to assume about the gain in national output which this productivity gain in the SET sector would bring. One extreme view would be to say that there would be no gain at all, because the people displaced from the SET industries as a result of higher productivity would simply remain unemployed, because they would be unsuitable for other industries. Protagonists of this view would argue that it cannot be pushed on one side by assuming macro-economic policies which secure the same balance between potential supply and aggregate demand, because the displaced labour would either retire from the labour force, or become 'frictionally' unemployed. For reasons explained in Chapter XIV, we reject this argument, whilst recognizing that there might be a very small increase in such types of non-employment.

At the other extreme, one might assume that the gain in aggregate output would be very large in relation to the number of workers involved. This might be argued on *short-term* grounds, by saying that in order to get the other industries to expand their employment, there would have to be a very substantial stimulus to demand for their output, because the first effect of an increase in demand is largely to take up the slack in the industries, rather than to induce higher employment. It might also be argued, on *long-term* grounds, that the availability of more labour for use in manufacturing (coupled with the necessary rise in demand) would make the potential supply rise very substantially.

Without really arguing the point, we decided not to apply either of these arguments in favour of very high figures to the problem which we are considering. The short-term analysis seems to be concerned primarily with a transitional situation in which a higher proportion of productive potential is being used, so that overhead labour is more fully utilised, and this is not the problem with which we are concerned. The long-term argument rests on an analysis which is the subject of considerable controversy, and is right outside our terms of reference: it does not seem wise to mix up a conclusion about SET with the acceptance of a controversial view on this topic.

We decided, therefore, to take a simple 'proportionate' assumption — that the increase in GDP made possible by the fact that productivity has been raised by x per cent in the SET sector is taken as equal to x per cent of the net output in that sector. One particular reason in favour of this conclusion was explained in Chapter XIV: the rise in GDP will raise the level of aggregate demand and so cause the output of the SET sector to be larger than it would have been without the rise in productivity. This rise in *output* goes some way to offsetting the effect of higher *productivity* on the number of workers employed in the SET sector.

The effect of combining this assumption and the assumed improvements in productivity is shown in Table XVII.3: the GDP comes out as being nearly £300

Table XVII.3 *Rise in GDP caused by SET: Illustrative Figures*

			£ million
Industry	Net output[(a)]	Assumed rise in productivity	Resultant addition to GDP
Construction	2,640	2%	53
Distribution	4,524	3%	136
Insurance, Banking and Finance	1,552	2%	31
Miscellaneous Services	3,545	2%	71
Total			291

(a) As given in 1971 Blue Book, Table 17; before providing for depreciation and stock appreciation. (See also notes to Table XI.2).

million (at 1970 prices) higher than it would otherwise have been, an increase of about two-thirds of one per cent.[1]

Let me end this section by repeating that the figures are for purposes of illustration, and that the assumptions have been deliberately chosen to give a minimum picture. One could make a plausible case for using illustrative figures which were 50% higher.

Allocation to End-Uses

The allocation of this additional GDP between end-uses depends in large measure on the type of macro-economic actions adopted by the Government to ensure that aggregate demand for goods and services would be at the right (higher) level to produce the same level of employment as with the alternative tax. We have assumed that this package of measures would cause exports and imports to rise by the same amount, above the alternative position (taking into account the effects produced by the incidence of SET on exports, for which we calculate a revised figure below). In the absence of any reason to the contrary, we assume a pro rata allocation between personal consumption, public authorities' current expenditure and investment.

Effect on Prices

We may now attempt a rather more sophisticated analysis of price effects. We still make the conventional assumption that SET has no effect on profits, on the argument that we are concerned with the long run. But instead of assuming that this result is achieved wholly by passing on the cost of SET, we reckon that in each SET trade the amount passed on in higher prices is the amount paid in SET, *less* the saving in labour costs through higher productivity: this latter amount is found by applying the assumed productivity percentages to the 'income from employment' figures given in the 1971 Blue Book. The results are shown in Table XVII.4. The percentage increases in price shown in this table are about six-tenths of the size of those shown in Table XVII.2.

Changes in the Pattern of Consumption

It is natural to ask, with any selective indirect tax, how large an impact it has had on the pattern of personal consumption: alternatively, one might take a wider field,

1 Against this one might have to set some loss of real income caused by taking action to maintain an acceptable position in the balance of payments.

and examine how usage of the things taxed had been affected in relation to total usage, covering investment and Government consumption also.

Table XVII.4 *Price Effects of SET: Illustrative Figures for U.K.*

			£ million			
Industry	Net SET burden, 1970	'Saving' through assumed productiv-ity gain[a]	Amount falling on each end-use			
			Personal consumption	Government consumption	Invest-ment	Exports (goods and ser-vices)
Construction	1·15	39	14	5	55	2
Distribution	185	85	78	4	8	10
Miscellaneous Services	212	80[b]	86	16	12	18
Other SET-payers	21	7	8	2	1	3
Total	533	211	186	27	76	33
% increase in price			0.6	0.3	0.8	0.3

(a) This is taken as 3% of 'income from employment' (as given in 1971 Blue Book) for distribution and 2% for the other main items: a token figure is included for the residual row.

(b) Estimated from number of employees, since the Blue Book figure has too wide a coverage, and is only a residual.

This is a rather tricky question to define precisely when one is dealing with SET, because it is a tax which is levied on particular *industries*, rather than on particular *products*. This distinction is not very important when the industry is producing services used directly by consumers (e.g. in the case of watch repairs), but it is absolutely fundamental where the service is of a 'business' kind (e.g. accountancy). Moreover in the very important case of the distributive trades, the consumer normally thinks of himself as buying 'goods' rather than 'distributive services' as such: he may think of his purchase as representing a package of goods-plus-distributive-services, but he seldom isolates the distributive element. It would be unrealistic therefore to attempt any assessment of the change in the proportion which that element represents in total consumption.

It seems best, therefore, to interpret the question as asking to what extent SET has caused consumer services proper to become a smaller proportion of consumers' expenditure than one would otherwise have expected. It is clearly more meaningful to do the exercise at constant prices.

This is a rather similar problem to the one which we had to investigate in Chapter XIV, when we were assessing the effect of SET on the labour employed in the SET sector as a whole. There we had to consider first the effect which SET had had on productivity, since this affected the number of workers needed for producing any given output in the SET sector: this is a matter which does not concern us here. But we also had to consider how much larger or smaller the output of SET goods and services had been, as a result of having that tax rather than an alternative. This second question fell into two parts: given our basic assumption that the Government would manage its macro-economic policies so as to produce the same level of employment under SET as under the alternative tax, the total level of GNP would be higher with SET (a point which we have investigated in more detail in this chapter), and this would raise the level of demand for all types of output; but the higher prices for SET goods and services would cause a small switch of demand away from them, towards other goods and services. The conclusion of Chapter XIV was that the first factor would be rather more powerful than the second, so that the output of the SET sector was rather *higher* than it would have been with an alternative tax.[1]

If we now wish to consider only the *proportion* which taxed consumer services represent of total personal consumption, then we can ignore the effect of SET in raising total output, and so raising the demand both for the taxed services and for consumption generally: the numerator and denominator of our fraction might not be raised by exactly the same percentage, but the effect of any difference would be very small, and incapable of being assessed without a very large investigation (and much better basic statistics).

We are left, therefore, with the need to assess the 'switch' effect away from consumer services caused by higher prices, with a possible refinement of studying whether there seems to have been a further fall in consumption of these services, which might be due to worse quality (not reflected in the price index) or decreased availability in certain parts of the country (e.g. if the only laundry in the area closed down). We can say straight away that, although the statistical evidence is not very good, we are convinced that the combined effect of these two factors is almost certainly too small to be of any real interest.

On the 'switch' effect caused by higher prices, the analysis in Chapter XII showed that the effect of SET on the prices of the consumer services examined averaged rather under 5% in 1969/70. SET was then at its peak rate, and the percentage would have been rather less in 1970 (because of the rise in other elements of cost), as well as in earlier years (when SET was a good deal lower). Moreover the services examined were all ones in which the labour element is very high − they do not, for example, cover any form of catering − so that a price-rise of 4% for 1970 is a reasonable assumption. For the reasons explained in Chapter XIV, the effect of this price-rise on the quantity bought would probably be to reduce it by perhaps 1%, given that aggregate personal consumption is assumed unchanged in real terms and that SET was raising prices over a wide field of competing services (rather than within a narrow area). In other words, if these services would otherwise have represented 10% of personal consumption, then the SET switch would lower this percentage to 9.9% in real terms (whilst of course raising the percentage in money terms).

As regards the possible 'residual' effect on consumption of taxed services (through quality, etc.) our assessment could only be indirect, but yielded just the sort of results which one would expect if this effect were negligible. The research project which is in progress in the Department of Applied Economics attempts to 'explain' the level of consumption in each year, for each category of consumption distinguished in the National Income Blue Book, by reference to the total consumption for that year, and relative prices (as deduced from that source). If there were a

1 But the labour employed was smaller than was to be expected without SET, owing to the productivity effect − a result which we also observed directly.

tendency for SET to lower the consumption of taxed services otherwise than through its effect on price, then the unexplained residuals emerging from that analysis would be predominantly negative for the relevant categories in the years when SET applied.[1] In fact, the residuals were divided about equally between positive and negative: this does not *prove* that the 'quality and availability' effect of SET on consumption of taxed services was negligible, but it gives no support at all for the belief that it was of any quantitative importance.

---

1 Since this analysis is obviously subject to errors, one can only apply the assessment in this 'grouped' way, and not to individual categories separately — see Chapters XII and XIII.

XVIII
Some Concluding Reflections

After working on this research project for nearly five years, I would have liked to end up with a nice clear picture of 'the effects of SET', which could be set out succinctly in a final chapter. The realities of an economist's life are not, however, so simple as that: the results of the research are complex and in many ways only tentative — i.e. they represent what seems most probable, but they are subject to a margin of uncertainty which is sometimes so large that one cannot exclude the possibility that the results were really of a very different character.

It seems right, however, to close with a brief review of the more interesting findings, although this will consist largely of rather dogmatic statements, coupled with references to the parts of the two Reports in which the matter is mainly discussed. It seems legitimate also, in this concluding chapter, to speculate briefly about *why* some of the results have emerged. The main Reports have been deliberately kept as free from theory as possible, to avoid any confusion between what was to be expected on theoretical grounds and what had been established empirically; moreover such theory as there was was segregated into a preliminary chapter (e.g. Chapter X of the First Report), designed to show what one should be looking for, and kept at a very simple level. But now that the fact-finding has been concluded (albeit on a very incomplete basis, because of the curtailment of the enquiry) it seems legitimate to try to investigate very briefly how theory might explain the facts.

We divide the chapter into three sections, dealing respectively with the broad characteristics of SET, its working and administration, and its effects.

Broad Characteristics of SET
This section summarises the most important characteristics of SET from an analytic point of view, with some inevitable overlap between the various items. Many of the points are 'obvious', but this does not take away from their importance.

A Selective Tax
SET is deliberately selective in its incidence, but this is a characteristic which it shares with almost all indirect taxes: even the value added tax has a zero rating for a very substantial field, including nearly all food. Consequently the idea that there must be something wrong, or even immoral, about SET just because it is selective rests on a complete misunderstanding of the role of an indirect tax. Very possibly this idea springs from the fact that the tax paid by the employer is based on the number of his employees, rather than on some inanimate item. (See First Report, pp. 16/17).

Given that there is nothing wrong with a selective tax as such, the first criterion for judging its merits is the basis adopted for making the selection. On this, one point can be made with conviction: the judgement of an indirect tax must always be based on a review of how it fits into the tax system as a whole, and any assessment which relies on a scrutiny of one tax in isolation is almost bound to be misleading. Thus there was a good logical case for introducing a selective tax on consumer services in 1966, precisely because these escaped most other types of indirect taxes, irrespective of one's views about the desirability of those services.[1]

A second point can also be stated with confidence, namely that the criteria adopted for deciding what is to be liable to any particular tax must be administratively workable. Opinions may differ about the relative importance to be attached to an improvement in workability as against a loss on other objectives, but a certain level of workability is clearly essential.

Apart from the above points, opinions differ a good deal about the criteria for judging whether the selection of what comes under any indirect tax is a good one or not, even amongst disinterested parties. In particular, some people attach great importance to the principle of *uniformity* in the total effective tax rate on each type of consumption (no matter in what form(s) the taxes are imposed), whilst others regard deliberate *variations* in the effective rate as a means of securing social objectives — whether the discouragement of smoking, or the heavier taxation of luxuries than of necessities. My own position in this matter is an indecisive one somewhere in the middle, but I favour a move towards uniformity unless there is some special reason against it in a particular case. (See First Report, pp. 7–8).

Goods versus Services

As regards the actual scope of SET, the most important point to make is probably a negative one. SET is frequently described as a tax on the service trades, but it was never a tax which fell on all services and no goods: one very large industry producing goods — i.e. construction — was included within the ambit of the tax from the outset, whilst many important service industries were exempted by name — notably almost all forms of transport — and many were almost wholly exempted because of the employer's status — e.g. most educational and medical services are run by a Local Authority or a charity. Consequently one is only introducing a red herring if one argues that SET was wrong in principle, because it is logically impossible to draw a line between 'services' and 'production of goods'.

What is of course true is that the absence of a single, simple principle for determining liability to SET is an unfortunate fact of life, but this is equally true in relation to purchase tax, or even value-added tax. This means that the law must make some 'arbitrary' decisions in relation to each of these taxes, but our Parliamentary process is designed to make such arbitrary decisions reflect the popular judgment of what is right or desirable.

A Low Tax over a Wide Area

Although SET is a selective tax, it nevertheless covers a large part of the economy —

1 This argument was not, however, as strong a support for SET as was often implied, because SET fell on many things besides consumer services. See First Report, pp. 12–14.

broadly one-third, whether reckoned in terms of numbers engaged or of contribution to GNP. (See Chapter XI).

At all times, however, it has been a *light* tax in comparison with almost any other selective tax. There are some difficulties in making comparisons, partly because SET rested on the establishment principle and partly because of its unusual incidence (both of which are discussed below). But it we take a simple case on which SET has an unusually high incidence — e.g. domestic service in 1970, when SET was at its peak rate — SET represented a lower percentage of what the consumer paid than purchase tax did for goods charged at the lowest PT rate. Or one can take a more topical example, and say that if VAT is charged at 10% it will be a distinctly heavier tax than SET ever was. (See Chapters III and XI).

This point about the lowness of the tax is in some ways even more apparent if one considers more complicated cases, outside the field of consumer services. Thus in construction the peak figure for the cost of SET in relation to the price of an average Local Authority house was only about 3%, partly because over half the cost of the house consists of materials, which virtually escape SET (see Chapter X). And in distribution SET is so small in relation to the selling price of the goods that we considered its size mainly in relation to the *gross margin* (i.e. the distributor's selling price, less his buying price). (See First Report, Chapter V.)

This combination of wide coverage and a low tax rate meant that the revenue received by the Government (after deducting refunds) was important, but not very important, amounting in 1969/70 to about 4% of the total revenue from taxation (see Chapter XI).

Finally, the fact that the tax has always been a low one has two technical consequences. First, it has meant that our job in trying to assess the effects of SET has required us to attempt extremely fine statistical comparisons: we have been trying to disentangle something which was bound to be small, as the difference between (say) the actual price-rise and what was to be expected on account of other changing factors, with a clear danger of errors in both of these items. And secondly, it means that our assessments reflect the consequences of SET *at a low rate*, and cannot be used in any simple manner to assess what the consequences of a much higher rate would be. This is particularly important in relation to productivity.

Unusual Incidence

SET has an incidence which is very different from that of most indirect taxes. This is true not only of its *legal* incidence — 'who pays it in the first instance' — but also of its ultimate incidence.

Chapter XVII examined the incidence of SET as between the four main categories of final expenditures in the country — personal consumption, Government consumption, investment and exports — and also emphasized that a substantial part[1] of the burden 'disappears' through the extra productivity induced by SET. The most striking feature is the high incidence on *investment*, caused by the inclusion of construction within the ambit of the tax. There was also a significant impact on *exports*, which reflects the fact that there is no method of giving a rebate of SET paid in the

---

1   This was shown in Table XVII.4 as about 40% of the whole, but the figures for productivity gain were only illustrative (though intended to be on the conservative side).

course of producing these, even at the final stage of production, let alone at the earlier ones. The boundaries of SET were chosen in such a way as to reduce this factor — e.g. by exempting not only manufacturing, but also transport, and by such devices as the effective exemption of manufacturers' distributive establishments (which includes most of their exporting organisations). Nevertheless there is a significant export content (direct or indirect) in the activities of the SET sector, and this was bound to be true if the field of the tax was defined in terms of establishments, rather than by reference to activities: the use of employment as the basis of the tax makes the latter approach administratively impossible, unless apportionment is used to a frightening extent.[1]

The incidence of SET on particular items within the consumption field was also unusual. Percentagewise, it was naturally highest on consumer services such as hairdressing, domestic service or dry cleaning, which largely escape other taxes. Nearly half of the revenue attributed to this field, however, came from the distribution of goods bought by consumers (see Table XVII.2): here the tax represents a very small part of the price of the goods, and applies whether they have already been subjected to heavy taxes of a different kind (e.g. cigarettes, fur coats), or have escaped altogether (most food, newspapers) or even been subsidised.

My own shorthand summary of the incidence of SET on personal consumption is to think of it as applying at varying rates to almost all forms of consumption, but with all the rates being *very* low, except in the case of consumer services, where the rate was merely 'low'.

The Working and Administration of SET

Every tax is peculiar in one way or another, so far as its working and administration are concerned; and every tax creates anomalies and involves costs of collection. SET had however a number of really special features, which make it particularly necessary to study its administrative details and working: one must, however, always remember that SET is not to be condemned because it is not perfect in these matters, because no tax ever is. (See First Report, page 7).

Methods and Costs of Collection

I have nothing to add to what was said in the First Report (pages 10—12). At first sight, it *seems* a strange way of proceeding to collect some £2,000 million in 1970 by adding SET to the national insurance stamp of all employees, and then to pay back three-quarters of it as refunds: but in fact it was an efficient way of doing the job (though obviously open to improvement in detail), which kept the total costs

---

1   In my view, however, it is not a very serious criticism of an indirect tax that it is unremitted on exports, provided that the tax has only a small impact on any particular item and this is widely dispersed over most types of exports. In that case the effect is primarily to influence the equilibrium level of the exchange rate associated with any particular level of money wage-rates etc.

   This view is set out in my article in *The British Tax Review* for March 1958, and discussed on pages 8—9 of the First Report.

of administration down to a low level, both for the Government and for the employers.[1]

Forced Loan from Non-SET Sector

One feature of the collection system attracted an amount of attention which seems to me to have been mis-conceived. Manufacturers and others who were eligible for refunds had to invest working capital in paying SET when it was introduced, and this constituted effectively a forced loan to the Government, which would remain outstanding until the tax was abolished and the refunds had all been made. The size of this loan was increased when the rate for SET was raised, and reduced in 1971 when the rate was halved. The whole procedure was attacked as constituting a terrible burden on industry.

The first point to be made about this forced loan is that it did not constitute a drain on national savings, or anything of that kind. If the Government had not borrowed the money in this way, it would have borrowed it in some other way. The 'organisational' effects of the loan can only be considered in the light of the changes in monetary policy which it induced.

Similarly, the fact that the loan was interest-free did not constitute a drain on the national income: industry's loss was the Government's gain, and both are part of the national community. Even the distributional implications were probably much less than they might seem: if the Government had had to pay interest, it might well have increased taxation.

To get beyond these almost tautological (but nevertheless important) points, one can adopt three different approaches.

The first is to make a rough assessment of how much money was really at stake (whilst recognising that this will be a *gross* figure, with no allowance for alternative action which the Government would probably have taken in the absence of this loan — e.g. by raising taxation). On this, we can say that in 1970 the total refunds made (excluding the 'imputed' one in respect of Government employees) were about £1,364 million. If we put the average interval between in-payment by the employer and refund at 3 months,[2] the average size of the loan would be £340 million Interest on this at 8% would be about £27 million per year — and of course this would in most cases have been liable to direct taxes, if it had in fact been paid.

---

1 Perhaps I *should* add one topical comment to what was said in the First Report. The value-added tax, which is to replace SET, rests even more heavily on the principle of paying-in and getting-back. It is true that the refund on a trader's inputs is secured by subtracting the amount due to him from the in-payment due on his output, and the refund is not simply a claim to get back what the trader himself has paid in. This may seem to armchair critics to remove the 'absurdity' inherent in the SET procedure, but to the man on the job it merely means a lot more work. And of course some traders (notably exporters) will receive an actual cash refund.

2 Claims for refunds could be made quarterly, so that *if* the insurance stamps were bought at the due date (or equivalent measures adopted for bulk payments) the minimum interval was 1½ months, even if claims were made and handled instantaneously. In fact the delay in the Department of Employment had become very short, unless there were a dispute. Employers' delays varied a lot, and claims for two quarters on one form were quite common. (See Appendix G).

One can compare this figure with all sorts of yardsticks, but one interesting one is the net revenue collected from SET in 1970 of £533 million: if the £27 million is regarded as taxation accidentally collected from the wrong people, it is not very large in relation to the amount paid by the intended victims. Moreover it was spread fairly evenly over about two-thirds of the whole economy, so that the burden on any particular employer was very small, and the difference between this and the burden of a substitute tax was even smaller. One must also remember that 1970 was the peak year for SET and so for the size of the forced loan.

The second approach is to judge from the behaviour of industrial spokesmen and commentators, both before the introduction (or increase) of SET, and after the event. My impression is that there was considerable worry about the forced loan before SET was introduced, and that this was by no means confined to interested parties: the concern was not so much about the loss of interest, but about the difficulty for many businesses which were in an illiquid position of finding the finance. When the tax became payable, however, there seemed to be an almost total absence of authenticated cases of difficulty on this account:[1] presumably the financial system proved sufficiently flexible in practice to cover the requirement (just as it did in most cases when import deposit receipts created a much more severe problem). Furthermore, the warnings about impending difficulties arising out of the forced loan barely reappeared when the increases in SET were announced, although this would increase its size, and I am not aware of any real difficulties being reported after the increases had become effective.

The third approach is to judge from the actions of individual employers in claiming refunds. The slowness with which many of these claims were submitted — including the practice of covering two quarters on one claim — does not suggest that the advance payments were creating an acute shortage of finance.

The Establishment Principle

In one important matter, SET differs from most indirect taxes: the basic general rule is that effective liability is determined on an *establishment* basis, for the whole establishment, rather than applying to those parts of its activity which are regarded as within the scope of the tax, and not to the rest. This inevitably produces anomalies, which have been discussed at some length in Chapter XVI of this Report and in Chapters XVI to XIX of the First Report. The anomalies are particularly acute in construction (see Chapter XVI), and also in the competition between wholesalers and manufacturers' distributive organisations (see First Report, Chapters XVI and XIX).

The Public Sector

Another source of anomalies was the fact that certain employers were entitled to refunds on the basis of their *status*, rather than the industrial classification of their activities. We discussed this matter in Chapter XVI of this Report, and also on page 186 of the First Report. In brief, our main conclusion was that the quantitative

---

1 The discussion is of course confined to the non-SET sector, in which the tax would be refunded. We did get a number of cases reported to us of businesses closing or contracting greatly because they could not find the money to pay SET, but these were in the SET sector, so that the payment would not be refunded.

effects of the anomalies were not very great, but that it would have been economically more rational to get away from this dual approach, and to make industrial activity the effective criterion: this could usefully have been coupled with an extension of the number of industries made eligible for refund (e.g. to cover health services and education) and an increase in the grant from the Central Government to Local Authorities (see pages 141 to 142).

Quite apart from any gain in economic efficiency, this is a matter in which it is wise that justice should be seen to be done between the public and private sectors.

Earnings as Basis for the Tax?

The First Report discussed the economic case for relating the tax to the *earnings* of workers in the selected industries, rather than having a flat rate for each of four age-and-sex groups, with concessions for part-timers and elderly workers (see pages 182–183). We have little doubt that it would be more logical to have a selective *payroll* tax rather than a selective *employment* tax, and the administrative reason for adopting the latter (to fit in with the flat-rate system of national insurance stamps) would disappear with a change of the national insurance contribution to an earnings-related basis.

Exemption of Self-Employed Workers

The economic case against the exemption of self-employed workers was set out in the First Report, pages 177 to 181, which also considered the administrative problems; we have added further points on pages 142 to 144 of this Report, based on our investigations in the field of near-distribution.

Here again the administrative problem would have been greatly changed under the Labour Government's proposal to collect SET through the P.A.Y.E. machinery. (See First Report, page 179, quoting the Chancellor's statement of 17th July, 1969.)

The Economic Effects of SET

The main task given to us was to examine the effects of SET on prices, margins and productivity in the SET sector. We have had to be very careful to emphasize that this is not the same thing as making a comparison between pre-SET and post-SET years ('the historical record'), and to insist that our job was to compare what did happen with what would have happened 'in the absence of SET': and we have defined the hypothetical alternative position as one in which the Government would have introduced an alternative tax, and perhaps changed other policies as well, so as *inter alia* to produce the same level of employment as actually prevailed. (See especially Chapters I and XVII.)

It is useful to start by considering what results traditional analysis would lead one to expect from a conventional indirect tax, which had the same characteristics as SET — wide coverage and low rate — whilst making the same assumptions about Government policies on the level of employment. We can then contrast these results with what we have concluded about the effects of SET, and speculate about the reasons for the differences.

Traditional View of Effects of Indirect Tax

Whilst many different ways of portraying the process are adopted, the conventional answers show the following features as their central point of reference, from which one measures minor deviations which might be caused by special circumstances:

  (a) In the long run the tax would be passed on to the buyer in the form of higher prices, but it might not be fully passed on at first.
  (b) The output of the goods would be slightly reduced, but the reduction might well be very small even in the long run.
  (c) The effect on profitability might be slightly adverse in the short run, but would be negligible in the long run.
  (d) The effect on productivity would probably be negligible in the long run, and might be downwards at first.[1]

It must be confessed that this general view rests more on *a priori* reasoning and the experience of officials than on formal empirical research, and there have been many discussions about the special circumstances which would cause departures from it. But so far as I am aware one would not expect these to be of much importance for a low selective tax, which applied to about one-third of the economy.

Comparisons with Findings on SET

Our findings on SET show departures from this picture at several points, as explained below. There is however one difference which seems to play a key role — our finding that SET seems to have induced an increase in productivity. The rest of the findings seem broadly to correspond with what one would expect from the conventional analysis, if one superimposes on it a rise in productivity.

In looking at our findings one must obviously remember the limitations of the statistical analysis on which they rest, and also that they do not necessarily apply equally to each trade within the various groups. Nevertheless it is reasonable to emphasize that such consistency tests as we could apply showed that the assessments which we made of different elements were in fact surprisingly consistent, even though made quite independently. (See First Report Chapter XIII and Chapter VI of this Report.) In the case of distribution their conformity was indeed so close as to cause us amazement, and I had to keep saying to myself that I *knew* that the component parts had been produced independently by different people.[2]

Productivity

As the findings on productivity seem to play a key role, we start with them. They are surprisingly well-established (given the inherent difficulties of research of this kind) in the case of distribution, where the whole set of results — for different years, and for wholesaling and retailing taken separately — holds together remarkably well. They suffer however from the serious drawback that the statistics cannot separate the effects of SET from those of the progressive ending of resale price maintenance,

---

1 I should emphasize once again that all these 'results' are comparisons between what would happen under the tax which is being investigated and what would happen with some other arrangement: they are not concerned with historical movements through time.

2 Cf. First Report, page 115: 'In view of the hazardous nature of the statistical exercise, we were frankly amazed to find that the residuals were so small. Indeed the fact that they are as small as they are, rather than two or three times as big, is largely a matter of good fortune: it is naturally comforting, but it has little real significance'. See also Chapter XIII generally.

which took place over much the same period:[1] the actual figures are in consequence too high to reflect the effect of SET by itself.

For the other trades the evidence is statistically very weak – see the last section of Chapter X for construction and Chapter XIII for services other than distribution. Nevertheless I personally find the evidence for a modest productivity gain moderately persuasive, especially when taken with the price results shown in Chapter XII and the consistency test for near distribution in Chapter VI. If there were a method of establishing the true answer, and I were asked which way I would like to bet before the assessment was made, I would choose the positive side, as against a combination of nil and negative.

Prices

For prices, our findings in each of the three sectors were that SET had caused a rise in prices, but that the rise was less than would have been produced by a full passing-on of the tax. The position may be broadly summarised as follows:

(a) For distribution, the combined effects of SET and the ending of RPM seemed to leave gross margins (which are the logical counterpart of prices in this trade) at much the same level in the second year of SET as one would have expected in the absence of these two factors, or even a little lower. (See First Report, Chapter XIII, or Appendix A of this Report, which reproduces the final chapter of that Report, and so includes a summary statement).

Since the ending of RPM would clearly lower margins, the most natural conclusion about the effects of SET by itself in that year is that it raised gross margins in both retailing and wholesaling, but by an amount which was, in my view, probably less than the full amount of the tax. We have no evidence for later years, when there were increases both in SET and in our estimate of the productivity gain, but it would be very odd if this general result were disturbed.

(b) For other services to consumers Chapter XIII seems to show conclusively that the introduction of SET caused a rise in prices, and that the increases in rate caused further rises. Our finding was that these increases were probably rather less than would be produced by a full passing-on of the tax, but this differential cannot be regarded as beyond dispute.

(c) For construction we could only apply the test to Local Authority houses, and even for these the statistics are much weaker: but our conclusion was the same as in (b). (See Chapter X, last section)

In all three sectors, therefore, the outcome on prices is what we would expect from the conventional assumption of full passing-on, coupled with a partial off-set through the reduction in costs caused by the gain in productivity.

Output

Our terms of reference did not call on us to study the effects of SET on the level of output in the trades covered by it, but one can draw some limited deductions by combining the work which we did on numbers engaged (Chapter XIV) and on

1 See in particular First Report, pages 99–100.

productivity. The analysis reported briefly in Chapter XVII, dealing with the pattern of consumption, is also of some relevance.

From all this, one can deduce an implicit finding, which is essentially that output of the SET sector was a little greater than it would have been in the alternative position. This reflects the fact that the productivity gain raised the level of the gross national product (since we assumed Government policy would have produced the same level of employment in either case): the resultant increase in aggregate real demand outweighed the loss of SET-sector output through the diversion of demand.

This finding rests on a mixture of theoretical assumption and empirical research, but there is sufficient empirical research involved to justify its inclusion (since the facts could have contradicted the theoretical assumption). The departure from the conventional result (a fall in output) is clearly attributable to the productivity gain.

Profitability

Our findings here are limited to distribution and near-distribution, because of the curtailment of our research. For distribution, Chapter XIII of the First Report leaves me in no doubt that profitability in both retailing and wholesaling had been reduced, both in 1967/8 and in 1968/9, relatively to what would have been expected in the absence of abnormal new factors. This reflected, however, the combined effects of SET and the ending of RPM, and it requires a complete act of faith to say anything about what the effect of SET by itself would have been. My own belief that it would have lowered profits somewhat probably reflects *a priori* views, rather than statistical findings, but at least these did not contradict it.

On near-distribution the tentative conclusion of Chapter VI was that SET had slightly reduced profitability both in 1967/8 and 1968/9, but the evidence is not very strong.

It would be presumptuous to assert positively that these findings correspond to what one would expect from the conventional analysis, plus a productivity gain, because both the findings and the expectations are uncertain. But at least there is no obvious conflict between them.

We are left, therefore, with the problem of explaining why SET had a positive effect on productivity: if that can be explained, the other departures from the conventional results fall into place. Nevertheless, our attempts at an explanation need not assume only a one-way process of causation: in so far as there may be factors which make it difficult for traders to pass on the whole of SET in higher prices, this may help to enforce a rise in productivity.

Reasons for SET Effect on Productivity

It is easiest to examine the possible reasons why SET led to increased productivity by concentrating first on the particular case of retailing, about which we have the best information: we can then add a few, more speculative remarks about the main differences between that trade and others. We start also with some rather drastic simplifying assumptions, which help to bring out certain points, and then see how the possibilities are enlarged when these are relaxed.

Simplifying Assumptions

Initially, then, we make the following assumptions:

(a) Differences between retailers are not important, either as regards the size of their business or their trading method.

(b) We ignore all normal trend developments — e.g. growth in the volume of trade caused by the rise in the national income, the secular rise in productivity. (This enables us to concentrate on the *effects* of SET, as against the historical record).

(c) There is no change in the purchase prices of the goods, paid by the retailers, or in wage-rates, or in any other cost item (apart from the addition of SET).

(d) The total volume of goods sold is unaffected.

(e) We ignore problems arising out of the exemption of self-employed workers from SET.

With these simplifications, the traditional analysis in its simplest form might portray the process something like this. All traders would suffer an increase in costs as a result of SET, and each would know that his rivals were also suffering from the same increase. Hence each would consider that he could increase his margin to cover the extra cost, without losing sales volume, because his rivals would be doing the same thing.[1] Consequently all do raise their margins, and as the total volume of sales is unchanged (because demand is increased, in money terms, by the absence of the alternative tax) the original position is reproduced, so far as the volume of sales and employment are concerned.

A slight modification of this would be to say that retailers might lower their standard of service somewhat, by employing less labour per article sold: labour is now more expensive relative to the cost of the goods, and each trader may reckon that consumers would prefer to deal with him if he made a smaller increase in margin (perhaps none at all), and gave rather worse service — e.g. if he more frequently kept them waiting for attention (or gave them less of it when their turn came). In this way one would get a rather spurious rise in productivity, as conventionally measured, and a rise in margins which did not reflect a full passing-on of SET.

As has been repeatedly emphasized in our two Reports (and indeed in my 1966 article, reproduced in Appendix A of the First Report), the 'quality' problem makes clear-cut answers almost impossible.

First Weakness in Traditional Approach

There is one important weakness in this traditional analysis, which applies even within the field set by our simplifying assumptions. This is that in retailing many selling prices are fixed by adding a *percentage* margin to the price paid by the retailer.[2] These percentages have shown a long-term tendency to rise somewhat in most types of retailing, but the margins have of course been enormously more stable than they would have been if they had been fixed in *cash* terms (as they are for a

---

1 Those who like to analyse the matter by drawing a cost curve for the individual retailer and the (expected) demand curve for his wares will realise that the demand curve would be raised by SET, because his expected sales at any price depend on what he assumes his rivals to be charging.

2 See First Report, pages 73–74.

packet of cigarettes): the general course of inflation, and particular changes affecting retailers (e.g. the rise of local rates as a percentage of turnover) have left various key rates (e.g. '$33\frac{1}{3}$% on returns') almost unaffected. The resultant stickiness of gross margins greatly weakens the force of the argument that each retailer will cover his increased costs by putting up his margin, in the confident hope that others will follow suit. It implies that, in comparison with the traditional approach, the pressure will be much more to cut costs, even if that has an adverse effect on the quality of the service.

The strength of this point must not however be exaggerated. To start off with, our figures for the gross margin in retailing showed it as significantly higher in each of the post-SET years than it was in 1965/6. (See First Report, Table XIII.2 on page 112); our conclusion that it was *lower than was to be expected* in the absence of the SET/RPM combination rested on our allowance for the upward trend in gross margins, deduced mainly from the Censuses of Distribution (See First Report, pp. 301–308). One clearly cannot *both* assume that gross margins have an upward trend anyhow *and* argue that they are so rigidly conventional that an increase in costs through SET can have no effect on them.[1]

Apart from this, our information from retailers — especially some of the interviews — showed clearly that pricing was not *simply* a matter of adding a standard percentage on everything within a given product group: there was quite a lot of discretion for the price-fixers, and they were much concerned to achieve a certain target percentage for each department or other unit. These percentages for gross margins were not immutable from year to year, and were indeed influenced by what was happening to costs. One very helpful trader described how he and his rivals had behaved as follows: 'When SET was announced we all knew that we had to get the over-all gross margin up, and we watched each other like tiger-cats to see where we could do it without losing competitive power'. This applied, however, to a particularly competitive part of the field.

Our provisional conclusion was that the existence of conventional margins and the smallness of SET (equivalent to some 1% of turnover when it was introduced) had put more of the emphasis on cost-saving (even at the expense of quality of service) than the traditional analysis would lead one to expect, and had also probably led to some acceptance of the extra cost without a sufficient departure from conventional margins to cover it, at the expense of profits. But in some parts of the retail field this factor was not of much importance, and in none was it decisive: gross margins could be affected by SET, and indeed were.

More Realistic Analysis

If we now relax some of the simplifying assumptions made above, we find a number of reasons why the effect of SET on productivity would probably be bigger than our simple picture suggests, and represent a more 'genuine' gain.

Difference Between Traders

The fact that traders are not all alike has a number of implications, which are particularly important because SET is not a tax on turnover, but rather a tax on the

---

1 See also the historical movements for different types of retailing, given in Chapter VI of the First Report.

principal item of expenses — labour. We have already seen that this would tend to lead retailers to reduce the amount of labour employed per article sold, even if retailers were all alike. But the existence of differences between retailers adds to this effect in the following ways:

(a) SET raises costs more severely (in relation to turnover) for retailers who give an elaborate service than for those who use simpler and less labour-intensive methods. This not only gives the managers of such shops a special incentive to try to improve their efficiency, without lowering the standard of their service, but may also induce them to change to a less elaborate way of doing business. As explained in the First Report, such a change may not imply any loss of welfare to the consumer (see First Report, pages 74—75), although in other cases it may do so. An alternative outcome may be that the retailer sells out to a rival or newcomer with more 'modern' ideas — perhaps a multiple, in process of expansion. Any of these results is likely to raise the recorded level of productivity, and this would also happen if customers were induced to shift their business to other shops, because the old-fashioned shop raises its margins by more than the average amount.

(b) SET also raises costs more severely, in relation to turnover, for the shop which is simply inefficient in its use of labour, without thereby giving a superior service.[1] This tends to hasten the disappearance of the inefficient managements: they may be replaced by new shopkeepers (possibly on a take-over basis) operating in the same premises, or the shop may be converted to some other use, leaving the more efficient shops to do extra business. In either case, the productivity of the industry should benefit.

As an extension of this last point, the theory has been advanced that the gain in productivity would come very largely from the effect of SET in concentrating the trade into a smaller number of shops than would otherwise have been in business, which would be able to make the sales without having to make a proportionate increase in their staff. We worked hard on attempts to test whether this factor had actually been important or not, and set out our results in Chapter IX of this Report. The conclusion was that our statistical and other information provided no real evidence that this factor had been of any quantitative importance, although the statistics are not accurate enough to rule out the possibility of its having made some contribution.

Acceleration of Trends

Our simplifying assumptions included one which ruled out the existence of trends of all kinds, in the interests of simplicity of presentation. This is liable, however, to mean that one misses something which is of real importance. If one is comparing two static positions, one is apt to assume that each of them represents an equilibrium, in which all the adjustments which are worth making have been made. In real life, however, new methods are always in process of being substituted for old, and it is much easier to envisage that an increase in labour-costs would *accelerate* some such

---

1 As explained in the First Report, page 16, the inefficient shop will pay more in SET than an efficient rival doing the same amount of turnover, whereas under a value-added tax the payments would be equal, and under a corporation tax the efficient firm would pay more.

development, than it would be to envisage its *initiating* a trend which did not exist. This was, indeed, the story which we were repeatedly told both on our question-naires and in our interviews: 'SET did not lead to anything being done which would not have been done anyhow, but it did lead to its being done more rapidly'.

Looking at the same point from a slightly different angle, it seemed as if SET had to some extent produced a 'shock' effect by concentrating attention on the need to move more rapidly.

Having made this point, I should perhaps add that it does not imply that SET would lead to a spurt in method-improvements, followed by an unusually quiet period. Knowledge is not something of which there is a limited amount to be ac-quired and applied, but rather something where experience leads to further ideas.

Exemption for the Self-Employed

The above factors have, on the whole, been producing reasons why the outcome on productivity would be better than might appear from the simple analysis, although we have also sought to indicate limitations on the probable strength of some factors which might seem likely to operate.[1]

When we come to the fact that self-employed workers are exempt from SET, however, it seems that we are dealing with a factor which will to some extent counter-act the ones making for a gain in productivity. Thus the firms which might most easily have been put out of business, because they used a lot of labour in re-lation to turnover, are largely firms in which a high proportion of the workers escape SET because they are self-employed. There may even be some tendency for the num-ber of these businesses to increase, relatively to what would otherwise have happened.

This whole matter is discussed in the First Report, pages 177–182, including the social considerations.

Summary on Retailing

This collection of factors does not lend itself to any simple summary, but it does perhaps provide some theoretical analysis as to why a selective tax on the employ-ees in the industry should have led to a gain in recorded productivity. As was fore-shadowed, the explanation lies partly in the impact of the pricing system on methods of working and productivity, even though in the previous section we stressed the fact that a gain in productivity essentially explained why the rise in prices was less than one traditionally expects from an indirect tax.

Position in Other Trades

So far as *wholesaling* is concerned, nearly all the considerations mentioned above apply, but there is one special factor which needs to be emphasized. For many wholesalers, there really was very little possibility of raising their margins to the full

---

1 Even in the case of the inefficient shops, which would pay more in SET than their efficient rivals, the importance of the tax factor should not be exaggerated. The inefficient firm is already having to pay wages to more workers, and this fact is quantitatively more important than the additional handicap imposed by paying more SET. The imperfection of the retail market which made the continued existence of the inefficient firm possible in the face of the big handicap on wages may be sufficient to cover the smaller handicap on SET as well: but of course the latter may be the last straw which breaks the camel's back.

extent needed to cover SET on their old method of working (or indeed of raising them at all), because they were in competition with direct sales by manufacturers, who escaped SET. This put the emphasis very much on cost-saving (and reduction of profits), and in many respects the cost-saving was secured at the expense of a reduced quality of service to their customers. Thus in the grocery field there was a rapid development of cash-and-carry wholesaling, which brings certain advantages to the customer, but offers him much less in other ways. And wholesalers were also led to reduce the frequency of their calls on small retailers, or to insist on minimum-size orders: this may have been thoroughly justifiable in terms of the economics of the previous service rendered, but clearly meant a deterioration of quality. (See First Report, Chapters XVI to XIX).

As regards *other service trades*, the main difference from the analysis presented for retailing is in the opposite direction: there was little or nothing to correspond with the stickiness of conventional gross margins, but the other factors broadly applied.

Reversibility?

Finally, the obvious question which one would *like* to answer is whether the effect of SET on productivity (and indeed its other effects) will simply be reversed when SET is removed. On this our statistical research throws no light but the qualitative information which we obtained about the reasons for the gain — plus the speculative analysis in this section — do suggest that some of the gain will be retained. Unfortunately there will be no way of testing this except by also assessing the effects of the value-added tax which replaces SET.

Appendix A
Main Findings in the First Report

*This Appendix reproduces, with minor corrections, Chapter XX of the First Report:
all cross-references in it relate to pages and chapters of that Report.*

This chapter is in no sense a summary of the Report, much of which does not lend itself to such treatment. It states the principal findings of a statistical kind, adding enough exposition of the problems involved to explain their broad meaning. Apart from that, it gives a brief guide to the structure of the Report, which may help readers to find where the problems in which they are interested are discussed, and how they fit with the rest of the analysis; and on occasions it indicates briefly some of the conclusions.

Logical Nature of the Enquiry

First, it is essential to be clear that the enquiry is concerned with the effects of having a selective employment tax as an *alternative* to having additional taxation of some other kind, which would have a broadly equal effect on the balance between overall demand in the economy and potential supply. When SET was introduced in 1966 it constituted a net addition to taxation, rather than a replacement of some other tax, but the Report is *not* concerned with this side of the matter. (See pages 3 and 21.)

Secondly, the Report tries to assess these effects by comparing what *has* happened with what *would have happened* under an alternative tax. The straight comparison between 'before SET' and 'after SET' — which we call 'the historical record' — can tell us little or nothing about 'the effects of SET': these can only be assessed by comparing 'what actually happened' with what would otherwise have been 'expected' under similar general conditions, on the basis of an econometric analysis of pre-SET statistics.

Thirdly, one must be clear what the econometric analysis can and cannot do in saying what would otherwise have been expected. Broadly speaking, it can allow for the basic trend in the item under investigation and for all factors which affect the distributive trades through the *level of demand* or through the *general state of the labour market* — which means that allowance has been made for the effects of the general squeeze on internal demand in the various years; naturally, one cannot expect any statistical analysis to do this perfectly but some guidance is available about its accuracy, and is given in the text.

On the other hand the econometric analysis does *not* allow for such factors as the ending of resale price maintenance, which affect distribution by altering the nature of the competitive process. Our statistical results must, therefore, be regarded as measuring the combined effects of SET and other 'abnormal new factors' of this kind – of which the really important one is the progressive ending of resale price maintenance on more and more goods.

Productivity, Margins and Expenses

The assessment of the effects of abnormal new factors on productivity are given in Chapter XI (retailing) and Chapter XII (wholesaling). Particular attention is drawn to the discussion of reliability in the last part of each chapter, which leads to the conclusion that the figures can be used with fair confidence for broad purposes, but that assessments of fine differences (e.g. between the gain in productivity in wholesaling for 1967 and 1968) are subject to a large proportionate error. Movements in output were assessed by reference to changes in the 'volume' of goods sold, without any allowance for changes in the average quality of the service supplied with the goods.

Table A.1 shows the *actual* level of productivity in each year, taking 1965 as 100, in contrast with the level which would have been *expected*, on the basis of pre-SET experience: there are various ways in which this 'expected' figure can be assessed (see the concluding part of Chapter XI), but, to take an example, we think it unlikely that any reputable method would have altered the 1968 figure by much more than 1½ units. The final column shows the percentage gain in productivity above the level which was 'expected'.

TABLE A.1 *Gain in Productivity as a Result of Abnormal New Factors*

(Index Numbers, 1965 = 100)

	Actual productivity	'Expected' productivity (on pre-SET experience)	Difference as a percentage of 'Expected' productivity
Retailers			
1966	102.5	100.8	1.7
1967	106.0	102.6	3.3
1968	111.1	105.6	5.1
Non-Industrial Wholesalers			
1966	103.1	101.0	2.0
1967	105.9	100.5	5.4
1968	110.2	104.2	5.8

The gain in productivity may also be expressed by saying that without it the distributive trades would have required more labour than they in fact had: the difference (in terms of full-time-equivalent persons) comes out for 1968 at rather over 100,000 in retailing and 30,000 in wholesaling. It is not possible to say what types of people would have been recruited or retained to produce this difference, or what they were doing in 1968.

Payroll Costs

The saving of labour through higher productivity has helped to keep down the cost of payroll as a percentage of sales; on the other hand the payment of SET has of course raised payroll costs. Table A.2 shows the *actual* movement of payroll costs, as derived from our samples of traders, and the figures for these two elements.

It will be seen that the saving in payroll costs through higher productivity went a long way towards off-setting the cost of SET.

Margins

Table A.3 shows the movements in gross margins and in net margins which we derived from our combined sample of retailers, together with the movements which were 'expected' on the basis of the econometric analysis, and hence the 'effects' of the abnormal new factors.

TABLE A.2 *Payroll Costs and SET*

(All figures are percentages of sales)

	1965−6	1966−7	1967−8	1968−9
Retailing				
Actual payroll (excluding SET)	12.38	12.63	12.56	12.47
Additional payroll needed if productivity had been at 'expected' level	—	0.21	0.41	0.64
SET payment	—	0.33	0.72	0.83
Effects of abnormal new factors on payroll cost (including SET)	—	+0.12	+0.31	+0.19
Wholesaling				
Actual payroll (excluding SET)	5.51	5.58	5.57	5.58
Additional payroll needed if productivity had been at 'expected' level	—	0.11	0.30	0.32
SET payment	—	0.15	0.31	0.34
Effects of abnormal new factors on payroll cost (including SET)	—	+0.04	+0.01	+0.02

Note:
The retailing figures cover our returns from both 'large retailers' and 'smaller retailers'.
The wholesale figures relate to those from 'traditional wholesalers' only.

TABLE A.3 *Movements[a] in Retail Margins since* 1965−6

(Percentage Points)

	1966−7	1967−8	1968−9
Gross Margins			
Actual movement (to year shown)	0.28	0.66	(0.57)
Expected movement (to year shown)	0.41	0.42	1.25
Effects of abnormal new factors	−0.13	0.24	(−0.68)
Net Margins			
Actual movement (to year shown)	−0.47	−0.55	(−0.75)
Expected movement (to year shown)	0.07	−0.25	0.22
Effects of abnormal new factors	−0.54	−0.30	(−0.97)

(a) All figures represent the difference between the percentage margin in the year shown and the percentage in 1965−6, when the figures were: gross margin 25.86 per cent, net margin 6.51 per cent. Net margins are calculated before any allowance for rent or interest.

The 'actual' figures for 1968−9 are based on a smaller number of returns linked through 1967−8.

186

The reliability of these figures is discussed in Chapter XIII, and (very briefly) in the next section.

A similar analysis was attempted for wholesalers, but we could not find sufficient data about pre-SET experience for a proper econometric analysis. The data and analysis presented in Chapter XIII give some support to the idea that one should use an adjusted version of the factors which were used for retailing, but it does not seem right to do more in this summary than say that the abnormal new factors have reduced net margins. (See Table XIII.7.)

Overall View

The above results are of course subject to considerable statistical uncertainty, and have been prepared by quite independent methods, so that there was a real danger that they might be seriously inconsistent – i.e. that the effect on gross margins would not be equal to the sum of the effects on costs and on net margins. The tests of this point in Chapter XIII were, however, quite surprisingly reassuring – though they cannot, of course, eliminate the danger of there being a serious error in (say) gross margin, which is balanced by a serious error in the same direction in net margin.

Having regard to the dangers of statistical errors, we consider it best to draw on all our statistical results for both 1967–8 and 1968–9, and make a broad statement of our conclusions for retailing and traditional wholesaling together: this might be regarded as applicable to the second year of SET (ending in September 1968), when the rate of tax was 25s. per week for a man. It is as follows:

(a) Gross margins were higher than before the introduction of SET, but the average rise was if anything rather smaller than one would have expected on the basis of past experience.

To put this another way, in conditions of progressive ending of RPM, the distributors *as a whole* did not make any recovery from the consumers to set against the cost of SET, and indeed probably received *less* in the way of gross margins than was to be expected on past experience.

This outcome was the result of different experiences in different trades, some of which received a considerably smaller gross margin than would have been expected in the absence of abnormal new factors – presumably because the ending of RPM had a large effect on them.

(b) The volume of sales per person engaged in distribution (reckoned in terms of full-time-equivalents) showed a considerably greater rise compared with 1965–6 than past experience would have led us to expect. This abnormal increase in productivity led to a saving on payroll costs which, in the trade as a whole, went a long way towards covering the cost of SET.

(c) The distributors earned a net profit (before rent, interest or taxation) which represented a decidedly lower percentage of sales than prevailed before the introduction of SET. Allowing for the movement which one would have expected in view of the conjunctural factors, the combined effect of SET and the RPM changes was to lower profits (on average) by the equivalent of more than half the cost of SET.

A rather more formal statement of these conclusions is to be found in the final section of Chapter XIII.

Other Statistical Findings

The above findings are in rather cold statistical terms. Chapters XIV and XV set out our findings about the effects of abnormal new factors on such matters as the quality of service, methods of working, the composition of the labour force and the number of shops (or rather their 'selling capacity').

The main finding was, in a sense, that these effects had been unsensational, but that they might nevertheless be of some importance, particularly in the longer run. The impact of SET and/or RPM seems to have been largely to *accelerate* the taking of action which would have been worthwhile anyhow — e.g. introduction of more self-service or more self-selection.

Understandably enough, there has been a move away from the employment of part-timers working for twenty-one to thirty hours a week, which involves the payment of the full amount for SET. There seems also to have been some slight shift towards female labour.

The investigation of the effects on the selling capacity of the retail industry was greatly handicapped by the fact that certain official statistics were not available beyond March 1967, so that the conclusions (given at the end of Chapter XIV) are very tentative.

Anomalies in SET

The Report considers, in Chapter II, various general arguments about the allegedly anomalous nature of SET: most of these are regarded as mis-understandings of the functions of the tax — which has also suffered greatly in public esteem through the almost universal mis-understanding of its objective (see pages 5 and 21).

The anomalies which the Report seeks to examine are essentially those in which one competitor pays the tax and another does not. These arise most acutely in wholesaling, and the issues are discussed at some length in Chapter XVI (for traditional wholesalers) and Chapter XIX (for industrial wholesalers). The main cause of the anomalies is competition between a taxed wholesaler and a manufacturer selling direct, since the latter usually escapes SET even in his distributive establishments: there are also, however, important anomalies — particularly in industrial wholesaling — where some wholesalers secure complete or partial refunds and others do not.

The discussion includes a review of the various ways in which the anomalies might be mitigated, either by extending the scope of SET to establishments which now escape or by widening the scope for refunds. In each case consideration is given to the creation of new anomalies around the revised border-line.

Other types of anomaly are discussed in Chapter XVII, notably those arising out of the exemption of self-employed workers, the method of assessing SET and competition with the Public Sector.

The Historical Record

Although the effects of SET, or any other factor, can only be assessed by a comparison between what actually happened and an 'expected' position, nevertheless the historical record is of considerable interest in itself. The information which we assembled on this is given systematically in Chapters VI to IX: it is in much greater detail than could be used for the subsequent analysis, and gives (for example) separate figures for individual trades.

This is preceded by Chapter V, which shows the size of SET in relation to a wide variety of yardsticks: without this it is very easy to have a quite false idea of the size of the thing under discussion.

Appendix B
The DAE Surveys

This Appendix describes the methods used in our own enquiries into the near-distributive trades, and the surveys of tenanted public houses which were carried out by the National Federation of Licensed Victuallers and John Tyzack Consultants Ltd.

We consulted the appropriate Trade Associations about the choice of sample, the design of questionnaires, and the method of approach to firms. We are very grateful for the Associations' help in these and other matters: especially for their active support for our requests to their members to cooperate with our enquiries. The Associations and other bodies which assisted us are listed at the end of this Appendix.

The Choice of Sample

We assumed from the outset that the problems of non-response would be such as to preclude truly scientific samples, and that the results we obtained would have to be based on an 'indicative' sample. The method of selection adopted in each case is outlined below.

Catering

(i) *Hotels.* The British Hotels and Restaurants Association (B.H.R.A.) and the Caterers Association of Great Britain (C.A.) selected a sample of 'independent' hoteliers from their lists of active members. We asked them to pick the members to provide a good spread by size, geographical area and type of hotel. The B.H.R.A. also selected a number of 'chains' of hotels from its lists; we requested that all the largest chains should be included. The chains of hotels were asked to select the individual hotels within their groups to give '... a reasonable reflection of your group's hotel activities ...', and most of the chains were asked to provide returns for six hotels.

(ii) *Industrial Caterers.* The questionnaires were sent to all the members and the two largest non-members of the Industrial and Staff Canteens Division of the C.A.

(iii) *Restaurants.* The sampling method was basically the same as that described for hotels except in this case the C.A., not the B.H.R.A., selected the 'chains'. Also, the Restaurateurs' Association of Great Britain provided us with a list of their members from which we selected a random (interval) sample.

(iv) *Managed Public Houses.* The Brewers' Society gave us the names of the six largest brewery companies and a sample of smaller companies. The companies themselves were requested to select individual houses to give a reasonable reflection of their activity by picking different types of public house roughly in proportion to their importance within the company. The number of returns they were asked to make was very roughly proportional to the size of the company.

(v) *Tenanted Public Houses.* We made supplementary, brief surveys of firms drawn from two samples. The reason for not making a full survey was that we were obtaining data, which, at the time, we thought to be comparable, from a study performed in two separate parts for the National Federation of Licensed Victuallers (N.F.L.V.). The sample selected by the Licensed Victuallers Central Protection Society of London Ltd. (Central Board) was a random sample of 119 drawn from their lists of active members. The sample from the N.F.L.V. was a random sample of 100 branch associations. The secretary of each branch association was then asked to select three houses from his membership list and send each of them a form with a covering letter.

Hairdressing

(i) *National Hairdressers Federation (N.H.F.).* This Federation basically represents the small 'independent' hairdresser, and its members employ roughly one-third of the employees in hairdressing. Men's hairdressers are more strongly represented than women's and the sample drawn (380 members) was biased to obtain twice as many women's hairdressers as men's. All the members selected *should* have had employees and therefore been liable to pay SET.

(ii) *Incorporated Guild of Hairdressers, Wigmakers & Perfumerers (Incorporated Guild).* The members of this Guild are normally hairdressers who own a chain of salons, and the membership is probably biased towards women's hairdressers. A random sample (excluding hairdressers known to be operating in retail establishments) was taken.

(iii) We also approached six other hairdressers whom we knew to have large businesses.

(iv) *Local Associations of the N.H.F.* A random sample was selected by the N.H.F. The form used was not designed for the same purpose as the questionnaire to the individual members of the associations, but was purely to obtain information about trends in the numbers of hairdressers in business.

Motor Traders

(i) *Large Motor Traders.* We took a random sample (of 185) of all the main and retail dealers on the membership lists of the Motor Agents' Association (M.A.A.) plus the thirty-eight largest (by turnover) members in England and Wales, plus the ten largest members of the Scottish Motor Trades Association (S.M.T.A.).

(ii) *Small Motor Traders.* A random sample was taken from the membership lists of the M.A.A. and a further selection of the members of the M.A.A. in its Cambridge, Coventry and Norwich Districts was added.

(iii) *Vehicle Builders and Repairers.* A random sample was taken from the Association's Yearbook and to this was added nineteen firms suggested by the Association as being of particular interest (for our investigation of anomalies).

Shoe Repairing

(i) *National Association of Shoe Repair Factories (N.A.S.R.F.).* All fully paid-up members of the Association were sent a form.

(ii) *St. Crispin's Boot Trades Association (St. Crispin's).* The sample was selected by the Association to give a representative cross section of its active members.

(iii) *Local Associations of St. Crispin's.* The form was sent to all the local associations thought to be active at the time. It was not used for the same purpose as the two questionnaires mentioned above, but to obtain background information on the state of the trade.

The Design of the Questionnaires
The aim of the D.A.E. enquiries was, in general, to collect two different types of information: information of an 'accounting' nature covering such things as sales, profits, expenses and employment; and information of a more qualitative nature dealing with the policy of the company and changes in that policy since the introduction of SET.

The discussions with the Trade Associations, and also our experience in the Distributive Trades Enquiry, indicated that the problem of non-response would become impossibly large if we imposed strict requirements for the information we requested in the 'accounting' part of the form, especially since we were often dealing with small business units. We therefore encouraged respondents to give *reasonable estimates* when actual figures were not available, and stated that consistency over the period was more important than conforming to one of our 'standard definitions' if to do so would involve an effort disproportionate to the result achieved. The number of years for which data was requested varied basically with the timing of the questionnaire, as did the format of the tables; some trades were not required to give financial data for the year immediately following the 'pre-SET' year.

Our enquiry into Tenanted Public Houses was a rather more specialised enquiry designed to obtain information to complete gaps in the data which we had received from the N.F.L.V. survey carried out by John Tyzack Consultants Ltd. for submission to the N.B.P.I. in connection with the latter's investigation into beer prices. It therefore only collected information on employment (split into SET rate categories), prices and total sales.

A very low response rate was achieved with the first form for Industrial Caterers which was drawn up after a meeting with representatives of the Industrial Catering and Staff Canteens Division of the C.A. The major reason for this was that the form was rather complicated because this particular trade is one of those in which there are SET anomalies and the form was designed to give a full picture of how these worked out in practice and how important they were. A second, simpler, form was designed, again in consultation with the Association, and was sent with an explanatory letter to those members who had not replied to the earlier request. The response was somewhat improved by this.

Because of the way we sampled chains of hotels and restaurants, and managed public houses, and the fact that hairdressing salons and tenanted public houses are normally owned as single units, we really only had to face the problem of mergers and takeovers in the large motor traders enquiry. Separate figures were obtained for the original business and each of the subsidiaries acquired, whenever this was possible.

The Approach to Firms

Catering Trades

(i) *Hotels*. A form was sent to 'independent' hoteliers (i.e. owners of one, or at most two hotels) early in February 1969. Late in the same month, forms were sent to owners of chains of hotels; each company received one form for the 'group as a whole', and a number of forms (almost identical with those for the 'independent' hotels) to be completed for a number (normally six) of the individual hotels within the group.

A supplementary questionnaire was sent to certain 'independent' hoteliers in July 1969 or later (see below).

After the postal returns had been analysed, a number of hotel owners were interviewed.

(ii) *Industrial Caterers*. The first attempt to obtain information from industrial caterers (in June 1969) was along the lines employed for chains of hotels. The second attempt (in 1970) only asked for a return for the group as a whole, and the forms for individual catering units were abandoned.

No supplementary questionnaire was used, and no interviewing was carried out.

(iii) *Restaurants*. The scheme for collecting data from restaurants was broadly the same as that employed for hotels. The questionnaires to the 'independents' were mailed in April 1969, and those to the chains in May 1969. The supplementary questionnaire was mailed in July 1969 or later. A limited amount of interviewing was done after the postal returns had been analysed.

(iv) *Managed Public Houses*. For this trade, the method adopted was broadly similar to that used for hotel chains. The questionnaires were mailed in July 1969. Some interviewing was carried out after the analysis of the returns had been completed.

Hairdressing

The forms were sent to members of the N.H.F. in October 1969, and to members of the Incorporated Guild in April 1970. The forms were identical and the respondent was asked to complete the form for all the establishments which he owned and which were mainly engaged in hairdressing. No supplementary questionnaire was used, and no interviewing was done.

The questionnaire on 'numbers of hairdressers' was sent to the sample of local associations of the N.H.F. in March 1970.

Motor Trades

Postal enquiries were sent to the 'large motor traders' in February and March 1969, to the 'small motor traders' in March and April 1969, and to the specialist repairers in April and May 1969. When the results had been analysed, a number of interviews were conducted.

The large motor traders were offered a choice of replying for the group as a whole or, after arranging details with us, submitting returns for individual establishments. The other two sections were considered to be composed basically of 'independent' units, so that the choice was not offered.

In addition to the material collected from our sample, we obtained information from large organisations connected with the motor trades who regularly collect operating returns from main dealers. This data, originally in the form of returns for

Table B.1   *Response Rates*

Trades	Forms sent out[(a)](b)	Usable replies received[(b)]	%	Number used in questionnaire analysis	Number used in financial analysis
Hotels – independent	116	58	50	58	44
Hotels – chain	231 (38)	97 (19)	42	95	87
Industrial Caterers	26	11	42	(c)	(c)
Restaurants – independent	146	62	42	60	42
Restaurants – chain	192 (32)	52 (13)	27	50	37
Managed Public Houses	190 (17)	130 (11)	68	130	124
Tenanted Public Houses	420	130	31	130	130
Hairdressers	462	185	40	185	118
Hairdressers Local Associations	51	33	65	(d)	(d)
Large Motor Traders	188	60	32	48	48
Small Motor Traders	187	69	37	30	30
Specialist Motor Repairers	117	41	35	34	34
Large Shoe Repairers (NASRF)	64	31	48	31	29
Small Shoe Repairers (St. Crispin's)[(e)]	508	105	21	105	67
Shoe Repair Local Associations	27	25	93	(d)	(d)

(a) Figures corrected for a few cases in which firms were wrongly addressed or turned out not to be part of the sample wanted.
(b) The figures in brackets refer to the number of 'chains'.
(c) These forms were not rigorously analysed.
(d) These forms were used for the special purposes described in the text.
(e) Includes those shoe repairers with a turnover of less than £5,000 in their pre-SET year.

194

Table B.2   *Reasons for Non-Return and Non-Use of Forms*

Trade	Reasons for non-return of forms[a]			Reasons for non-use in financial analysis of forms returned		
	No reply	Not paying SET	Other	Refusal to supply or correct data	Not open over whole period	Other
Hotels – independent	44	0	14	11	2	1
Hotels – chain	(4)	(0)	(15)	0	3	7
Industrial Caterers	14	0	1	(b)	(b)	(b)
Restaurants – independent	68	1	15	17	0	2
Restaurants – chain	(8)	(0)	(11)	9	7	0
Managed Public Houses	(0)	(0)	(6)	5	0	1
Tenanted Public Houses	287	2	1	0	0	0
Hairdressers	205	43	29	52	15	0
Large Motor Traders	82	0	46	12	0	0
Small Motor Traders	109	0	9	30	9	0
Specialist Motor Repairers	59	0	17	7	0	0
Large Shoe Repairers (NASRF)	29	0	4	2	0	0
Small Shoe Repairers (St. Crispin's)[c]	241	49	103	32	4	1

(a) The bracketed figures refer to the number of 'chains'.

(b) These forms were not rigorously analysed.

(c) Includes those shoe repairers with a turnover of less than £5,000 in their pre-SET year.

different sizes of dealers of varying complexity, was consolidated on the basis of the definitions used in our sample returns for vehicle dealers: in this way, we were able to obtain an independent series of figures, comparable to our sample definitions for the period 1961–69. As a result of this, and the problems experienced by traders in filling out our return, we did not go back to our sample for additional material for 1968–69.

Shoe Repairing
The forms were mailed to the members of N.A.S.R.F. in July 1969, and to the individual members of St. Crispin's in November 1969.

The form to the large repairers (N.A.S.R.F.) was for the 'group as a whole' and no data were requested for individual units within the group.

No supplementary questionnaires were needed, thanks to the timing and wording of the original form. A number of interviews were carried out.

The 'background information' questionnaires to the Local Associations of St. Crispin's were mailed in June 1969.

The Response and Coverage of the DAE Enquiries
The response rates are set out trade by trade in Tables B.1 and B.2; and Table B.3 indicates the coverage of our enquiries in terms of turnover.

As can be seen from Table B.1, the percentage of forms returned which were usuable in any way is not, on average, very high despite several reminders from us and the urgings of the appropriate Trade Associations. These response rates are, however, broadly in line with our expectations and experience from earlier enquiries, and are in many cases (notably that of managed public houses) somewhat higher than the Trade Associations had predicted. The large number of traders who did not reply to our enquiries was a disappointment, especially in view of the complaints which had been made by these trades about SET.

Table B.3   *Coverage of DAE Enquiry in Terms of Turnover*

Trade	(1) Total turnover in DAE enquiry (£'000)	(2) Total turnover in benchmark enquiry (£'000)	(1) as % of (2)
Hotels[a]	31,572	259,208	12.18
Restaurants[a]	7,252	412,971	1.76
Managed Public Houses[a]	5,579	369,800	1.51
Hairdressing[b]	1,263	135,823	0.93
Motor Traders[c]	111,936	3,230,705	3.46
Shoe Repairers[b]	9,722	26,039	37.34

(a) B.o.T. Catering Enquiry Turnover 1964; DAE Enquiry Turnover 1965–6; (N.B. the definitions for hotels are not consistent.)
(b) Census of Distribution Turnover 1966 (Ratio Estimate: Establishment Data) DAE Enquiry Turnover 1965/6. (N.B. The definitions for shoe repairing are not consistent.)
(c) B.o.T. Enquiry Turnover 1967 (for classes included, see Appendix D): DAE Enquiry Turnover 1967–8.

Supplementary Questionnaires

As has been mentioned earlier in this Appendix, a supplementary questionnaire was sent to those 'independent' hotels and restaurants which had not been able to supply data for the year 1968–9 on their original return. The timing of the form allowed questions to be included about reactions (either before or after the event) to the July 1969 increase in SET. The response rates for the supplementary questionnaires are set out in Table B.4.

Table B.4   *Response to Supplementary Questionnaires*

Trade	Forms sent out	Forms returned and usable	% response
Hotels ('independent')	30	26	86.7
Restaurants ('independent')	23	14	60.9

Not all firms were able or willing to supply data for their 1968–9 financial year, so the financial data for this year had to be linked to that for 1967–8 in most trades.

Analysis of Returns

On receipt, the forms were checked for accuracy and consistency, and any obvious errors were queried with the respondent. Certain key ratios — such as net margin, payroll as a percentage of sales, SET as a percentage of sales, etc. — were then

196

calculated for each firm and any large movements or paradoxical results were checked with the respondent. We are most grateful for the tremendous amount of time and trouble many respondents obviously spent in completing the forms and later correcting or standardising data for us.

When the results had been fully analysed and ratios calculated for each trade, we interviewed a number of owners/managers of 'independent' firms, and also senior officials of large companies. The aims of the interviews were to clear any remaining doubtful points on the forms received from that company and to explore in greater depth the policy of that company in particular and that trade in general. We are very grateful to those people who made time available to be interviewed.

Unfortunately, we were unable to complete our planned interview programme, because of the change of Government.

End Date of Financial Year

The end dates of the financial years of the companies included in the trades in this Report are spread over the whole year, with bunching occurring for certain trades at certain times of the year. The most common date for the financial year end of brewery companies and hotels was September, but for the other trades, December or March were most common.

In all cases, the 'pre-SET' year was defined as the last full financial year ending on or before 30th September 1966. Although this meant that some 'pre-SET' years would include one month of SET payments, we felt that to be absolutely correct and use a year ending on or before August 31st 1966 would lead to many returns for the 'pre-SET' year (especially in the catering trades) being for a year ending in September 1965.

Table B.5 shows the average terminal date of this 'pre-SET' year for each trade; as a rough generalisation, for the trades as a whole one can think of the years as corresponding with fiscal years.

Table B.5   *Average Terminal Dates of Pre-SET Year*

Trade	'Average' terminal date of 'pre-SET' year
Hotels	mid-April 1966
Restaurants	end-March 1966
Managed Public Houses	mid-June 1966
Motor Traders	April 1966
Hairdressers	March 1966
Shoe Repairers	mid-March 1966

When our survey results are presented, 1965–6 refers to the 'pre-SET' year as defined above, 1966–7 to the following financial year, 1967–8 to the next but one financial year (i.e. a financial year ending between 1st October 1967 and 30th September 1968) etc.

The N.F.L.V./Tyzacks Enquiry

This is, in fact, two enquiries, both of which were processed by the University of London Atlas Computing Service for the National Federation of Licensed Victuallers.

The questionnaire data was collected by the N.F.L.V. itself by interview, but the questionnaire was designed – in collaboration with the N.F.L.V. – by John Tyzack Consultants Ltd., who also carried out by post the financial enquiry for the same public houses.

The sample of tenanted public houses (all outside London) was a balanced random one of 800 drawn from the membership list of the N.F.L.V. The response rates, possibly due to the speed with which the enquiry was conducted, were not very high and we only received information from 321 questionnaires and 105 financial returns. All the questionnaires were analysed despite some strong doubts about the accuracy of the data, but we could only analyse 54 of the financial returns. The remainder were not used either because they did not cover the years at which we were looking, or in a few cases because they contained gross inaccuracies – e.g. profits plus expenses did not equal revenue – which could not be corrected. The results of this analysis are not included in our main tables for reasons mentioned above and also because the items about which they asked were, in many ways, not at all consistent with the definitions in our own enquiries.

For what they are worth, we present the results of the financial analysis in Table B.6.

Table B.6   *Summary of Financial Results from Tenanted Public Houses Survey by the N.F.L.V.*

Item	1965–6 %	1966–7 %	1967–8 %	1968–9[a] %	% change 1967–8 c.f. 1965–6	% change 1968–9 c.f. 1965–6
Cost of goods sold	78.2	78.0	78.3	78.2	+0.13	+0.02
Payroll (inc. SET)[b]	3.4	3.5	3.5	3.6	+3.38	+4.63
Other expenses[c]	6.7	6.6	6.5	6.7	−2.45	+0.19
Tenant's wife's wages	2.3	2.5	2.5	2.5	+6.97	+7.02
Net profit[d]	9.4	9.4	9.2	9.0	−2.31	−3.67
Productivity[e]	100.0	93.37	91.86	94.31	−8.14	−5.69

(a) These figures were linked on 81% of the firms.
(b) Excludes remuneration of tenant and wife.
(c) Excludes rent, rates and interest.
(d) Includes rent, rates and interest and tenant's remuneration, but excludes wife's wages and Inland Revenue assessment for 'benefits in kind'.
(e) Deflated sales per pound of deflated payroll (including wife's wage). The deflators used were the same as those for managed public houses, though they were only calculated quarterly, not monthly.

We also calculated from our own enquiry into tenanted public houses that SET as a percentage of sales amounted to 0.89% for those (108) houses which paid SET. Over all (130) houses it amounted to 0.74%. This data relates to the period when the SET rate for a full-time male employee was 37/6 (187½p.) and therefore corresponds most closely with the results of our other surveys for the year 1968–9.

Counting a part-time employee as half a full-time employee, 19.1% of full-time-equivalent employees were part-time, and 80.9% were full-time in March/April/May 1970. This contrasts rather sharply with the experience of managed public houses where the full-time workers as a percentage of F.T.E. workers was only 45% in April 1969.

List of Cooperating Bodies

We have listed below the Trade Associations and other bodies who assisted us in one or more of the following ways: by providing membership lists to be used as bases for our sample; by giving advice on the composition of questionnaires; by completing questionnaires; by supplying data or other forms of assistance. We are extremely grateful to these organisations, and to all the other organisations (too numerous to mention individually) who assisted us in our enquiries.

Catering Trades
Atlas Computing Service (University of London)
Brewers' Society
British Hotels and Restaurants Association
Caterers Association of Great Britain
John Tyzack Consultants Ltd.
Licensed Victuallers Central Protection Society of London Ltd.
National Consultative Council of the Retail Liquor Trade
National Economic Development Office (Hotel and Catering E.D.C.)
National Federation of Licensed Victuallers
Restaurateurs Association of Great Britain

Hairdressing
Incorporated Guild of Hairdressers, Wigmakers and Perfumerers
National Hairdressers Federation

Shoe Repairing
National Association of Shoe Repair Factories
St. Crispin's Boot Trades Association Ltd.

Construction Trades
Federation of Civil Engineering Contractors
Federation of Master Builders
National Federation of Building Trades Employers
Nationwide Building Society
Royal Institute of British Architects

Motor Trades
Automobile Association
National Board for Prices and Incomes
National Economic Development Office (Motor Vehicles and Repair E.D.C.)
Scottish Motor Trades Association Ltd.
Society of Motor Manufacturers and Traders Ltd.
Vehicle Builders' and Repairers' Association

Questionnaires Used

Listed below are the questionnaires used in the Department's enquiries. We have not reproduced any since they essentially follow the spirit of those used in our enquiries into the distributive trades. Copies are available on request to the Department (at a charge of 10p. each, post free).

(a) Form for 'independent' hotels (and individual chain hotels)
(b) Form for 'group as a whole' for hotel chains
(c) Form for 'independent' restaurants (and individual chain restaurants)
(d) Form for 'group as a whole' for restaurants chains
(e) Form for managed public houses
(f) Form for 'group as a whole' for managed public houses
(g) Form for tenanted public houses
(h) First form for 'group as a whole' for industrial caterers
(i) First form for 'individual units' of industrial caterers
(j) Second form for industrial caterers
(k) Form for hairdressers
(l) Form for local associations of N.H.F.
(m) Form for 'large' (N.A.S.R.F. members) shoe repairers
(n) Form for 'small' (St. Crispin's members) shoe repairers
(o) Form for local associations of St. Crispin's
(p) General notes for motor traders
(q) Form for 'small' motor traders
(r) Form for 'large' motor traders
(s) Form for vehicle builders and repairers

Appendix C
Notes on Preparation of Statistics in the Text

The information given here is in addition to that given in the detailed appendices on Prices (F), Output and Employment (E) and Construction (H). It starts with a general note about weighting systems used in compiling DAE surveys, and then takes in order the tables on which notes are needed.

Throughout this Appendix all Minimum List Headings relate to the 1958 version of the Standard Industrial Classification; the same is true throughout the Report unless the contrary is stated.

Weighting Systems Used in Compiling Results of DAE Surveys
The methods used are essentially similar to those described in the First Report, Appendix B.

(a) Within samples
Within individual samples, and when the ratio was expressed in terms of sales (the majority of cases) we took an unweighted average of the ratios for individual firms. The justification for this procedure is the assumption that the sampling fraction is roughly proportional to the size of the firm. It is impossible to check the accuracy of this assumption for many of the trades because there are no appropriate benchmark data available.

If we wished to express a figure as a ratio of some other item (e.g. net profit) we calculated two ratios with sales as the denominator, and took the ratio of these.

(b) Between samples
For *Shoe Repairing* we took an unweighted average of the ratios for the samples for 'multiples' (i.e. sales over £100,000 in 1965) and 'large independents' (i.e. sales of between £5,000 and £100,000 in 1965).

For *Motor Traders*, the ratios from the samples for 'Large Motor Traders', 'Small Motor Traders' and 'Vehicle Builders and Repairers' were combined in the ratio 89.96:8.36:1.67. The weights were derived from the 1967 B.o.T. enquiry into the Motor Trades.

Notes on Individual Tables

Table V.1 Price Indices
The figures in this table represent, for the 'average financial year'[1] of the trade

---

1   See Appendix B.

concerned, the price series used for deflating sales for our own enquiries. They were arrived at in different ways.

(i) *Hotels, Restaurants, Managed Public Houses.* To obtain the sales deflators for these trades, we used various combinations of indices for 'Tobacco', 'Beer', 'Wines and Spirits' (all parts of the index of retail prices), 'Meals bought and consumed outside the home' and 'Accommodation' (both obtained from the C.S.O.). The weights used were derived from the B.o.T.'s 1964 Catering Enquiry. The same deflator was used for tenanted public houses as for managed public houses.

We also used the same source data to calculate the deflators for the turnover series for the projection of net output in Appendix E.

(ii) *Motor Traders.* The deflators for the trade were the relevant components of the retail price index (purchases of motor vehicles, maintenance of motor vehicles, petrol and oil). The weights used were provided by the departmental breakdowns of sales for firms in the sample for the pre-SET year.

(iii) *Hairdressers.* The components of the retail price index for men's hairdressers, women's hairdressers and mixed hairdressers were applied appropriately. The figures actually shown are a composite of these three.

(iv) *Shoe Repairers.* We used the component of the index of retail prices for boot and shoe repairing.

Table V.6 Productivity

(i) *Sales.* A monthly price index was derived for each trade (see note on Table V.1). From these we calculated, for each possible financial year end, a price index covering the years 1965–6 to 1968–9. The sales index for each firm was then deflated by the price index which covered the twelve month periods which constituted the firm's accounting years.

For shoe repairers, output data was also adjusted to take account of increased retail output and the effects of such diversification upon productivity.

(ii) *Payroll.* On timing the system used was as described for sales. The deflators used were:

(a) *Hotels, Restaurants and Hairdressers.* An index derived from the 'certain miscellaneous services' data from the D.E.P. half-yearly enquiries into earning of manual workers.

(b) *Public Houses.* The data used were from the same source as that used for hotels and restaurants, but the earnings of motor traders were excluded.

(c) *Motor Traders.* The D.E.P. half-yearly enquiries into earnings of manual workers in motor repairing, garages etc.

(d) *Shoe Repairers.* The earnings of workers in the Boot and Shoe Repair trades as shown by the D.E.P. half-yearly enquiries.

In all cases, National Insurance contributions were added to earnings before the six-monthly figures were interpolated and the payroll deflators calculated.

202

Table V.7 Productivity Comparisons
The combined figure for catering productivity was obtained by weighting together the productivity indices for Hotels, Restaurants and Managed Public Houses from our own enquiries. The weights used were the net outputs in 1963.

Table VII.6 Percentage of Part-timers
The full analysis of the composition of employment, from which Table VII.6 was derived, is given in Table C.1.

Tables VIII.6 and VIII.7 Productivity Gains in Retailing and Manufacturing
Table C.2 gives the properties of the equations used in producing these tables.

Table XIV.1 FTE Numbers Engaged
Full-time-equivalent employments were calculated in the following manner:

(a) *SET sector*
    (i) MLH 500 — As described in (b) below.
   (ii) MLH 709, 860, 871, 873, 879, 881–9, 891, 899 — As shown in Appendix E.
  (iii) MLH 810, 820 — As shown in First Report (Tables D.14 and D.12 respectively) (N.B. A number of double-jobbers are therefore included.)
  (iv) MLH 831, 832 — By following the method used for MLH 810 in the First Report.

(b) *All industries and services except Public Administration and Defence, Medical and Dental Services, and Educational Services*
  (i) FTE employment was calculated for all MLH except 872, 874, 901, 906 and those defined as being in the SET sector. The resulting estimate was added to that for the SET sector.
 (ii) The actual calculation was performed by adding the D.E. June count of employees in employment to a series for self-employed workers derived by interpolating the Censuses of Population and projecting from 1966 with respect to the June-to-June movements in all self-employed workers shown by the D.E. The number of part-time workers included was derived by interpolating between percentages of part-time workers derived from the censuses and applying the results to the total numbers engaged; the resulting numbers of part-time workers were converted to an FTE basis by scaling by a factor derived from the 1966 C.o.P. (hours worked by part-timers) and the 'Historical Abstract of British Labour Statistics' (hours worked by full-timers).

(c) *All Industries and Services*
The estimates obtained in (a) and (b) were added to an FTE series for MLH 872, 874, 901 and 906 derived by the same general method as described in (b).

Table C.1   Composition of Labour-force in Near Distribution
(The figures give the percentage of F.T.E. [a] labour-force contributed by each category)

	Full-time workers[b]				Part-time workers[b][c]				Total	of which self employed[d]
	Adult male	Adult female	Juvenile	Total full-time	Under 8 Hours	8–20 Hours	21 hours & over	Total part-time	Total	of which self employed[d]
	%	%	%	%	%	%	%	%	%	%
Vehicle builders										
April, 1966	74.7	5.1	18.7	98.5	0.4	0.6	0.5	1.5	100.0	n.a.
April, 1967	76.6	6.0	15.8	98.4	0.4	0.7	0.6	1.7	100.0	n.a.
April, 1968	77.6	6.2	14.6	98.4	0.4	0.6	0.6	1.6	100.0	n.a.
Large motor traders[1]										
April, 1966	71.2	16.4	9.0	96.6	0	1.3	0.9	2.2	98.8	n.a.
April, 1967	70.1	16.1	10.2	96.4	0	1.3	0.8	2.2	98.6	n.a.
April, 1968	71.2	16.1	8.9	96.2	0	1.3	0.9	2.3	98.5	n.a.
Managed public houses										
April, 1966	24.4	18.4	—	42.8	2.2	24.6	30.4	57.2	100.0	—
April, 1967	25.6	18.8	—	44.4	2.5	22.1	31.1	55.6	100.0	—
April, 1968	26.8	18.9	—	45.8	2.6	22.9	28.8	54.2	100.0	—
April, 1969	26.6	18.4	—	45.0	3.2	25.1	26.7	55.0	100.0	—
Hotels[2]										
I.[3]										
November, 1965	43.0	40.9	4.7	88.5	1.1	3.6	6.8	11.5	100.0	n.a.
November, 1966	43.8	40.3	4.9	88.9	1.2	3.4	6.5	11.1	100.0	n.a.
November, 1967	44.6	39.4	4.9	88.8	1.1	3.8	6.2	11.2	100.0	n.a.
November, 1968	44.5	38.7	5.3	88.6	1.4	3.8	6.2	11.4	100.0	n.a.
II.[4]										
July, 1966	42.1	40.9	5.9	89.0	1.0	3.5	6.6	11.0	100.0	n.a.
July, 1967	41.7	41.2	5.7	88.7	1.0	3.7	6.6	11.3	100.0	n.a.
July, 1968	42.5	39.9	5.5	88.0	1.1	4.1	6.8	12.0	100.0	n.a.

Restaurants[2]

I.[5]										
November, 1965	34.9	43.6	3.5	82.1	2.2	4.3	11.4	17.9	100.0	n.a.
November, 1966	35.3	43.1	3.8	82.3	2.2	4.4	11.1	17.7	100.0	n.a.
November, 1967	36.0	43.0	3.5	82.6	2.8	5.0	9.7	17.4	100.0	n.a.
November, 1968	34.8	41.6	4.2	80.6	2.9	5.7	10.8	19.4	100.0	n.a.
II.[6]										
July, 1966	34.1	43.3	4.6	82.0	2.1	4.7	11.2	18.0	100.0	n.a.
July, 1967	34.5	42.6	4.8	81.8	2.3	5.0	10.9	18.2	100.0	n.a.
July, 1968	33.8	42.0	4.8	80.7	2.6	6.1	10.6	19.3	100.0	n.a.
Hairdressing										
August, 1966	n.a.	n.a.	21.4[7]	97.1	1.1	1.3	0.5	2.9	100.0	19.5
June, 1968	n.a.	n.a.	20.3[7]	96.2	1.4	£1.5	0.8	3.7	100.0	21.2
October, 1969 to May, 1970 (i.e. at time of enquiry)	n.a.	n.a.	18.8[7]	96.0	1.4	1.5	1.0	3.9	100.0	23.8
Shoe repairing[8]										
April, 1966	n.a.	n.a.	n.a.	85.7	0.5	2.3	2.2	5.0	90.7[9]	9.3
April, 1967	n.a.	n.a.	n.a.	85.4	0.5	2.5	2.3	5.3	90.7[9]	9.3
April, 1968	n.a.	n.a.	n.a.	84.6	0.5	2.7	2.0	5.2	89.8[9]	10.2
April, 1969	n.a.	n.a.	n.a.	83.6	0.6	3.1	2.0	5.6	89.2[9]	10.8

(a) Part-time worker working less than 8 hours = 1/5 full-time; 8–20 hours 2/5 full-time; 21 & over 3/5 full-time.

(b) Includes 'self-employed' except in the case of shoe repairing.

(c) Defined as less than 36 hours for hotels and restaurants; less than 35 hours for hairdressers; less than 34 hours for public houses; and less than 30 hours for shoe repairers, vehicle builders & motor traders.

(d) Includes 'working proprietors' etc. i.e. those not liable to SET

(1) For large motor traders the lines given do not sum to 100.0 since in a number of instances firms were not able to allocate all workers between the various categories of employment.

(2) These figures are not based on the same group of firms as the financial data.

(3) Hotels group I; based on 120 hotels operating throughout the year.

(4) Hotels group II; based on 138 hotels open in July, but either shut in November or unable to provide data for that month.

(5) Restaurants group I; based on data from 91 restaurants open throughout the year.

(6) Restaurants group II; based on 99 restaurants open in July, but either shut in November or unable to provide data for that month.

(7) For hairdressing the figures given under juveniles relate in fact to apprentices, and thus may not be strictly proportions of juveniles as defined for the other trades.

(8) Includes only those businesses with turnover of £5000 and over p.a.

(9) Excludes self-employed.

Table C.2 Properties of the Equations

$$\Delta E = a + b_1(\Delta 0_t - \overline{\Delta 0}) + b_2(V - \overline{V}) + b_3 D$$

		a	b_1	b_2	b_3	R^2	SE	DW
Retailing	(1)	0.79 (0.21)	0.79 (0.17)	-2.01 (1.00)	1.25 (0.44)	0.62	0.67	1.30
	(5)	0.83 (0.21)	0.67 (0.18)	-0.59 (0.96)	0.78 (0.44)	0.55	0.67	1.78
Manufacturing	(1)	0.74 (0.23)	0.33 (0.07)		0.43 (0.10)	0.74	0.74	0.78
	(5)	0.82 (0.22)	0.33 (0.06)		0.56 (0.12)	0.80	0.68	0.81

$$\Delta E = a + b_1(\Delta 0_t - \overline{\Delta 0}) + b_2(\Delta 0_{t-1} - \overline{\Delta 0})$$

		a	b_1	b_2	b_3	R^2	SE	DW
Retailing	(2)	0.59 (0.27)	0.53 (0.20)	0.10 (0.16)		0.31	0.89	1.73
	(6)	0.74 (0.26)	0.51 (0.18)	0.09 (0.14)		0.37	0.80	2.36
Manufacturing	(2)	0.54 (0.22)	0.26 (0.06)	0.27 (0.06)		0.76	0.72	1.23
	(6)	0.64 (0.22)	0.26 (0.06)	0.31 (0.07)		0.80	0.68	1.74

$$\Delta E = a + b_1(\Delta 0_t - \overline{\Delta 0}) + b_2(\Delta 0_{t-1} - \overline{\Delta 0}) + b_3 t$$

		a	b_1	b_2	b_3	R^2	SE	DW
Retailing	(3)	1.54 (0.54)	0.51 (0.17)	0.01 (0.14)	-0.15 (0.08)	0.50	0.76	2.45
	(7)	1.37 (0.57)	0.50 (0.17)	0.02 (0.15)	-0.11 (0.09)	0.41	0.77	2.75
Manufacturing	(3)	1.25 (0.41)	0.28 (0.06)	0.28 (0.05)	-0.12 (0.06)	0.82	0.62	1.71
	(7)	1.17 (0.46)	0.28 (0.06)	0.30 (0.06)	-0.10 (0.08)	0.81	0.65	1.87

$$\log_e \text{Prod.} = a + b_1 t + b_2(V - \bar{V})$$

		a	b_1	b_2	R^2	SE	DW
Retailing	(4)	4.5662	0.0246	0.0202	0.99	0.0069	1.75
		(0.0045)	(0.0006)	(0.0066)			
	(8)	*4.5680*	*0.0241*	*0.0162*	*0.99*	*0.0070*	*1.72*
		(0.0054)	*(0.0008)*	*(0.0081)*			
Manufacturing	(4)	4.3413	0.0282	0.0579	0.97	0.0174	1.70
		(0.0113)	(0.0016)	(0.0167)			
	(8)	*4.3388*	*0.0283*	*0.0593*	*0.95*	*0.0185*	*1.52*
		(0.0142)	*(0.0022)*	*(0.0214)*			

Roman numerals refer to equations fitted to the period 1954–1965; those in italics to the equations fitted to the period 1954–1964. The standard errors of the coefficients are in brackets.

$\Delta 0 - \overline{\Delta 0}$ = deviations of percentage changes in output from the average percentage change in output over the period to which the equation is fitted. D = initial-deficiency in employment as a percentage of the required level. $V - \bar{V}$ = deviation of tightness in the labour market (measured in terms of unfilled vacancies) from the average tightness for the period to which the equation is fitted. These terms are more fully explained in 'Effects of the Selective Employment Tax, First Report on the Distributive Trades'.

t (time) assumes an initial value of one for the period 1954/5 in equations (3) and (7) and a value of one for 1954 in equations (4) and (8). For the purposes of calculating the expected values for the post-SET period from equations (3) and (7), t is held constant at the level attained in the last year of the period to which the equations are fitted (see text). Equations (4) and (8) are calculated using $\log_e$ and the coefficients and standard errors given in the table are expressed in terms of logarithms.

The coefficient of determination (R^2), the standard error of the residuals (SE), and the Durbin-Watson statistic (DW) are shown on the right of the table. Bracketed figures on the left refer to Tables VII.6 and VII.7.

Table XIV.2 Self-Employed in SET Sector

The figures for employers and self-employed were derived as follows:

(a) MLH 500 — Census of Population data interpolated logarithmically. The 1967 to 1969 data were supplied by the D.H.S.S.

(b) MLH's 810 and 820 — As calculated for the First Report (Tables D.4 and D.13).

(c) MLH 709, 831, 832, 860, 871, 873, 879, 881—899 — Census of Population data interpolated (and extrapolated to 1969) by the D.E. exchange of cards series. Where this series did not exist for a trade, the C.o.P. data were interpolated logarithmically.

The figures for employees in employment were derived as follows:

(a) MLH 500 — D.E. June card counts data (linked).

(b) MLH 810, 820 — As calculated for First Report (Tables D.9 and D.13). A number of double-jobbers are therefore included.

(c) MLH 709, 831, 832, 860, 871, 873, 879, 881—889. D.E. June card counts data (linked).

Appendix D
Notes on the Near-Distribution Trades

These notes are intended to give background information on some aspects of the near-distributive trades which are relevant to the analysis of Part II: major mergers, technical changes, trade practices which may not be widely known, and the like. No attempt has been made to provide a comprehensive description of the trades.

Catering
The 1958 SIC defines MLH 884 as 'Establishments (whether or not licenced for the sale of intoxicating liquor) providing meals, light refreshments, drink or accommodation. Included are the Hotel and Catering Services Division of the British Transport Commission; NAAFI; school canteens and industrial canteens run by catering contractors; social and political clubs; residential clubs and hotels; holiday camps; the letting of furnished apartments for short tenancies. Canteens run by industrial establishments for their own employees are excluded and classified with the main establishment. Sports clubs are excluded and classified in MLH 882'.

The 1966 Census of Population showed 253,000 males and 438,000 females engaged in this industry.

Our enquiries concentrated on hotels, restaurants, and managed public houses, which amongst them account for about 47% of the total sales of the MLH.[1] We also looked for evidence as to whether the inclusion of industrial canteens' employees with those of the main establishment had led to a serious anomaly, and we also looked at tenanted and free public houses to obtain background information to add to our detailed investigation of managed public houses. If the sales of these categories are included we 'covered' some 77% of the MLH.

Three main categories of public house may be distinguished. Managed public houses are owned by a brewery, which receives the profit and pays a salary to the manager. Many of the largest public houses and those with the best sites fall into this category. Tenanted public houses are owned by a brewery but let to a (self-employed) tenant who is charged a rent. Profits are normally retained by the tenant, but are sometimes divided between him and the brewery. 'Free' public houses are those owned and run by a self-employed person, or an independent company, who is not usually limited in the makes of beer sold.

Many public houses employ staff on a casual basis, including 'double-jobbers' whose National Insurance cards are stamped by another employer (and who are therefore not included in official employment statistics for the catering industry).

1 As shown by the B.o.T. Catering Enquiry 1964 (which itself did not comprehensively cover the MLH).

In some parts of the country licenced or registered clubs compete strongly with public houses.

The total of licenced outlets includes 'off licences', and some hotels and restaurants as well as public houses; of this total, brewers owned approximately 50% at the end of 1967. Further detail is given in the Monopolies Commission Report, 'Beer' (April 1969), from which these figures are taken.

Between the beginning of 1966, and 1970, the brewers agreed to a series of Government requests not to increase the recommended price of beer in public bars, except for minor types, or as a result of increases in the excise duty. Prices in other bars were not controlled in this way, although they were of course affected like other prices by the general prices and incomes policy.

A second aspect of Government policy which has affected catering since 1966 is the system of investment incentives. Service industries did not qualify for investment grants in the same way as manufacturing industries, but under the Industrial Development Act 1966, as under previous Local Employment Acts, new hotels in Development areas would receive a 25% building grant.

From January 1967 to March 1968, a 'cheap loan' scheme was operated by the Government, to assist all hotel development schemes likely to increase earnings from overseas visitors.

In 1968, a new 'Hotel Development Incentives' scheme was introduced, offering (broadly) grants of 20% for new hotels, extensions and improvements above a minimum size; in Development Areas the rate of grant was 25%. Also, provision was made for Government loans to assist these schemes.

Thus, since 1966, investment incentives for hotels have become more generous in several ways. The grants available to new hotels in development areas have been extended to cover improvements and enlargements, and to other parts of the country (at a lower rate), and cheap loans are also available to help investment projects.

Motor trades

The 1958 SIC definition of this industry (MLH 887) is: 'Repairing all types of motor vehicles; wholesale or retail distribution of motor vehicles (including motor cycles), tyres, parts and accessories and the retail distribution of petroleum products. Lock-up garages are excluded and classified in MLH 860 and the wholesale distribution of petroleum products is excluded and classified in MLH 810'.

Within this general rubric, the Board of Trade for census purposes subdivides the motor trades into 10 classes. These classes, the number of organisations involved in each and the turnover in each in the census years of 1962 and 1967 appear in Table D.1.

Our present enquiry into the effects of SET concerns itself primarily with classes 1, 4, and 5 in Table D.1. Class 9 has been dealt with in the First Report. As the three classes involved sell over three quarters of the new and used vehicles, petrol, accessories and repairs in the trade, the coverage of our enquiry is fairly broad.

There are two main types of dealer appointed by manufacturers to trade in their vehicles: Distributors (also called Main Dealers) and Retail Dealers. Distributors, unlike Retail Dealers, are authorised to sell to other traders and are under an obligation to stock continuously new, unregistered motor vehicles. Both types of dealer are obliged to maintain stocks of spares for the manufacturer's vehicles. In June 1969

Table D.1   *Number of Organisations in the Motor Trades and their Turnover, 1962 and 1967*

Description of Business (by principal activity)	1962		1967	
	No. of Organisations	Turnover (£'000)	No. of Organisations	Turnover (£'000)
1. New Vehicle Dealers	9,922	2,058,274	9,646	2,905,757
2. Motor Cycle Dealers	2,301	64,864	1,553	43,356
3. Second-hand Vehicle Dealers	4,454	200,919	4,181	200,249
4. General Repairers	11,838	164,300	10,547	270,069
5. Specialist Repairers	2,599	38,284	3,102	53,879
6. Motor Accessories Dealers	983	25,458	1,460	51,870
7. Tyre Dealers	1,264	88,929	1,120	124,854
8. Petrol Stations	12,696	260,581	10,416	412,821
9. Wholesalers of Motor Accessories and Spares	449	40,687	584	104,675
10. Caravan Dealers	336	20,100	273	29,731
	46,842	2,962,397	42,882	4,197,261

Source: *Board of Trade Journal,* 6 May 1970

there were 1,561 main dealers and 7,524 retail dealers attached to British manufacturers.

Manufacturers issue recommended prices which in practice are not to be exceeded but may be undercut. The discount structure in the trade is roughly as follows:

Cars   Retailer's buying price — 17½% discount off recommended price excluding purchase tax.

Wholesaler's discount on above — 4% of net invoice value or 5% of the gross for the car, excluding purchase tax.

Loyalty Bonus for retail sales exclusively for one manufacturer — 1% of net or gross invoice value for the car only.

Commercial Vehicles

Wholesaler's buying price — 20% discount off recommended price.

Retailer's buying price — 17½% discount off recommended price.

Loyalty bonus — as above

Where a dealer makes a casual sale of a vehicle for which he does not hold a franchise he negotiates with a franchise holder a margin of 10–15%. A vehicle repairer making a casual sale receives an introductory commission of 5–12½% through negotiation. The vehicle is actually sold by the distributor or dealer who supplies it directly to the vehicle repairer's customer. Sales to fleet owners involve discounts of between 5 and 15%

About 80% of new car transactions involve the part exchange of an older vehicle. These vehicles taken in part exchange are either sold to retail customers or cashed out to the trade. The sales of these used cars normally involve additional trade-ins. Generally speaking, there are thought to be approximately 2.8 used car purchases associated with every new car sold. The existence of used car transactions makes most sales of vehicles joint transactions where the seller of the original vehicle must reckon his profit margin on the total transaction (i.e. on the sale of a new vehicle plus the sales of the associated used vehicle). This type of transaction allows considerable room for bargaining and before the abolition of RPM in 1965 reduced the effects of RPM on sales of new vehicles.

In addition to the manufacturers' parts which dealers may be obliged to stock, there is a wide range of proprietary motor goods for which both the franchise holder and the normal garage may act as agents. These proprietary goods are handled by wholesalers or factors who act as a connecting link between manufacturers and the retail trade, which includes specialised shops and specialist transport operators. These factors, who may operate over a wide range of goods or specialise in one type of good (tyres, garage equipment or electrical components) were covered in the First Report. For this reason we need not examine the structure of their margins, but the margins for the trade as a whole are of some import.

Manufacturers' tied parts released to distributors and retail dealers carry recommended prices which are generally observed, except to fleet owners. The discounts to distributors on such parts, plus rebates on turnover arrangements, normally range between 25 and 35%. Retail dealers normally earn a flat discount of 15–25% and traders and repairers receive proportionately smaller discounts depending on negotiations.

For accessories supplied through the factor network the retailers would receive discounts of $25-33\frac{1}{3}\%$ on recommended prices. For tyres the discounts are 25–30% on major makes and 30–35% on minor makes.

All petrol companies normally issue recommended selling prices for their petrol and oil products. The margins to the retailer were roughly as follows:[1]

		Best	Premium	Regular
Difference between recommended	1965	6.75d	6.50d	5.50d
selling and buying prices per gallon	1968	6.30d	6.05d	5.05d

In addition, the great majority of dealers for major companies sign *solus* or exclusive selling agreements and receive a rebate which will vary with the terms of the agreement, but range from slightly below 1.25d to 1.5d; these rebates did not change between 1965 and 1968. Such rebates are not as common among minor companies, which also tend to allow lower margins per gallon. The margins shown may be eroded by increased prices for small deliveries.

Petrol prices to the motorist increased quite sharply between 1965 and 1968, primarily as a reflection of higher duties. The 'inner zone' recommended retail prices were:

	Best	Premium	Regular
1965	5/5d	5/2d	4/10½d
1968	6/5¾d	6/3¾d	5/11¾d

1 As reported by the Petroleum Information Bureau.

The *overwhelming majority* of vehicle repairs are charged out to the customer at an hourly rate, known as the charge-out rate. The time against which this rate is normally charged is a standard time prepared by the manufacturer of the vehicle concerned. The manufacturer derives this standard time from studies of repairs to road-used vehicles, using generally available tools and excluding the use of power tools, hydraulic lifts or other such equipment. These times commonly form the basis for wage-incentive schemes, whereby the mechanic involved receives wages for the manufacturer's scheduled time no matter how long he takes for the job. These times also form the basis for manufacturers' payments to dealers for warranty work. They are not, however, used for extremely difficult jobs where the vehicle is heavily rusted or dirty, and for certain other jobs, and where these times do not find use, the firm concerned may charge for the elapsed time in doing the job; or it may charge a price recommended by an oil company for, say, jobs such as lubrication; or it may charge a price agreed with an insurance company.

In addition to sales of the above goods and services, firms engaged in the motor trade normally engage in other activities. These include car hire, driving schools, taxi services, bus services, and sales of cigarettes and confectionery, not to mention sales of bicycles and motor cycles. In 1967, the Census reports that turnover in car hire and other activities of the type mentioned above was £18,734,000 and £107,628,000 respectively (equal to over one-half the value of sales of new commercial vehicles).

Hairdressing and Manicure

The 1958 SIC definition of MLH 889 is simply 'Men's and women's hairdressers, manicurists and beauty parlours'. In addition to establishments whose receipts come mainly from men's or women's hairdressing, manicure, beauty treatment etc., the Census of Distribution includes all establishments combining hairdressing with the sale of cigarettes and tobacco, except those whose receipts from hairdressing were less than 10% of their total turnover.

Distinct trends are apparent in the amount of business done by men's and women's hairdressers: whilst the former has shown a slight decline in real output since the middle 1950's, the latter has shown a very rapid increase, though the signs are that this rate of growth is beginning to level off. Over the same period men's prices have risen more rapidly than women's. A recent phenomenon, widely criticised in the trade, has been the growth of home hairdressers not registered with Local Authorities under the Shops, Offices and Railway Premises Act.

In 1966 the number of persons engaged in the industry was 40,000 males and 124,000 females. The turnover, according to the Census of Distribution of the same year, was £136m. The trade is characterised by a large number of small units: the Census of Distribution showed that in 1966, 32% of the total number of persons engaged were working in their own business. The trade is also notable for the relatively high number of indentured apprentices, whose period of training lasts for three years.

Repair of Boots and Shoes

This industry is defined in the 1958 SIC as MLH 888, 'Repairing boots, shoes, slippers and clogs'. About 16,000 males and 4,000 females were engaged in this industry in 1966.

213

Both output and numbers engaged have been declining rapidly; for example, they halved between about 1958 and 1966. This has resulted from a change towards replacing shoes rather than having them repaired, probably associated with a tendency for cheaper shoes to take a larger share of the market.

The types of business engaged in shoe repairing may be broadly classified into the following categories:

(i) The small independent shoe repairer with one branch — the self-employed man, sometimes working with his wife and one or two other assistants. Such repairers are liable to pay little or no SET.

(ii) The medium-sized independent repairer with perhaps one or two branches and up to say 10 assistants.

(iii) Multiple repair businesses operating up to 200 repair shops, the majority of operatives falling into the 'employee' rather than the 'self-employed' category.

(iv) Manufacturers undertaking repair work either (a) at their manufacturing establishment; (b) at a central repair workshop; or (c) by sub-contracting to categories (i), (ii), (iii) above and (vi) below.

(v) Heel-bars of the type found in Department stores etc. — as distinct from the independent offering 'while-you-wait' service as an option.

(vi) A few specialised trade repairers often operating from central repair workshops and accepting work from other repairers, retailers, manufacturers or institutions such as hospitals. Some multiples, whilst owning street repair shops, may have their own centralised repair workshops where they carry out specialised jobs such as colouring.

(vii) Retailers undertaking their own repairs on a very small scale, primarily as a service to their customers. Retailers pass a substantial volume of work to repairers, receiving a commission for doing so.

Few independent shoe repairers now concentrate solely on repairs, diversification into other lines having taken place especially during the past five years in an attempt to maintain profitability.[1]

Most multiple repairers are members of the National Association of Shoe Repair Factories (NASRF) which accepts into its membership any organisation having ten or more employees. The typical member of NASRF with 10 employees has 2 or 3 branches. The largest five members, however, accounted for a repair turnover of £5½ million and operated some 850 branches at the time of our enquiry. Whilst the overall scale of these businesses' repair activities has declined, this has been accompanied by policies of rationalisation which have included the opening of new branches and the acquisition of others.

Repairs undertaken by or on behalf of manufacturers are relatively unimportant, being in the main either repairs of specialised, or high quality, or guaranteed footwear. Whilst manufacturers do undertake some of these repairs themselves, others may be sent to independent, multiple or trade repairers. The shoe repair Trade Associations considered that manufacturers operating upon this basis did not

---

1 Some of these units may now fall into the Census classification of retailer rather than repairer, although still considering themselves to be repairers. It is apparently the independent repairers that have experienced the most rapid rate of absolute (and relative) decline.

constitute any severe competitive threat since the heavy transport costs and other overheads involved more than outweighed any other advantage that might arise (e.g. exemption from SET). The Associations also felt that many of these repair services operated by manufacturers are probably run at a loss.

The past five or six years have witnessed a rapid increase in the number of heel-bars carrying out on-the-spot/while-you-wait repairs. Although there are a few independently owned heel-bars, the majority are owned by three companies. Much of the 'traditional' repair trade feels that the most lucrative business is being creamed off by heel-bars; N.A.S.R.F. considered that turnover per employee per week is generally some £20 to £30 above that of the small independent trader. However, operating costs are generally higher owing to the fact that most heel-bars are in 'prime sites', such as department stores.

The Trade Associations considered that central repair factories and specialised trade repairers were unlikely to constitute any serious competitive threat to the on-street repair shops owing to the transport/collection costs involved. They have of course, also to pay a commission to the collecting agent. It was the opinion of the Trade Associations that these trade repairers served a useful function in the trade in general in so far as they undertake specialised repair jobs and could also assist independent repairers with excess work during staff holidays.

Appendix E
Estimating Productivity Movements from Aggregative Statistics

Chapter XIII discussed the conclusions which might be drawn from our estimates of productivity changes in the SET-paying sector. This Appendix describes in more detail how these estimates were prepared from official statistics.

Labour Input
To estimate changes in productivity, it is necessary first to estimate changes in labour input and in real output. Our approach to the first of these problems was to calculate changes in the 'Full-Time Equivalent' (FTE) of the people engaged in each trade (whether self-employed or employees), and making due allowance for part-time workers. We could not use the alternative method, of deflating the total pay-roll in each industry by an index of the average earnings per worker, because the necessary information is not available at the level of detail required.

Sources of Information
The sources of information for estimating changes in the FTE numbers engaged are:

(a) *Censuses of Population.* In April 1951 and 1961 there were full Censuses of the U.K. population (though in 1961 only 10% of the respondents were asked to give details of their jobs) and a 10% sample Census was carried out in 1966. From these three Censuses, we have estimates of the number of people working in each trade as employees and on their own account, and of how many of them were part-time workers.

Unfortunately, for our purposes the Census questions were not ideal. For example, people who had a second (part-time) job in addition to their main occupation were not asked what it was, so that the figures of employees in each trade are too small by the number of 'double-jobbers' at work in it. These workers are important in some trades, such as public houses. There are other reasons why the Census of Population figures have to be treated with caution, as we explain below.

(b) *Censuses of Distribution.* These Censuses, which were carried out in 1950, 1957, 1961 and 1966, were the main source of detailed information about labour which we used in our First Report. They have the very solid merit, for estimates of productivity changes, of collecting figures of output and employment at the same time and from the same firms. Unfortunately, they only cover a small part of the service sector outside distribution: shoe repairers and hairdressers were included in all years and laundries and dry cleaners in 1961 and 1966. They are also liable to be incomplete.

(c) *National Insurance cards.* Every employee and self-employed person, except some married women, is supposed to have a N.I. card, and to exchange it each year for a new one. These cards can be classified according to the business of the employer, and they show the sex of the owner of the card and whether he/she is an employee or self-employed (since different rates of stamp are needed).

Some of this information is recorded by the Department of Employment, who use it to estimate for each MLH the number of employees in June each year, and the number of self-employed (but the latter figures are not published, and are far below the true level for numbers engaged — see *First Report*, page 272 and Table D.2).

The main disadvantages of estimates based on N.I. cards, for our purposes, are firstly that people with two jobs will have their card stamped and exchanged by their main employer, so that 'second jobs' go unrecorded. Also, not everybody exchanges their card on time, and some people may not have cards, so that the estimates are subject to a margin of error; this in itself is of course normal, but Chapter XV shows that these errors may be connected with the number of self-employed people, and could therefore have increased directly because of SET.

However, the N.I. cards exchanged are the main source of information about changes in the numbers engaged in each trade between Census years.

(d) *The 'L' returns.* The employment Ministry sends questionnaires to a sample of medium and large businesses in each trade, asking for information about employees. The replies are used to produce monthly estimates of the number of employees in each trade — though these are not published for all trades, as they are not always considered reliable. The 'L' returns also allow estimates to be made for each June of the proportion of female employees in each MLH who are working part-time.

These two estimates are both subject to some error. The monthly employment figures are revised, after the figures from the next card count become available, to bring them into line with the movements shown between the two counts. The estimates of female part-time employees are not published, because they are regarded as unreliable; this is partly because small businesses (which are numerous in some SET-paying industries) are not included in the sample.

Methods Used

The method which we preferred for combining this data to give FTE estimates was as follows:

(a) Take D.E. figures for total male and female employees each year as correct (using the annual average where this is available, but otherwise the June figure). These figures were 'linked' so as to be consistent through time, whenever this was made necessary by a change in the SIC or other cause.

(b) Take male and female self-employed numbers from the three C.o.P.'s, and estimate the numbers in other years from the movements shown by the card-counts.

(c) Take the proportions of male employees and self-employed who are part-time from the three C.o.P.'s, estimating other years' figures by interpolation and extrapolation.

Table E.1   Indices of FTE Numbers Engaged, 1961 = 100

Year	Miscellaneous Transport Services and Storage (MLH 709)	Insurance Banking & Finance (MLH 860)	Accountancy Services (MLH 871)	Legal Services (MLH 873)	Other Professional & Scientific Services (MLH 879)	Cinemas, Theatres, Radio etc. (MLH 881)	Sport and Other Recreations (MLH 882)	Betting (MLH 883)
1951	63.96	78.47	80.54	87.33	66.41	102.47	116.05	80.23
2	61.64	79.18	80.88	87.78	70.10	99.96	110.59	81.79
3	68.46	80.00	84.34	86.78	70.87	99.73	108.31	84.57
4	70.17	82.48	85.46	89.19	74.95	98.65	107.65	84.89
5	74.39	83.64	86.17	90.74	76.64	98.64	104.67	82.50
6	78.58	84.94	87.87	91.38	82.33	100.74	100.69	79.95
7	76.60	87.71	92.34	92.12	88.61	99.14	98.33	80.84
8	76.85	89.25	92.87	93.54	89.64	98.87	98.27	85.43
9	88.60	94.62	96.38	93.44	93.20	100.49	98.54	92.35
60	96.26	96.37	95.77	95.60	92.90	98.06	100.06	95.27
1	100.00	100.00	100.00	100.00	100.00	100.00	100.00	100.00
2	103.49	103.14	102.61	103.10	104.53	99.50	101.61	106.48
3	114.03	107.87	104.25	104.90	106.73	99.71	105.00	104.37
4	119.91	110.96	104.78	106.48	105.52	98.08	113.87	113.66
5	124.54	113.09	106.48	110.74	112.22	96.49	115.50	119.97
6	129.43	113.04	105.18	109.31	112.88	95.80	115.66	123.70
7	131.23	115.03	105.44	109.96	113.70	95.36	118.03	123.92
8	128.98	117.86	105.33	114.65	115.42	93.82	116.74	121.08
9	136.31	122.43	106.43	112.84	120.56	95.81	112.43	115.78
1961 no.	65,178	551,833	91,948	101,001	185,776	127,134	52,334	47,347

Table E.1 (cont'd).

Year	Catering, Hotels etc. (MLH 884)	Laundries (MLH 885)	Dry Cleaning (MLH 886)	Motor Trades (MLH 887)	Boot & Shoe Repair (MLH 888)	Hairdressing & Manicure (MLH 889)	Private Domestic Service (MLH 891)	Other Services (MLH 899)
1951	106.48	117.54	94.86	75.94	145.19	62.95	161.59	76.39
2	105.57	114.25	98.14	78.84	146.75	63.12	151.70	78.37
3	106.12	113.30	96.01	81.65	138.43	62.60	145.46	82.55
4	105.19	109.66	100.86	82.78	135.80	65.37	145.48	82.62
5	104.64	109.34	98.90	86.06	131.87	66.36	141.90	85.27
6	104.91	108.03	100.03	88.60	126.86	69.76	134.52	87.19
7	100.61	105.51	101.69	87.15	124.99	74.18	131.50	92.81
8	101.56	104.81	100.85	89.22	118.32	76.29	119.67	93.60
9	102.85	102.01	100.87	92.55	111.01	86.00	117.71	88.30
60	102.78	100.55	99.20	96.85	104.81	94.29	108.73	94.69
1	100.00	100.00	100.00	100.00	100.00	100.00	100.00	100.00
2	102.84	99.58	102.43	101.99	96.25	101.64	92.23	108.06
3	100.33	97.95	103.98	106.07	90.70	110.22	87.59	109.65
4	105.30	94.72	104.00	109.93	83.80	110.33	80.65	121.53
5	103.61	95.13	100.14	115.01	74.87	109.03	70.76	124.46
6	102.65	89.81	96.32	116.96	67.79	106.68	64.03	132.89
7	99.44	83.14	92.73	114.50	60.47	105.68	57.56	132.60
8	98.53	75.43	84.31	114.88	53.19	105.22	51.47	139.55
9	101.09	66.63	73.94	113.34	43.31	100.76	48.08	145.25
1961 no.	566,220	110,966	41,913	387,309	27,481	130,147	195,370	312,667

(d) Take the proportion of female workers who are part-time from the 1961 and 1966 C.o.P.'s (the 1951 C.o.P. figures cannot be used). For employed females, use the changes from year to year shown in the 'L' return series to estimate the figures for non-Census years. For self-employed females, other years' figures are estimated by interpolation and extrapolation.

In deciding on this method, and which were the precise figures to use, we considered and rejected numerous possible alternatives, some on points of detail and others on principle. We must however put on record that alternative procedures, which might have been considered equally legitimate, would have made a substantial difference in some cases: this was true even in relation to the percentage movements of the final FTE figure, which is the only thing with which we were concerned. For movements in particular components of that figure, or for the actual numbers, the differences were suitable only for a statistician's chamber of horrors.

Our next step was to express part-time workers as Full-Time Equivalents. The 1966 C.o.P. shows the average hours worked by part-timers in each MLH, and the 1968 New Earnings Survey shows the average hours worked by full-time workers. Using this information, we calculated the following figures as reasonable indicators of the number of full-time workers which are equivalent to a part-time worker.

(i) One part-time male (motor trades) = 0.40 of a full-time male
(ii) One part-time male (other trades) = 0.33 of a full-time male
(iii) One part-time female (all trades) = 0.40 of a full-time female

Table E.1 presents the indices of the FTE numbers engaged in each MLH which we derived in this way. Lack of output data prevents some of these series from being used to estimate productivity changes, and others have to be used in combination, but we publish them all here as being of interest in their own right.

It should be noted that, up to 1959, the June card counts of employees for MLH's 882 and 883 ('Sport and other Recreations' and 'Betting') were combined, so that the resulting FTE indices before this date are even less accurate than the other series. The method used to 'split' the card count was, in short, to interpolate between the proportion of employees shown for each MLH from the 1951 and 1961 Censuses of Population, and apply those interpolated percentages to the total of employees shown by the card counts of each year.

Output

There are well-known general problems connected with the measurement of output in the service industries. Often these arise from the difficulty of measuring changes in the quality of service offered.

Output at current prices can in principle be measured in the same way in most service trades as in other industries: that is, gross output can be measured by recording the total expenditure of customers on the services sold, or by recording the receipts of the businesses;[1] and net output by adding up their wages, salaries and profits. If one wishes to deflate the current price output to constant prices, a record of price changes in the industry is needed. Such a record should in theory allow for

---

1 There are difficulties in various cases – e.g. banking – because it is not clear what constitutes the service which is sold, or what should count as 'receipts'.

quality changes, but in practice the difficulty of identifying quality changes generally prevents this from being done. As a result, the estimates of constant price output made in this way may be misleading.

A second approach to the problem of estimating changes in real output is to attempt to record the quantities produced directly. This is generally much easier in manufacturing than in service industries; changes in, for example, the number of tons of steel of different kinds can fairly safely be taken to show changes in the output of the steel industry, whilst it may lead to error to make similar use of, say, the number of cheques cleared or the number of tax assessments to shown changes in the output of parts of the service sector.

Difficulties in applying one or other of the methods are not equally severe in all service trades, and attempts are in fact made to overcome them, by careful choice of direct output indicators and/or in the selection of price series. The Central Statistical Office has in fact produced estimates of the output of the service trades, both in current prices and at constant prices, which they incorporate in their figures for the national product as a whole, and these were made available to us. These figures are, however, regarded by the C.S.O. only as the 'best' (i.e. least bad) way of completing their aggregate table for the whole economy, rather than as figures which should be used 'in their own right'. For our particular purpose – estimating changes in productivity – it is indeed obvious in some cases that they are totally unsuitable, because the output is *assumed* to move proportionately to the numbers employed.[1] With others it is obvious, both from the nature of the method used and from a scrutiny of the figures, that the series are not suitable for deducing anything about the trade in question, taken by itself. We decided, however, to persevere with them in the hope that one could make some tentative generalisations about the trades as a group.

Table E.2 shows the estimates of movements in real output used in our calculations of productivity. All except those for Catering and Hairdressing are as supplied by the C.S.O.: the different way in which we used the official material for these two trades is described below. In view of the (inevitably) weak basis for these series, it seems necessary to outline what this is in each case. The series for near-distribution trades on which we did more work, are discussed after the others.

Insurance, Banking and Finance (MLH 860)

The basic indicator used by the C.S.O. to measure the net output of the insurance industry is a 3-year average of premiums less claims deflated, according to class of insurance, by a representative price index. In the case of life assurance, however, the indicator used is consumers' expenditure deflated by the consumers' price index.

In the banking sector, the C.S.O. combines four indicators: the number of cheques cleared by the London Clearing Banks, the value of bank advances, the value of deposits with the London Clearing Banks, and the amount remaining invested in national savings (the last 3 deflated by the consumers' price index).

The remaining financial sector includes Building Societies, stockbrokers and jobbers, and Hire Purchase Companies. Here the C.S.O. combines indices for the

1 This applies to MLH 709 (Misc. Transport Services and Storage), MLH 879 (Other Professional and Scientific Services) MLH 891 (Private Domestic Service) and MLH 899 (Other Miscellaneous Services).

Table E.2   Indices of Real Net Output: 1963 = 100

	Insurance, Banking, Finance, Property Owning (MLH 860)(a)	Accountancy Services (MLH 871)	Legal Services (MLH 873)	Cinemas, Broadcasting, Entertainments Sport (MLH 881, 882)(b)	Betting (MLH 883)	Catering (MLH 884)	Laundries, Dry Cleaning (MLH 885, 886)	Motor Trades (MLH 887)	Shoe Repairs (MLH 888)	Hairdressing (MLH 889)
1950	64.0	67.2	54.9	149.3	n.a.	n.a.	n.a.	n.a.	178.8	n.a.
1	64.3	69.4	58.1	148.8	n.a.	n.a.	n.a.	n.a.	172.4	n.a.
2	64.1	68.9	60.6	145.4	n.a.	n.a.	n.a.	n.a.	173.2	n.a.
3	66.0	69.6	59.4	144.6	n.a.	n.a.	n.a.	n.a.	162.0	n.a.
4	69.5	71.8	58.9	145.5	n.a.	n.a.	n.a.	n.a.	162.7	n.a.
5	71.8	74.0	60.6	140.5	n.a.	n.a.	n.a.	58.0	161.1	n.a.
6	72.2	76.5	63.9	136.3	n.a.	n.a.	n.a.	54.6	153.9	n.a.
7	75.4	79.6	68.6	126.0	n.a.	n.a.	n.a.	55.2	155.5	65.7
8	78.0	83.8	79.2	117.3	71.7	n.a.	90.3	65.0	151.5	70.7
9	86.7	87.4	82.0	109.3	79.3	n.a.	93.6	72.3	133.9	76.2
60	90.5	90.1	84.6	105.8	87.2	100.2	98.5	81.9	130.3	83.6
1	93.8	96.6	92.8	103.5	91.3	99.9	98.6	82.3	117.9	92.0
2	95.4	98.9	98.4	100.7	97.9	100.9	97.0	85.1	113.9	95.2
3	100.0	100.0	100.0	100.0	100.0	100.0	100.0	100.0	100.0	100.0
4	105.3	106.6	100.0	100.8	106.9	102.8	101.3	113.4	92.5	103.3
5	108.0	104.6	102.6	100.0	107.1	101.5	101.5	112.1	87.5	106.2
6	111.8	111.3	107.4	98.0	111.5	101.4	97.5	111.8	83.0	108.6
7	118.3	115.6	115.3	96.4	118.7	98.2	92.9	117.9	73.8	105.6
8	127.7	125.2	114.7	93.2	111.9	100.7	90.0	122.0	65.3	105.6
9	133.0	126.9	119.1	90.8	105.5	99.6	86.6	120.8	57.3	105.7

Note: All series provided by the C.S.O., except that we used the official statistics in a different way for catering and hairdressing.
(a) Supplied as 4 separate indices: combined on 1963 weights
(b) Supplied as 2 separate indices: combined on 1963 weights

numbers of mortgage advances, balances due on mortgage, total Building Society liabilities, the number of transactions on the London Stock Exchange, stamp duty on share transfers, the value of new capital issues, new hire purchase credit extended, and the balance of hire purchase credit outstanding – with all the value series being suitably deflated.

Estimates of the net output arising in each sector in 1963 are used for combining the series.

Accountancy (MLH 871)

The index is calculated from changes in the number of Schedule D tax assessments made on individuals or partnerships and the number of assessments for corporation tax (formerly income tax) made on companies. Assumptions are made about the proportion of each type of assessment handled by professional accountants. No heed is taken of any other type of work done by this industry.

Legal Services (MLH 873)

The index is calculated from changes in the numbers of cases in various courts and the number of grants of probate made in each year. No account is taken of conveyancing, although this comprises a large part of the work of many solicitors (as shown, for example, by the Reports of the National Board for Prices and Incomes).

Entertainment etc. (MLH 881, 882)

The series used are the number of admissions to cinemas, the numbers of radio and television licences current, and the amounts estimated from the Family Expenditure Survey as being spent on other entertainment and sport (deflated by the consumer price index). No heed is taken of the advertising revenue of independent television companies or of the number of programmes transmitted.

Betting (MLH 883)

This index is based on the amounts wagered on various types of betting, as derived from the Family Expenditure Survey, deflated by the consumer price index.

Laundries and Dry Cleaning (MLH 885, 886)

From 1958 to 1962 the C.S.O. used consumers' expenditure data deflated by the relevant section of the retail price index, and for subsequent years an index of turnover obtained from sample returns collected by the Board of Trade, similarly deflated. This sample does not cover launderettes, and is exposed to the usual problems of new businesses and deaths.

On making a comparison between the movements shown by various series we found, however, that there was radical disagreement between the movements shown for laundries. Thus the Censuses of Distribution, the consumers' expenditure figures and the B.o.T. series give the following figures in value terms for 1961 and 1966 (in £ million).

	1961	1966	Change
Census of Distribution (incl. launderettes)	72	117	+45
Census of Distribution (excl. launderettes)	67	99	+32
Board of Trade sample (excl. launderettes)	67	82	+15
Consumers' expenditure (based on F.E.S.)	57	63	+ 6

The consumers' expenditure figures naturally do not cover expenditure by businesses: the labour figures (with which the output series has to be combined for our analysis) cover launderettes as well as laundries.

Rather than face the formidable (and probably insoluble) problems of trying to reconcile these conflicting figures, and make them suitable for our analysis, we decided to use the dry-cleaning figures alone, which did not seem to present serious discrepancies. We compiled these only for the years needed for the analysis in Chapter XIII, using the same basic sources.

Motor Trades (MLH 887)

Since 1963 movements have been estimated on the basis of the movements in monthly sales shown by a sample of firms, collected by the Department of Trade and Industry. These statistics give separate series for three categories of sales — new vehicles, used vehicles and the remainder. The C.S.O. deflates these value figures by the best available price indices, and as the ratio of net output to sales clearly varies greatly between (say) the sale of a new car and repair work, the C.S.O. has also estimated the 'likely gross margins' for each of the 3 types of sale. These percentages are applied to the 3 deflated value series before they are combined.

Prior to 1963 the movements were based on a combination of three indicators: new registrations, deliveries of petrol and the number of licences current.

We did some work on a comparison of the movements between 1962 and 1967 shown by the two Censuses and those derived from the D.T.I. sample, which was moderately reassuring for total sales (though the components showed significant discrepancies).

Shoe repairing (MLH 888)

Since 1958 the C.S.O. series has been based on the Family Expenditure Survey, which gives value figures, and the shoe repair component of the consumer price index. Before 1958 it was based on employment.

The other main source of information is the Census of Distribution, which covered shoe repairing in 1950, 1957, 1961 and 1966. Unfortunately the first two censuses are not comparable with the last two in important respects: thus the first two did not include work done for the trade in their definition of turnover, but this was included in the last two.

It should be noted that the Census of Distribution defines shoe repair establishments (and organisations) as being those whose receipts from such repairing amounted to 50% or more of their turnover. Those selling footwear, as well as repairing it, are however only included if their receipts from shoe repairing amounted to 80% or more of their turnover; those with less than 80% are included as boot and shoe retailers. Any comparison between the C.S.O. and Census of Distribution data should make allowance for these factors, since the C.S.O. figures (being based on family expenditure) cover all shoe repairs but not goods sold by shoe repairers.

The Census of Distribution and C.S.O. data in fact show markedly different movements in repair receipts (at constant prices) of shoe repair establishments and in real net shoe repairing output (based on consumers' expenditure data). The percentage movements for the two periods, measured at constant prices, are as follows:

	1957–1961	1961–1966
Census of Distribution		
Repair receipts of shoe repair establishments	−4.8%	−16.8%
C.S.O.		
Real net output in shoe repairing	−24.2%	−29.6%

The causes of the discrepancies may be several. First the 1957 Census of Distribution did not include repair work 'done for the trade' whereas the 1961 and 1966 Censuses did. Secondly, as explained above, the series are different in coverage, the C.S.O. data being more extensive in coverage of repairs and including repair work done by retailers. It is quite possible that the share of the total work done by the latter has declined. And finally, it is quite possible that the two sets of data contain various errors, although one might expect some of these errors to average out.

In view of the problems with the data and the lack of suitable information with which to adjust it, we decided to use the C.S.O. net output series, since this was on an annual basis and seemed as appropriate an output indicator to combine with the D.E. employment data as would be the Census of Distribution output, which was only available for four years and suffered a serious break of continuity between 1957 and 1961.

Employment data are also available for shoe repairing from the Censuses of Distribution. We considered whether it could be used to adjust the figures given by the Censuses of Population and Department of Employment so as to make them more comparable with the C.S.O. output series, for example by allowing 'double-jobbers' to be included. However, the definition used to classify firms as shoe repairers in the Censuses of Distribution prevented this; in fact, these Censuses record fewer employees than the other sources. We therefore decided that the best basis for estimates of productivity were the C.o.P./D.E. figures, as used for other industries. This amounts to assuming, in the absence of relevant information to the contrary, that the numbers of people working as shoe repairers in establishments classified to other industries, the numbers of people working as (e.g.) retail assistants in shoe repair establishments, and the numbers of unrecorded double-jobbers or family workers, have on balance changed in line with the numbers recorded by the C.o.P./D.E. These assumptions will have introduced a margin of error into the figures used, which was probably substantial.

Catering (MLH 884)

As we wanted our output series to be as nearly comparable as possible in coverage with the employment statistics, we decided that we must use the data provided by the C.S.O. in a different manner from theirs. We also had to cope with the major break in continuity in the monthly turnover figures for the different types of catering, which took place between 1963 and 1964. This reflected the fact that the second Catering Trade Enquiry, conducted in 1964, showed that the first one, made in 1960, had been seriously incomplete, to an extent which could not be estimated.

Since the two Enquiries were not comparable we decided that we would not take them both as benchmarks, and instead we assumed that the levels of turnover recorded in the 1964 Enquiry were correct, and also that the *movements* shown in the

225

Table E.3   *Estimated Turnover Indices for the Catering Trades*
(1963 prices: 1963 = 100)

Trade	1960	1961	1962	1963	1964	1965	1966	1967	1968	1969
Licensed Hotels & Holiday camps	100.00	98.71	101.54	100.00	104.09	103.56	103.06	99.53	101.83	103.18
Restaurants, Cafes, Snack Bars etc. (a)	104.45	102.09	102.67	100.00	101.10	100.32	98.79	95.29	94.26	93.13
Fish & Chips Shops	102.39	102.00	101.15	100.00	102.29	101.79	100.14	98.83	96.61	94.46
Tenanted & Free Public Houses	97.36	100.62	99.56	100.00	102.39	98.08	99.48	95.96	98.32	98.12
Managed Public Houses	90.19	94.86	96.23	100.00	103.17	102.72	107.56	107.90	109.55	113.58
Canteens & Catering Contractors(a)	104.78	101.21	101.01	100.00	100.47	98.04	94.29	89.00	88.59	86.02

(a) This series should be treated with greater reservation due to a change in definition in 1964.

monthly series were correct. This enabled us to construct a turnover index for each group for the years 1960 to 1969, based on 1964. These were rebased on 1963 = 100 and deflated by the price indices discussed in Appendix F; the resulting volume series are shown in Table E.3. As with all such series these may underestimate the true growth of turnover to the extent that the system used to calculate the movements fails to take complete account of the turnover of businesses coming into operation; this is probably not too serious, however, since the output of additional establishments operated by groups is included, and the omission of new independent establishments is balanced to some extent by the correction which would be needed to allow for businesses going out of operation.

Our next problem was to combine these series so as to secure the best possible comparability between employment and output data. The major sources of information about employment in catering are the counts of N.I. cards and the Censuses of Population. As the former (on the 1958 SIC) classified all catering to MLH 884 it was not possible to adjust the employment figures to make them correspond with the output data: on the other side, the turnover series do not in fact cover all the types of catering covered by the labour statistics. We therefore combined the turnover series for different types of catering by weighting each of them according to the importance not only of the sector from which it is derived but also of any other sector which we assumed would show similar movements.

Table E.4   *Calculation of Weights for Catering Series*

C.S.O. Net Output Figures		1964 Catering Enquiry		Calculated Figures	
Trade	1963 Net Output (£m)	Catering Enquiry Groups	1964 Turn-over (£m)	1963 Output split by turnover ratios	1963 Net Output to be projected by the B.o.T. 'monthly' series
Hotels etc. Restaurants etc.	199	Hotels etc.	285.5	199.0	282.6[a]
Canteens etc.	288	Restaurants etc. Fish and chip	413.0	178.7	178.7
		shops	100.9	43.6	43.6
		Canteens etc.	151.7	65.7	13.3[b]
Public Houses	111	Tenanted Public Houses	663.3	71.3	115.9[c]
		Managed Public Houses	369.8	39.7	51.1[d]
Clubs	56	Licensed	51.9	11.4	−
		Registered	203.0	44.6	−

(a) Net output scaled up to allow for boarding-houses etc.
(b) Net output scaled down to allow for canteens not covered by labour statistics
(c) Net output scaled up to allow for Registered Clubs
(d) Net output scaled up to allow for Licensed Clubs

The C.S.O. supplied the estimated net output in 1963 for four sectors of the catering trade. We assumed that these net outputs applied to the groups (or combinations of the groups) shown in the 1964 Catering Enquiry and we derived our weights for the turnover series by allocating them appropriately and adjusting for parts of the trade (e.g. boarding-houses) which were in the labour figures but not covered by the Catering Enquiry. The details are shown in Table E.4.

Table E.5 shows the final set of net output index numbers, and compares the movement in the aggregate with that supplied by the C.S.O. The differences are not very great.

Hairdressing (MLH 889)

The basic sources of information relating to the output by value of the hairdressing trade are:
  (i) Census of Distribution turnover: 1950, 1957, 1961, 1966;
  (ii) The Family Expenditure Survey, introduced in 1958 (which includes expenditure on hairdressing whether or not done by establishments classified to MLH 889);
  (iii) The D.T.I. monthly turnover series introduced in 1961 (and discontinued after 1971).
To deflate these value series, information is also available on the movements in the price of a man's haircut and a woman's shampoo and set: these indices are combined with fixed weights to derive the 'All Hairdressing' component of the Retail Price Index.

The C.S.O. produce an index of hairdressing real net output which has been based upon a series of different indicators. Until 1958 the series relied solely on the movement in employment, but from 1958 onwards the C.S.O. switched to using consumers' expenditure (in which the F.E.S. gives only a single figure for men's and women's taken together). In addition, between 1961 and 1963 only, use was made of information from the D.T.I. monthly turnover series. For deflation, the C.S.O. has always applied the 'All Hairdressing' component of the Retail Price Index.

Despite the availability of this ready-made index, we were critical of certain features of its construction upon which we felt we could improve. In particular, we feared that the method of deflation which had been used was seriously wrong owing to two factors operating in combination:
  (a) the growing proportion of women's hairdressing, which is visible from the Censuses (see Table E.6);
  (b) the fact that prices have shown a much slower rate of increase for women's hairdressing than for men's — e.g. between 1960 and 1969 the men's index rose by 83%, against 48% for the women's
In addition, we were critical of the use — between 1961 and 1963 only — of a D.T.I. turnover series which was later found to have seriously underestimated the growth of turnover, possibly by inadequate reflection of the birth and growth of new establishments.

For the Census years, we therefore attempted to estimate net output figures by value and volume for men's and women's hairdressing separately, as reported by establishments classified to the hairdressing trade, which we then combined to derive an index for hairdressing output done by the trade. Similarly, we estimated

Table E.5　　*Net Output of the Catering Trades (MLH 884)*
(£m at 1963 prices)

Series used for projection[a]	1960	1961	1962	1963	1964	1965	1966	1967	1968	1969
Hotels etc.	282.6	279.0	287.0	282.6	294.2	292.7	291.2	281.3	287.8	291.6
Restaurants etc.	186.6	182.4	182.4	178.7	180.7	179.3	176.9	170.3	180.6	166.4
Fish and chip shops	44.7	44.5	44.1	43.6	44.6	44.4	43.7	43.1	42.2	41.2
Tenanted public houses	112.8	116.6	115.4	115.9	118.6	113.6	115.3	111.2	111.4	113.7
Managed public houses	46.1	48.5	49.2	51.1	52.8	52.5	55.0	55.2	56.0	58.1
Canteens	14.0	13.5	13.5	13.3	13.4	13.1	12.6	11.9	11.8	11.5
Total	686.9	684.5	691.6	685.3	704.3	695.6	694.7	672.9	689.8	682.5
Index (1963 = 100)	100.23	99.89	100.91	100.00	102.77	101.51	101.37	98.20	100.66	99.59
C.S.O. series (1963 = 100)	*96.8*	*99.1*	*99.3*	*100.0*	*102.5*	*101.7*	*101.2*	*98.7*	*99.2*	*99.8*

(a) See Table E.3.

229

Table E.6   *Receipts from Hairdressing by Type of Business*

(*£'000*)

Type of Business	1950 Receipts from Hairdressing	As % of Total	1957(a) Receipts from Hairdressing	As % of Total	1961 Receipts from Hairdressing	As % of Total	1966(b) Receipts from Hairdressing	As % of Total
All types	28,275	100.0	50,487	100.0	85,081	100.0	122,891	100.0
of which								
(i) Men's	5,387	19.1	(7,169)	(14.2)	9,820	11.5	15,803	12.9
(ii) Men's-Tobacconists	2,236	7.9	(3,887)	(7.7)	6,486	7.6	2,534	2.1
(iii) Women's	14,079	49.8	(30,545)	(60.5)	56,653	66.6	91,672	74.6
(iv) Men's and Women's	6,572	23.2	(8,835)	(17.5)	12,120	14.2	12,883	10.5
Estimate for women's hairdressing(c)	18,554	65.6	36,694	72.7	65,378	76.8	100,184	81.5
Estimate for men's hairdressing(c)	9,720	34.4	13,742	27.2	19,701	23.2	22,708	18.5

(a) The percentages in brackets for 1957 were interpolated between the 1950 and 1961 figures and then applied to the total receipts to give a turn-over breakdown by kind of business.

(b) For 1966, a detailed breakdown is only available on an organisation basis. All figures have been proportionately scaled up to an establishment basis.

(c) Using Census allocations between men's and women's for 1961 and 1966, and assuming a similar allocation for the mixed businesses in other years.

a separate value and volume series for receipts from the sale by hairdressers of goods such as tobacco and toilet requisites, in order that the (declining) retail element of the trade could be combined with the pure service element on a compatible added-value basis (where its share in the total was about 3% in 1966). In this way we derived a series for the output of the hairdressing industry as a whole.

The next step was to compare the movement in the Census totals by value, for hairdressing as such, with the movement in consumers' expenditure based on the F.E.S., and we were reassured to find that the agreement was reasonably good.

The figures for consumers' expenditure were then divided between men's and women's, using the proportions derived above for the Census years, and interpolating or extrapolating these for the other years. These value figures were then deflated separately by the appropriate indices, and added together to produce a revised series for consumers' expenditure on hairdressing at 1963 prices. This series showed very similar movements between the Census years to the one derived above for the volume of output by the industry (including its retail sales): we therefore used it to interpolate and extrapolate the Census figures, to give the index numbers shown in Table E.2.

Attempts at Alternative Measures of Output

We gave some thought to the question whether the type of output indicator sought by the C.S.O. was really the best instrument to use in our calculations, and whether, if it were not, it would be possible to devise anything better with the available statistics.

On the *logic* of the matter, it seems clear in principle that we are ultimately interested in assessing the effects of SET on productivity, rather than with securing a historical measurement of what happened to it: the C.S.O., on the other hand, is concerned with the historical task of measuring what happened to output, and doing so in a way which will fit into the picture for the national aggregates.

The logic of our procedure is seen most clearly if we take the case (which underlay our work on distribution, and is normally a good approximation) in which it is assumed that the *output* of the industry in any post-SET year would have been the same, whether or not SET had been introduced. In that case, we do not need to *measure* the output for its own sake, because it is common to both the positions being compared: what we have to do is to compare the *actual* employment with what we would have *'expected'* to accompany the actual output in the absence of SET (or other abnormal new factors). What we require, therefore, is the best guide to what amount of labour was to be 'expected': this must clearly involve a measure of the industry's output of some kind, but it need not necessarily be of the kind which fits into the national income statistics.

An example from the insurance industry may make this clearer. The C.S.O. measure the output of the motor insurance section by using the *difference* between premiums received and claims paid — and this may well be the best measure for their purposes. If the introduction of the breathalyser leads to fewer claims, however, this indicator will show a substantial rise in output, although clearly it should *reduce* the amount of labour required: consequently our estimate of the effects of SET will be greatly exaggerated if we say that the amount 'expected' to be used in this post-SET year is to be assumed to have been *raised* on account of the rise in output. We would have a better basis for our 'expectation' about the labour required if we used the *sum* of premiums and claims as our guide to the labour that we would 'expect' to find. This might be called an indicator of the volume of 'work-generating output'.

This is clearly a very tricky subject, in which one is in danger of throwing away the baby with the bath-water: one must not include in the 'work-generating output' a list of processes which *were* undertaken in the past, because the firms may introduce a change of method — perhaps as a direct result of SET — which enables the same effective output to be produced without involving some process at all, or with a much smaller amount of it. Nevertheless, particularly in the tricky field of services (where a unit of the 'quantity' of service produced is often very elusive) one should be seeking to get a measure of output which reflects its 'work-generating' characteristics, so far as these are due to factors external to the industry.[1]

In practice the deficiencies of the statistics (and our limited knowledge and resources) made it impossible for us to pursue this matter at all systematically, but we experimented with two industries: we would have welcomed the opportunity to discuss the problems with people in the various trades, but this was not possible in view of the truncation of our enquiry. (We did not feel that action of this kind was needed in any of the trades in near-distribution.) The immediate use of the results was to see whether they pointed to a higher or a lower answer than the ones derived from our main calculations for the 'difference' in Table XIII.1, which we used as a guide to the effect of SET on productivity.

Insurance Banking and Finance (MLH 869)
In accordance with the principles sketched above, we used rather different indicators for the various sections of the trade.

For life assurance (ordinary and industrial), we took the total of premiums, claims paid and outstanding life and annuity funds each year. Changes in this total were deflated by the consumers' price index to give an index of work performed by the sector.

For the other types of insurance, fund management is much less important, and our index was derived from the total of premiums plus claims paid each year, deflated by price indices appropriate to each section.

The current price series referred to above were adjusted, with the help of the C.S.O., to take account of changes in the coverage of the statistics resulting from the 1967 Companies Act, which raised problems for the 1969 figures.

The constant price series were combined using C.S.O. weights to give an index of changes in the amount of work-generating output for insurance companies as a group.

In the banking sector, we omitted most of the C.S.O. indicators as not reflecting 'work-generation' — e.g. we felt that it might involve more work to hold down the total of advances and deposits than to allow it to rise; the series for the number of cheques cleared, taken by itself, seemed a much better indicator of the work-

---

1 This point is allied to — but not identical with — the question of allowing for changes in the net-output-content of a unit of gross output, caused by (e.g.) the use of more highly fabricated materials or of fewer 'outside' services.

generating output. We would have liked to have had this for a wider field than the London Clearing Banks, and also to cover other methods of making payments (e.g. credit transfers), but in the time available we could not solve the various problems. So we used the series for the London Clearing Banks alone, recognising that it would have a downward bias — but even so it rose more rapidly than the C.S.O. series for the real net output of banking.

For Building Societies we finally decided to use simply the number of advances made. We are grateful to the Building Societies Association for providing us with unpublished information which enabled us to make this calculation.

For stockbrokers and jobbers we decided to rely simply on the number of transactions marked.

For hire purchase companies, we followed the C.S.O. by using the total of new credit extended and instalments outstanding, deflated by the durable goods component of the Retail Price Index.

For property owning and managing, we followed the C.S.O., who use three indicators — the transfer costs of land and buildings (representing estate agents etc.) the stock of commercial and industrial buildings (representing the real estate industry) and the movement calculated for the rest of the Order (representing the parts of finance and property owning not covered elsewhere).

In order to combine the indicators just described for the different parts of the Order, we used weights taken from the 1966 Census of Population, which gives details of the number of people engaged in each. This procedure differs in principle from that used for the national accounts, where estimates of the net output arising in each sector constitute the weights, but seemed more appropriate for our purpose.

Table E.7   *Insurance, Banking and Finance: Alternative Measures of Output*
(Index Numbers, 1963 = 100)

Year	'Work-generating output'	C.S.O. output series
1960	89.3	90.5
1961	92.7	93.8
1962	93.7	95.4
1963	100.0	100.0
1964	106.0	105.3
1965	107.3	108.0
1966	111.1	111.8
1967	119.0	118.3
1968	131.1	127.7
1969	137.5	133.0

Results. The series for 'work-generating output' derived in this way is given in Table E.7, with the C.S.O. output series for comparison. It will be seen that it rises rather more rapidly in the period from 1965 to 1969, but shows much the same increase between 1960 and 1965.

In consequence of this, when the two output series were combined with the labour figures we found that productivity rose with the new series by 18.3% between 1965 and 1969, against 13.7% on the C.S.O. series. As 'trend productivity' was affected much less by the change of series (the index for 1969, with 1965 = 100, being raised only from 101.3 to 101.8), the difference between the actual and the trend was significantly increased — from 12.2% of the trend index to 16.2%. Thus the use of this alternative figure in Table XIII.1 would not, as it happens, have had any effect on the median value for the 10 trades, because this one was already well above the median.

Cinemas, Theatres, Radio etc. (MLH 881) and Sport (MLH 882)

We were worried about the C.S.O. series for this combined industry for two reasons: on principle, it seemed unsuitable for our purposes to have a set of indicators in which the radio and television component was represented solely by the number of licences current, when a large part of the work was generated by the (increasing) number of programmes and by the commercial side of the independent television companies; and on a pragmatic approach, the big fall in output shown by the C.S.O. series seemed surprising (see Table E.2) and the consequent fall in productivity meaningless for our purposes (see Table XIII.1).

We therefore decided to experiment with a rather simple approach, which took as indicator the sum of two items, both measured at 1963 prices: total consumers' expenditure on 'entertainment and recreational services' (as given in the 1971 Blue Book), and the net advertising revenue of television companies.[1] The resultant outcome is shown in Table E.8, with the C.S.O. series for comparison, and also the index numbers for numbers engaged (which show little movement).

Table E.8   *Entertainment etc.: Alternative Measures of Output*
(Index Numbers, 1963 = 100)

Year	'Work-generating output'	C.S.O. output series	Numbers engaged (F.T.E.)
1960	83.2	105.8	97.4
1	88.4	103.5	98.8
2	92.9	100.7	99.0
3	100.0	100.0	100.0
4	109.2	100.8	101.4
5	114.1	100.0	100.6
6	115.0	98.0	100.2
7	119.9	96.4	100.5
8	123.7	93.2	99.1
9	123.5	90.8	99.3

The alternative series is radically different, and seems to us a good deal more plausible, at least for our purposes. The reason for the contrast is something of a mystery to us. When we embarked on the exercise we had expected that some such changes might arise, though hardly on this scale, because we were including a completely new figure for the advertising revenue of ITV companies, and this had an upward trend: we assumed that the 'volume' of consumers' expenditure would show much the same movement as the C.S.O.'s existing series for real output, since they covered much the same ground.

---

1   We are grateful to the Independent Television Companies Association for supplying the figures (before deduction of the levy) for the years 1963 to 1969, based on audited returns. The figures for earlier years had to be estimated.

In the event, however, the inclusion of the ITV component was not of very great quantitative importance. In the base year (1963) it carried only 16% of the total weight; more important still, it and the consumers' expenditure series *both* show rising trends, which are not radically different — between 1963 and 1969 the movements are, indeed, rather similar. The main explanation for the different movements shown in Table E.8 is simply the fact that the Blue Book series for the volume of consumers' expenditure shows a radically different movement from the C.S.O.'s real output series for the industries: between 1963 and 1969 the former shows a rise of 23% and the latter a fall of 9%.

Whatever the explanation, the use of the alternative series produces a radically different productivity movement, showing a substantial upward trend instead of a decline. This applies however both to the pre-SET period and to the post-SET period, and indeed is substantially greater in the earlier period. In consequence, our calculation of the 'difference' figure, on the lines set out in Table XIII.1, is revised as follows:

	With new index	*With C.S.O. index*
Index numbers for 1969 (1965 = 100)		
(1) Output	107.8	90.8
(2) Numbers engaged (FTE)	98.7	98.7
(3) Productivity	109.2	92.0
(4) 'Trend' productivity	125.3	93.0
Difference, (3) minus (4), as % of (4)	−12.8	−1.1

It would obviously be absurd to take this calculation as implying that SET had the effect of reducing productivity in this industry by 12.8% — just as it would have been absurd to take the calculation for insurance banking and finance as implying that SET raised productivity in that industry by 16%. As explained in Chapter XIII, we had to take the figures for all available trades *as a group*, and hope that the errors — whether due to bad statistics or to the very simple econometric procedure used — would tend to cancel out. In this case the result has been crucially affected by the high rise in productivity taken as 'expected', which in turn simply reflects the rise between 1960 and 1965.

As it happens, a change-over to the alternative set of figures for entertainment and sport would not have affected the median for the 10 trades, because this one was already below it. As this was true also of the revised series for insurance banking and finance, the introduction of the alternative output series would not have affected our conclusion at all.

Appendix F
Prices

Data availability

Price data are available from several sources, the most important for our purposes being the Department of Employment which made available to us a number of unpublished components of the monthly Index of Retail Prices. These series form the basis of our analysis of prices presented in Chapter XII, but we only used those series which we felt could sensibly be interpreted for possible effects of SET upon prices. Some series could not be usefully included in one section or both, *either* because they were unsuitable for short-term analysis, prices typically being changed perhaps only once or twice a year, *or* because we possessed insufficient information about earnings or other necessary factors to be able to undertake a meaningful long-term analysis.[1]

Other sources of information about prices include the Central Statistical Office (C.S.O.), the reports of the National Board for Prices and Incomes (N.B.P.I.) and our own enquiries. The information available from these sources was carefully considered and was drawn upon at various points in this Report, but little of it was used in Chapter XII. This is because the data from our own enquiries and from the N.B.P.I. reports do not cover a sufficient period of time for us to be able to establish any pre-SET trends or relationships, but in the case of the C.S.O. data, the problem was rather different. Such data as the C.S.O. does gather is collected for the purposes of estimating output or expenditure at constant prices for inclusion in the national income accounts. Whilst their data may be adequate for these purposes, it is not generally suitable for use in the type of analysis undertaken in Chapter XII.

In brief we aimed to include any series which was at all suitable, in the hope of making up for the inevitably rather poor quality of the data by having a large number of series, with (hopefully) no common bias. The number of series which passed our combined tests of quality and time-period was unfortunately rather small.

Methods of analysis

Two methods of analysis were used in Chapter XII, one based on short-term movements in prices over three month periods, the other based on long-term movements

---

1 Football admission charges present a good example of a series which we have excluded from both sections of our analysis. Admission charges are normally increased once a year – at the beginning of the season. Hence a short-term analysis would be inappropriate since the very purpose of the approach, namely to increase the importance of SET in relation to other costs and hence to 'isolate' its effects on prices, would be defeated. We also had insufficient information about footballers' earnings, transfer fees and the effects of the abolition of the maximum wage to be able to undertake a long-term analysis.

over four year periods. The two approaches were designed to supplement each other in an attempt to overcome some of the difficulties inherent in such an exercise. Briefly these stemmed from the existence of secular, cyclical, seasonal and random factors influencing prices, as well as errors in the data.

Chapter XII outlines the two approaches, their advantages and their disadvantages. The following section of the Appendix describes the methodology of these approaches in more detail.

Short-term analysis

The short-term analysis of price movements, based on changes in prices from mid-July to mid-October, was primarily designed to overcome the problems associated with cyclical movements in the economy and seasonal price-changes. By considering price movements over such short periods, one should be able largely to 'isolate' the effects of SET from the effects of other general increases in costs; for if businesses adjusted their prices at the times when SET was introduced or increased, the impact of SET upon total costs would be disproportionately greater than the impact of other cost increases, when considered over a period as short as three months.

The period from mid-July to mid-October (mid-June to mid-September in the case of 1969) was chosen because it straddled the dates at which SET became effective and was subsequently increased. A period of three months seemed to be the shortest period over which we could hope to measure the effect that SET might have had upon prices. The period chosen needed to be as short as possible to minimise the effect of cyclical forces, which might be producing movements in opposite directions in one year from those in another.

Such a short-term approach did, however, contain a number of shortcomings, of which the most serious is that of adjustment lags. If, for example, businessmen did not raise prices at the times when SET was introduced or increased but rather adopted a 'wait and see' attitude, then obviously our short-term approach would completely fail to register a 'SET effect'. If, on the other hand, businessmen only made small increases in prices, while intending to make further ones at a later date, then the short-term analysis would under-record the SET effect. Perhaps more serious is the danger that the introduction (or increase) of SET might be made the 'occasion' for concentrating into one price change not only the influence of SET but also the trader's reaction to other cost increases, such as are continually accruing in an era of generally rising prices: in such a case the single large increase made when SET was introduced would be followed by an unusually long period of stability, and the short-term analysis would over-estimate the SET effect on prices.

The operation of the Prices and Incomes Policy may have tended to produce this last result; for under the policy businesses were only allowed to increase prices under certain circumstances, one of which was the introduction of SET.[1] The extent to which such 'concentrated' increases would in practice have been possible is

1 The relevant White Paper, Cmnd. 3073, introducing the prices and incomes standstill from July, 1966 to January 1967 says: 'This standstill period will apply except to the limited extent that increases in prices or charges may be necessary because of marked increases, which cannot be absorbed, in costs of imported materials, or which arise from changes in supply for seasonal and other reasons or which are due to action by the Government such as increased taxation' (para. 4).

probably fairly small, given the existence of the National Board for Prices and Incomes. However, it may have been sufficient to provide an upward bias to the results obtained from our short-term approach, especially in 1966.

Other limitations of a short-term approach include the effects upon the results of random variations or errors in the data: there is a danger that these may be proportionately greater in relation to the underlying price increase, the shorter the period under study. And one may get 'perverse' results, such as the fact that football admission charges are only varied at one date in the year, to reflect a whole year's developments.

For the above reasons we decided to supplement our short-term approach with an analysis of price movements over somewhat longer periods of time.

Long-term analysis

We commenced our long-term analysis by studying movements in prices on a year to year basis, using annual average data. Such an approach had the immediate advantage of overcoming problems of seasonal variations in the data. It also considerably reduced the problem of initial over- or under-adjustment of prices, especially when one considers the cumulative effect of SET on prices. The problems associated with any 'concentration' effect resulting from the operation of the prices and incomes policy were also considerably reduced.

Using annual data meant however that SET also assumed proportionately less significance as against other cost factors. An essential of such an approach was thus to make allowance for the effects of variations in other cost factors from year to year. For this purpose we constructed indices of average weekly labour costs (exluding SET) for the services under study, based on average weekly earnings and employers' National Insurance and graduated pension contributions.[1] Such indices seemed to be appropriate as indicators of variations in cost increases for two main reasons. First, they related directly to the largest single item of cost faced by many services. This factor becomes even more relevant if businesses adopt a pricing policy based on any form of mark-up on labour costs. Secondly, such indices — when adjusted for the relationship between prices and wages in the way described below — ought to provide reasonable indicators of annual variations in costs in the economy as a whole and hence in the other costs borne by these service trades. Obviously these indicators can only provide an approximation to such cost movements, but bearing in mind the general data limitations which we faced, they seemed to be the best for which we could hope.

After experimenting with other methods we decided to adopt for our long-term approach an analysis of prices based on movements over a sufficiently lengthy period of time to minimise the effects of cyclical influences, random influences and

---

1 We used the following weekly labour cost indicators for the following trades:

Trade	Labour cost indicator used based on earnings in
Shoe repairing	Shoe repairing
Laundering	Laundering
Dry-cleaning	Dry-cleaning
Hairdressing	Average of above 3 series
Watch-cleaning	Average of above 3 series

errors in the data. We chose a four-year period as a basis for study as this approximated to the normal length of the post-war cycle. We again used annual average data, but rather than use calendar year averages, we took years running from August of one year to July of the next. (The reason for this choice is explained in Chapter XII).

We then calculated the ratios between price and wage-cost relatives over various four year periods. From these figures we then made 3 separate estimates for each item of the pre-SET relationship between the 4-year relatives for prices and labour costs. These estimates were applied to post-SET movements in labour costs to arrive at the price increases that might have been expected in the absence of SET. The difference between the expected and actual price increase for any item gave us a measure of the effect of SET or other abnormal new factors upon prices in 1969/70. The results of this exercise are shown in Table F.1, which shows the answers obtained by each of the 3 separate methods and the average of the three methods. It is the latter set of results that is presented in Table XII.3 of Chapter XII.

The nature of the three methods used in Table F.1 was as follows. *Method One* works with successive, overlapping four-year periods running from 1955/6 to 1965/6 (i.e. 1955/6 to 1959/60, 1956/7 to 1960/1, 1957/8 to 1961/2 etc.); for each of these the ratio of the price relative to the labour-cost relative is found, and these are then averaged. This approach effectively gives smaller weight to the early and later years of the forecast period than to the middle years (i.e. 1955/6 and 1965/6 are only included once). *Method Two* calculates similar ratios for the two periods 1957/8 to 1961/2 and 1961/2 to 1965/6 and averages these, thereby giving all years an equal weighting. *Method Three* simply uses the ratio for the latest four-year period available — i.e. 1961/2 to 1965/6 — as a basis for the forecast.

The price-labour cost movement ratios are set out in Table F.2. As will be seen from the table, the three methods gave somewhat different answers for individual items, but each gave much the same answer for the average of the 7 items, the figures being .9638, .9615 and .9609.

The estimates for 1967/68 were obtained in a similar way to those for 1969/70, but with an appropriate adjustment of the price-labour cost ratio to take account of the period being two years instead of four. We used the pre-SET relationships as a basis for estimating the likely price increase over the two year period 1965/6 to 1967/8 in the absence of SET and compared this estimate with the actual price increase to obtain a measure of the SET effect in 1967/8.

Table F.1   'SET Effect' on Prices in 1969/1970
(All figures are percentages)

Item	Price-increase between 1965/6 and 1969/70	Estimate of SET Effect(a) by Different Methods			
		Method One(b) (based on mean of successive price-labour cost relationships)	Method Two(b) (based on mean of 1957/8–1961/2 and 1961/2–1965/6 price-labour cost relationships)	Method Three(b) (based on 1961/2–1965/6 price-labour cost relationship)	Average of methods
Dry-cleaning	19.4	9.8	9.6	6.3	8.6
Laundering	26.3	-0.9	-0.5	-2.3	-1.2
Hairdressing: man's haircut	33.1	1.3	2.0	5.0	2.8
woman's shampoo & set	24.5	3.1	4.2	8.0	5.1
Shoe repairing: man's sole & heel repair	22.1	6.1	6.8	8.7	7.2
woman's heel repair	31.3	4.5	4.5	3.8	4.3
Watch cleaning	30.1	5.6	4.6	2.3	4.2
Average of above items	26.7	4.2	4.5	4.5	4.4

(a) The figures show the percentage by which the prices charged exceeded those which would have been 'expected' in the absence of SET.
(b) See text for explanation of methods.

Table F.2   Price/Labour-Cost Ratios[a]

Item	Method One Mean of successive ratios 1955/6–1959/60 to 1961/2 to 1965/6	Method Two Mean of two ratios 1957/8–1961/2 and 1961/2–1965/6	Method Three Pre-SET ratio i.e. 1961/2–1965/6	Mean of 3 Methods
Shoe repairing: men's	0.9241	0.9180	0.9020	0.9147
women's	1.0098	1.0090	1.0158	1.0115
Dry-cleaning	0.8769	0.8785	0.9061	0.8872
Laundering	0.9866	0.9830	1.0010	0.9902
Hairdressing: man's haircut	1.0325	1.0255	0.9961	1.0180
woman's shampoo & set	0.9488	0.9386	0.9058	0.9311
Watch cleaning	0.9682	0.9776	0.9993	0.9817
Mean of above items:	0.9638	0.9615	0.9609	0.9621

(a) Based on years running from August to July.

Appendix G
SET Payments and Refunds

In this Appendix we describe the statistical procedures used in estimating the net burden of SET by industry, and also some of the checks used to see whether these estimates were reasonable. We also consider some problems over the allocation of the burden of SET between end-uses.

The Estimation of SET payments by Industry

The first stage of our task was to obtain, for the year 1970, estimates of the average number of people in respect of whom SET was paid in Great Britain, irrespective of whether a refund was subsequently obtained or not. These estimates had to be divided by various industrial categories, for reasons which will appear below, and not merely between the SET-sector and the non-SET sector: moreover, since we wanted to use these numbers to estimate the amount of SET paid, they had to be divided between males and females and to show the people under 18 separately, since the rate of SET varied between the four age-and-sex categories.

Estimation of numbers for the whole economy

The first method which we used for estimating the required numbers for the whole economy was designed to provide, as part of the same operation, the analysis by industry, and also by sex and age. Its starting point was the Department of Employment series for employees in civilian employment, from which various deductions were made (as described below) to allow for the fact that SET would not be paid in respect of various classes of people included in those figures (e.g. the sick). When we came to write a formal account of the method, however, we realised that there were logical flaws in our procedures, and we therefore devised two alternative ways of arriving at the required answer for the economy as a whole, which yielded separate figures for males and females, but did not provide a ready basis for making the industrial and age subdivisions. Fortunately, however, the averages of the two new estimates agreed very closely with the estimates for the aggregate prepared by our original method: we therefore used the industrial allocation derived from the original method to allocate the total males and total females between the relevant industries, and we also split the figures by age in the proportions derived from our original calculation.

For purposes of exposition, we refer to the original method as the 'old indirect method', because it started from a figure for the total active civilian population, and made rather substantial deductions to cover various classes in respect of whom SET was not paid. Our two later methods are referred to as the 'new indirect method', because it also started from the total active population and made substantial deductions, and the 'direct method', which started from figures which (apart from one adjustment) were directly a measure of the number of people in respect of whom SET was paid.

The Old Indirect Method

As explained above, the starting point for this method was the published D.E. figures for employees in employment, broken down between males and females: these are based on the June card-counts, but for many industries are available in the form of a monthly series which we averaged over the year. The number of males and females under 18 in each industry was obtained by using the proportions shown for June 1970 (which covered the unemployed as well as the employed).

As we later realized, these figures were not well adapted for our purpose: their basic starting-point is the card-count, less the number of people registered as unemployed on a particular date, whereas we wanted the deduction to reflect the number who were unemployed *for the whole week* (since an insurance contribution, and hence SET, is payable unless the employee is unemployed for the whole week), but also to cover the unemployed who did not register.

From these basic figures, we then made three deductions for classes of people in respect of whom SET would not be paid, as follows:

    (a) *The sick,* whose numbers we estimated from the New Earnings Survey and the D.H.S.S. figures for insured persons incapacitated by sickness: here again we failed to allow for the fact that SET would be payable, unless the sickness covered a whole week.

    (b) The *very-low-income* group, whose income was less than £4 per week, or who worked less than eight hours per week: a special insurance stamp is used for these people, to which SET was not added, and our estimate was based on the number of contributions in the year which took this special form.

    (c) *Students* who hold an insurance card and are included in the card-count: since students do not typically register as unemployed in the weeks when they are not working, we assumed that 5-6ths of the number should be subtracted as not paying SET in an average week, on the assumption that the average period of employment in the year would be two months.

The weakness in the old indirect method was therefore that we made excessive deductions for the unemployed who did register and for the sick, but that we made no direct allowance for a number of categories of employees who did not pay a contribution (and so SET) in any particular week, either because they were unregistered unemployed, or because they intended to work only for part of the year, or were taking an unpaid holiday, or were 'between jobs' (and did not register, because they would draw no benefit).

The New Indirect Method

Our first alternative method rested on the principle of trying to find better estimates for the various deductions which had to be made from the figure for the active population of employees, which in turn we estimated from the card-counts. The main source of this information was the series of quarterly ½% samples which the D.H.S.S. carried out on all the people coming within its ambit (including, for example, the retired and the married women who no longer seek employment). These samples provide a figure for the number of people in particular categories, so far as the payment of insurance stamps is concerned, in the final week of the contribution-year for the relevant class; and they also give figures for the total number of credits granted in the previous twelve-month period to contributors who were sick or unemployed.

In rather more detail, we estimated the average number of employees (whether employed or unemployed) in 1970 on the basis of the three card-counts which gave the figures for the middle of 1969, 1970 and 1971. Since the numbers for each of these three years were closely similar, it was possible to arrive at an estimate by interpolation which could be regarded as reasonably reliable.

Deductions from this figure for the active employee population were then made for the following factors:

(a) The first deduction was for the unemployed and sick, on the basis of the credit statistics. We made five independent estimates for the 1970 average number of people not paying SET for this reason, by using samples covering the five 12-month periods ending in June 1970, September 1970, December 1970, March 1971, and June 1971. In each case, we adjusted the recorded number of credits by means of an index of the number of people sick or unemployed in the relevant 12-month period, as compared with the number in the calendar year 1970. We took the average of these five independent estimates, and were pleased to find that the average discrepancy between an estimate and the average (taken without regard to sign) was only a little over one per cent of the average, both for males and for females.

From these figures we deducted the long-term sick (i.e. those who were sick throughout the year), because they are excluded from the figures for the card-count.

(b) We next deducted the number of students who did not pay a stamp, (or get a credit), taking the average of the four sample weeks of 1970.

(c) The samples also showed a figure for employees paying a stamp at the very-low-income rate, and we took the average for the four sample weeks here also.

(d) The samples also showed a number of other categories of people who did not pay a stamp or get a credit in the sample week, and it was clear that a proportion of various headings would have been included in the card-count, and ought therefore to be subtracted. Fortunately, the Government Actuary's department had been working on a similar problem, and kindly provided us with estimates for the number of males and females who should be deducted for these miscellaneous reasons. This estimate was inevitably based on somewhat imprecise data, but it was an essential part of the calculation, and we would like to record our gratitude to the Government Actuary's department.

(e) Finally, the Department of Employment card-count includes a number of persons to whom cards had not yet been issued (e.g. unemployed school leavers under 16 years of age), and the Department kindly gave us the figure which should be subtracted to cover this category when estimating the number of people paying SET.

We would not pretend that all the loose ends were effectively tied up in this calculation, but we felt fairly confident that we had got the main items, and there did not seem to be any particular bias in the final figures. In total, the deductions which we made came to 1,454,000 males and 1,180,000 females, and the resultant estimates for the number of people paying SET are given in Table G.1 below, along with the other estimates. To obtain the total of SET in-payments we divided the males and females by industry on the basis of the figures derived from the old indirect method, and then split each industry's figure to get the number under 18, again by using the figures from the old indirect method.

Table G.1   *Estimates for Numbers of People Paying SET in Great Britain in 1970*

	(Averages for the year, thousands)			
	New indirect method	Direct Method	Average of (1) and (2)	Old indirect method
	(1)	(2)		
Total Males	12,829	12,945	12,887	12,903
Total Females	7,457	7,135	7,296	7,274
Total Males and Females	20,286	20,080	20,183	20,177
Total SET paid (£m.)	2,030	2,025	2,027	2,028

The Direct Method

The direct method also relied on the D.H.S.S. samples, but was very much simpler. It started from the figures for the numbers of males and females shown as paying a Class I contribution (or receiving a credit) in each of the four sample weeks in the year, but excluding the people who paid only the low-income stamp (since that did not involve payment of SET). We were reassured to find that the figures for the four sample weeks were very similar, and we treated the average of the four as giving the annual average for 1970.[1]

The numbers to be subtracted on account of contribution credits was the same as in the new indirect method, except that we did not subtract the long-term sick, because they were included in the basic figures.

As can be seen from Table G.1, the new indirect method and the direct method gave reasonably similar answers both for males and for females, and the divergencies were in opposite directions, so that the total for males and females agreed to within one per cent. The estimates for the total SET payments were in even closer agreement, because the higher number of people included a higher proportion of females.

As we had no strong reason for preferring one of the new methods to the other, we took a simple average of the results, which is also shown in Table G.1, and which we regard as our best estimate for the numbers involved. As will be seen, the agreement between this estimate and the one produced by our original method was most unexpectedly close, not only for the totals, but also for males and females taken separately.

We therefore felt justified in using the proportions of males and females in each industry, which we had derived from the original method, to produce figures for

---

1   In point of fact, the average absolute deviation of the four sample figures from the mean was 0.4% of the mean for males and 1.8% for females.

the numbers paying SET in each industry. These were used to produce Table G.2, which gives the estimated payments of SET for the industry groups which are most relevant to our work.

Table G.2   *Estimated Payments of SET in Great Britain, 1970*

1968 SIC Order or MLH	SET Payments £ million
Agriculture, Forestry and Fishing I	36
Manufacturing III–XIX	851
'Other Mainly Exempt Industries'[a]	545
Total Non-SET Sector	1,432
Construction XX	144
Distribution XXIII	205
Insurance, Banking and Finance XXIV	78
Accountancy, Legal and Other Professional Services 871, 873, 879	26
Miscellaneous Services XXVI	131
Other Road Haulage, Miscellaneous Transport and Services 704, 709	11
Total Payments	2,027

(a) These include – Mining and Quarrying II, Gas, Electricity and Water XXI, Transport XXII (excluding Other Road Haulage and Miscellaneous Transport Services, 704, 709), Educational Services 872, Medical and Dental Services 874, Religious Organisations 875, Research and Development Services 876, Public Administration and Defence XXVII.

The total of £2,027 million estimated in this way agreed well with the actual figure of £2,029 million published in Financial Statistics. Further checks on the reliability of the figures are developed in the final section of this Appendix.

Refunds to the SET Sector, Analysed by Industry
In this section we describe the methods used to estimate the amount of in-payments of the SET sector industries which would be likely to be repaid. The net burden by industry is then established as the difference between the in-payment and the amounts refunded.

Refunds in respect of part-time employees and employees aged 65 and over
In 1970 an employer could claim a two-thirds refund of SET for any employee aged 18 or over who worked less than 21 hours per week, and also in respect of full-time employees aged 65 and over. Refunds in respect of part-timers and employees aged 65 and over were made by the Department of Health and Social Security, which published a figure of £18 million for the total amount refunded in 1970 in its Annual Report.

Suitable employment data for estimating refunds by industry for 1970 in respect of part-timers and employees aged 65 and over are not available. To allocate this total of £18 million we were forced therefore to rely on the age and hours-worked breakdown by industry given in Part III of the 1966 Sample Census. As might be expected, this calculation gave over half the total to distribution.

Refunds in respect of employees reclassified to manufacturing

Employees classified to the SET sector for statistical purposes may be reclassified to manufacturing for refund purposes on a variety of grounds, which have been described in our discussion of distribution (in the First Report) and of construction (see Chapter XVI). It was important to devise a method of measuring the size of this reclassification not only for this statistical investigation, but because the extent of the practices is important in itself.

The method which we devised rested on unpublished returns of SET refunds made available by the Department of Employment for the five quarters beginning at the start of 1970. These analysed the refunds according to the MLH to which the employees in question were allocated *for this purpose*, and not according to their classification in the Ministry's normal labour statistics. Hence if a building employer secured recognition of a split establishment for part of his work-force as manufacturers of builders' woodwork, the refund for these workers would appear under MLH 471–2 'Other woodwork for buildings', although in the ordinary employment statistics they would remain in construction (MLH 500); and similarly if a Court ruling said that workers constructing a steel rolling mill were to be regarded for refund purposes as coming under MLH 341 as makers of industrial plant.

Basically, therefore, our method rested on a comparison of the actual refunds in various manufacturing industries, as shown in the DE statistics, with what we would have expected on the basis of the number of people shown as employed in that MLH in the ordinary labour statistics: we made these comparisons (which were rather time-consuming) for all the manufacturing industries which seemed to us likely to be important in the reclassification of workers normally classified to building or distribution.[1] In most of these cases (but not all) the actual refunds were above the expected level by a substantial percentage, and we assumed that this percentage reflected the number of workers transferred to that part of manufacturing for refund purposes.

In more detail, our method of calculating the 'expected' refund was first to reduce the number of employees shown in the ordinary labour statistics for each MLH examined so as to allow for those not paying SET; then to divide these into categories to whom different rates of 'refund' would apply, using the information given on the claim forms about age, sex and whether or not in a Development Area;[2] to allow, in respect of each quarter, for the probable distribution of the lags between in-payment by the employer and out-payment of refund (insofar as this might affect the number of workers and the amount repayable per head, because of the 1969 changes in SET and the ending of the premium); and to average the results for the five quarters for which we had refund statistics. These averages were then compared with the average of the actual refunds for those quarters.

1 As is shown below, the *total* refunds which we predicted for manufacturing (in the SIC sense) agreed quite well with the total recorded by the DE as made to 'manufacturing', after this and other adjustments.

2 The numbers given on the claim forms could not be directly compared with the number of employees in the ordinary labour statistics, because employers often claim for more than one quarter at a time: the quarterly average of the numbers on the forms would therefore be a good deal too low.

The Area information was necessary because the DE's refund statistics included the premium paid during part of the period to manufacturers in Development Areas.

Table G.3   *Number of Employees in Certain Trades Reclassified for Purposes of SET Refunds in Great Britain, 1970*

MLH (1968 SIC)	Number of employees 000's	Percentage of employment in that MLH
212 Bread and flour confectionery	33.0	22.9
214 Bacon curing, meat and fish products[a]	4.0	3.7
215 Milk and milk products[b]	61.7	121.9
442 Men's and boys' tailored outerwear	–	–
443 Women's and girls' tailored outerwear	–	–
472 Furniture and upholstery	0.6	0.7
473 Bedding, etc.[c]	1.0	4.8
Total estimate for employees reclassified from Distribution	100.3	
336 Construction and earth-moving equipment	19.8	46.7
337 Mechanical handling equipment	2.1	3.0
339 Other machinery	–	–
341 Industrial plant and steelwork[d]	58.7	32.8
349 Other mechanical engineering n.e.s.	–	–
394 Wire and wire manufacturers	–	–
399 Metal industries n.e.s.	–	–
469 Abrasives and building materials n.e.s.	21.1	17.8
471 Timber[e]	17.0	16.0
474 Shop and office fitting	1.6	4.5
Total estimate for employees reclassified from Construction	120.3	

(a) includes making of sausages, meat pasties etc.
(b) includes pasteurising and homogenizing.
(c) includes making up curtains and loose covers.
(d) includes constructional steelwork.
(e) includes woodwork for buildings.

Table G.3 gives the results of this analysis, expressed in terms of numbers of employees, including the cases where the statistics did not show any apparent addition to the ordinary labour force by this reclassification. We divided the recipient industries into two groups, according to whether the workers were more likely to have come from distribution or from building: it is of course quite possible that in some industries (e.g. MLH 471, 'Timber') some of the reclassification was from each of these, or indeed from some other SET trade.

One statistical point should be added: if anything, these estimates are likely to be biassed downwards, because the ordinary employment statistics for each MLH include employees in head offices, in respect of whom refunds will normally not be made if they are geographically separated from the factory. For all manufacturing, the section below shows that this factor would exaggerate the expected refund by rather under 1%, and one might argue that the percentages shown in Table G.2 should be raised by rather less than one unit.[1]

1   To test whether there might be any abnormal factors raising the actual refund payments in 1970/71 and so generating spurious figures for reclassification (for example late registrations or establishments becoming eligible as a result of a tribunal decision), actual and expected refunds were calculated quarterly for all manufacturing from 1967. Compared with the early period no abnormal factors appeared to be operating in the five quarters for which the above analysis was undertaken.

The amount of SET estimated to be refunded in respect of these reclassified employees was £23 million.

Refunds to employers in the SET sector by virtue of their organisational status

Certain employers in the SET sector receive refunds not on the grounds of their industrial status but rather on the grounds of their organisational status – i.e. because they are charities, or part of the public sector. The most important category is the employees of Local Authorities classified under SIC Order XX – Construction and *not* employed on works of 'major' construction.

The numbers of employees working for Local Authorities and the Central Government in June 1970 are published in *Economic Trends* for June 1972, with a separate figure for construction. These include the number engaged on works of major construction, but we estimated the split with the aid of the figures collected by the Ministry of Public Buildings and Works (as it then was) and published in the Monthly Bulletin of Construction Statistics. The total number of workers shown there is considerably larger, but the excess was attributed mainly to repair workers (who are often classified to local Authorities in the DE card count, because they do not work from a separate 'building' establishment). The MPBW figures were used to adjust from a June figure to an annual average, which was some 120,000 workers.

Other Local Authority employees attracting a refund but classified under industries in the SET sector are employees working in catering establishments of Local Authorities (classified under MLH 885), and Local Authority cemetery and crematorium employees (classified under 899). The Department of Employment publishes[1] an industrial breakdown of Local Authority employees which enables employees classified under MLH 885 to be approximately identified. For the other Local Authority employees classified under MLH 899 we were again obliged to rely on the 1966 Sample Census.

The amount of SET refunded in respect of all Local Authority employees classified in the SET sector was estimated at £17 million.

Charities. The refund statistics indicate that about 300,000 employees attract a refund of SET by virtue of their employment by charities, but provide no industrial breakdown. Manifestly a large part of these employees will be in education (MLH 872) and health (MLH 874), where most non-Government organisations are registered as charities (e.g. universities, public and direct-grant schools, nursing homes etc.): these we must not count, since we have treated the whole of these 'industries' as being in the non-SET sector. We were therefore forced back on the use of the 1966 Sample Census of Population, which shows about 100,000 employees under the heading 'Welfare and Charitable Services' (MLH 899-3 in the 1968 SIC). We added an arbitrary 10% to cover charities not classified under this heading, and arrived at an estimate of £9 million for SET refunds in 1970.

Other refunds in respect of employees in the SET sector

Certain parts of industries in the SET sector have been specifically declared eligible

---

1   Department of Employment Gazette June 1968.

for a refund – e.g. the processing of scrap metal and waste paper (classified under MLH 832), hotels operating in certain areas of the country (classified under MLH 884), the production of cinematographic film (classified under MLH 881). Refunds in respect of employees in these industries were shown in the refund statistics at £5 million.

Refunds are also made in respect of persons rendering domestic and nursing assistance at a qualified household – i.e. a household which includes someone who is aged seventy or over, someone who is sick or a child under the age of 16. Refunds in respect of these employees are made by the DHSS and we attributed the 1970 refund of £1.5 million wholly to MLH 891 Private Domestic Service.

Refunds in respect of employees sent overseas, which amounted to less than £0.5 million, were assumed to have been allowed for in our estimates of the non-SET sector refunds.

Net Burden on Industries Outside the SET Sector

We could only make rough estimates for the non-refundable payments of tax by industries that we classify to the non-SET sector, but the figure is not likely to be large – our final estimate was only £10 million, though we may have missed some cases.

The major sources of such in-payments arise firstly in the case of firms with head offices away from the main location of their activities, and secondly in the case of employees of doctors, dentists and private (non-charitable) schools.

For payments in respect of separate head office employees, quantitatively the most important will be for the head offices of manufacturing companies. The number of employees in separate manufacturing offices in the City of London was obtained from a survey based on returns under the Office, Shops and Railway Premises Act of 1963.[1] Estimates for other areas of central London were calculated using estimates for all office employees of manufacturing in central London given in the Sample Census 1966. To obtain the number of those in independent offices we used the ratio of independent manufacturing office employees to all manufacturing office employees in the City of London. An allowance was made for offices dispersed from central London[2] in the 1960's and to allow for other offices in provincial cities we added an arbitrary 10% of the independent manufacturing office employees in London. The number of employees in separate head offices of manufacturing firms was estimated to be 85,000 and the in-payments of SET in respect of these employees was calculated as £7 million.

In-payments in respect of employees of doctors, dentists and private schools are particularly tentative and liable to error. We have assumed that on average each doctor or dentist employs one assistant in respect of whom SET is paid but not refunded. Although it is possible in some cases for dentists to claim that their technical assistants are engaged in a 'manufacturing activity' (for example the manufacture of artificial teeth) an analysis based on the refund statistics to identify reclassifications of employees to MLH 353 – 'Surgical Instruments and Appliances' gave a zero answer.

1   The results of this survey are published in 'An Economic Study of the City of London' by J.H. Dunning and E. Victor Morgan.

2   Annual Reports of the Location of Offices Bureau.

The estimate of in-payments not refunded for employees of private schools was equally arbitrary. The major difficulty here is that very little is known about the extent to which independent schools have been able to obtain refunds by virtue of their charitable status. We have assumed that one-third of the employees of independent schools do not attract refunds of SET payments made.

The SET in-payments not refunded in respect of employees in medical and educational services was estimated at £3 million.

Net Burden of SET

The figures for refunds described in this section are combined with those for in-payments to give the net burden of SET for various groups of industries in Table XVII.1 on page 160.

Consistency Checks

The figures obtained in the above sections enable three further consistency checks to be made.

Total Refunds

First, we can prepare an estimate of the total refunds 'expected' on the basis of our figures, to compare with the figures for actual payments.

There are some slightly awkward timing problems involved. Our estimate for refunds to the non-SET sector is based on in-payments of £1432 million made in 1970, less the small amount (£10m.) not refundable: this would most naturally be treated as predicting refunds in the year ending about 31 March 1971, or perhaps a little later. For the SET sector, where the amount is much smaller (only £75 million in total) the timing basis varies between calendar year 1970 and fiscal 1970/71. Effectively, therefore, we might take fiscal 1970/71 as the natural period for which to seek a 'control' figure, but the postal strike in the first quarter of 1971 seems to have caused some delay in making payments. As the flow of refunds in the relevant quarters was not seriously disturbed by changes in SET rates or in the level of employment, one might say that the year to June 1971 provides an equally relevant test.

The control figure has to relate to Great Britain and to include an allowance for the imputed refunds in respect of Central Government employees (for whom no actual cash passes). This latter element is available from the Estimates for the fiscal year, and the same figure (£136m.) was also used for the year to June 1971: the ordinary refunds are available for each year from Financial Statistics.

The check then comes out as shown in Table G.4, and may be considered satisfactory.

Manufacturing

Our estimates give an expected figure of £844m. for refunds to the manufacturing part of the non-SET sector, which is most naturally applicable to the fiscal year 1970/71.

The DE refund statistics give figures for what they classify as manufacturing, but these include SET premiums paid to manufacturers in the Development Areas (£5m. in 1970/71), and there are two important differences in coverage from the

Table G.4   *Consistency Test for Total Refunds*

(£ million)

Our Estimate for Non-SET Sector		
1970 in-payments	1432	
Less Not refundable	10	1422
Out Estimate for SET Sector		
(a) Elderly and part-timers	18	
(b) Reclassified workers	23	
(c) Local Authorities and charities in SET sector	27	
(d) Miscellaneous	7	75
Our Total		1497
Control Figures		
Year to 31 March 1971		1500
Year to 30 June 1971		1505

normal SIC definition of manufacturing:

(a) They include the refunds (which we estimate at £23 million) paid in respect of reclassified workers, normally treated as part of building or distribution.

(b) On the other hand they do not include refunds in respect of those manufacturing workers employed by the Central Government, Local Authorities and Public Corporations, which are not made by the Department of Employment but by the Government Department with which these Bodies have their normal financial contacts. (Examples are Royal Ordnance, naval dockyards, HMSO, railway workshops).

Our estimate for the second of these adjustments (which we did not need for any purpose except this check) is based simply on the numbers shown by the Central Statistical Office[1] as employed in manufacturing by the Public Sector in June 1970, *less* the number employed by the British Steel Corporation (which is covered by DE). The CSO warns that the industrial allocation of the Public Sector employees does not conform exactly to the allocation used in the ordinary card-count, but none of the examples given seem to affect manufacturing and we did not check up on possible discrepancies.

This gave a figure of some 140,000 employees, and an estimated refund of £16 million.

The consistency check then runs as shown in Table G.5, in which we give two control figures so as to guard against the disturbance caused by the postal strike.

Agriculture, forestry and fishing

Our figure of £36 million for expected refunds, based on the in-payments in 1970, agreed very closely with the actual refunds recorded for 1970/71.

Allocation of Burden by End-Uses

In preparing Table XVII.2 of the main text, we allocated the net amount paid by each of the industries shown between end-uses in the light of the figures given in Table 6 of 'Input-Output' Tables for the U.K., 1963', produced by the Central

1   See Economic Trends for June 1972.

252

Table G.5 *Consistency Test for Refunds to Manufacturing*

		(£ million)
	Our estimate for manufacturing	844
Add	Allowance for reclassified workers	23
Subtract	Estimate for Public Sector not covered by DE refunds	− 16
Gives	'Expected' figure for DE refunds to 'manufacturing' (after subtracting premia)	851
	Actual DE refund figures less *premia*[a]	
	Fiscal year 1970/71	846
	Year to 30 June 1971	850

(a) Figures for these are given in Financial Statistics.

Statistical Office. This table shows how much of the net output of each industry in 1963 is reckoned to end up as a constituent of each type of final expenditure.

For distribution and miscellaneous services we used the proportions derived from the table as they stood. For construction however we first eliminated the output of the Public Sector workers who are exempted on grounds of the status of their employer, estimating how much of this output would go to personal consumption (in respect of house maintenance) and how much to Government consumption. We also eliminated an amount of output estimated to correspond with the workers who are 'reclassified' to manufacturing for SET purposes, assuming that this would all go to investment. The burden of SET was then distributed in proportion to the figures for each end-use which remained.

For the small miscellaneous category we allocated each part separately in a manner which seemed plausible.

Appendix H
Construction Statistics

This Appendix deals with the statistics produced by the Ministry of Public Buildings and Works,[1] from which we hoped to be able to get a measure of what had happened to productivity in the construction industry. Inevitably, this involves consideration of the figures for value of output, price deflator, volume of output and number of workers, and also of the *consistency* between the various measures. We start with a brief explanation of how this arises.

Interconnections between Statistics

It is not possible to measure the output of the construction industry effectively in terms of physical units, because there are so many different kinds of work, and the products vary so greatly in size, quality etc. Hence the attempts to measure movements in the volume of output proceed by first getting the value for each period at current prices, and then deflating this by a series to represent the movement of prices. The accuracy of the volume figures depends on both these series being reliable.

As explained in Chapter X, the price series used by M.P.B.W. was not based on actual prices charged by firms in the building industry, but was based on the prices of their *inputs* of labour and materials. The assumption was made that overheads plus profits would represent a constant percentage of the price charged, so that these were left out of the index. There is, however, an obvious need to allow for changes in labour productivity, rather than simply taking the cost of employing a man for one hour as measuring 'labour costs'.

This produces a 'chicken and egg' problem, according to which one cannot measure the movements in the volume of output without a price index, but one needs to measure changes in the volume of output per head to arrive at the labour-cost element of the price index.

---

1 Now the Department of the Environment. The descriptions in the appendix relate to the position as we found it in 1969/70, hence our use of the past tense. Since that date there have been some changes. Research on more fundamental changes is still proceeding within the Department of the Environment, in close consultation with the Standing Consultative Committee on Construction Statistics of the National Consultative Council for the Building and Civil Engineering Industries.

Early in our study we received at our request from M.P.B.W. a draft of a subsequently published report of research sponsored by M.P.B.W. with the aim, amongst others, of critically considering suitable methods of constructing indices of building costs and prices. (Professor M.E.A. Bowley and W.J. Corlett, University College, London: Report on the Study of Trends in Building Prices: M.P.B.W. Research and Development Directorate of Research and Information.)

M.P.B.W. met this logical conundrum by assuming, for purposes of producing the price index, that the volume of output of the firms making returns to their survey could be assumed to move proportionately to the 'volume' (i.e. value at constant prices) of the materials which they had (apparently) used. This movement in the volume of materials was set against the movement in the number of workers shown on the forms, to obtain a 'productivity corrector', which was combined with figures obtained from the Department of Employment about movements in earnings and National Insurance etc., to give movements in the labour-cost element.

The problem of sub-contracting was ostensibly met by instructing each firm to deduct from the value of its output the amounts which reflect the work done by sub-contractors: this raises particular problems if the returns do not cover labour-only sub-contractors, since the materials used by these firms will have been included, but not their workers.

From this brief review, it is clear that a judgement of the reliability of these statistics involves a comprehensive study both of the method by which the basic data were secured (including its coverage), the probable accuracy of the entries made by the firms, and the procedures adopted by M.P.B.W. in working up the results.

Data used by M.P.B.W.

Details of quarterly output and monthly employment were collected by M.P.B.W. from firms on the Ministry's statistical register. Response to this enquiry is compulsory under the Statistics of Trade Act. In those months in which details of quarterly output are collected, details of employment are requested on the same enquiry form, a procedure which might seem to assure that even if the register is deficient and/or 100% of replies are not received, nevertheless there should be consistency of coverage of output and employment series for the purpose of any productivity calculation.[1]

The first quarter's output enquiry in each year is a full census of firms on the register. In the other three quarters, sampling of the register is very intensive as shown below.

Employment of firm recorded in census quarter	Nil	1	2–7	8–13	14–24	25–34	35 and over
Sampling fraction in other quarters	1/44	1/22	1/6	1/7	1/4	1/2	1/1

Despite response to the enquiry being obligatory, about 3% of firms do not at first respond to the first quarter census. Non-respondents are sent a second enquiry, asking for details of employment only, on the basis of which global output is estimated by assuming equal value of output per head between respondents and non-respondents.

The quarterly samples of output are grossed up by assuming that the firms sampled produce the same proportion of the output of their size groups as they did in the first quarter census. The coverage of firms included in the statistical register is, then, very complete.

1 But this is not in fact true, as we demonstrate later.

There is however, no grossing-up procedure to include the value of output of firms not on the register. The Ministry relied on the examination of trade director-ies and classified telephone directories, followed by the despatch of enquiry forms, telephone calls and visits from its regional officers, to up-date the register. This pro-cedure was supplemented by examination of registrations of new companies by Business Statistics Office, and cross-checks of registers with Inland Revenue. As we shall see later, the derivation of the volume indicator of output is dependent on the inclusion of *all* small firms and self-employed workers in the output enquiry, and the coverage has in fact become progressively less complete.

The value of output recorded by the respondent firms is supposed to be an esti-mate of the amount chargeable to their customers in the quarter, including the value of any work (e.g. speculative building) done on the contractor's own initiative. Contractors are asked to exclude the value of work done for them by sub-contrac-tors, which should be reported in turn directly by sub-contractors on their own returns of output. This exclusion is also to apply to payments made by main con-tractors to labour-only sub-contractors, although the value of materials supplied to this type of sub-contractor is to be included in the main contractors' returns of out-put. The returns of the payments for labour services are assumed to be made by the labour-only sub-contractors themselves.

Contractors are asked to divide the value of their output by the classification of type of work (e.g. housing, non-housing, repairs) and by the type of client (public or private), the most important distinction being between new work and repair work. They are also asked to allocate the reported number of operatives employed between these types of work.

Employment reported is to include all persons male or female and full or part time whose National Insurance cards are held by the respondent firm. Their num-bers should exclude any employees of other firms, or self-employed, who have sub-contracted for the respondent firm. Employment is stated under three headings — (i) administrative, professional, technical and clerical, (ii) working principals, and (iii) operatives. Self-employed owners should be included in (ii) if they do manual work, or in (i) if they do not. When returning their own employment, self-employed labour-only sub-contractors should include themselves under (ii). In those months where the enquiry is of employment only, the same detail of employment is re-quired as in the quarterly output enquiry, except that operative labour is not allo-cated to the type of work on which it is engaged.

Data collected by other Departments

The earnings series used for multiplication with the number of employees found above 'to produce an estimate of the industry wage and salary bill' are based on the Department of Employment's annual (formerly twice yearly) enquiries into weekly earnings of adult male manual workers, and of male administrative professional technical and clerical workers in construction.

Department of Employment sends the annual enquiry, which is voluntary, to all firms thought likely to respond. The resulting coverage is about 40% of workers in construction. Respondents supply totals of payments to labour (including over-time, bonus and commission) and the number of employees to whom these were paid. The total of payments and numbers of workers from all respondent firms are then added to provide, after division, average earnings figures for these groups of workers. The October earnings figures were interpolated and extrapolated (by M.P.B.W.) so as to provide a monthly series, by use of the D.E.'s less accurate monthly index of average earnings of all employees in construction.

The Department of Trade and Industry produces an index of wholesale prices for construction materials. The weighting of individual material prices was devised by the M.P.B.W. on the basis of sales recorded in the Census of Production, after allowance for sales to purchasers outside the construction industry.

M.P.B.W. Calculations

From the data just described M.P.B.W. devised a price index known as the index of the cost of new construction, which is published. This is used to deflate current price output to give a series of the volume of output, also published, and which is taken as the Index of Industrial Production indicator for new construction. By division of the volume of output series by its employment series the Ministry also produced a series for gross output per head, which is not published but used for the purpose of answering parliamentary questions etc., and which was supplied to us when we asked for information about productivity. M.P.B.W. also produced a deflator for repair work, which is not itself published, although the resulting series for the volume of repair work and of all work are. There would be little point in producing a series for repair output per head, as the calculation of the deflator assumed this to be constant.

In the case of new work the first step by M.P.B.W. was to derive the quarterly value of materials used, by deducting from the value of new work reported estimates of the total cost of labour (including administrative workers etc.)[1] and an (assumed) allowance for overheads and profits.

The estimate of the cost of labour was made by multiplication of 'average total labour costs per worker' by the number of workers attributed to new work. Average total labour costs per worker were found by adding to the Department of Employment earnings series for adult male operatives and APTC workers amounts for employers' contributions to National Insurance, redundancy fund and SET, all at the adult male rate. (All workers were assumed to be adult males, as the M.P.B.W. employment statistics did not discriminate between male and female or young and adult workers.) The addition of SET to labour costs, while keeping the proportion of overheads and profits constant, assumed of course from the start that no part of SET would be absorbed out of profits; and that no refund is received.

In finding the number of workers engaged on new work, there was no difficulty in the case of employed operatives, as these are allocated between new and repair work by reporting firms. But in the case of APTC workers, the assumption had to

---

1 We were informed that the treatment of APTC wages and salaries as a variable cost, and this inclusion of APTC numbers in the denominator of the 'productivity correction' calculation was formally originated in early 1969, when the price series were re-based on the year 1968 and re-calculated back as far as the year 1963. Prior to this, the 'productivity correction' calculation had included operative numbers only, and regarded APTC wages and salaries as part of the 'fixed' proportion of overheads and profits. Continuation of the earlier method, as demonstrated to us by M.P.B.W., would have produced an index figure as low as 116.1 for 1969, as against the figure of 121.8 published after consideration of the results of the revised calculation.

be made that their numbers are attributable to new or repair work in the same ratio as the value of new to repair work.

The allowance for overheads and profits was deemed to include all expenses other than this labour cost and the purchase of materials; it included the earnings of working principals. The allowance made was a constant proportion of the value of output, this proportion being taken from the Census of Production for the base year of the calculations, which was of course the latest census available.

The residual value of materials found in this way seems likely to give the materials delivered to the site in the period, rather than the materials used, because we understand that many builders prepare their 'output' figures on that basis, so as to reflect 'the amount chargeable to customers' and avoid elaborate allowances for changing stocks. It was deflated by the wholesale price index for construction materials, after lagging this index by one quarter, on the assumption that construction materials are on average used one quarter after they are purchased.

The resulting series for the volume of materials used is very unstable; if it were treated as measuring the volume of output and divided into the value of output, it would produce an output price index which would be unstable and show seasonal variation. What was in fact done was to divide the index of the volume of materials by the index of employment (operative and APTC workers) to derive an indicator of labour productivity, henceforth called the 'productivity correction index'. This index was then used in the calculation of the labour cost component of the index of the cost of new construction (on the basis of input costs).

M.P.B.W. derived the index of the cost of new construction by weighting together (on the basis of the Census of Production) indices of material and labour costs. The starting-point for the latter was the earnings (plus National Insurance and SET) of adult male workers, including APTC: this series was then adjusted by the productivity correction index described above. To produce a smoothed series, the productivity correction index was taken as the mean of its value in the current and three preceding quarters.

This index of the cost of new construction could then be divided into the index of value of new output to produce the constant price output series. Finally, division of the constant price output by an employment series gave output per head.

For the purpose of clarity, and for later reference when we come to examine the sensitivity to error of the calculations described above, they are represented algebraically below. But for the purpose of simplicity, no distinction is made here between the earnings and numbers of operative and APTC workers.

$$I_p = \frac{pO_t - W_t N_t}{M_{t-1} N_t} \cdot \frac{M_{-1} N_0}{pO_0 - W_0 N_0}$$

$$I_c = \frac{w \dfrac{W_t}{W_0}}{\dfrac{1}{4} \sum\limits_{t-3}^{t} I_p} + m \dfrac{M_t}{M_0}}{w + m}$$

where I_p is the unsmoothed productivity correction index, I_c is the index of the cost of new construction

O is the value of output

M is the materials price index

N is the number of employees

W is the earnings of labour plus NI, SET etc.

p,w,m are the proportions of price represented by prime costs, labour costs, and purchases of materials respectively, so that $p = w + m$.

Subscripts t, $t-1$, 0, and -1 denote time where t is the current and 0 the base period.

$$\text{Constant price output} = \frac{\text{current price output}}{\text{index of the cost of new construction}}$$

$$\text{Output per head} = \frac{\text{constant price output}}{\text{number of employees plus working principals}}$$

It may well seem strange that this calculation embodied an assumption about productivity (in the productivity correction index), based on the assumption that the volume of output moves proportionately to the volume of materials, but ended up with a new figure for output per head, obtained by deflating the value of output. It can however be shown algebraically that *if* one ignores certain complications – i.e. the exclusion of the small number of working principals in the first calculation of productivity, the smoothing of I_p, the lagging of the materials price index and the fact that the weights do not correspond exactly with the base-year proportions in the series used – then the results of the calculations of the productivity correction index and output per head would be equal. In practice, because of inclusion of working principals in output per head, lagging, smoothing and the use of Census of Production weights the correspondence is not exact.

In the case of repair work there is very little method to describe. Value of repair output is recorded in the output enquiry. This was deflated to constant prices by an index similar to the index of the cost of new construction except that (i) the weights for material and labour prices, derived from the Census of Production, were given different values from those for new work, and (ii) no 'productivity correction' was introduced, labour productivity being assumed always to remain constant through time for this purpose. The indices of operative labour and material costs included were the same as those used in the calculation for new work.

Sensitivity Analysis

In view of the complex nature of the M.P.B.W. calculations, and also the precarious nature of some of the data and assumptions, it is useful to see how sensitive the results are to small changes in the basic information (or assumptions) which entered into the calculations. In Table H.1 we examine the effects of raising p, O, M, N, and W in turn by 1% of itself, and then of combining a 1% increase in M, N, and W with a 1% reduction in p and O.[1]

1 The results were produced by assuming the values set out below (which are probably similar, in their general effect, to the ones used by M.P.B.W. for 1965 and 1969) and then changing the 1969 figures by 1%.

$p_0 = p_t = 0.84$; $w = 0.39$; $m = 0.45$
$O_0 = £m\ 2,631$; $O_t = £m\ 3,167$
$M_0 = 106$; $M_t = 119$
$N_0 = 971,000$; $N_t = 891,000$
$W_0 = 987.6$; $W_t = 1329.6$

Table H.1 *Sensitivity Analysis for M.P.B.W. Indices*

Factor(s) changed in later year	Percentage change in			
	Productivity correction	Cost index	Output at constant prices	Output at constant prices per head
Effect of increase of 1% in:-				
Prime cost proportion	−1.80	0.87	−0.87	−0.87
Value of output	−1.80	0.87	−1.86	−1.86
Price of materials	1.01	−1.00	1.01	1.01
Number of employees	1.82	−0.85	0.86	1.88
Wage (plus N.I. etc.)	0.80	−0.85	0.86	0.86
Combined effect of 1% increase in M, N, W and 1% fall in P and O	+7.36	−4.23	+5.46	+6.52

The results show that a small error in the measurement of only one variable, output or employment, could produce an error almost double the size in output per head. An unfortunate combination of 1% errors would lead to an error of 6½% in the productivity index.

Smoothing

The above calculations have deliberately ignored the smoothing of series carried out by M.P.B.W. which was designed to produce more stable index series for price, constant price output, and output per head. One consequence of this smoothing is that, however necessary it may have been to produce credible results, it would smooth away any abnormal movement which might have been produced, quite legitimately, by a factor such as SET. For instance, if we were to look at the level of the index of the cost of new construction in year t, this was produced by taking the mean of the levels in the four quarters of that year. Each of the quarterly figures used a 'volume of materials' indicator averaged over the current and three preceding quarters to arrive at the productivity correction index. So, price in year t was produced by attaching weights of 1, 2, 3, 4, 3, 2 and 1 respectively to the volume indicator in quarters II, III and IV of year $t-1$ and quarters I, II, III and IV of year t.

Besides mechanical, smoothing of a more subjective nature was also adopted, in the light of M.P.B.W.'s knowledge of the state of the trade. Thus, the published results are incapable of being reproduced by the methods described.

Other Factors

Apart from methods of calculation, errors are produced by the methods of collection of output and labour statistics, and the assumptions made before calculation begins. It is through the interaction of assumptions, methods of collection, and industrial trends and cycles, that large trend and cyclical errors are produced. The most dubious assumptions were (i) that overheads and profits form a constant proportion of the value of output, and (ii) that real output is in a constant ratio to the volume of materials used.

The weaknesses of collection are (i) the incomplete coverage of small firms and self-employed sub-contractors on the statistical register; (ii) the design of the question on output; (iii) the non-discrimination between male and female employment, and (iv) the confusion of material stock-piled and materials consumed. The industrial trends exacerbating the situation are (i) the trend from employment to self-employment (ii) increasing female participation in the labour force, and (iii) increasing off-site prefabrication of building components.

The Register of Firms

Complete collection of the value of output and employment obviously depends on the inclusion of all firms and self-employed workers on the statistical register of firms. In construction, however, this requirement must also be met if *consistent* output and employment series are to result, which would give an accurate productivity estimate. This condition arises because main contractors are asked to exclude from their reported output payments for work done by sub-contractors, including labour-only sub-contractors (LOSC), but to include the value of the materials which they supply for use by LOSC. The payments for labour services, together with the number of LOSC employees and working partners, should be reported directly by LOSC, but of course this can happen only if the LOSC are included on the register of firms.

There are two special points to be made here. First, if the system works at its best, and all LOSC are included on the register, a trend to self-employment such as has occurred in construction becomes inconsistent with the assumption made about overheads and profits. This can best be explained by reference to a simple example in which we ignore changes in the volume or price of output and inputs. In the first year, main contractors do not sub-contract, but employ exclusively their direct labour to produce an output of £1,000. In the second year, main contractors sub-contract one-fifth of their activity on a labour-only basis, to self-employed individuals, or groups of these. The two periods' returns of output and employment, are shown in Table H.2, together with the calculations performed by M.P.B.W.

Table H.2.   *Calculation of Productivity Correction Index*

| | Period 1: no sub-contracting | Period 2: sub-contracting to self-employed LOSC | | |
		Main con-tractor	LOSC	Total
Returned on Forms				
(1) Gross output (£)	1,000	922	78	1,000
(2) No. of employees	10	8	–	8
(3) No. of working principals	–	–	2	2
Calculated Figures				
(4) Overheads and profits at 16% (£)	160	(148)		160
(5) Wages	390	(312)		312
(6) Residual (taken as materials)	450	(462)		528
(7) Productivity correction index ((6) ÷ (2))	45	(58)		66

(The figures in brackets reflect the calculation which would be made if no return were received from the LOSC: they are not needed at this stage, but are used later.)

In the analysis of the combined returns, M.P.B.W. as before, assumed 16% of the value of output to be overheads and profits, and no separate deduction was made for the income of self-employed working principals (which is assumed in the table to be equal to their previous wages). Because of the 'fixed' assumption about overheads and profits, the analysis inflated the apparent value of materials by the amount of this income, and it also excluded the number of working principals from the 'productivity correction' calculation. So, if one-fifth of the labour force were to become self-employed as LOSC on new work, the productivity correction to the price of labour would be overstated by almost one half, from 45 to 66.

This represents the analysis of productivity working as designed, on the basis of a complete register. But secondly, we must examine the effect of incomplete coverage.

When collection of statistics started there was an almost complete register of firms as a result of the requirements of building licensing. After the abolition of licensing in 1953 there was no longer any incentive to be on the register; inclusion resulted only in the obligation to complete enquiry forms. With the coming into fashion of self-employment, and labour-only sub-contracting, the maintenance of a full register became impossible: LOSC do not need to maintain any office or other business premises, to provide for the purchasing and stocking of materials; the organisation of groups of LOSC can take place at home, in public houses, or on site; and self-employed men doing small repairs must be very hard to trace too.

This inevitable deterioration of the register shows up in the figures. The number of working principals recorded by M.P.B.W. shows an apparent decline through time, while the number of self-employed, as estimated from the 1966 Census of Population extrapolated by D.H.S.S. card counts, has risen rapidly.

We recognise that other self-employed partners, etc. *not* doing manual work should be included elsewhere on the quarterly statistical return under 'APTC workers'. These would tend to be mostly employers. But the 1966 Census showed 'self employed without employees' to have increased greatly in number compared with 1961, whereas the M.P.B.W. figure declined — see Table H.3. The conclusion is that most LOSC and small repairers were by 1970 missing from the register. The deficiency of the register can also have the effect of excluding numbers and output of the *employees* of small employers, as well as self-employed.

Table H.3.   *Self-employed in Construction in Great Britain*

At April each year	Working principals[a]	Self-employed[b] (thousands) All	Without employees
1961	92	166	93
1962	91		
1963	90		
1964	89		
1965	88		
1966	82	212	147
1967	81	238	
1968	79	252	
1969	76	268	
1970	72	268	

(a) Source: M.P.B.W.
(b) Source: Census of Population and D.H.S.S.

The growing incompleteness of the register is of course a serious matter for estimates of the value of output. For the productivity correction index *as it has been described*, however, the complete omission of self-employed LOSC's from the statistical register might be rather less disastrous than their inclusion would be in a period of increasing use of LOSC. Table H.2 shows how the calculation would then have run: the smaller exaggeration of the estimate for materials reduces the exaggeration produced by that factor, but the under-statement of the number of workers handling the materials is as great as before.

The Questionnaire on Output and Employment

We have seen that the collection of all output depends on obtaining response from many units which are impossible to find. From the consideration of collecting a complete output series, then, it would be preferable if the questionnaire were to request details of work sub-contracted by traceable firms, as is done in the Census of Production. This would also help to overcome the problem of non-deduction of the value of sub-contracted work from the output return, which we understand is a common omission among respondents.

Another weakness is the failure to distinguish between male and female employment, or to have made any allowance for the difference in their earnings when calculating the residual for materials. For this purpose, employment was assumed to be all male, but Department of Employment statistics show that there has been a trend towards more female employment in construction. This growth is presumably largely among APTC workers where the sex differential in earnings is high.

Whether or not contractors, in reporting the value of their output, are likely to deduct the value of payments made to sub-contractors depends partly on the method of response chosen. Several methods of response exist, and the ambiguity of the question on the value of output sent to firms permits considerable flexibility in response. Firms are asked for 'estimates of the amount chargeable to your customers for building, civil engineering and associated work done directly by you between ...... and ...... Include the value of work done on your own initiative in the period on buildings .... for eventual sale or lease.' No further guidance was issued, either on or with the enquiry form, as to what methods should be used in the derivation of these estimates. The use of the word 'estimate' is in itself perhaps unfortunate. It might indicate reference to the back of an envelope, rather than to a firm's accounts. The treatment of retention monies, margins, and even perhaps sale of land, is open to speculation.

Enquiries have been made on at least two occasions into the various methods of estimation used by firms in returning their value of output. In 1968, M.P.B.W. approached fifty firms directly, and later more firms were interviewed in the course of an enquiry into statistics of expenditure and output.[1]

Neither of these enquiries was concerned mainly with the relationship between value of output and employment reported. The first enquiry examined the feasibility of producing output statistics monthly, and the second the reconciliation of output and expenditure series. Both enquiries produced broadly similar results,

---

1 Lady Eleanor Lea – The Value of New Construction Work; an Enquiry into the Statistics of Expenditure and Output – draft report to the Department of Environment.

although not surprisingly the Ministry's direct enquiry found less firms which reported using the least satisfactory methods of response.

About half the firms approached based their estimates of the value of work done on valuation certificates issued for progress payments. These seem most likely to be the larger firms. Of these firms, some based their estimates on cash payments received rather than the value certified.

Apart from this, about two fifths of all the firms approached based their response on costing systems, and the final one tenth used a variety of methods. Of these, multiplication of the number of operatives employed by a typical output per head was the most common, but the reporting of some fraction of turnover for the last accounting year also featured.

The first enquiry included five firms doing speculative work. Of these, three used valuations made by their surveyors, one used costing, and one used the completion value of houses for which contracts had been signed by clients during the period.

Of all the methods reported, the greatest importance must be attached to the use of valuation certificates as the basis for estimation by main contractors. The first enquiry included two sub-contractors, both of whom were among the firms using costing systems as the basis of estimation.

Much the greater part of new construction work (probably about 80%) is carried out under the provisions of formal contract between main contractor and client. Other work not subject to this arrangement will include speculative building, especially of private housing, and small works including much repair and maintenance work. In the case of work done under formal contract, the usual arrangement is for the client to make monthly progress payments to the main contractor, on the basis of the architect's certification of the value of work done. The main contractor similarly makes progress payments to sub-contractors. Interim valuations are made by measurement of work done as specified in bills of quantities. The valuations include the value of materials brought onto the construction site, but as yet unused, by the contractor. From this valuation, a deduction is made against the possibility of defects becoming apparent before the end of the maintenance period. The architect's certification of course includes, but does not specify, the value of work done by sub-contractors engaged by the main contractor.

Thus architect's certificates provide a convenient source of reference for firms in answering the question of output, and it is likely that estimation of the greater part of reported output is based on these. Returns of employment are likely to be drawn from the wage sheets, although the allocation of operatives to types of work reported must presumably draw also on costing systems.

It is necessary to examine the implications of these methods of response. We are not so much concerned with *levels* of output and employment, but with movements of the two series in relation to each other.[1] In the case of the enquiries which were used as data, the emphasis was on the level of output and the speed with which this could be reported. Thus answers to some points of primary importance to us are not available, or only partial, but the next few paragraphs will discuss the possible treatments by reporting firms of sub-contracted work, material stocks, overheads and profits, retention monies, and the sale of land.

1 This is not to detract from the importance of levels to other users, e.g. in national accounting.

It was noted in the second enquiry that some firms using valuation certificates, and some using costing systems, failed to deduct the value of sub-contracted work. This is not surprising: after valuation certificates have been used as an easy source of reference for estimates of the gross value of output, there must be some extra effort involved in further reference to valuations of sub-contracted work. It was noted too, that there was difficulty in separating sub-contractors from other suppliers, in company accounts. We consulted Lady Lea about how widespread the failure was, and she replied that there was some ambiguity in the interview questions and notes, but that on the whole she did not think this was a very significant feature: it is, however, likely to be more serious with labour-only sub-contracts.

It seems fairly certain that sub-contractors' labour will correctly be excluded from main contractors' employment returns. Generally, there would be no purpose for a main contractor to keep detailed records of sub-contractors' labour, and even in the worst cases of bogus self-employment, where LOSC are paid at an hourly rate, this labour seems likely to be kept off the wages sheet for the purpose of consistency with National Insurance records.

To summarise, we think that all sub-contractors' labour will be correctly excluded from main contractors' employment returns. As regards the output and labour of supply-and-fix sub-contractors, employment should on the whole be correctly reported, but non-deduction by main contractors means that some output will be reported twice. In a general trend towards more sub-contracting, this will cause distortion in productivity estimates. Lastly, as regards the output and labour of LOSC, their employment and income is largely not reported, but the value of materials they put in place will be reported by main contractors, who also fail to deduct some payments to LOSC.

If sub-contracting of both types and self-employment increase, then all the factors discussed in the previous paragraph will cause upward bias in productivity estimates.

An important consideration is the treatment of materials delivered and stockpiled on site. As we noted earlier, the value of these materials is included in valuation certificates, and estimation from valuation certificates forms the most important method of response to the output question. There will be a tendency for these stocks to fluctuate seasonally, and between periods of low and high demand. These changes in the level of stocks will cause the output series to become out of phase with the employment series, and with the true level of construction activity. This contributes to the need for smoothing of the 'productivity correction' series: but, more importantly, it can also distort the movement of output, productivity and hence price from one year to the next. When the industry quickly approaches capacity working as in 1964 and 1967, the increase of stocks of materials preceeds the increase in construction activity. Further, shortages of materials are expected to arise, and contractors increase the level of their stocks on site, as well as double ordering, etc. The effect of this is to overstate the value of output, and hence the value of materials derived by M.P.B.W. for use in their productivity corrector. Thus, in years such as 1964 and 1967, the increase in productivity is over-stated, and the price index obstinately refuses to rise.[1]

1 This is not apparent from the published statistics, because of the 'smoothing' described above. The statistics published at the time showed a drop in the index of construction costs in 1967, which was smoothed away in the revised series.

Value of output reported on the basis of certificates will of course include the overhead and profit element. Where firms use costing systems as the basis of response, however, the result may be unsatisfactory. The first enquiry found that only one firm failed to make allowance for overheads and profits. But the second noted that some firms failed to include any allowance for overheads and profits, while others added a standard percentage to labour and material costs. It seems likely that this addition, where included, would be based on the results of the last accounting year, rather than on current experience.

Where the amounts reported are of cash received as progress payments (less cash paid to sub-contractors), rather than the value certified, the retention percentage will be excluded; this was the practice of 6% of firms in the first enquiry, and 10% in the second. If the final payment (made after completion of the work) is duly reported, the total value of work reported should be right, but distortions in the movements of output between periods may be serious.

The remaining consideration is the treatment of the sale of land by firms engaging in speculative building. The first enquiry mentions firms doing speculative work. Of five firms, one used the completion value of houses for which contracts had been signed by clients during the period. This value would include the site value. The use of costing systems should avoid this complication, but raises problems in relation to the profit element. In the absence of more information the outcome is very uncertain, but the increase in the price of land relative to building costs seems likely to contribute to the overstatement of productivity increases.

The methods of response used by some 10% of firms (according to the second enquiry) which were based on the number of men employed, or the turnover of a previous period, are unworthy of detailed consideration. As regards movements in productivity, the fact that some returns are on this basis can only make one more sceptical of the usefulness of the statistics.

Overheads and Profits

There are two ways in which overheads and profits featured in M.P.B.W. calculations; these were (i) weighting of input costs in the price calculation and (ii) the earlier calculation of material input by residual from the value of output when forming the volume indicator, and hence the 'productivity correction index'. It is the second which has the greater importance, the effect of errors being shown in Table H.1.

As no more information became available on the level of overheads and profits until the next quinquennial Census of Production, M.P.B.W. assumed that overheads and profits measured as a proportion of turnover remain constant for five to ten yearly periods.[1] The justification claimed for this assumption, apart from that no further information is easily obtainable, was put to us as follows:

> (1) In the short term, overheads and profits each taken as a proportion of turnover, will move, if at all, inversely, and so taken together they will form a nearly constant proportion; thus, if demand falls, fixed overheads will proportionately rise, but profits will fall.

---

1 In 1970, the latest available information was based on the proportion of overheads and profits found in 1963.

(2) Contractors do not aim to increase their margins in favourable conditions, but seek a fair return; if unfavourable conditions make them tender low for contracts, they will during the course of the work, by constant subterfuge and dispute with architects and clients, restore a reasonable margin.

(3) By the long nature of the construction process, and phased starts and completions, short-term variations in the proportion of overheads and profits will be smoothed away.

As regards (3), it must be remarked that if movements become so smoothed by the long nature of the construction process, then the need for even further smoothing by M.P.B.W. statisticians mentioned above is surprising. In the case of (1), five to ten years cannot be regarded as the short term, and it must be expected that some trend will become apparent during such a period. Inland Revenue analysis of company turnover (now discontinued) shows that for companies engaged in construction trading profit as a percentage of turnover increased from 6.0% to 8.0% between 1952 and 1964. During this period, it is most likely that overheads would also have increased as a percentage of turnover, due to mechanisation, increased capitalisation etc. Further, the Inland Revenue analysis demonstrates cyclical movement in percentage trading profit, with margins increasing during boom and falling during depression.

Finally, turning to (2), there can be *many* theories of pricing policy. It is worthy of remark though, that in the light of changing rates of taxation, etc., it would be surprising if the notion of 'a fair return' did not also change over five to ten years.

It seems likely, and is supported by such observation as we can make that as demand increases, tendering will be less keen and contractors will raise their margins. This could be reinforced by the practice of tendering high prices for jobs which are not really wanted during over-loading: if all firms are busy, some of these 'unwanted' tenders may well be accepted.

If profit plus overheads increase as a percentage of turnover the M.P.B.W. calculation will show a false rise in the residual value of materials. This produces a false rise in the 'producitivity correction factor', and a downward bias in the price index. Thus, the movement of price and productivity will be distorted on trend, but also cyclically (and it is worth remembering that 1967, the first SET year, was a year of upturn in demand).

There is, however, a point of more general consideration. We have noted here, that the volume indicator may be upward-biassed during boom and, conversely, downward-biassed during slack. We also noted earlier (in the section on 'the questionnaire on output and employment') that the inclusion of material stocks in the reported value of output would tend to have the same effect. Clearly then, some part of the reported cyclical movement in construction output will be spurious.

Returning to the consequences of direct importance to this enquiry, it has been remarked before but should not be forgotten that (i) the assumption of a constant proportion of overheads and profits is inconsistent with a trend to self employment while income from self-employment is deemed to be part of 'overheads and profits', and (ii) that the assumption made from the start is that no part of SET will be absorbed out of profits.

Gross Output and Net Output

The M.P.B.W. statisticians followed the 'normal' practice of assuming that the industry's gross output and materials show the same percentage movements in 'volume' terms: they therefore took the index of gross output as applicable to net output also, and used it for productivity purposes.

This is liable to produce serious errors in a period of shift towards the use of more prefabricated materials, and the error was increased by the Ministry's method of using the 'volume' of materials as a proxy for output in calculating the productivity correction index. This effect can be illustrated by a numerical example.

Suppose a contractor builds one building in year 0 and an identical building in year t. In year 0 he purchases £100,000 of bricks which are assembled on site by 100 men earning £1,000 each. This gives gross output of £200,000 in year 0 (as profits and overheads were assumed by M.P.B.W. to be a constant proportion of turnover, these are ignored here). At the end of year 0, one man leaves the contractor's labour force to work for a brick company prefabricating brick panels at the same wage. In year t the contractor purchases £101,000 prefabricated brick panels which are assembled on site by 99 men earning the same £1,000 each. Gross output is £200,000 as in year 0, and no prices have changed. Gross output per head by the contractor's labour force would seem to have risen from £200,000/100 to £200,000/99, i.e. by 1%. But M.P.B.W. methods doubled this. They would see the value of materials used per man as being £100,000/100 in year 0 and £101,000/99 in year t, so the productivity correction index goes up by 2%. The cost index falls by 1%, though prices have been constant, value of output at constant prices rises by 1%, and value of gross output per head rises by 2%. True productivity (as measured by net output per head at constant prices) should be regarded as unchanged.

Attempts to Quantify Errors

In the nature of the case it is impossible to know the quantitative effect of all the various shortcomings described in this appendix, whether in the data collected or the methods of calculation. We thought it right however to attempt a summary view, which would give rough quantitative figures where possible, and indicate the *direction* in which the factor was producing an error where that was not possible: only occasionally did we have to say that the direction was unknown.

We concentrated our attention on the index of the cost of new construction, because one can reasonably hope to get some idea of a 'price' movement without having returns from all firms: deficiencies in the value of output in any year depend (*inter alia*) on the incompleteness of the register, on which we cannot say much except that it seems to us to be serious, whilst *movements* in that value are affected by changes in the degree of incompleteness.

We also concentrated our attention on the movement in the index from 1963 to 1969: by taking a long period the importance of purely cyclical factors is minimised, and it is these on which we have least information.

We wish to emphasize that this section does not claim to give exact figures for any item: it represents an attempt to make some sort of reasonable estimates, which in places rest on very 'heroic' assumptions — but ones which we hope are unbiassed in their total effect.

Results of the Analysis

It may be easiest to start with an over-all statement of our results. These are:

(a) Over the six years 1963–1969 the 'productivity correction index' used by M.P.B.W. in assessing the movement of labour costs was calculated to rise by 35.7%: our attempt at a revised figure is some 17 to 18 per cent, which seems a good deal more probable.

(b) The index of the cost of new construction (as worked by M.P.B.W.) showed a rise over this period of 20.5%, whereas our assessment is some 28 to 29%.

(c) One can get some test of the degree of under-statement in the cost of new construction index by reference to the tender price index for Local Authority housing (which is based on actual prices). As the latter relates to prices given at the time of tender, whereas the cost index relates to costs when the work is done, we allowed a one-year lag, and compared the movement in the tender index from its base in 1964 to 1968 with that in the cost index between 1965 and 1969: we did not think that a later terminal date would be meaningful, because tenderers might not foresee the rapid increases in costs which occurred in 1970.

On this basis the cost index (as worked) rose by 14.1%, but the tender index rose by 19.6%. This understatement of about 5% over a four-year period is broadly in line with the understatement of 6 to 7% which our calculation showed for a six-year period.

Methods for estimating LOSC effects

The main cause of trouble has, fundamentally, been the *growth* of labour-only subcontracting. If it had been roughly constant, then the consequences for the index of the cost of construction would not have been very serious, because the errors in the basic data (and the ones introduced in the calculations) would have tended to be much the same in all periods, whether they were due to LOSC or to some other factor.

This growth affected the calculation of the index (and especially of its first stage, the productivity correction index) in many ways, and we have tried to adopt a 'swings and roundabouts' approach in deciding on the method of quantifying each one. Some of the factors are:

(*a*) *Non-deduction of payments to LOSC from value of output returned by main contractors.* In so far as main contractors fail to deduct these payments, the value of their output is over-stated, and hence the residue for 'materials' is over-stated; with a growing amount of LOSC work, this factor would lead to over-statement of the productivity corrector, but in our calculations we take this factor as *zero* (since there is no real information) thereby under-stating the error.

(*b*) *Failure to secure returns from labour-only sub-contractors.* As explained above, this leads to some under-statement of the value of output, but to a serious exaggeration of the productivity correction index, because the value (and hence 'volume') of materials is exaggerated and the number of people handling them under-stated: the effect varies somewhat according to whether the people missing are self-employed

269

(or employers) — i.e. the contractors themselves — or people employed by the contractors.

Our method of calculating the number of missing LOSC workers (described below) is to find the change in the *total* number of people missing from M.P.B.W. statistics by the use of the numbers derived from the card-counts for employees and self-employed, and to assume that *all* this increase (in so far as it was not on repairs) was on LOSC work. The estimate of the total is probably too small, because of increased evasion and statistical deficiencies (see Chapter XV), but some of the extra 'missing' workers would be in small firms not doing this work.

Our calculation requires an allowance for the *falling* number of working principals actually reported to M.P.B.W. The statistical treatment adopted by M.P.B.W. for handling such workers introduces two errors, which lead to under-estimates of the productivity corrector: no deduction is made for their income in calculating the value of materials, and they are not counted as 'workers' handling the materials. The *smaller* number reported therefore lowers the productivity corrector, as a partial offset to the exaggeration produced above.

(*c*) *Estimation of missing LOSC workers.* The number of self-employed (and employers) not on the M.P.B.W. statistical register was calculated by subtracting from the card-count figure for self-employed the number of working principals reported to M.P.B.W. *plus* an allowance of 7,000 for self-employed included in the APTC figure.

For employees we compared the D.E. employment figures for MLH 500 with the M.P.B.W. figure, roughly adjusted to that basis by taking only the *operatives* in the Government and Local Authority sector. The two series were in rough agreement up to 1961/2.

It was assumed that missing workers were divided between repairs and new work in the same proportions as reported operatives.

For assessing the effects on the productivity correction index, it was assumed that a self-employed LOSC worker earned the equivalent of an average operative plus the employer's share of the insurance stamp (including SET). This was statistically convenient: if the true earnings were really higher, our estimate of the error is too small.

Other Factors

Other items in our list can be described rather summarily.

Female employees. M.P.B.W. did their calculations on the assumption that all employees are adult males, but D.E. figures show a rising proportion of females, whom we assume to be APTC workers.

The M.P.B.W. assumption led to an under-estimate of the rise in the value of materials, thereby making the productivity corrector too low; it also failed to allow for the use of a bigger proportion of female labour in 1969, when assessing the rise in earnings per worker, and so further exaggerated the rise in the labour cost element of the index of the cost of new construction.

Table H.4   *Effects of Various Factors in Distorting M.P.B.W. Index Numbers*

(The figures are the percentage by which the calculated index for 1969 (1963 = 100) is thought to have exceeded the true one).

Factor	Effect on	
	Productivity Correction Index	Cost of New Construction Index
LOSC Factors		
Non-deduction of payments to LOSC Contractors	Positive, taken as 0	Negative, taken as 0
Missing LOSC workers: self-employed	+10.6	−4.5
employees	+5.0	−2.2
Decline of no. of working principals reported	−2.2	+1.1
Other Factors		
Assumption in calculations of no female employment	−0.8	+0.8
Increased use of prefabricated materials	+3	−1.5
Inclusion in output returns of additions to stocks	Negative	Positive
Assumption of constant percentage for overheads and profits	Unknown	Unknown
Index derived from M.P.B.W. calculations	*135.7*	*120.5*
Our reassessment	*117–118*	*128–129*

> *Note:*
> As we adopted a 'swings and roundabouts' approach, the entries for individual items should be regarded primarily as calculating figures, designed to reach a reasonable estimate for the total effect.

Increased use of prefabricated materials. The figures used are derived from correspondence with M.P.B.W.

Additions to stocks. In 1963 stocks on sites were probably rising, and in 1969 probably falling. Their inclusion in at least some returns of output means that the productivity corrector for 1969 is too low.

Overheads and profits as % of price. This item may well have both a trend and a cycle, but we can only enter it as 'unknown' for this comparison.

Results

The results of our calculations are brought together in Table H.4. As emphasized in the note, some of the figures for individual items are to be regarded primarily as a means of reaching the total effect, rather than as important in themselves.

This table makes it apparent why we felt unable to base any analysis on the M.P.B.W. series which were deduced from the cost of new construction index.

Suggestions for Improvement

The above investigation led us to the conclusion that the cost index (which although it may be called a cost index is in fact implied to be a price index by its use as a deflator) was unsatisfactory as an indicator of changes in price, and that the productivity information was too weak to form the basis of an analysis such as we have carried out on other trades.

Major ways in which we thought the statistics could be improved are:
(i) Deflation should be by an index produced by a variant of the methods used for existing tender price indices, under which the information for the various stages of the production process would be allocated to the months when the work was certified for payment, rather than all being allocated to the time when the tender was submitted.

The requirement, for a price index used as a deflator, of timing the measurement of price to correspond with execution of work, will be more easily met by the use of indices based on unit rates from bills of quantities than by the use of alternative indices based on standardised total tender prices.
(ii) Output should be collected by asking main contractors to report output including that part sub-contracted, with payments to sub-contractors and LOSC as separate items. Work done as a sub-contractor by the respondent should also be distinguished from other work. Output by smaller firms including sub-contractors and repairers should be collected by means of a very much simpler form, using small sampling fractions.

The present method of collecting output and of deflation involves attempting, unsucessfully (and, we feel, very expensively) to gather complete information from every firm large and small. This should not be continued.

The effect of our recommendations would be that all new output would be reported, and productivity estimates (even though including smaller firms on a sample basis only) could be more reliably derived. We would prefer, thinking still of productivity estimates, that details of employment should continue to be collected on the same form as output.

Appendix I
Rates of SET

The Selective Employment Tax rates quoted below were effective in Great Britain from the dates shown. All rates are given net of refunds for part-time and elderly workers.

Hours employed	5th September 1966		4th September 1967		2nd September 1968*		7th July 1969*		5th July 1971*	
Over 21 hours per week	s.	d.	s.	d.	s.	d.	s.	d.	s.	d.
Men	25	0	25	0	37	6	48	0	24	0
Women; boys under 18	12	6	12	6	18	9	24	0	12	0
Girls under 18	8	0	8	0	12	0	16	0	8	0
Men over 65	25	0	25	0	12	6	16	0	8	0
Women over 65	12	6	12	6	6	3	8	0	4	0
Over 8 hours and under 21 hours per week										
Men (including over 65)	25	0	12	6	12	6	16	0	8	0
Women (including over 65)	12	6	6	3	6	3	8	0	4	0
Boys under 18	12	6	12	6	18	9	24	0	12	0
Girls under 18	8	0	8	0	12	0	16	0	8	0
Under 8 hours per week	No tax paid									

* These rates did not apply to hotels situated in the areas specified in Schedule 17 of the 1968 Finance Act (Rural Development Areas). A full refund could be claimed on any employee of any such hotel which had '... not less than four rooms which .... were available for use .... as sleeping accommodation by guests ....'

N.B. The rates above are expressed in shillings and pence. The decimal equivalents are:

s.	d.	£	p.		s.	d.	£	p.
4	0	0	20		18	9	0	94
6	3	0	31		24	0	1	20
8	0	0	40		25	0	1	25
12	0	0	60		37	6	1	87½
12	6	0	62½		48	0	2	40
16	0	0	80					

University of Cambridge Department of Applied Economics
Occasional Papers

274

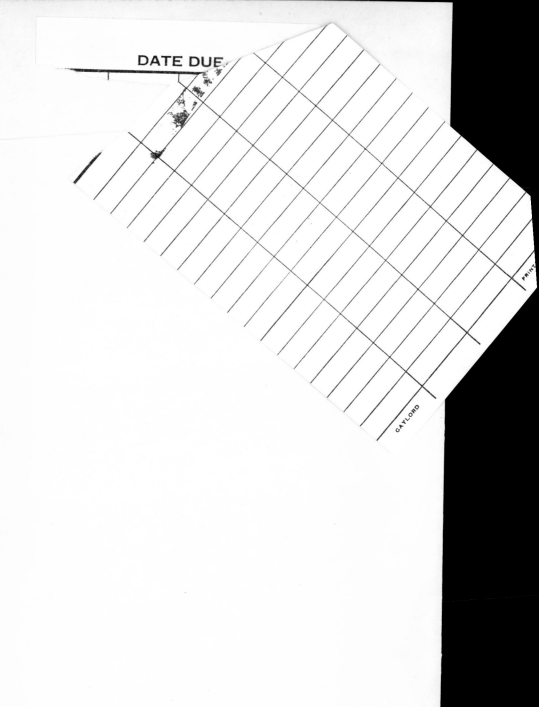

DATE DUE

GAYLORD

PRINT